# HIGH COURT CASE SUMMARIES

# CONTRACTS

Keyed to Farnsworth's
Casebook on Contracts,
7th Edition

**WEST**®

A Thomson Reuters business

Mat #40870522

© West, a Thomson business, 2002
© 2009 Thomson Reuters
    610 Opperman Drive
    St. Paul, MN 55123
    1–800–313–9378
Printed in the United States of America

**ISBN:** 978–0–314–20710–4

# Table of Contents

# Alphabetical Table of Cases

*

# CHAPTER ONE

## BASES FOR ENFORCING PROMISES

### Hawkins v. McGee

**Instant Facts:** Dr. McGee (D) guaranteed that an operation would be "a hundred percent" successful, but Hawkins (P) was permanently injured as a result of the surgery.

**Black Letter Rule:** The question of whether a contract is formed is a factual question and is to be decided based on the words spoken, as well as the context in which they are spoken.

### Bayliner Marine Corp. v. Crow

**Instant Facts:** Crow (P) purchased a boat manufactured by Bayliner (D) that did not perform as well as Crow (P) expected.

**Black Letter Rule:** Statements that do not relate to the particular item purchased, or that merely commend the quality of goods, do not create express warranties.

### United States Naval Institute v. Charter Communications, Inc.

**Instant Facts:** Naval (P) bought an action against Charter Communications (D) and Berkeley Publishing Group (D) for breach of licensing contract not to publish book before the month of October.

**Black Letter Rule:** Courts will not grant punitive damages for a breach of contract.

### Sullivan v. O'Connor

**Instant Facts:** Plastic surgeon disfigures patient in the course of performing a nose job.

**Black Letter Rule:** Clear proof of a doctor's promise of specific medical results may give rise to an enforceable contract.

### White v. Benkowski

**Instant Facts:** White (P) recovered a judgment against Benkowski (D) for breach of a contract to supply water, and the court reduced the damages awarded by the jury to one dollar in compensatory damages and no punitive damages.

**Black Letter Rule:** Punitive damages may not be recovered for breach of contract.

### Hamer v. Sidway

**Instant Facts:** William E. Story Sr. (D) promised his nephew, William E. Story Jr. (P) , that he would pay William Jr. $5,000 if William Jr. would refrain from drinking, using tobacco, swearing, and gambling, until William Jr. Was 21 years of age, which William Jr. did.

**Black Letter Rule:** The party who abandons some legal right in the present or limits his legal freedom of action in the future as an inducement for a promise, gives sufficient consideration to create a legally binding contract.

### Fiege v. Boehm

**Instant Facts:** Hilda Boehm (P) alleged that Louis Fiege (D) promised to pay all her medical expenses and compensate her for her loss in salary caused by her child's birth, for which Fiege (D) was the alleged father.

**Black Letter Rule:** Forbearance to sue for a lawful claim or demand is sufficient consideration for a promise if the party forbearing had an honest intention to prosecute litigation which is not frivolous, vexatious, or unlawful, and which he believed to be well-founded.

### Feinberg v. Pfeiffer Co.

**Instant Facts:** Pfeiffer Co. (D) stopped making pension payments, pursuant to a resolution adopted by the Board of Directors, to Feinberg (P) after she retired.

**Black Letter Rule:** Past services is not sufficient consideration to support a promise.

### Mills v. Wyman

**Instant Facts:** Seth Wyman (D) failed to pay Daniel Mills (P) as promised for the expenses Mills (P) incurred from providing care for Wyman's (D) ill son.

**Black Letter Rule:** Past expense is not sufficient consideration to support a later promise to pay for the expenses.

### Webb v. McGowin

**Instant Facts:** Joe Webb (P) saved Greeley McGowin (D) from death or serious bodily harm during Webb's (P) course of employment, for which McGowin (D) agreed to pay Webb (P) $15 every two weeks for the remainder of Webb's (P) life.

**Black Letter Rule:** Past act of saving a party from death or serious bodily injury, that results in injuries to the saving party, is sufficient consideration for the saved party's subsequently induced promise to pay the saving party.

### Kirksey v. Kirksey

**Instant Facts:** A widow attempts to impose contractual liability for a promise made by her brother-in-law which induced her to leave her residence and move to his estate.

**Black Letter Rule:** A bargained-for exchange is required for all contracts, and merely changing position in reliance on a statement is insufficient to impose contractual liability in absence of any bargain.

### Lake Land Employment Group of Akron, LLC v. Columber

**Instant Facts:** Columber (D) worked for Lake Land (P) for several years before signing an agreement not to compete with Lake Land (P) and later claimed that the agreement was not supported by consideration.

**Black Letter Rule:** The continuation of an at-will employment relationship after the employer imposes a new requirement on the employee is sufficient consideration for the employee's agreement to that requirement.

### Strong v. Sheffield

**Instant Facts:** Strong (P) attempts to obtain payment for a note from the guarantor, although Strong (P) convinced the guarantor to sign the note merely by promising not to demand payment until he felt like it.

**Black Letter Rule:** In order to be legally binding, a promise must be supported by consideration and cannot be illusory.

### Mattei v. Hopper

**Instant Facts:** A seller attempts to back out of a real estate sale on the ground that the buyer's satisfaction clause rendered the buyer's promise illusory.

**Black Letter Rule:** A contract that is dependent on one party's subjective satisfaction with related matters may nevertheless be enforceable.

### Eastern Air Lines, Inc. v. Gulf Oil Corporation

**Instant Facts:** In the midst of an oil embargo, Eastern Air Lines (P) seeks an injunction to prevent Gulf Oil (D) from breaching the requirements contract between the parties.

**Black Letter Rule:** Requirements contracts are neither indefinite nor lacking in mutuality.

### Wood v. Lucy, Lady Duff-Gordon

**Instant Facts:** A famous fashion designer attempts to invalidate an exclusive-dealing arrangement by arguing that the supplier never made any promise to market her goods.

**Black Letter Rule:** Exclusive dealing arrangements impose an obligation by the seller to use his best efforts to distribute and market goods.

### Ricketts v. Scothorn

**Instant Facts:** A woman who quit work in reliance on her grandfather's promise to support her sues when the executor of her grandfather's estate fails to pay.

**Black Letter Rule:** Where a person changes position in detrimental reliance on a promise, the promisor may be estopped from later denying the promise.

### Feinberg v. Pfeiffer Co.

**Instant Facts:** Feinberg (P) retired from her employment, induced by her employer's promise to pay retirement benefits, and Feinberg (P) sues when the payments are eventually discontinued.

**Black Letter Rule:** Retirement in reliance on pension benefits is sufficient reliance to estop the employer from paying retirement benefits.

### Cohen v. Cowles Media Company

**Instant Facts:** Cohen (P), who leaked a newspaper story on the assurance that his name would be kept confidential, sues when the newspaper editors publish his identity.

**Black Letter Rule:** Promissory estoppel is applicable only where enforcement of a promise is *required* in order to prevent an injustice.

### D & G Stout, Inc. v. Bacardi Imports, Inc.

**Instant Facts:** A liquor distributor, who rejected a purchase offer in reliance on a supplier's promise not to terminate the relationship, sues the supplier after the supplier withdrew its account.

**Black Letter Rule:** Promissory estoppel allows recovery of reliance damages and not expectancy damages.

### Cotnam v. Wisdom

**Instant Facts:** Wisdom (P) was a physician who responded to an emergency call from a spectator to perform emergency surgery on Harrison (D), decedent, in an effort to save Harrison's life, but the operation was unsuccessful, and Harrison died without regaining consciousness.

**Black Letter Rule:** When a physician renders emergency medical services to a person, who due to his medical or mental condition is not capable of agreeing to the treatment, the law will imply a contract for the reasonable value of the services.

### Callano v. Oakwood Park Homes Corp.

**Instant Facts:** Operators of a nursery seek to recover payment for shrubbery from the home builder, although a contract existed only with the now-deceased home owner.

**Black Letter Rule:** Quasi-contractual recovery is not available when an alternative remedy based on an actual contract exists.

### *Pyeatte v. Pyeatte*

**Instant Facts:** After spouses agree to put each other through graduate school, the husband uses the wife's money to graduate law school, then divorces her.

**Black Letter Rule:** While ex-spouses are not entitled to restitution for performing usual duties incidental to marriage, restitution is available if the spouses had an agreement and one spouse made extraordinary efforts which benefited the other solely.

# Hawkins v. McGee

(Patient) v. (Surgeon)

84 N.H. 114, 146 A. 641 (1929)

WORDS THAT CONSTITUTE A PROMISE MAY BE THE BASIS OF A CONTRACT

■ **INSTANT FACTS** Dr. McGee (D) guaranteed that an operation would be "a hundred percent" successful, but Hawkins (P) was permanently injured as a result of the surgery.

■ **BLACK LETTER RULE** The question of whether a contract is formed is a factual question and is to be decided based on the words spoken, as well as the context in which they are spoken.

■ **PROCEDURAL BASIS**

Appeal from a judgment for Hawkins (P).

■ **FACTS**

McGee (D) performed surgery on Hawkins's (P) hand. The surgery involved taking skin from Hawkins's (P) chest and grafting onto his hand, to replace scar tissue from a burn. Before the surgery, McGee (D) stated that "I will guarantee to make the hand a hundred per cent perfect hand or a hundred per cent good hand." There also was evidence that McGee (D) asked Hawkins's (P) father repeatedly for permission to perform the surgery, and the attorney for Hawkins (P) advanced the theory that McGee (D) wanted to experiment with skin grafting, a field in which he had little experience. In addition, there was testimony that Hawkins's (P) father asked how long Hawkins (P) would be in the hospital, and that McGee (D) replied "[t]hree or four days, not over four; then the boy can go home and it will be just a few days when he will go back to work with a good hand."

McGee (D) argued that no reasonable man would understand his words as being used with the intention of entering into a contractual relationship. McGee (D) claimed that it was common knowledge that the results of all surgeries are uncertain, and that it was improbable that a surgeon would ever contract to make a damaged body part "one hundred per cent perfect." The trial court held that there was a contract, and that McGee (D) breached that contract.

■ **ISSUE**

Did McGee's guarantee constitute an inducement to make a contract?

■ **DECISION AND RATIONALE**

(Branch, J.) Yes. The question of whether a contract is formed is a factual question and is to be decided based on the words spoken, as well as the context in which they are spoken. The jury had a reasonable basis for determining that McGee (D) intended that his words should be taken at face value, and that he meant them to be an inducement to the granting of consent to the surgery.

The statement that Hawkins (P) would be home after three or four days in the hospital can only be construed as an opinion, not as a guarantee. It is the promise that Hawkins's (P) hand would be "one hundred per cent perfect" that provides the basis for the finding that McGee (D) made a guarantee. Reversed and remanded for a new trial on the issue of damages.

**Analysis:**

This case is popularly known as the "Hairy Hand" case, and has a firm place in the folklore of American legal education. The court emphasizes that it is merely upholding the findings of the jury that McGee's (D) statements, in their context, created a binding promise. It can be inferred that, had the jury found there was no guarantee, the court would have deferred to that finding as well. The question of whether particular words are sufficient to form a contract is a question of law to be decided by the court, but the ultimate question of whether the "sufficient" words do in fact make a contract is a factual one for the jury.

# Bayliner Marine Corp. v. Crow

(Boat Builder) v. (Buyer)
257 Va. 121, 509 S.E.2d 499 (1999)

WARRANTIES ARISE FROM STATEMENTS OF FACT

■ **INSTANT FACTS** Crow (P) purchased a boat manufactured by Bayliner (D) that did not perform as well as Crow (P) expected.

■ **BLACK LETTER RULE** Statements that do not relate to the particular item purchased, or that merely commend the quality of goods, do not create express warranties.

■ **PROCEDURAL BASIS**

Appeal from a judgment for Crow (P).

■ **FACTS**

Crow (P) purchased a "3486 Trophy Convertible," a sportfishing boat manufactured by Bayliner (D). He intended to use the boat for offshore fishing. Before the purchase, Crow took an excursion of approximately twenty minutes on the boat, and piloted the boat for a short period of time. There was no speed measurement equipment onboard the boat during the test, so Crow (P) could not determine its speed. A salesman told Crow (P) that he had no experience with that particular model boat, and had no knowledge of its performance. He gave Crow (P) copies of "prop matrixes," documents that showed the recommended propeller and engine sizes for each model made by Bayliner (D). The matrix showed that the 3486 Trophy Convertible had a top speed of thirty miles per hour with a "20x20" propeller. The matrix also stated that the data was for "comparative purposes only," and did not account for variables such as weather conditions. The matrix explained that testing was done with approximately 600 pounds of crew and equipment weight. Crow (P) was also given a brochure showing a 3486 Trophy Convertible fully rigged for offshore fishing. The brochure stated that the model "deliver[ed] the kind of performance you need to get to the prime offshore fishing grounds."

The boat purchased by Crow (P) had a "20x17" propeller. Crow (P) also purchased various accessories, such as navigational and fishing equipment, covers, an extra radio, an icemaker, and heating and air conditioning equipment, to be installed by the dealer. The total weight of the additional equipment was approximately 2,000 pounds. After Crow (P) took delivery of the boat, he found that he could not reach a top speed of more than 13 miles per hour. He returned the boat to the dealer, and various repairs and adjustments were made over the course of the next twelve to fourteen months. Despite those repairs and adjustments, the top speed reached by the boat was seventeen miles per hour, except for one time when the boat reached twenty-four miles per hour. A representative of Bayliner (D) told Crow (P) that the published figures he received were inaccurate, and that the maximum speed the boat could reach was twenty-three to twenty-five miles per hour.

Crow (P) brought suit against Bayliner (D), alleging breach of express and implied warranties of merchantability and fitness for a particular purpose. Crow (P) testified that the boat's low speed made it worthless to him, and that he would not have purchased it if he had known that the maximum speed was only twenty-three to twenty-five miles per hour. He testified that he could not use the boat for offshore fishing. Other witnesses testified that a typical offshore fishing site in the area was approximately ninety miles offshore, and the speed at which a boat could reach those fishing grounds had an impact on the amount of time left for fishing. The trial court ruled in Crow's (P) favor, and held that Bayliner (D) breached express and implied warranties of merchantability and fitness for a particular purpose.

## ■ ISSUE

Did Bayliner (D) make a warranty that was breached?

## ■ DECISION AND RATIONALE

(Keenan, J.) No. Statements that do not relate to the particular item purchased, or that merely commend the quality of goods, do not create express warranties. Express warranties are created by affirmations of fact, and the question of whether a particular statement creates a warranty is a factual question for the jury. A statement relating to the quality of particular goods may create a warranty. In this case, however, the statements in the prop matrix did not relate to the boat purchased by Crow (P), or even to a similar boat. Crow's (P) boat had a different propeller from the one referred to in the matrix and was loaded with substantially heavier equipment. The statements in the prop matrix could not constitute an express warranty with regard to Crow's (P) boat.

Similarly, the statements in the brochure did not create a warranty. The brochure was only a commendation of the boat's performance, and was only Bayliner's (D) opinion. Statements of opinion cannot create a warranty. Reversed.

---

### Analysis:

Why did Crow (P) think that the prop matrix contained anything about the performance of his boat when, at the very least, the propellers were different? Advertisements and marketing documents routinely carry disclaimers, so it should have come as no surprise to him that there would be some limitations or qualifications on the statistics set out. The case here concerns only Crow's (P) claim against Bayliner (D), but he also brought a claim against the dealer who sold him the boat. The opinion—addressing as it does only the claims against Bayliner (D)—does not say what, if anything, the dealer might have told Crow (P) when he selected the propeller and ordered the additional equipment.

---

## ■ CASE VOCABULARY

EXPRESS WARRANTY: A warranty created by the overt words or actions of the seller. Under the UCC, an express warranty is created by any of the following: (1) an affirmation of fact or promise made by the seller to the buyer relating to the goods that becomes the basis of the bargain; (2) a description of the goods that becomes part of the basis of the bargain; or (3) a sample or model made part of the basis of the bargain. UCC § 2–313.

IMPLIED WARRANTY OF FITNESS FOR A PARTICULAR PURPOSE: A warranty—implied by law if the seller has reason to know of the buyer's special purposes for the property—that the property is suitable for those purposes.—Sometimes shortened to *warranty of fitness.*

IMPLIED WARRANTY OF MERCHANTABILITY: A warranty that the property is fit for the ordinary purposes for which it is used.

# United States Naval Institute v. Charter Communications, Inc.

(Assignee of Copyright) v. (Publishing Lessee)

936 F.2d 692 (2nd Cir. 1991)

■ **INSTANT FACTS** Naval (P) bought an action against Charter Communications (D) and Berkeley Publishing Group (D) for breach of licensing contract not to publish book before the month of October.

■ **BLACK LETTER RULE** Courts will not grant punitive damages for a breach of contract.

■ **PROCEDURAL BASIS**

Appeal following remand for relief for breach of contract.

■ **FACTS**

Naval (P), as the assignee of the author's copyright of the book entitled "The Hunt For Red October," entered into a licensing agreement granting Charter Communications, Inc. (D) and Berkeley Publishing Group (D) an exclusive license to publish a paperback edition of the book *not sooner* than October 1985. But, the retail sales of the paperback began September 15, 1985. Early sales were sufficiently substantial that the book was near the top of the paperback best seller lists before the end of September. Naval (P) learned of Berkeley's (D) plans for early shipments, but could not get a preliminary injunction. After the trial, the District Court ruled that Berkeley (D) had not breached the contract because it was to ship prior to the agreed publication date, in accordance with industry custom. On appeal, the Circuit Court reversed the case holding that the contract was breached because of the retail sales prior to October 1985. The Circuit Court remanded the case back to the trial court for judgement and appropriate relief. On remand, the trial court concluded that Naval (P) was entitled to recover actual damages for copyright infringement and, in addition, profits wrongfully received by Berkeley (D) for that infringement. Both parties appealed the relief.

■ **ISSUE**

Will a court grant profits that are in addition to the actual damages on a breach of contract?

■ **DECISION AND RATIONALE**

(Kearsee). No. The purpose of damages for breach of contract is to compensate the injured party for the loss caused by the breach. Those damages are generally measured by the plaintiff's actual loss. While on occasion a defendant's profits are used as a measure of damages, this generally occurs when those profits tend to define the plaintiff's loss. The central object behind the system of contract remedies is compensatory, not punitive. Punitive damages are not recoverable for breach of contract unless conduct constituting the breach is also a tort, for which such damages are recoverable. Reverse the award for profits and affirm the award for damages.

**Analysis:**

One fundamental assumption made by courts in enforcing promises is that the law is concerned mainly with damages to redress the breach and not with the punishment of a promisor by compelling performance of a promise. Here the inclusion of profits in the calculation of damages was in addition to actual damages and thus equated to a punitive recovery. Courts normally attempt to put the plaintiff in the position he would have been in had the contract been performed, not a better one.

■ **CASE VOCABULARY**

ERRONEOUS: Groundless, characterized by error.

PUNITIVE: Relating to punishment; having the character of inflicting a punishment or penalty.

REMAND: To send back; the sending by the appellate court of the case back to the same court out of which it came, for the purpose of having some further action taken on it there.

# Sullivan v. O'Connor

(Patient) v. (Plastic Surgeon)
363 Mass. 579, 296 N.E.2d 183 (1973)

SUPREME COURT OF MASSACHUSETTS ENFORCES A DOCTOR'S PROMISE REGARDING A SUCCESSFUL NOSE JOB

■ **INSTANT FACTS** Plastic surgeon disfigures patient in the course of performing a nose job.

■ **BLACK LETTER RULE** Clear proof of a doctor's promise of specific medical results may give rise to an enforceable contract.

■ **PROCEDURAL BASIS**

Appeal from a jury verdict for the plaintiff in a breach of contract action.

■ **FACTS**

Sullivan (P), a professional entertainer, want to O'Connor (D) to have plastic surgery performed on her nose. O'Connor (D) promised to do the surgery. He also promised that it would make Sullivan (P) more beautiful and would enhance her appearance. In fact, the surgery was a disaster. O'Connor (D) told her the nose job would only require two operations, but it required three. He told her she would be more beautiful, but Instead, she was left with an asymmetrical nose which was flat and broad in some places and bulbous in others [aren't all noses?]. Her appearance could not be improved by further surgery. Sullivan (P) subsequently sued O'Connor (D) for malpractice. She also sued for breach of contract based on O'Connor's (D) representations prior to the surgery. It seems that O'Connor (D) never took this claim seriously since it appeared to be without precedent in Massachusetts. The jury ruled in Sullivan's (P) favor on the breach of contract Issue and O'Connor (D) appeals this verdict.

■ **ISSUE**

Can an agreement between a doctor and a patient for a specified medical result be enforced?

■ **DECISION AND RATIONALE**

(Kaplan) Yes. Courts have occasionally enforced agreements between doctors and patients. However they generally enforce these agreements reluctantly and with certain considerations in mind. Medical practice is Inherently uncertain. The physical needs and reactions to treatment vary from patient to patient. Doctors cannot be he??liable for every optimistic opinion of a patient's condition [not a problem for Dr. Kevorklan]. Unfortunately, patients are likely to interpret these opinions as promises, especially when things do not work out as planned. In addition, patients must be protected from unscrupulous doctors who fraudulently promise miraculous results. The difficulty lies in the grey area between optimistic opinions and unfounded promises. It is necessary to balance the protection which individual doctors require against the need to protect the integrity of the medical profession. As a result, courts have required clear proof before considering a breach of contract action in a doctor/patient relationship. In this case, ?? no error in permitting the breach of contract claim to go forward. Judgement Affirmed.

**Analysis:**

Justice Kaplan appears to support an Inquiry Into the patient's subjective interpretation of a doctor's opinion in order to determine if a promise has been made. This approach is not necessarily at odds with the objective intent theory. Courts will frequently assume that parties to business contracts have a working knowledge of the terms and conditions that are generally associated with their business. In this case, the court is simply charging doctors with the knowledge that their objectively harmless opinions may have a significant impact on a distraught or confused patient. This seems reasonable, since doctors are sought out precisely because they take control of situations that are beyond the abilities of their patients. Another possible approach to this problem is used in Michigan, where agreements regarding the success of medical treatment are now statutorily void unless signed and in writing.

■ **CASE VOCABULARY**

BILL OF EXCEPTIONS: Formal written statement of the objections by a party during trial to the trial judge's decisions, rulings or instructions.

CASE AT BAR: Case before the court.

CHARLATAN: A quack or fraud; one who makes a noisy, showy pretense to knowledge or ability.

COUNT: (n.) One of the plaintiff's causes of action.

EXCEPT: (v.) To leave out of an account or consideration; to object.

EXPECTANCY: That which is expected or hoped for, sometimes conditioned on or dependent on an expected event.

NONSUITED: A case that has a judgment given against it because plaintiff is unable to prove his case (Involuntary nonsuit) or refuses or neglects to proceed to trial (voluntary nonsuit).

SEDULOUS: Diligent in application or pursuit.

SPECIAL QUESTION: A point in dispute which is submitted for the decision of a jury.

STATUS QUO ANTE: The state of things before.

# White v. Benkowski

(Water Purchaser) v. (Water Supplier)

37 Wis.2d 285, 155 N.W.2d 74 (1967)

■ **INSTANT FACTS** White (P) recovered a judgment against Benkowski (D) for breach of a contract to supply water, and the court reduced the damages awarded by the jury to one dollar in compensatory damages and no punitive damages.

■ **BLACK LETTER RULE** Punitive damages may not be recovered for breach of contract.

## ■ PROCEDURAL BASIS

Appeal from an order reducing a jury award for White (P).

## ■ FACTS

The Whites (P) bought a house with no water supply of its own, but with a connection to a well on Benkowski's (D) property. The Whites (P) and Benkowskis (D) entered into a written agreement under which the Benkowskis (D) agreed to supply water to the Whites (P) for ten years. The Whites (P) agreed to pay three dollars per month plus half the costs of future repairs or maintenance. Eventually, the relationship deteriorated. On nine occasions, Benkowski (D) shut off the water for periods of less than an hour. Benkowski (D) acknowledged shutting off the water, and said it was done either to allow accumulated sand in the pipes to settle or to remind the Whites (P) that their water usage was excessive. On one of these occasions, the lack of water in the bathroom caused an odor, and on two other occasions, the Whites (P) had to take their children to a neighbor's house to bathe.

White (P) brought suit for breach of contract, asking for compensatory and punitive damages. The trial court instructed the jury on nominal damages, telling the jury that a nominal award was appropriate when the no pecuniary damages had been proven. The court based this instruction on the calculation that the Whites' (P) loss in proportion to the contract price for their water was approximately twenty-five cents. The jury awarded the Whites (P) compensatory damages of $10 and punitive damages of $2,000. The trial court reduced the award to $1 in compensatory damages and no punitive damages.

## ISSUE

Are punitive damages available in breach of contract cases?

## DECISION AND RATIONALE

(Wilkie, J.) No. Punitive damages may not be recovered for breach of contract. Punitive damages are permitted in some tort actions to punish, but, with the limited exception of claims for breach of contract to marry, have never been allowed in contract cases. Cases from other jurisdictions hold that punitive damages are unavailable in breach of contract cases without exception. This is true even though the breach, as it was here, is willful.

The trial court's instruction on compensatory damages was erroneous. The calculation of the amount of the Whites' (P) loss did not consider the inconvenience to them of the water shut-off. In viewing the evidence most favorable to the Whites (P), there was some injury, and the Whites (P) were not required to prove their damages with mathematical precision. The jury found that the appropriate amount of damages was $10, which is more than nominal. The trial court was in error when it reduced the compensatory damages award, and that award should be reinstated. Reversed in part.

## Analysis:

The court can give no stronger rationale for its refusal to allow punitive damages than to say that it just isn't done. The usual reasoning is that contract law does not seek to punish, but to compensate. In this case, in which Benkowski (D) acted out of malice (at least some of the time), the lines between tort and contract seem to blur. Shutting off the water doesn't fit into one of the traditional tort causes of action, and the only legally recognized "wrong" done was to go against the terms of the contract. This makes the action a contract action, even if it may seem tortious.

## ■ CASE VOCABULARY

NOMINAL DAMAGES: A trifling sum awarded when a legal injury is suffered but when there is no substantial loss or injury to be compensated; a small amount fixed as damages for breach of contract without regard to the amount of harm.

PECUNIARY DAMAGES: Damages that can be estimated and monetarily compensated. Although this phrase appears in many old cases, it is now widely considered a redundancy, since damages are always pecuniary.

PUNITIVE DAMAGES: Damages awarded in addition to actual damages when the defendant acted with recklessness, malice, or deceit.

# Hamer v. Sidway

(Assignee of Right of Nephew) v. (Executor of Uncle)

124 N.Y. 538, 27 N.E. 256 (1891)

---

FORBEARANCE OR GIVING UP SOME LEGAL RIGHT IS GOOD CONSIDERATION TO SUPPORT A PROMISE

---

■ **INSTANT FACTS** William E. Story Sr. (D) promised his nephew, William E. Story Jr. (P) , that he would pay William Jr. $5,000 if William Jr. would refrain from drinking, using tobacco, swearing, and gambling, until William Jr. Was 21 years of age, which William Jr. did.

■ **BLACK LETTER RULE** The party who abandons some legal right in the present or limits his legal freedom of action in the future as an inducement for a promise, gives sufficient consideration to create a legally binding contract.

---

■ **PROCEDURAL BASIS**

An appeal from the supreme court reversing the trial court judgment that awarded judgment for Hamer (P), the assignee, against Sidway (D), the executor.

■ **FACTS**

On March 20, 1869, William E. Story, Sr.(D) promised William E. Story, Jr. (P) that if William Jr. would refrain from drinking, using tobacco, swearing, and playing cards or billiards for money until William Jr. became 21 years of age, William Sr. would pay him $5,000. On January 31, 1875, after William Jr. (P) had become 21 years old, William Jr. wrote his uncle, William Sr. (D), and informed him that he had performed his part of the agreement and was entitled to the $5,000. William Sr. (D) wrote his nephew back and stated that "I have no doubt but you have, for which you shall have five thousands dollars as I promised you." However, William Sr. insisted that William Sr. continue to keep the money in the bank for William Jr. until William Jr. was capable of making good decisions about the use of the money, when he would then receive the $5,000 with interest. William Jr. (P) agreed to these terms. On January 29, 1887, William Sr. (D) died without having paid William Jr. (P) the $5,000 and interest. William Jr.'s right was subsequently assigned to Hamer, the plaintiff, who sued William Sr.'s executor, Sidway, the defendant in this action.

■ **ISSUE**

Is forbearance to do that for which one has a legal right to do sufficient consideration to support a promise made to induce the forbearance?

■ **DECISION AND RATIONALE**

(Parker) Yes. A valuable consideration in the sense of the law may consist either in some right interest, profit, or benefit accruing to the one party, or some forbearance, detriment, loss, or responsibility given, suffered, or undertaken by the other. The forbearance does not have to benefit the promises or a third party, or have any substantial value to any one. It is enough that something is promised, done, forborne, or suffered by the party to whom the promise is made as consideration for the promise made to him. William Jr. (P) used tobacco, occasionally drank liquor, and he had a legal right to do so. He abandoned these rights for a period of years upon the strength of William Sr.'s (D) promise that for such forbearance William Sr. would give him $5,000. It is not of any legal importance whether or not the forbearance benefitted William Sr. (D). The judgment of the supreme court is reversed and the special term judgment for plaintiff, Hamer, is affirmed.

**Analysis:**

The waiver of the legal right in this case was clearly induced by the promise of the uncle. The court pointed out that the consideration given may in fact have benefitted the nephew even more than the uncle. However, the degree of benefit is not measured by the court to determine the validity of a contract. The determining factor is that William Sr. (D) "bargained" for the surrender of William Jr.'s (P) legal right to drink alcohol, use tobacco, and gamble. The abandonment of these rights may have saved William Jr. (P) money or contributed to his health, nevertheless this same abandonment, when bargained for, is sufficient consideration to uphold the promise.

■ **CASE VOCABULARY**

MESNE ASSIGNMENT: An previous assignment of a right or interest that occurred prior to the current assignment.

# Fiege v. Boehm

(Claimed Father) v. (Pregnant Woman)

210 Md. 352, 123 A.2d 316 (1956)

FORBEARANCE OF A LAWFUL CLAIM IS SUFFICIENT CONSIDERATION IF BASED ON GOOD FAITH BELIEF OF RIGHT

■ **INSTANT FACTS** Hilda Boehm (P) alleged that Louis Fiege (D) promised to pay all her medical expenses and compensate her for her loss in salary caused by her child's birth, for which Fiege (D) was the alleged father.

■ **BLACK LETTER RULE** Forbearance to sue for a lawful claim or demand is sufficient consideration for a promise if the party forbearing had an honest intention to prosecute litigation which is not frivolous, vexatious, or unlawful, and which he believed to be well-founded.

■ **PROCEDURAL BASIS**

An appeal from the trial court judgment for Boehm (P).

■ **FACTS**

Boehm (P) alleged that Fiege (D) had sexual intercourse with her, and the result of that intercourse was that she became pregnant. Boehm (P) further alleged that Fiege (D) agreed to pay all her medical and hospital expenses, to compensate her for loss of salary caused by the pregnancy and birth, and to pay her ten dollars per week for the support of the child, upon condition that she would refrain from instituting bastardy proceedings against him. Boehm (P) further testified that Fiege (D) paid a total of $480 from September 17, 1951, to May, 1953, pursuant to the agreement. In September, 1953, after Fiege (D) stopped making payments to Boehm (P), she brought bastardy proceedings against him in Criminal Court. Fiege (D) was found not guilty solely on the Landsteiner blood-grouping testimony. The blood test showed that Flege's (D) blood group was Type O, Boehm's (P) was Type B, and the infant's was Type A. The physician who performed the test, further testified at the criminal trial that on the basis of the blood tests, Fiege (D) could not have been the father of the child, as it was impossible for a mating of Type O and Type B to result in a child of Type A. Subsequently, Boehm (P) brought this action in civil court for the sum of $2,415.80, the balance due under the agreement, for which Flege (D) failed to pay Boehm (P). Following the Court's instruction that Flege's (D) acquittal in Criminal Court was not binding upon them, the jury found a verdict in favor of Boehm (P) for $2,415.80.

■ **ISSUE**

Is forbearance to assert a claim sufficient consideration to support a promise if the parties entering into it thought at the time that there was a bona fide question between them, although it may eventually be found that there was in fact no such question?

■ **DECISION AND RATIONALE**

(Delaplaine) Yes. The forbearance to assert a claim is sufficient to support a promise if there is a subjective belief in a bona fide claim, and there is an objective reasonable basis to support the claim. The claim forborne must be neither absurd in fact from the standpoint of a reasonable man in the position of the claimant, nor obviously unfounded in law to one who has an elementary knowledge of legal principles. Forbearance to sue for a lawful claim or demand is sufficient consideration for a promise to pay for the forbearance, if the party forbearing had an honest intention to prosecute litigation, which is not frivolous, vexatious, or unlawful, and which he believed to be well-founded. Boehm (P) gave testimony which indicated that she made the charge of bastardy against Fiege (D) in good faith. For these reasons the Court acted properly in overruling Flege's (D) demurrer to the complaint and Fiege's (D) motion for a directed verdict. The jury verdict and the trial court judgment is affirmed.

### Analysis:

Maryland had a civil statute that provided that whenever a person was found guilty of bastardy, the court had to issue an order directing such person to pay, for the maintenance and support of the child, an agreed-upon amount, or in the absence of an agreement, such sum as the court may fix. If the party failed to give the required bond as security for payments, then the party could be punished by commitment in jail. The court pointed out that, although prosecutions for bastardy are treated in Maryland as criminal proceedings, there prosecutions are actually civil in purpose. Therefore, Boehm (P) was promising to forbear pursuing a lawful civil claim resulting from a criminal act. Boehm (P) testified that on January 21, 1951. Fiege (D), after taking her to a moving picture theater on York Road and then to a restaurant, had sexual intercourse with her in his automobile. The court observed that the jury believed her story, and this tends to prove that a reasonable man in the position of the claimant would have a subjective bona fide belief in the claim.

### ■ CASE VOCABULARY

BONA FIDE: An absence of deceit or fraud; a genuine good-faith belief in a position or claim.

# Feinberg v. Pfeiffer Co.

(Employee) v. (Employer)
322 S.W.2d 163 (Mo. App. 1959)

A PROMISE MADE IN CONSIDERATION OF A PRIOR PERFORMANCE IS NOT SUFFICIENT TO CREATE A BINDING CONTRACT

■ **INSTANT FACTS** Pfeiffer Co. (D) stopped making pension payments, pursuant to a resolution adopted by the Board of Directors, to Feinberg (P) after she retired.

■ **BLACK LETTER RULE** Past services is not sufficient consideration to support a promise.

■ **PROCEDURAL BASIS**

An appeal from Circuit Court that rendered a judgment for Feinberg (P).

■ **FACTS**

In 1910, when Feinberg (P) was 17 years old, she begin working for Pfeiffer Co. (D). She continued to work for Pfeiffer Co. (D), and by 1947, Feinberg (P) had attained the position of bookkeeper, office manager, and assistant treasurer. On December 24, 1947, the Board of Directors adopted the following resolution: "Resolved, that the salary of Anna Sacks Feinberg be Increased from $350.00 to $400.00 per month and that she be afforded the privilege of retiring from active duty in the corporation at any time she may elect to see fit so to do upon retirement pay of $200.00 per month, for the remainder of her life." The Chairman stated that the company desired to show its appreciation to Feinberg (P) for her many years of long and faithful service, and that the resolution was to be adopted to afford Mrs. Feinberg security for the future and in the hope that her active services would continue with the corporation for many years to come. Feinberg (P) was notified of the resolution the same day it was adopted. Feinberg continued to work for Pfeiffer Co. (D) through June 30, 1949, on which date she retired. Pfeiffer Co. (D) made the $200 payments to Feinberg (P) until April 1, 1956, at which time Pfeiffer reduced the payment to $1.00. Feinberg (P) declined to accept the reduced amount, and brought this action based on Pfeiffer Co.'s (D) agreement.

■ **ISSUE**

Is past performance sufficient consideration to support a promise?

■ **DECISION AND RATIONALE**

(Doerner) No. A valid contract requires mutuality of obligation bargained for and given in exchange for the promise. The consideration sufficient to support a contract may be either a benefit to the promisor or a loss or detriment to the promisee. There is nothing in the resolution adopted by Pfeiffer Co. (D) that made its effectiveness conditional upon Feinberg's (P) continued employment. Feinberg (P) was not under contract to work for any length of time but was free to quit whenever she wished. Feinberg (P) had no contractual right to her position and could have been discharged at any time. Feinberg (P) made no promise or agreement to continue in the employ of the Pfeiffer Co. (D) in return for its promise to pay her a pension. The judgment of the Circuit Court is reversed.

**Analysis:**

The chairman stated that it was hoped that Feinberg would continue working in the future (which she did). Arguably, she would have quit at that moment and may have planned to do so, but continued on because of the pension. But Feinberg's (P) past years of faithful service were not bargained for in return for the promise to pay her a retirement pension of $200. In reality, the pension was merely a present gift. If the retirement plan existed prior to her employment, and she was notified of this plan prior to accepting employment, then there is a strong argument that her long faithful service with the company would have been bargained for. When the issue is whether the performance was bargained for, the court does not have to consider the issue of the degree of benefit given.

# Mills v. Wyman

(Good Samaritan) v. (Father of Ill Person)
20 Mass. 207, 3 Pick. 207 (1825)

A PROMISE TO PAY FOR PAST EXPENSES IS NOT SUPPORTED BY CONSIDERATION

■ **INSTANT FACTS** Seth Wyman (D) failed to pay Daniel Mills (P) as promised for the expenses Mills (P) incurred from providing care for Wyman's (D) ill son.

■ **BLACK LETTER RULE** Past expense is not sufficient consideration to support a later promise to pay for the expenses.

■ **PROCEDURAL BASIS**

An appeal from a judgment granting nonsuit of Mills' (P) claim.

■ **FACTS**

Mills (P) incurred expenses arising out of caring for Levi Wyman, who fell ill on his return from a sea voyage. Mills (P) gave Levi Wyman shelter and comfort for about two weeks until Wyman died. A few days later, after Mills' (P) expenses had been incurred, Levi Wyman's father, Seth Wyman (D), promised in writing to pay for the expenses. Seth Wyman (D) then decided not to pay.

■ **ISSUE**

Does a past expense incurred support a later promise to reimburse the expenses?

■ **DECISION AND RATIONALE**

(Parker) No. It is only when the party making the promise gains something, or he to whom it is made loses something, that the law gives the promise validity. Mills's (P) kindness and services towards Wyman's (D) sick son were not given at Wyman's request. Wyman's (D) promise to pay for the expenses incurred, influenced by a transient feeling of gratitude, was made without any legal consideration. Judgment ordered for nonsuit is affirmed.

**Analysis:**

This case stands for the principle that a "moral obligation" that motivates a promise for some benefit previously received is not sufficient consideration to create a binding contract. Exceptions to this rule are (1) a promise to pay a debt that is no longer enforceable because the statute of limitations has run; and (2) a promise made as an adult, subsequent to the same promise made as a minor, that was avoided on the basis of the age of the party.

■ **CASE VOCABULARY**

NONSUIT: Judgment ordered on nonsuit results when the plaintiff has no legal basis for his action based on the proof presented at trial.

# Webb v. McGowin

(Life-Saving Employee) v. (Executor of Saved Person)

27 Ala. App. 82, 168 So. 196 (1935)

THE ACT OF SAVING A PARTY FROM DEATH OR GRIEVOUS BODILY HARM IS SUFFICIENT CONSIDERATION TO SUPPORT A SUBSEQUENTLY INDUCED PROMISE

■ **INSTANT FACTS** Joe Webb (P) saved Greeley McGowin (D) from death or serious bodily harm during Webb's (P) course of employment, for which McGowin (D) agreed to pay Webb (P) $15 every two weeks for the remainder of Webb's (P) life.

■ **BLACK LETTER RULE** Past act of saving a party from death or serious bodily injury, that results in injuries to the saving party, is sufficient consideration for the saved party's subsequently induced promise to pay the saving party.

■ **PROCEDURAL BASIS**

An appeal by Webb (P) from a judgment of nonsuit at trial court.

■ **FACTS**

Webb's (P) work required him to clear the upper floor of a lumber mill by dropping heavy pine blocks from the upper floor of the mill to the ground below. During one such occasion, on August 3, 1925, while Webb (P) was working within the scope of his employment, Webb (P) diverted a 75-pound block, that he was clearing, from dropping on Greeley McGowin (D) below, by falling with the block to the floor below. Webb (P) was successful in preventing any injuries to McGowin (D). However, Webb (P) received serious bodily injuries, resulting in his right leg being broken, the heel of his right foot tom off and his right arm broken. He was badly crippled for life and rendered unable to do physical or mental labor. On September 1, 1925, McGowin (D) agreed to pay Webb (P) $15 every two weeks from the time he sustained his injuries to and during the remainder of Webb's life. It was agreed that McGowin (D) would pay this amount to Webb (P) for Webb's maintenance. McGowin paid the sum so agreed up until McGowin's (D) death on January 1, 1934, at which time they were discontinued. Webb (P) sued McGowin's (D) estate for the balance of the payments due.

■ **ISSUE**

Are past acts of saving a party from death or serious boldly injury sufficient consideration to support a subsequently induced promise?

■ **DECISION AND RATIONALE**

(Bricken) Yes. Any holding that saving a man from death or grievous bodily harm is not a material benefit sufficient to uphold a subsequent promise to pay for the service, necessarily rests on the assumption that saving life and preservation of the body from harm have only sentimental value. Had McGowin been accidentally poisoned and a physician, without his knowledge or request, had administered an antidote, a subsequent promise by McGowin (D) to pay the physician would have been valid. Likewise, McGowin's (D) agreement to compensate Webb (P) for saving him from death or grievous bodily injury is valid and enforceable. In the business of life insurance, the value of a man's life is measured in dollars and cents according to his expectancy, soundness of his body, and his ability to pay premiums. In the act of saving McGowin (D) from death or grievous bodily harm, Webb (P) was crippled for life. This was part of the consideration of the contract McGowin (D) made with Webb (P). Benefit to the promisor or injury to the promisee is a sufficient legal consideration for the promisor's agreement to pay. The court below erred in sustaining the demurrer, and for this error the case is reversed and remanded.

■ **CONCURRENCE**

(Sanford) Yes. "I do not think that law ought to be separated from justice, where it is at most doubtful." Chief Justice Marshall in *Hoffman v. Porter*, Fed Cas. 6,5777; 2 Brock, 156, 159.

■ **CONCURRENCE**

(Foster) Yes. McGowin (D) benefited substantially from the performance by Webb (P), and when this is considered with the injuries to Webb (P), this constituted sufficient consideration to support McGowin's (D) subsequent promise to pay Webb (P).

---

**Analysis:**

The court here discussed the value of a life and the severity of the injuries suffered by Webb (P). Although the case is arguably a case where a "moral obligation" was held to be sufficient consideration, the distinction in this case is the degree of the injuries to Webb (P) and the act of saving a life. One of the concurring opinions quoted Chief Justice Marshall as stating, "This case is about achieving justice." This type of rationale has been condemned by legal scholars, who claim that it is a wanton departure from legal principles and replaces sound legal logic with sentiment. New York is one jurisdiction that has given legal effect to promises based on consideration consisting of a past performance, when the promise is in writing and it meets other requirements.

---

■ **CASE VOCABULARY**

ASSUMPSIT: In contracts this refers to oral promises made without written record as evidence of the promise.

DEMURRER: In court pleadings this is a claim that even if all of the allegations are accepted as true, the party claiming the allegations still has not shown a legal basis for recovery.

# Kirksey v. Kirksey

(Widow) v. (Brother-in-Law)

8 Ala. 131 (1845)

RELIANCE DOES NOT IMPOSE CONTRACTUAL LIABILITY IN THE ABSENCE OF A BARGAINED-FOR EXCHANGE

■ **INSTANT FACTS** A widow attempts to impose contractual liability for a promise made by her brother-in-law which induced her to leave her residence and move to his estate.

■ **BLACK LETTER RULE** A bargained-for exchange is required for all contracts, and merely changing position in reliance on a statement is insufficient to impose contractual liability in absence of any bargain.

■ **PROCEDURAL BASIS**

Appeal from judgment for damages for breach of contract.

■ **FACTS**

Antillico Kirksey (P) lived in a home approximately sixty miles away from her brother-in-law, Mr. Kirksey (D). After Antillico's (P) husband died, Mr. Kirksey (D) wrote to Antillico (P) and expressed concern with her living situation. He stated that if Antillico (P) would come down and see him, he would give Antillico (P) a place to raise her family and some land to tend. He stated that, considering her plight, he wanted Antillico (P) and her children to do well and have a nice place to live. Within a month or two of receiving the letter, Antillico (P) abandoned her home and moved to the residence of Mr. Kirksey (D). He gave Antillico (P) a comfortable house and land to cultivate for two years, but then he forced Antillico (P) to move into an uncomfortable house in the woods. Later, he even required Antillico (P) to abandon this house. Antillico (P) sued, alleging that Mr. Kirksey (D) had made a promise and that she had fulfilled her obligations under the contract, but that he had breached. The trial court granted a $200 judgment for Antillico (P). Mr. Kirksey (D) appealed.

■ **ISSUE**

Is a change of residence in reliance on a promise to provide a new residence sufficient consideration to impose contractual duties upon the promisor?

■ **DECISION AND RATIONALE**

(Ormond, J.) No. A change of residence in reliance on a promise to provide a new residence is not necessarily sufficient consideration to impose contractual duties upon the promisor. In this situation, the promise of Mr. Kirksey (D) has been interpreted by the majority of the court as a mere gratuity. As such, Mr. Kirksey (D) did not enter into a binding contract with Antillico (P). I tend to disagree. In my mind, the loss and inconvenience that Antillico (P) suffered in moving to Mr. Kirksey's (D) land is sufficient consideration to support Mr. Kirksey's (D) promise to furnish her with a house and land to cultivate. However, my brothers on this court disagree. Reversed.

**Analysis:**

This case is one of the prime examples of the difficulty of interpreting contractual language and behavior. The central issue in this case is the intent of Mr. Kirksey (D), the promisor. Was Mr. Kirksey (D) making a bargained-for exchange, in which he promised to provide a house and land in exchange for Antillico's (P) action of moving to his estate? Or was Mr. Kirksey (D) simply offering a gift to which no contractual duties attach? Sound arguments can be made for each position. On one hand, it appears that Mr. Kirksey (D) was bargaining for Antillico's (P) performance. For example, he states that he feels that he wants Antillico (P) and the children to do well, which seems to indicate that he will obtain some psychological benefit from her performance. On the other hand, it can be argued that this was clearly a gift, and that her moving down to his estate was simply the condition that had to be met in order to obtain the gratuity. In either case, Antillico (P) certainly relied on Mr. Kirksey's (D) words, and her actions seem to constitute valid consideration. But this consideration is meaningless if, as the Court concluded, Mr. Kirksey (D) was not making a bargain, but rather was simply offering a mere gratuity.

---

■ **CASE VOCABULARY**

GRATUITY: Something voluntarily given and acquired without a bargained-for exchange.

# Lake Land Employment Group of Akron, LLC v. Columber

(Former Employer) v. (Former Employee)

101 Ohio St. 3d 242, 804 N.E. 2d 27 (2004)

## CONTINUED EMPLOYMENT IS SUFFICIENT CONSIDERATION FOR A NON–COMPETE AGREEMENT

■ **INSTANT FACTS** Columber (D) worked for Lake Land (P) for several years before signing an agreement not to compete with Lake Land (P) and later claimed that the agreement was not supported by consideration.

■ **BLACK LETTER RULE** The continuation of an at-will employment relationship after the employer imposes a new requirement on the employee is sufficient consideration for the employee's agreement to that requirement.

■ **PROCEDURAL BASIS**

Appeal from an order affirming a grant of summary judgment.

■ **FACTS**

Columber (D) began working for Lake Land (P) in 1988. In September 1991, he signed a non-compete agreement with Lake Land (P) that provided that Columber (D) would not, for a period of three years after termination of his employment with Lake Land (P), engage in any competing business within a fifty-mile radius of Akron, Ohio. Columber (D) received no additional pay or benefits in connection with signing the non-competition agreement.

Columber's (D) employment with Lake Land (P) ended in 2001, and Columber (D) opened a business similar to Lake Land (P). Lake Land (P) brought suit against Columber (D), and Columber (D) pleaded lack of consideration. He testified that he remembered little about the noncompetition agreement, but admitted signing it. He could not remember if he was told that his continued employment depended upon his signing the agreement. The trial court granted Columber (D) summary judgment, finding that there was no consideration for the agreement. The trial court did not address the reasonableness of the time and geographic restrictions in the agreement. The Ohio Court of Appeals affirmed.

■ **ISSUE**

Was the noncompetition agreement supported by consideration?

■ **DECISION AND RATIONALE**

(Moyer, C.J.) Yes. The continuation of an at-will employment relationship after the employer imposes a new requirement on the employee is sufficient consideration for the employee's agreement to that requirement. In an at-will employment relationship, either the employer or the employee is free to propose changes in the employment relationship at any time. The employee who is dissatisfied with an employer's proposal may quit. Similarly, the employer who does not agree to a proposal from the employee may either negotiate a change or accept the loss of the employee. Presentation of a noncompetition agreement is, in effect, a proposal to renegotiate the terms of the at-will employment. Acceptance of the agreement is accepting employment on new terms, and is supported by consideration. Assent to the agreement is given in exchange for the forbearance from terminating the employee.

Traditionally, courts have carefully scrutinized noncompetition agreements. Restraints of trade were long disfavored, and restrictions on competition could either destroy a person's means of earning a livelihood or bind him to an employer for life. Modern economic realities do not justify a strict prohibition on noncompetition agreements. Noncompetition agreements allow the parties to work together, without fear that one will leave with confidential information and secrets, to engage in a competing business.

Jurisdictions that have held that continued employment is not sufficient consideration have stressed that an employee has little bargaining power once employed and is subject to coercion. By signing a noncompetition agreement, an employee gets no more than he or she already has. The noncompetition agreement is not a protection of the employer's investment, but a barrier to the employee's mobility. Recently, however, some courts have found sufficient consideration when there has been a substantial period of employment after the noncompetition agreement is executed, particularly when continued employment is accompanied by raises, promotions, or other tangible benefits. These courts have found, in effect, that the employment relationship is changed from one purely at-will to employment for an indefinite, but substantial, term.

Recognition that continued employment is sufficient consideration for a noncompetition agreement does not preclude an inquiry into the reasonableness of the agreement. Examination of the factors relating to the reasonableness of an agreement should be separate from an inquiry into the adequacy of consideration. Reversed and remanded.

■ DISSENT

(Resnick, J.) The only difference between the parties' relationship after the execution of the noncompetition agreement was the agreement itself. If the same relationship continues, where is the consideration? The employer has relinquished nothing, and the employee has gained nothing. The employer ends up with the agreement and the continued right to terminate the employee. The majority's opinion would uphold a noncompetition agreement signed one day before the employee was terminated.

■ DISSENT

(Pfeifer, J.) Continued employment in exchange for signing a noncompetition agreement does not constitute consideration—it is coercion. Any promise of continued employment makes the relationship something other than employment at will, and imposes on the employer an obligation to continue employing the employee for some period of time, but the majority does not define that time period.

---

**Analysis:**

The circumstances under which Columber (D) stopped working for Lake Land (P) are not discussed, but it is stated that he was "discharged," meaning that he did not leave voluntarily. In a number of jurisdictions, noncompetition agreements are unenforceable if the employee did not quit voluntarily. In other jurisdictions, involuntary termination does not make a noncompetition agreement unenforceable unless the termination was in "bad faith." "Bad faith" is hard to define in this context, but could include Judge Resnick's scenario of an employee fired the day after signing a noncompete agreement.

---

■ CASE VOCABULARY

AT WILL: Subject to one's discretion; as one wishes or chooses; especially (of a legal relationship), able to be terminated or discharged by either party without cause.

# Strong v. Sheffield

(Creditor) v. (Guarantor)

144 N.Y. 392, 39 N.E. 330 (1895)

## ILLUSORY PROMISES DO NOT CREATE BINDING CONTRACTS

■ **INSTANT FACTS** Strong (P) attempts to obtain payment for a note from the guarantor, although Strong (P) convinced the guarantor to sign the note merely by promising not to demand payment until he felt like it.

■ **BLACK LETTER RULE** In order to be legally binding, a promise must be supported by consideration and cannot be illusory.

■ **PROCEDURAL BASIS**

Appeal of reversal of judgment for payment of promissory note.

■ **FACTS**

Benjamin Strong (P) sold his business on credit to Louisa Sheffield's (D) husband, Gerardus. Strong (P) sought a promissory note from Gerardus for this antecedent debt, and Strong (P) wanted Louisa (D), his niece, to endorse the note as security for the debt. Strong (P) promised that he would not put the note away, but rather that he would keep it until such time as he would demand payment. Strong (P) did not promise to forbear on collection for any specific period of time. Based on this promise from Strong (P), Louisa (D) endorsed the note. After the note was executed, Strong (P) waited for two years before demanding payment. Louisa (D) refused to satisfy her undertaking, and Strong (P) sued for payment on the note. The trial court granted a judgment for Strong (P), and the New York Supreme Court reversed. Strong (P) appeals.

■ **ISSUE**

Does a promise not to take some action for an unspecified period of time constitute sufficient consideration to create a contract?

■ **DECISION AND RATIONALE**

(Andrews, J.) No. A promise not to take some action for an unspecified period of time does not constitute sufficient consideration to create a contract. Gerardus' debt, secured by the promissory note, was already past due. The only possible consideration for Louisa's (D) endorsement was that Strong (P) promised to forbear the collection of the debt, and that this promise was followed by a forbearance of two years. However, at the time of making the promise, Strong (P) did not promise to forbear for any specific period of time. The note did not extend the period for paying the debt, as the note was payable on demand at any time. Gerardus and Louisa (D) may have hoped that Strong (P) would forbear, and indeed he did forbear for two years. However, there was no agreement to forbear. Consideration must be tested by the agreement itself, not by what actually occurred under the agreement. This was a case of mutual promises, with no consideration exchanged for Louisa's (D) endorsement. Accordingly, the endorsement on the note did not create a valid contract. Affirmed.

**Analysis:**

Although a contract can be formed with a promise exchanged for a promise, both promises must be valid. This case provides an example of an illusory promise. Strong (P) made no promise of any substance to the Sheffields (P), because he could demand payment on the note at any time. Likewise, Strong's (P) "promise" to forbear was not sufficient consideration for Louisa's (D) endorsement, since Strong (P) did not agree to any specific period of forbearance. If Louisa (D) had bargained for a two-year forbearance, and Strong (P) had agreed in order to get Louisa (D) to endorse the note, then a valid contract most likely would have been created. But promises must have some substance; they cannot be illusory.

---

## ■ CASE VOCABULARY

ILLUSORY PROMISE: A purported promise that entitles the promisor to perform or not perform, at his own choice and with no binding commitment either way.

NUDUM PACTUM: An illusory promise or agreement, not supported by any consideration.

UNDERTAKING: A promise or security by one party which does not necessarily imply any consideration.

# Mattei v. Hopper

(Buyer) v. (Seller)

51 Cal.2d 119, 330 P.2d 625 (1958)

## SATISFACTION CLAUSES DO NOT RENDER CONTRACTS ILLUSORY OR LACKING IN MUTUALITY

■ **INSTANT FACTS** A seller attempts to back out of a real estate sale on the ground that the buyer's satisfaction clause rendered the buyer's promise illusory.

■ **BLACK LETTER RULE** A contract that is dependent on one party's subjective satisfaction with related matters may nevertheless be enforceable.

## ■ PROCEDURAL BASIS

Appeal from judgment denying damages for breach of contract.

## ■ FACTS

Mattei (P), a real estate developer, and Hopper (D), a landowner, entered into a written agreement for the sale of Hopper's (D) property. The written agreement was evidenced by a deposit receipt, under which Mattei (P) paid $1000 of the total purchase price of $57,500. Mattei (P) was given 120 days to examine the title and consummate the purchase, subject to Mattei's (P) bank obtaining leases satisfactory to Mattei (P). While Mattei (P) was in the process of securing the leases for this commercial property, Hopper (D) notified Mattei (P) that he would not sell the property. Thereafter, Mattei (P) offered to pay the balance of the purchase price, but Hopper (D) failed to tender the deed as provided in the deposit receipt. Mattei (P) sued for breach of contract. The trial court concluded that the agreement was illusory and lacking in mutuality. Mattei (P) appeals.

## ■ ISSUE

Can a contract that is dependent upon one party's satisfaction with a related matter be enforceable?

## ■ DECISION AND RATIONALE

(Spence, J.) Yes. A contract that is dependent upon one party's satisfaction with a related matter can be enforceable. Satisfaction clauses have been given effect and do not necessarily render a contract illusory or lacking in mutuality of obligation. Indeed, where parties attempt to make a contract with promises alone, the promises must be mutual in obligation in order to be supported by valid consideration. In other words, both parties must have assumed some legal obligations. The presence of the satisfaction clause does not mean that Mattei (P) assumed no legal obligations. There are two types of satisfaction clauses that have been given effect. First, in contracts where commercial quality is at issue, the standard of a reasonable person is used to determine whether the party judged satisfaction properly. Second, where the question is one of judgment, the promisor's good faith determination of his satisfaction controls. However, the promisor must exercise his judgment in good faith. The satisfaction clause at hand is of the latter variety. Mattei (P) was legally obligated to make a good faith determination of the satisfactory nature of the leases. Thus, Mattei (P) assumed a legal obligation, and his promise was not illusory. Both Mattei (P) and Hopper (D) assumed legal obligations, and their promises thus had the required mutuality of obligation. Parties to a real-estate sales contract may agree to make one party's performance dependent on his good-faith satisfaction with the leases obtained by him. Reversed.

**Analysis:**

Contracts containing satisfaction clauses, making one party's performance dependent on his good-faith satisfaction with a related matter, are neither illusory not lacking in mutuality of obligation, Mattei (P) was legally bound to make a good-faith determination. Suppose that Hopper (D) wanted to go forward with the sale, but that Mattei (P) refused on the ground that the leases were not satisfactory. In this case, Hopper (D) could call experts to testify to the satisfactory nature of the leases, and he would have to prove that Mattei's (P) dissatisfaction was not in good faith. The court held that the satisfaction clause was an issue of judgment, not of commercial value or quality, and therefore that Mattei's (P) subjective good-faith judgment controlled. Would it make more sense to require satisfaction based on commercial value or quality? In such a case, a reasonable person standard is used. The good-faith standard usually applies to something like a portrait painting, which is inherently personal and cannot be judged on a reasonable person standard.

■ **CASE VOCABULARY**

MUTUALITY OF OBLIGATION: The requirement that, when parties exchange promises in order to form a contract, both parties must have assumed some legal obligations in executing their promises.

VITIATED: Made void; destroyed.

# Eastern Air Lines, Inc. v. Gulf Oil Corporation

(Airline) v. (Oil Supplier)

415 F.Supp. 429 (S.D. Fla. 1975)

COURT UPHOLDS REQUIREMENTS CONTRACT BASED ON GOOD-FAITH LIMITATIONS

■ **INSTANT FACTS** In the midst of an oil embargo, Eastern Air Lines (P) seeks an injunction to prevent Gulf Oil (D) from breaching the requirements contract between the parties.

■ **BLACK LETTER RULE** Requirements contracts are neither indefinite nor lacking in mutuality.

■ **PROCEDURAL BASIS**

Hearing on motion for permanent injunction.

■ **FACTS**

Eastern Air Lines, Inc. (P) and Gulf Oil Corporation (D) had a long-standing contractual relationship involving the sale of jet fuel. Pursuant to their "requirements" contract, Eastern (P) agreed to purchase any and all aviation fuel at selected cities from Gulf (D), and Gulf (D) agreed to supply all of Eastern's (P) good-faith requirements. The relationship was, until 1974, beneficial to both parties. Eastern (P) paid a reduced base price for oil, determined by the West Texas Sour indicator. Gulf (D) had a long-term outlet for its jet fuel. In 1974 the Arab oil embargo and resulting two-tier system of United States governmental price controls caused chaos in the American oil market. The short supply of oil sent one tier of prices to $11 per barrel, while government-controlled oil, which was very limited in supply, was listed at the old price of $5 per barrel. The West Texas Sour index listed the old price throughout this period. Gulf (D) demanded that Eastern (P) pay a price increase in order to meet Gulf's (D) increased costs. Eastern (P) filed a complaint for a preliminary injunction, alleging that Gulf (D) had breached its contract. A preliminary injunction was entered by stipulation of the parties, and a motion for permanent injunction followed.

■ **ISSUE**

Are requirements contracts, in which the seller agrees to make a good-faith effort to meet all of the buyer's requirements, enforceable?

■ **DECISION AND RATIONALE**

(King, J.) Yes. Requirements contracts, in which the seller agrees to make a good-faith effort to meet all of the buyer's requirements, are enforceable. Gulf (D) argues that the contract is invalid because it is indefinite, lacks mutuality of obligation, and renders Gulf (D) subject to Eastern's (P) whims respecting the volume of jet fuel Gulf (D) would be required to supply. We disagree and hold that requirements contracts such as the one at issue are binding. Both parties have assumed some legal obligation. Eastern (P) agreed to purchase all of its required oil at select cities from Gulf (D), and Gulf (D) agreed to make good-faith efforts at meeting these requirements. The contract is not indefinite, since a court can determine the volume of goods provided for under the contract by reference to objective evidence of the volume of goods required to operate the specified business. Furthermore, the Uniform Commercial Code approves requirements contracts, such as the contract at hand, that are based on the parties' good faith. We therefore conclude that specific performance of the contract is warranted, and Eastern (P) is entitled to Gulf's (D) fuel at the prices agreed upon in the contract. Permanent injunction entered.

## Analysis:

In the typical market setting, requirements and output contracts provide insurance and stability for both purchasers and sellers. In a requirements contract, the seller agrees to provide whatever quantity the buyer requires. In an output contract, the buyer agrees to purchase whatever quantity the seller produces. These contracts are not indefinite or lacking in mutuality, because the U.C.C. imposes a good-faith requirement on both parties. Suppose, in the instant action, that Eastern (P) wanted to buy only 50% of its typical requirements from Gulf (D). If Eastern (P) were simply unhappy with Gulf's (D) prices and decided it wanted to purchase fuel from another supplier, this would not be a good-faith alteration of the terms, and it would not be allowed. Unless there was some good-faith basis other than simply finding a better deal—such as Eastern (P) experiencing diminished requirements after it was forced to close down certain non-profitable routes—Eastern (P) would have to stay reasonably close to its stated, estimated requirements. Note that requirements prices may be fixed price or variable. A seller would obviously want a variable price contract in a time of rising prices, and Gulf (D) though it had structured its agreement as a variable-price contract, based on a reliable oil index. Is it fair to hold Gulf (D) responsible for the unprecedented "two-tier" pricing system and Arab embargo which resulted in the West Texas Sour index being inaccurate?

## ■ CASE VOCABULARY

COMMERCIAL IMPRACTICABILITY: An excuse to contractual performance when unforeseeable events alter the premise on which the contract was based.

REQUIREMENTS CONTRACT: A contract in which the seller agrees to make a good-faith effort to meet the buyer's requirements, and the buyer agrees to purchase all of its requirements from the seller.

# Wood v. Lucy, Lady Duff-Gordon

(Distributor) v. (Fashion Designer)
222 N.Y. 88, 118 N.E. 214 (1917)

COURT IMPLIES DUTY TO MAKE REASONABLE EFFORTS IN AN EXCLUSIVE DEALING ARRANGEMENT

■ **INSTANT FACTS** A famous fashion designer attempts to invalidate an exclusive-dealing arrangement by arguing that the supplier never made any promise to market her goods.

■ **BLACK LETTER RULE** Exclusive dealing arrangements impose an obligation by the seller to use his best efforts to distribute and market goods.

■ **PROCEDURAL BASIS**

Appeal from order reversing denial of demurrer to complaint for breach of contract.

■ **FACTS**

Lucy, Lady Duff-Gordon (D) was a famous fashion designer. In order to profit from her fame, Lucy (D) employed Wood (P). Wood (P) was granted the exclusive right to endorse products using Lucy's (D) famous name for one year. In return, Wood (P) agreed to split the profits with Lucy (D). Wood (P) sued for breach of contract after he discovered that Lucy (D) had endorsed products without his knowledge and without splitting the profits. Lucy (D) demurred on the ground that a valid contract never existed between the parties. In granting the demurrer and dismissing the complaint, the Appellate division found that the contract lacked mutuality, as Wood (P) never promised to do anything. Wood (P) appeals.

■ **ISSUE**

May a court imply a promise to make reasonable efforts in an exclusive-dealing arrangement?

■ **DECISION AND RATIONALE**

(Cardozo, J.) Yes. A court may imply a promise to make reasonable efforts in an exclusive-dealing arrangement. Indeed, Wood (P) never expressly promised to use reasonable efforts to endorse Lucy's (D) products or to market her designs. However, such a promise may be fairly implied by the court. Lucy (D) gave an exclusive privilege to Wood (P), and his acceptance of the exclusive agency was an assumption of its duties. To hold otherwise would be to undermine the purpose of the agreement. Lucy's (D) sole compensation for the grant of exclusive agency was to receive one-half of all profits. He agreed to account monthly for all moneys received, and to take out the necessary patents, copyrights, and trademarks. Unless Wood (P) gave some reasonable effort, Lucy (D) could never get anything. In line with the intention of the parties, we determine that Wood (P) made an implied promise, and thus that the contract was not lacking in mutuality of obligation. Reversed.

**Analysis:**

One of the fundamental bases of contract law is that the parties should be free to establish the terms of the contract. Ordinarily a court will not interfere and create implied promises or duties. For this reason, the holding of the Court of Appeals of New York in this opinion is open to some criticism. Obligations should be created voluntarily by contracting parties, not imposed by courts. Although this opinion deviates from the typical "freedom of contract" analysis, it is nevertheless supported by the U.C.C. According to § 2–306, exclusive dealing contracts are valid and, unless otherwise agreed, impose an obligation on the seller to use his best efforts to supply the goods. Thus, the court and legislature may step in and alter the terms of a contract in some situations, typically where the interests of justice so require.

### ■ CASE VOCABULARY

EXCLUSIVE DEALING ARRANGEMENT: An agreement whereby a distributor expressly or implicitly contracts to supply all of a seller's goods, using the distributor's best efforts.

# Ricketts v. Scothorn

(Grandfather) v. (Granddaughter)
57 Neb. 51, 77 N.W. 365 (1898)

COURT ADOPTS PROMISSORY ESTOPPEL AS ALTERNATIVE TO BARGAINED-FOR EXCHANGE

■ **INSTANT FACTS** A woman who quit work in reliance on her grandfather's promise to support her sues when the executor of her grandfather's estate fails to pay.

■ **BLACK LETTER RULE** Where a person changes position in detrimental reliance on a promise, the promisor may be estopped from later denying the promise.

## ■ PROCEDURAL BASIS

Appeal from judgment for damages based on equitable estoppel.

## ■ FACTS

John C. Ricketts (D) executed a promissory note by which he promised to pay his granddaughter, Katie Scothorn (P), $2000 per year at 6% interest on demand. After Ricketts (D) died, Scothorn (P) sued his estate in order to recover payment on the note. Scothorn (P) alleged that the consideration for this note was that Scothorn (P) should surrender her employment and cease to work for a living, just like the rest of Ricketts' (D) grandchildren. Scothorn (P) also argued that Ricketts (D) was equitably estopped from denying to pay the note, since the note was given to induce her to abandon her occupation, and since she did give up her employment in reliance on the note. Scothorn (P) remained unemployed for more than a year after receiving the note, but she eventually went back to work with the consent of Ricketts (D). Ricketts (D) died approximately two years later, having paid only one year's interest on the note. The trial court granted judgment for Scothorn (P), and Ricketts' (D) executor appeals.

## ■ ISSUE

Where a person intends to cause, and does indeed cause, another to change position in reliance on a promise, can that person be estopped from denying the promise?

## ■ DECISION AND RATIONALE

(Sullivan, J.) Yes. Where a person intends to cause, and does indeed cause, another to change position in reliance on a promise, that person can be estopped from denying the promise. We find that the note was not given in consideration of Scothorn (P) pursuing any particular line of conduct. Scothorn never promised to do, or refrain from doing, anything. Nevertheless, the doctrine of equitable estoppel, or estoppel in pals, precludes Ricketts (D) from alleging that the note in controversy is lacking one of the essential elements of a valid contract. Ricketts (D) gave Scothorn (P) the note with the intent that she, like his other grandchildren, not work any longer. Thus, Ricketts (D) induced Scothorn (P) to alter her position to her detriment on the faith that the note would be paid on demand. It would be grossly inequitable to permit Ricketts (D) to resist payment on the ground that the promise was given without consideration. Affirmed.

**Analysis:**

The conventional equitable estoppel application precluded a party from alleging facts that would contradict an earlier representation, if some other party had taken action in reliance on the statement. The modern doctrine of promissory estoppel, by contrast, as stated in the Restatement of Contracts, provides: (1) a promise that the promisor should reasonably expect to induce action or forbearance, (2) and that does induce such action or forbearance, (3) is binding if injustice can be avoided only by enforcement of the promise. In the case at hand, the first two elements are clearly satisfied. Ricketts (D) made a promise and executed a promissory note to induce Scothorn (P) to quit work, and Scothorn (P) did indeed quit because of this promise. Further, the court concludes that it would be unjust to permit Ricketts (D) to escape his promise. Alternatively, in the instant case, the court could have concluded that Ricketts (D) and Scothorn (P) made a bargained-for exchange, with Ricketts (D) bargaining for the psychological comfort he would feel if Scothorn (P) quit work, and with Scothorn (P) bargaining for the money. In the end, no matter which theory is used, the courts seem to be placing a premium on doing the right thing. It a result is equitable, the court usually finds some legal basis for reaching that result.

---

■ **CASE VOCABULARY**

ESTOPPEL IN PAIS: The doctrine by which a person may be precluded from asserting some right where his acts or words have induced another person to change position in reliance; also known as equitable estoppel.

QUID PRO QUO: Something in exchange for something else, as in a bargained-for exchange.

# Feinberg v. Pfeiffer Co.

(Employee) v. (Employer)

322 S.W.2d 163 (Mo. Ct. App. 1959)

## RELIANCE MAY SUBSTITUTE FOR CONSIDERATION IN ORDER TO MAKE PROMISES ENFORCEABLE

■ **INSTANT FACTS** Feinberg (P) retired from her employment, induced by her employer's promise to pay retirement benefits, and Feinberg (P) sues when the payments are eventually discontinued.

■ **BLACK LETTER RULE** Retirement in reliance on pension benefits is sufficient reliance to estop the employer from paying retirement benefits.

## ■ PROCEDURAL BASIS

Appeal from judgment awarding damages based on promissory estoppel.

## ■ FACTS

Anna Sacks Feinberg (P) was employed by Pfeiffer Co. (D) for 37 years. In view of Feinberg's (P) long service, Pfeiffer (D) promised to pay Feinberg (P) $200 per month for life whenever Feinberg (P) decided to retire. Feinberg (P) continued to work for Pfeiffer (D) for one-and-one-half years, at which point she decided to retire. Pfeiffer (D) paid Feinberg (P) $200 per month for several years. However, when new management took the helm at Pfeiffer (D), they decided not to pay Feinberg (P) any more. Feinberg sued under two alternative theories: (1) that her continued employment and eventual retirement was a bargained-for exchange for the future retirement benefits; and (2) that Pfeiffer's (D) promise was enforceable because it induced Feinberg (P) to rely thereon. The trial court entered a judgment for Feinberg (P), and Pfeiffer (D) appealed. On appeal, the Appellate Court held first that there was no consideration sufficient to create a binding contract. The Appellate Court then considered Feinberg's (P) second purported basis of recovery.

## ■ ISSUE

Is retirement from a lucrative position sufficient reliance to estop an employer from denying the promise to pay retirement benefits?

## ■ DECISION AND RATIONALE

(Doerner, J.) Yes. Retirement from a lucrative position is sufficient reliance to estop an employer from denying the promise to pay retirement benefits. Feinberg (P) clearly retired in reliance on Pfeiffer's (D) promise to pay retirement benefits, and this act was certainly anticipated by Pfeiffer (D). Following her retirement, and after receiving years of retirement payments, Feinberg (P) was essentially unemployable. Thus, great injustice would occur if Pfeiffer (D) was allowed to renounce its promise to pay benefits to Feinberg (P). And even notwithstanding her ability to be employed, the mere act of retiring based on Pfeiffer's (D) inducement is sufficient to impose a duty to pay on Pfeiffer (D). Affirmed.

---

**Analysis:**

This case provides interesting insight into the doctrine of promissory estoppel. Feinberg's (P) previous work, plus her continuation of employment after Pfeiffer (D) made the promise, was not sufficient consideration to form a binding contract. However, Pfeiffer's (D) promise clearly was made with the intent to induce reliance, and Feinberg (P) did retire in detrimental reliance on the promise. The third prong of the promissory estoppel analysis—that the promise is binding if injustice can be avoided only by enforcement of the promise—seems to be an afterthought. The court essentially holds that, where a promisor intends to induce and does induce detrimental reliance, the promisor is estopped from later denying the obligation imposed by the promise. But it is important to note that the act done must actually be in reliance on the promise. If Feinberg (P) were planning on retiring anyway, promissory estoppel would not apply.

# Cohen v. Cowles Media Company

(Gubernatorial Aide) v. (Publisher)

479 N.W.2d 387 (Minn. 1992)

PROMISSORY ESTOPPEL APPLIES ONLY WHERE NECESSARY IN ORDER TO PREVENT AN INJUSTICE

■ **INSTANT FACTS** Cohen (P), who leaked a newspaper story on the assurance that his name would be kept confidential, sues when the newspaper editors publish his identity.

■ **BLACK LETTER RULE** Promissory estoppel is applicable only where enforcement of a promise is *required* in order to prevent an injustice.

■ **PROCEDURAL BASIS**

Appeal from judgment for $200,000, on remand from U.S. Supreme Court to apply doctrine of promissory estoppel.

■ **FACTS**

Dan Cohen (P), an associate of a gubernatorial candidate, informed reporters of newspapers owned by Cowles Media Company (D) of the arrests and conviction of the opposing candidate for lieutenant governor. The reporters had promised to keep Cohen's (P) identity confidential. However, the editors overruled these promises and printed Cohen's (P) name. Cohen was fired by his firm, and he sued Cowles (D) for breach of contract. The trial court awarded $200,000 in compensatory damages. However, on Cowles' (D) appeal, the Minnesota Supreme Court held that the parties were not thinking in terms of a legally binding contract, and that recovery based on promissory estoppel would violate the newspapers' First Amendment rights. The United States Supreme Court disagreed on the First Amendment holding, and it remanded to the Supreme Court of Minnesota.

■ **ISSUE**

Is promissory estoppel applicable only where enforcement of a promise is *required* in order to prevent an injustice?

■ **DECISION AND RATIONALE**

(En banc) Yes. Promissory estoppel is applicable only where enforcement of a promise is *required* in order to prevent an injustice. In the case at hand, both parties have good moral arguments as to why Cowles' (D) promise should or should not be enforced. Neither side clearly holds the higher moral ground. However, the record reveals that the harm to Cohen (P) requires a remedy in order to avoid injustice. At trial, the newspapers themselves conceded that they generally keep the confidentiality of any source. Cowles' (D) editors conceded that they have never since reneged on a promise of confidentiality. Other experts stressed the ethical importance of keeping promises of confidentiality. Based on these representations, we conclude that promissory estoppel should apply to prevent Cowles' (D) from reneging on their promise of confidentiality. Affirmed.

**Analysis:**

A promise that was intended to induce, and did indeed induce, reliance can be enforced only where *required* in order to prevent injustice. Here, however, the facts do not clearly state that Cohen (P) revealed the information only after being assured that his name would remain confidential. If the promise was given by the newspapers only after Cohen (P) supplied the information, promissory estoppel would not apply. The court itself notes that both parties are on equal moral ground. How, then, can the court be so sure that enforcement of the promise is required in order to prevent injustice? Couldn't the newspapers have validly argued that their First Amendment rights are equally important, and that printing Cohen's (P) name was required in order to prevent injustice to the newspapers? This case exemplifies the difficult balancing that must occur when considering the equitable issues underlying promissory estoppel.

### ■ CASE VOCABULARY

COUNTERMANDED: Took an action inconsistent with an earlier action or promise.

GUBERNATORIAL: Of or concerning an election for governor.

# D & G Stout, Inc. v. Bacardi Imports, Inc.

(Distributor) v. (Supplier)

923 F.2d 566 (7th Cir. 1991)

PROMISSORY ESTOPPEL ALLOWS RECOVERY FOR RELIANCE DAMAGES ONLY, NOT EXPECTANCY DAMAGES

■ **INSTANT FACTS** A liquor distributor, who rejected a purchase offer in reliance on a supplier's promise not to terminate the relationship, sues the supplier after the supplier withdrew its account.

■ **BLACK LETTER RULE** Promissory estoppel allows recovery of reliance damages and not expectancy damages.

## ■ PROCEDURAL BASIS

Appeal from order granting summary judgment dismissing action for damages based on promissory estoppel.

## ■ FACTS

D & G Stout, Inc. (P), operating under the name General Liquors, Inc. ("General") was distributing liquor in indiana in 1987. During this time period, the liquor suppliers in indiana undertook an effort to consolidate their distribution. As a result, two of General's (P) suppliers canceled their contracts in early 1987. General (P) began negotiating with another distributor, National Wine & Spirits, for a potential sale of General (P). However, Bacardi Imports, Inc. (D), one of General's remaining suppliers, assured General (P) that it would continue to act as its supplier for Indiana. Based on this promise, General (P) turned down National's offer to purchase General (P). One week later, Bacardi (D) withdrew its account. General (P), after losing another major supplier and several employees, then returned to its earlier negotiations, eventually selling the company to National for $550,000 less than the original offer. General (P) sued Bacardi (D) in order to recover this $550,000 difference. The district court entered summary judgment for Bacardi (D), holding that General (P) could not recover based on promissory estoppel because Bacardi's (D) promise was not one on which it should have reasonably expected General (P) to rely. General (P) appeals.

## ■ ISSUE

Does promissory estoppel allow recovery of reliance damages only and not expectancy damages?

## ■ DECISION AND RATIONALE

(Cudahy, J.) Yes. Promissory estoppel allows recovery of reliance damages and not expectancy damages. Pursuant to Indiana law, promissory estoppel does not afford recovery for an at-will employment relationship. Under such a relationship, any promises of future employment are only expectancy damages, since the employment relationship may be terminated by either party at any time. However, Indiana law does allow for recovery of some reliance damages, even in the at-will employment relationship. For example, where an at-will employee changes location in reliance on continued employment, he may recover his moving expenses incurred if he is later fired. This latter example is of reliance damages, since the employee moved in reliance on continued employment. In the instant action, we must determine whether General's (P) damages were based on a mere expectancy that

Bacardi (D) would continue as supplier, or based on reliance in Bacardi's (D) promise to remain a supplier. While we do not need to decide the issue, we hold that General (P) did have a reliance interest in Bacardi's (D) promise. National never assumed that Bacardi (D) would continue as a supplier if National purchased General (P). Rather, General (P) was damaged because it relied on Bacardi's (D) promise and chose not to accept National's original offer. All parties Involved, including Bacardi (D), realized that General (P) could continue in business only if Bacardi (D) remained one of General's (P) suppliers. Thus, Bacardi (D), because of its promise and its continuing reassurances to General (P) of its commitment, could have reasonably expected General (P) to rely thereon. While we do not reach the issue of whether General's (P) reliance was reasonable—as this is an issue for the trial court on remand—we hold that promissory estoppel may apply. Reversed and remanded.

**Analysis:**

Promissory estoppel applies, of course, only to allow recovery of reliance damages. Thus, where a party changes position based on the mere expectancy of a continuing relationship, that party may not recover. In the case at hand, it is possible to argue that General (P) did just that. It expected Bacardi (D) to continue as a supplier, and therefore it rejected National's offer. However, the condusion reached by the Court is more reasonable. General's (P) rejection of National's offer was not based on any future income from Bacardl (D), but on the fact that it could stay in business by having Bacardi (D) as a supplier. It was General's (P) reliance on the assurances, and not any future income, that induced General (P) to reject the original bid. It is interesting to note that, on remand, the district court found that Bacardi's (D) commitment was conditional on future events, but nevertheless that General's (P) reliance was not unreasonable. Accordingly, General (P) was awarded nearly $400,000 in damages.

■ **CASE VOCABULARY**

AT-WILL EMPLOYMENT: An arrangement whereby either the employer or employee can terminate the relationship at any time, for any reason, without liability.

QUANDARY: A logical predicament; a state of perplexity.

# Cotnam v. Wisdom

(Administrator of Decedent-Patient) v. (Emergency Surgeon)

83 Ark. 601, 104 S.W. 164 (1907)

---

## SERVICES PROVIDED BY A PHYSICIAN COMING TO THE EMERGENCY AID OF PARTY CREATES A CONTRACT IMPLIED BY LAW FOR REASONABLE VALUE OF SERVICES

---

■ **INSTANT FACTS** Wisdom (P) was a physician who responded to an emergency call from a spectator to perform emergency surgery on Harrison (D), decedent, in an effort to save Harrison's life, but the operation was unsuccessful, and Harrison died without regaining consciousness.

■ **BLACK LETTER RULE** When a physician renders emergency medical services to a person, who due to his medical or mental condition is not capable of agreeing to the treatment, the law will imply a contract for the reasonable value of the services.

■ **PROCEDURAL BASIS**

An appeal from Circuit Court that awarded judgment for Wisdom (P).

■ **FACTS**

Harrison(D) was thrown from a street car and received serious injuries which rendered him unconscious. While Harrison (D) was still unconscious, Wisdom (P), a physician, was summoned to his assistance by some spectator. Wisdom (P) performed a difficult operation in an effort to save Harrison's (D) life, but the operation was unsuccessful, and Harrison (D) died without regaining consciousness. Wisdom (P) brought an action against Cotnam, administrator of Harrison's (D) estate, to recover for the services rendered to Harrison (D). The trial court gave instructions to the jury that "(1) If you find from the evidence that plaintiffs rendered professional services as physicians ... in a sudden emergency ... then you are instructed that plaintiffs are entitled to recover ... reasonable compensation for the services rendered. (2) The character and importance of the operation, the responsibility resting upon the surgeon ... his experience and professional training, and the ability to pay of the person operated upon, are elements to be considered ... in determining ... reasonable charge...."

■ **ISSUE**

Is there an implied contract by law for the reasonable value of services rendered by a medical professional giving emergency assistance to a party not physically capable of agreeing to have the services performed?

■ **DECISION AND RATIONALE**

(Hill) Yes. Contracts by implication of law are almost as old as the English system of jurisprudence. They are usually called "implied contracts". More properly they should be called "quasi contracts" or "constructive contracts." Contracts implied by law contain no mutual understanding, and so no promise. It is a legal fiction, invented and used for the sake of the remedy. Since implied contracts do not require any evidence of mutual understanding, the fact that Harrison (D) was never conscious after his accident, and therefore, could not expressly or impliedly, assent to the action, is not determinative in finding the existence of a contract. The legal fiction that creates an implied contract merely requires a reasonable compensation for the services rendered. It was therefore error to instruct the jury in the second instruction that in determining what was a reasonable charge, they could consider the "ability to pay of the person operated upon." The subsequent evidence that Harrison (D) was a bachelor and that his estate was left to nieces and nephews was admitted into evidence in error. This was relevant to no issue in the case, and its effect might well have been prejudicial. Judgment is reversed, and the action is remanded.

## ■ CONCURRENCE

(Battle and Wood) Yes. However, it was not error to admit evidence of the value of the estate, and instructing that it might be considered in fixing the charge.

## Analysis:

As the court pointed out, implied contracts (or quasi or constructive contracts) exist only as a legal fiction. The courts apply the legal fiction only when one party has substantially benefited another and justice requires that the benefited party compensate the other party. In this case, the physician, Wisdom (P), was adhering to his oath taken as a doctor by responding to the medical emergency of Harrison (D). The general welfare of the public interest is furthered when physicians respond to the emergency medical needs of the public. The court compares these occurrences to physicians treating insane persons. The insane person needs medical assistance, but is unable to contract for the treatment. The legal fiction creates the contract in the interest of public welfare.

## ■ CASE VOCABULARY

ASSUMPSIT: A common law action to recover for nonperformance of some type of contract.

EX CONTRACTU: Actions arising from a contract.

EX DELICTO: Actions arising from a tort.

# Callano v. Oakwood Park Homes Corp.

(Nursery) v. (Home Builders)

91 N.J.Super. 105, 219 A.2d 332 (A.D. 1966)

QUASI-CONTRACTUAL RECOVERY IS AVAILABLE TO PREVENT UNJUST ENRICHMENT ONLY IN LIMITED SITUATIONS

■ **INSTANT FACTS** Operators of a nursery seek to recover payment for shrubbery from the home builder, although a contract existed only with the now-deceased home owner.

■ **BLACK LETTER RULE** Quasi-contractual recovery is not available when an alternative remedy based on an actual contract exists.

■ **PROCEDURAL BASIS**

Appeal from judgment based on quasi-contract.

■ **FACTS**

Oakwood Park Homes Corp. (D) contracted with Bruce Pendergast to sell a new home which Oakwood was building. Prior to the completion of the house, Julia and Frank Callano (P), the operators of a plant nursery, delivered and planted shrubbery pursuant to a contract with Pendergast. An Oakwood representative had knowledge of the planting. Pendergast failed to pay the Callanos (P) and Pendergast died shortly after the shrubbery was planted. After the death, Oakwood (D) and Pendergast canceled the house sale contract. Shortly thereafter, Oakwood (D) sold the property (including the shrubbery) to a new buyer. The Callanos (P) sued Oakwood (D) in order to recover payment for the shrubbery. Although no contract existed between the Callanos (P) and Oakwood (D), the Callanos (P) argued that Oakwood (D) would be unjustly enriched if it did not have to pay for the shrubbery. The parties agreed that the shrubbery increased the value of the property by $475. The trial court implied a quasi-contract and granted restitution, entering a judgment in favor of the Callanos (P) in order to prevent unjust enrichment. Oakwood (D) appeals.

■ **ISSUE**

May a party recover based on quasi-contract when an alternative remedy based on an actual contract exists?

■ **DECISION AND RATIONALE**

(Collester, J.) No. A party may not recover based on quasi-contract when an alternative remedy based on an actual contract exists. The law does recognize contracts implied by law, also known as quasi-contracts, as a means to prevent unjust enrichment in some situations. Pursuant to this theory, the Intention of the parties is entirely disregarded, and the law imparts an implied promise to pay where one party is enriched by benefits and the retention of the benefits without payment would be unjust. A common thread runs through all such cases, namely, that the plaintiff expected payment from the defendant at the time the benefit was conferred. In other words, there must be some direct relationship or mistake on the part of the person conferring the benefit. In the case at hand, there was no direct relationship between the Callanos (P) and Oakwood (D). The Callanos (P) did not expect remuneration from Oakwood (D) at the time they planted the shrubbery. In this situation, we hold that it would be unjust to hold Oakwood (D) liable. The Callanos (P) may seek recovery from Pendergast's estate based on the actual contract with Pendergast. Courts should not employ the legal fiction of quasi-contract to substitute one promisor or debtor for another. Reversed.

## Analysis:

Restitution is recovery based on preventing unjust enrichment, not any actual promise between parties. Thus, the law implies a promise (a quasi-contract) when it would be unfair for one person to obtain certain benefits without having to pay for them. Based on this framework, it would appear that the Callanos (P) could recover from Oakwood (D), since Oakwood (D) was certainly enriched by the increased value conferred on the land by the shrubbery. However, there are two important twists. First, there must be some relationship or dealings between the party seeking the quasi-contract and the party who was unjustly enriched. Second, where the party seeking the quasi-contract has an alternative remedy available—such as suing the original promisor for breach of contract—he cannot recover based on unjust enrichment. Courts are cautious in employing unjust enrichment theories, especially when alternative recovery based on actual contracts is possible.

## ■ CASE VOCABULARY

QUASI-CONTRACT: A contract implied at law, in which obligations are imposed not based on actual promises made but on the grounds of fairness and preventing unjust enrichment.

UNJUST ENRICHMENT: The basis for restitution, in which a party who receives benefits is required to pay for the benefits even if there was no actual contract.

# Pyeatte v. Pyeatte

(Ex-Wife) v. (Ex-Husband)

135 Ariz. 346, 661 P.2d 196 (App. 1982)

EX-SPOUSES ARE NOT ENTITLED TO RESTITUTION FOR USUAL MARITAL DUTIES, BUT MAY RECEIVE RESTITUTION FOR EXTRAORDINARY CONTRACTUAL EFFORTS

■ **INSTANT FACTS** After spouses agree to put each other through graduate school, the husband uses the wife's money to graduate law school, then divorces her.

■ **BLACK LETTER RULE** While ex-spouses are not entitled to restitution for performing usual duties incidental to marriage, restitution is available if the spouses had an agreement and one spouse made extraordinary efforts which benefited the other solely.

■ **PROCEDURAL BASIS**

In contract action seeking damages, appeal from appellate affirmation of judgement for plaintiff.

■ **FACTS**

Charles (D) and Margrethe (P) Pyeatte married. They agreed Margrethe (P) would put Charles (D) through law school without his working, and that Charles (D) would later pay for Margrethe's (P) graduate school. Margrethe (P) paid Charles's (D) bills, enabling him to graduate, obtain work at a law firm, and divorce her soon after. [Apparently, he learned the law too well.] Margrethe (P), who had not yet started graduate school, sued Charles (D) for breach of contract. Charles (D) defended, contending the agreement was too indefinite to be enforceable. At trial, the court found the agreement was enforceable, and awarded Margrethe (P) $23,000. On appeal, the Court of Appeal apparently found the contract was invalid, but granted Margrethe (P) the same amount as restitutionary damages. Charles (D) appeals.

■ **ISSUE**

If spouses agree to pay each other's graduate schooling, and one does, may he or she sue for restitution when the other leaves before performing?

■ **DECISION AND RATIONALE**

(Corcoran) Yes. While ex-spouses are not entitled to restitution for performing usual duties incidental to marriage, restitution is available if the spouses had an agreement and one spouse made extraordinary efforts which benefited the other solely. We find the agreement here was unenforceable. However, the agreement is still relevant in considering Margrethe's (P) claim of unjust enrichment, because it evidences both Margrethe's (P) expectation of compensation, and the injustice of allowing Charles (D) to retain the benefits of Margrethe's (P) extraordinary efforts. We find that restitution is sometimes an appropriate remedy in divorce proceedings, but only where there was a spousal agreement and one spouse made extraordinary or unilateral efforts which inured to the other's sole benefit. Where both spouses perform the usual and incidental activities of the marital relationship, upon divorce there can be no restitution. Reversed and remanded to recalculate restitutionary damages.

**Analysis:**

Usually, inter-spousal restitution claims are dismissed on the premise that spousal services are presumed gratuitous. This premise is still applied in the vast majority of cases, since even under *Pyeatte*, few spouses start off their marriage by making specific, legally valid contracts. There seems to be no sound basis for such a policy, other than courts' unwillingness to "denigrate" the marital relationship by admitting it is often partly a financial arrangement. However, the court here clearly believed that to deny Margrethe (P) any recovery at all would be a colossal injustice to her, and an undeserved windfall to her husband.

# CHAPTER TWO

## Creating Contractual Obligations

### Lucy v. Zehmer

**Instant Facts:** Two drunks agree to a farm sale written on the back of a bar bill.

**Black Letter Rule:** A contract is enforceable despite one party's subjective belief that the parties are joking.

### Owen v. Tunison

**Instant Facts:** Letters pass between a property owner and a prospective purchaser as they haggle over the value of the property.

**Black Letter Rule:** An invitation to negotiate is not binding as an offer to contract.

### Harvey v. Facey

**Instant Facts:** Prospective purchaser solicits Jamaican landowner by mail for lowest sale price.

**Black Letter Rule:** Stating a possible sale price is not binding as an offer to sell at that price.

### Fairmount Glass Works v. Grunden [Crunden]-Martin Woodenware Co.

**Instant Facts:** Letters are exchanged between a mason jar manufacturer and a prospective buyer.

**Black Letter Rule:** A price quote may give rise to an enforceable contract, depending upon its language.

### Lefkowitz v. Great Minneapolis Surplus Store

**Instant Facts:** A store refuses to sell a fur coat to a male buyer for the advertised price of $1.

**Black Letter Rule:** An advertisement which is definite, explicit, and which leaves nothing open to negotiation creates a binding contract upon the acceptance of a prospective purchaser.

### Elsinore Union Elementary School District v. Kastorff

**Instant Facts:** A general contractor made an error in a bid for a job and tried to get released from his bid.

**Black Letter Rule:** A contractor's error in calculating a bid can be grounds for rescission.

### International Filter Co. v. Conroe Gin, Ice & Light Co.

**Instant Facts:** A water filter manufacturer refuses to cancel an ice company's order for a filter.

**Black Letter Rule:** The offeror controls the method and means of acceptance by the language of the offer.

### White v. Corlies & Tift

**Instant Facts:** A builder accepts a construction contract by beginning to purchase lumber for the job.

**Black Letter Rule:** In the absence of express provisions in the offer, an acceptance must be by reasonable means given the circumstances surrounding the offer.

### Ever-Tite Roofing Corporation v. Green

**Instant Facts:** A roofing company arrives to start a job only to discover that their prospective client has hired someone else.

**Black Letter Rule:** In the absence of specific language in an offer, the offeror must allow a reasonable amount of time for acceptance.

### Allied Steel and Conveyors, Inc. v. Ford Motor Co.

**Instant Facts:** Ford sought to hold Allied to an indemnification agreement when an Allied employee was injured at the Ford plant.

**Black Letter Rule:** An offer which suggests a means of acceptance may become binding by performance by the offeree.

### Corinthian Pharmaceutical Systems, Inc. v. Lederle Laboratories

**Instant Facts:** A drug distributor sought to force a drug manufacturer to sell it a vaccine at a certain price.

**Black Letter Rule:** If a seller ships to the buyer non-conforming goods and gives notice that the shipment is an accommodation, the seller is not in breach of contract and is not obligated to deliver goods that conform to the buyer's order.

### Dickinson v. Dodds

**Instant Facts:** An offeror gave an offeree until Friday to accept an offer to sell property, but sold the property to someone else on Thursday.

**Black Letter Rule:** Without separate consideration, an offeror may revoke an offer anytime before the offeree's deadline to accept the offer.

### Ragosta v. Wilder

**Instant FActs:** A shop owner and a prospective buyer dispute the meaning of a cash-in-hand offer that the owner made for the sale of the shop.

**Black Letter Rule:** An offer is freely revocable until the offeror is bound by a valid acceptance.

### Dorton v. Collins & Aikman Corp.

**Instant Facts:** A carpet manufacturer wants to hold a dissatisfied retailer to an arbitration agreement pre-printed on the manufacturer's sales forms.

**Black Letter Rule:** Under UCC § 2–207, if an arbitration provision materially alters an existing agreement, it will not be incorporated into the contract unless expressly agreed to by both parties.

### Step-Saver Data Systems, Inc. v. Wyse Technology [and The Software Link, Inc.]

**Instant Facts:** A software dealer used a defective program in one of its commercial systems and sought to enforce a warranty against the producer of the program.

**Black Letter Rule:** UCC § 2–207 governs contracts for the sale of goods where the parties have multiple agreements with additional or different terms.

### ProCD, Inc. v. Zeidenberg

**Instant Facts:** A purchaser of a computer software database resold the database on the Internet in violation of the license included with the software.

**Black Letter Rule:** A license enclosed in a software package forms a binding contract between the software seller and buyer if the package provides notice that the purchase is subject to the license and the buyer can receive a refund if the buyer does not agree to the license's terms.

### Hill v. Gateway 2000, Inc.

**Instant Facts:** Hill (P) purchased a computer from Gateway (D) and claimed that the arbitration agreement included in materials enclosed inside the box, which purported to govern unless the computer was returned within thirty days, was unenforceable.

**Black Letter Rule:** A seller may provide that acceptance of an offer will be by conduct, and the buyer accepts by performing the acts that the seller proposes to treat as acceptance.

### Drennan v. Star Paving Co.

**Instant Facts:** A general contractor wants to enforce a subcontractor's bid on a construction job.

**Black Letter Rule:** An offer may not be freely revocable if the offeree has substantially relied on the offer.

### Hoffman v. Red Owl Stores

**Instant Facts:** A bakery owner wants to open a supermarket franchise but is rejected by the franchiser after making preparations at their request.

**Black Letter Rule:** It is not necessary for an offer to address every detail of an agreement in order to support a promissory estoppel claim.

### Cyberchron Corp. v. Calldata Systems Development, Inc.

**Instant Facts:** A computer hardware manufacturer produced equipment for a buyer without entering into a contract, and sued for promissory estoppel.

**Black Letter Rule:** A party who relies on a promise that a contract is forthcoming may recover under a promissory estoppel theory.

### Channel Home Centers, Division of Grace Retail Corp. v. Grossman

**Instant Facts:** A mall developer abruptly cancels lease negotiations with a prospective tenant.

**Black Letter Rule:** An agreement to negotiate in good faith toward a prospective contract may be binding if it satisfies the conditions to a binding contract.

### Toys, Inc. v. F.M. Burlington Company

**Instant Facts:** A lessor and lessee cannot reach an agreement when the lessee attempts to exercise a renewal option.

**Black Letter Rule:** An option provision may be sufficiently definite to be binding if it contains terms which enable the parties to satisfy their subsequent agreement.

### Oglebay Norton Co. v. Armco, Inc.

**Instant Facts:** After about 25 years of doing business pursuant to a contract, the parties could no longer agree on a price to be used.

**Black Letter Rule:** If parties to a contract have not agreed on the price, the court can set a price so long as the parties intend to be bound by the contract.

# Lucy v. Zehmer

(Farm Buyer) v. (Farm Seller)

196 Va. 493, 84 S.E.2d 516 (1954)

## SUPREME COURT OF VIRGINIA ENFORCES FARM SALE INTENDED AS A JOKE

■ **INSTANT FACTS** Two drunks agree to a farm sale written on the back of a bar bill.

■ **BLACK LETTER RULE** A contract is enforceable despite one party's subjective belief that the parties are joking.

■ **PROCEDURAL BASIS**

Appeal from a trial court judgement for the defendant in a breach of contract action.

■ **FACTS**

W.O. Lucy (Lucy) (P) and A.H. Zehmer (Zehmer) (D) were drinking at a bar when Lucy (P) offered to buy Zehmer's (D) farm for $50,000. Zehmer (D) thought it was a joke. In fact, he said that he was "high as a Georgia Pine" at the time. Nonetheless, he wrote up an agreement of sale on the back of a bar bill. Zehmer (D) and his wife signed the agreement and left it on the bar. When Lucy (P) picked it up, Zehmer (D) assured him that it was a joke. Lucy (P) insisted that he had purchased the farm and then left the bar. Lucy (P) brought a breach of contract suit against Zehmer (D), asking that the court enforce the sale of the farm by ordering specific performance of the agreement. The trial court denied Lucy's (P) request and this appeal followed.

■ **ISSUE**

Will a contract be enforced despite one party's subjective belief that the parties are joking?

■ **DECISION AND RATIONALE**

(Buchanan) Yes. The objective intent of the parties is central to a determination of their desire to be bound. This rule will be disregarded only when one party is aware of the other party's subjective intent not to be bound. In this case, Lucy (P) and Zehmer (D) haggled over the price of the farm, the wording of the agreement, and the need for a token payment to seal the deal. They appear to have dealt with each other as reasonable parties to a genuine transaction [okay...reasonable drunk guys]. Lucy (P) had no idea that Zehmer (D) was secretly joking and Zehmer's (D) behavior, judged objectively, gave no indication of this before the agreement was delivered. As a result, the contract is enforceable and specific performance will be ordered. Reversed and remanded.

**Analysis:**

The meeting of the minds doctrine, which required that each party to a contract have a subjective desire to be bound, is no longer the litmus test for a valid contract. In this case, a contract predicated on a joke remained enforceable even though Zehmer (D) was subjectively disinterested in selling his farm. Several mistakes can lead to the rescission of a contract, including transcription mistakes, jokes, ambiguities, and other problems. According to the Restatement (Second) of Contracts, when there is a mistake of fact that goes to a basic assumption of the contract, the party seeking to be excused from performance must show that they ought not to bear the risk of loss from the mistake. The analysis in mistake cases frequently hinges on which party was best situated to avoid the mistake. In this case, Zehmer (D) was best situated to avoid the confusion, because he had not made it clear that he was joking. However, a modem court would be unlikely to enforce the agreement under these circumstances.

## ■ CASE VOCABULARY

LAST CLEAR CHANCE: A doctrine usually associated with negligence law which places liability for an injury on the person with the last opportunity to avoid the accident by exercising reasonable care; it is not applied in every jurisdiction.

SPECIFIC PERFORMANCE: A contract remedy which provides for exact performance on the contract when money damages would not adequately compensate the injured party. It is most often available for the sale of real estate and for the sale of unique goods, but it is not a commonly ordered remedy.

# Owen v. Tunison

(Prospective Purchaser) v. (Property Owner)

131 Me. 42, 158 A. 926 (1932)

SUPREME COURT OF MAINE DISTINGUISHES BETWEEN AN OFFER TO CONTRACT AND AN OFFER TO NEGOTIATE

■ **INSTANT FACTS** Letters pass between a property owner and a prospective purchaser as they haggle over the value of the property.

■ **BLACK LETTER RULE** An invitation to negotiate is not binding as an offer to contract.

■ **PROCEDURAL BASIS**

Not stated.

■ **FACTS**

W.H. Owen (Owen) (P) wanted to purchase a piece of property owned by R.G. Tunison (Tunison) (D). He wrote to Tunison (D), telling him that he would be willing to pay $6,000 for the property. Tunison (D) wrote back, stating that he would want at least $16,000 due to improvements which he had made to the property. Owen (P) replied, accepting the "offer" and asking Tunison (D) to forward the deed to Owen's (P) bank. Tunison (D) wrote back, stating that he did not want to sell the property. Owen (P) brought-suit and sought enforcement of the alleged agreement of sale.

■ **ISSUE**

Is a statement of a desired price a binding offer to sell at that price?

■ **DECISION AND RATIONALE**

(Barnes) No. In order for this contract to be valid, there must be an actual offer to sell the property. In this case, Tunison (D) did not offer to sell his real estate. At best, his letter indicated a willingness to negotiate towards a potential sale. Judgement for Tunison (D). [You're a man of few words, Justice Barnes.]

---

**Analysis:**

It can be difficult to determine whether a party's communication is a potentially binding offer to enter into a contract. The general rule is that a communication is an offer if the person receiving the communication would be justified in thinking that he or she had the power to bind the other party to a legally enforceable agreement. In this case, the letter is phrased negatively—it would not be possible...unless." This language implies that Tunison (D) is not completely committed to the idea of selling the property. In addition, Owen (P) initiated the communication between the parties. As a result, a more affirmative response from Tunison (D) should be required before binding him to a contract.

---

## ■ CASE VOCABULARY

[SPOCK: A half-Vulcan, half-human member of the crew of the Starship Enterprise capable of performing the creepy Vulcan mind meld. This would be a very useful device for determining the subjective intent of the parties to a contract if courts took this into account—which they don't.]

# Harvey v. Facey

(Potential Purchaser) v. (Landowner)

[1893] A.C. 552 (Privy Council) (Jamaica)

PRIVY COUNCIL OF JAMAICA DISTINGUISHES BETWEEN AN OFFER TO CONTRACT AND A STATEMENT OF A POSSIBLE SALE PRICE

■ **INSTANT FACTS** Prospective purchaser solicits Jamaican landowner by mail for lowest sale price.

■ **BLACK LETTER RULE** Stating a possible sale price is not binding as an offer to sell at that price.

■ **PROCEDURAL BASIS**

On appeal from the Supreme Court of Jamaica's reversal of the trial court's dismissal of the breach of contract action.

■ **FACTS**

Harvey (P) wanted to purchase a piece of property owned by Facey (D). Harvey (P) sent Facey (D) a telegram asking him if he would consider selling Harvey (P) the property. He also asked Facey (D) to quote his lowest price. Facey (D) responded that the lowest price was £900. Harvey (P) accepted this "offer." When Facey (D) refused to sell the land, Harvey (P) sued him for breach of contract and requested specific performance on the contract. The trial court found that there was no completed contract between Harvey (P) and Facey (D) and dismissed Harvey's (P) claim. The Supreme Court of Jamaica reversed and Facey (D) appeals.

■ **ISSUE**

Is a response to a request for a lowest price binding, an offer to contract?

■ **DECISION AND RATIONALE**

(Morris) No. Harvey's (P) initial telegram posed two distinct questions: 1) will you sell this property? and 2) what is your lowest price? Facey (D) only answered the second question. This is not tantamount to an offer to sell Harvey (P) the property at this price. In fact, Facey's (D) telegram requires a response from Harvey (P), telling him whether he will pay £900 for the property. At that point, Facey (D) is free to accept or reject Harvey's (P) offer to buy at that price.

**Analysis:**

Consider the consequences if this case had come out against Facey (D), the landowner. By simply asking what the sale price was, a potential purchaser could obligate a landowner to sell the property. Looking at it this way, the court's decision is perfectly understandable. Also note that in offer and acceptance cases, it is always important to analyze the communications between the parties in strict chronological order. At every point, you should ask, "is this an offer?" As this case demonstrates, there can be no contract without a valid acceptance following a valid offer.

# Fairmount Glass Works v. Grunden [Crunden]-Martin Woodenware Co.

(Jar Manufacturer) v. (Prospective Buyer)

106 Ky. 659, 51 S.W. 196 (1899)

---

**KENTUCKY COURT OF APPEALS ENFORCES A CONTRACT BASED ON A DETAILED PRICE QUOTE**

---

■ **INSTANT FACTS** Letters are exchanged between a mason jar manufacturer and a prospective buyer.

■ **BLACK LETTER RULE** A price quote may give rise to an enforceable contract, depending upon its language.

---

■ **PROCEDURAL BASIS**

Appeal from a trial court judgment in favor of the plaintiff in a breach of contract action.

■ **FACTS**

A number of letters were exchanged between Crunden-Martin Woodenware Co. (Crunden) (P) and Fairmount Glass Works (Fairmount) (D). Crunden (P) was interested in buying mason jars from Fairmount (D), the manufacturer. They sent Fairmount (D) a letter asking them to quote a price for an order of ten car loads of mason jars. Fairmount (D) responded with price quotes, by jar size, which would be good for immediate acceptance on any shipment before May 15th, 1895. Crunden (P) sent a telegram on April 24th, before the deadline, requesting ten car loads at the quoted prices. They also sent a telegram detailing the specifications for their order, including the number of jars they desired in each size and a request that the jars be "strictly first-quality goods." When Fairmount (D) replied, before they received the specifications, they told Crunden (P) that they could not fill the order because they had sold all of their stock [due to the current mason jar boom]. Crunden (P) then sued for breach of contract. They claimed that their April 24th telegram closed the contract between Crunden (P) and Fairmount (D). Fairmount (D) claimed that the contract had not closed because they had the right to decline the order at any time. The trial court found for Crunden (P). Fairmount (D) appeals.

■ **ISSUE**

Can a price quote be the basis for an enforceable contract?

■ **DECISION AND RATIONALE**

(Hobson) Yes. Ordinarily, a contract does not close until the seller responds affirmatively to an order from a buyer. This order must conform to the terms which the seller has set for the buyer. However, the cases which support this view rely on the language used by the parties in order to determine their intent. In this case, the letters between Crunden (P) and Fairmount (D) gave rise to an enforceable contract as soon as Crunden (P) accepted the terms set forth in Fairmount's initial reply (D). This is because Crunden's (P) first letter made it clear that they were interested in an actual price at which they could place their order. Fairmount (D) not only gave them the price quotes, but told them that the prices were available for immediate acceptance. As a result, they opened themselves up to a contract which could be sealed by Crunden's (P) acceptance. Fairmount (D) claims that Crunden's (P) letters fail to conform to their stated terms because the language "strictly first-quality goods" was never agreed to, and the language, "ten car loads" was too indefinite to constitute a viable order. Both of these terms, however, have a commonly accepted trade meaning which did not alter the terms of the offer, or subject them to any confusion. Judgment affirmed.

**Analysis:**

Justice Hobson follows the trail of correspondence chronologically and with close attention to the language of each letter. Note that this case comes out differently than the earlier cases, because of the language of the letters and their precise sequence. Crunden (P) made it clear that they were interested in buying mason jars from Fairmount (D). Fairmount (D) not only stated a price, but said that it was available for immediate acceptance and laid out a number of other detailed terms. In the earlier cases, the sellers did not commit themselves with as much specificity as Fairmount (D) did in this case. It is also worth noting that justice Hobson Interpreted the correspondence with the assumption that Fairmount (D) is conversant in the language commonly associated with the trade, which is a rule of interpretation that is generally applied in commercial transactions.

### ■ CASE VOCABULARY

TRADE USAGE: The customary vernacular associated with a particular business.

# Lefkowitz v. Great Minneapolis Surplus Store

(Prospective Buyer) v. (Fur Seller)
251 Minn. 188, 86 N.W.2d 689 (1957)

MINNESOTA SUPREME COURT BINDS STORE TO AN ADVERTISED, FIRST-COME FIRST-SERVED PRICE

■ **INSTANT FACTS** A store refuses to sell a fur coat to a male buyer for the advertised price of $1.

■ **BLACK LETTER RULE** An advertisement which is definite, explicit, and which leaves nothing open to negotiation creates a binding contract upon the acceptance of a prospective purchaser.

■ **PROCEDURAL BASIS**

Appeal from a trial court judgement for the plaintiff in a breach of contract action.

■ **FACTS**

The Great Minneapolis Surplus Store (the Store) (D) published a newspaper advertisement in which they offered a single black lapin stole for sale at a price of $1 [the stole was a steal].  The stole would go on sale Saturday morning on a first come, first served basis.  Lefkowitz (P) was the first in line on Saturday morning but the Store (D) refused to sell him the fur.  They told him that they had a "house rule" that the offer was intended for women only.  Lefkowitz (P) sued for breach of contract and sought damages for the full value of the stole, minus $1.  The trial court held for Lefkowitz (P) and the Store (D) appeals.  They rely on the general rule that advertisements are not offers to enter into a contract.  They also claim that any offer which they made was modified by the Store's (D) house rule on selling only to women.

■ **ISSUE**

Can an advertisement create an enforceable contract to sell a particular good at the advertised price?

■ **DECISION AND RATIONALE**

(Murphy) Yes.  The Store (D) correctly states the general rule that advertisements are merely offers to negotiate for the sale of an item at the advertised price.  However, when an offer is clear, definite and explicit, and leaves nothing open to negotiation, then the advertiser can be bound by the acceptance of a prospective purchaser.  In this case, the Store's (D) advertisement fits this description.  Nor can they use their house rule to escape liability.  They cannot modify the advertised offer after it has already been accepted.  Judgement affirmed.

**Analysis:**

Justice Murphy believed that the "First Come-First Served" language was definite and explicit enough to create a valid, binding offer.  Recall that an offer is valid only if the offeree is justified in thinking that he has the power to bind the offeror to a legally enforceable agreement.  An open-ended offer, like those in most advertisements, does not justify this belief because the store might sell out of the advertised product before the buyer gets there. However, in this case, the Store (D) identified the first person there as the person who could accept. Lefkowitz (P) was justified in thinking that the Store (D) must sell him the fur coat if he was the first in line The Store's (D) secret condition that it would sell only to women is indeed invalid.

## ■ CASE VOCABULARY

CONDITION: A circumstance which must be satisfied before a contract, or a term within it, will become binding.

# Elsinore Union Elementary School District v. Kastorff

(School District) v. (Construction Contractor)

54 Cal.2d 380, 6 Cal.Rptr. 1, 353 P.2d 713 (1960)

SUPREME COURT OF CALIFORNIA GRANTS RESCISSION TO A CONSTRUCTION CONTRACTOR WHO MADE A MISTAKEN BID

■ **INSTANT FACTS** A general contractor made an error in a bid for a job and tried to get released from his bid.

■ **BLACK LETTER RULE** A contractor's error in calculating a bid can be grounds for rescission.

■ **PROCEDURAL BASIS**

Appeal from a trial court judgement for the plaintiff in a breach of contract action.

■ **FACTS**

Kastorff (D), a general contractor, intended to bid on a construction job for Elsinore Union Elementary School District (the School District) (P). However, he submitted his bid with an error which lowered his price somewhere between $6500 and $9285. His total bid was $89,994. The competing bids were opened at the School District (P) and Kastorff's (D) bid was found to be $11,306 lower than the next lowest bid. As a result, the superintendent and the school board members asked Kastorff (D) if he was sure that his figures were correct. He checked with his assistant and told them that his bid was correct. The school board subsequently voted to award Kastorff (D) the contract. This was on August 12th, 1952. The next day, Kastorff (D) double-checked his worksheets and discovered his mistake. He met with the architects who were overseeing the project, explained his mistake and asked to be released from his bid. The architects communicated all of this to the superintendent. On August 15th, the school board received a letter from Kastorff (D) again requesting that he be released from his bid due to the error. The school board met and voted to refuse his request. On August 28th, they notified Kastorff (D) in writing that he was awarded the contract. When they sent him the contract itself, he returned it and again explained his error and asked that they reconsider their refusal to release him from his bid. The School District (P) subsequently accepted bids from other contractors and hired the lowest bidder. They sued Kastorff (D) for breach of contract and asked for $12,906 in damages—the difference between his bid and the bid they ultimately accepted. The trial court found for the School District (P). Kastorff (D) appeals.

■ **ISSUE**

Is a contractor bound by a bid which contains an error of which both parties are aware?

■ **DECISION AND RATIONALE**

(Schauer) No. Kastorff (D) argues that, as in *M.F. Kemper Const. Co. v. City of Los Angeles* [California Supreme Court states the circumstances under which a contractor's bid may be rescinded], a contractor is entitled to rescind his bid when he has made a clerical error in its computation. This is true if the requirements set forth in *Kemper* are met. First, it should be noted that a contractor's bid gives the soliciting party an irrevocable option to bind the contractor to a construction agreement. This is a contract right which is subject to the requirements for rescission if the contractor wants to be released from the bid. In order for rescission to be granted, the contractor must show 1) that the soliciting entity knows or has reason to know that there is a mistake in the bid, 2) that the mistake was material and did not result from the neglect of a legal duty, 3) that enforcement of the contract would be unconscionable, 4) that the soliciting entity can be returned to the position they were in prior to contracting, 5) that the contractor promptly notified the soliciting entity of the mistake, and 6) the contractor restores or offers to restore to the soliciting entity everything of value they have received under the contract. Of these six requirements, the second and third are the most pivotal in this case. With regard to the second requirement, the School District (P) argued that the amount of the error was immaterial. However, this court has permitted rescission in similar circumstances when the percentage error was far smaller. In addition, Kastorff's (D) mistake, and his failure to recognize it when the board asked him to check his figures, does not rise to the level of neglect of a legal duty. With regard to the third requirement, it can only be said that if the School District (P) had committed an error which would deny them a significant portion of their construction, but force them to pay for it, they would be here demanding rescission rather than Kastorff (D). Likewise, it would be inequitable to force Kastorff (D) to suffer under the bargain which the School District (P) would like to impose. Reversed.

**Analysis:**

With regard to an action for rescission, courts will generally grant relief if both parties are aware of the mistake and neither party has relied on the contract. The seemingly complicated requirements for rescission are frequently interpreted in favor of an equitable outcome on a case-by-case basis. Consider the similarities between this case and *Lucy v. Zehmer*, in which the Supreme Court of Virginia upheld a contract of sale for real estate even though the seller was joking. *Lucy v. Zehmer* would probably be decided differently today, because both parties were aware that the seller was joking, albeit not until after the contract was signed and delivered. Courts will not be as solicitous when one party holds the last clear chance to avoid damages due to a misunderstanding but fails to exercise the power to let the other party out of the contract.

■ **CASE VOCABULARY**

GENERAL CONTRACTOR: A person responsible for assembling and overseeing the subcontractors necessary to the completion of a construction project. They will frequently do some of the construction work themselves, and are responsible for bidding on jobs and keeping track of the expenses associated with all of the work. When bidding on jobs with public entities, their bids are generally binding.

UNCONSCIONABILITY: A doctrine which strikes terms out of contracts or voids whole contracts. In order for a party to succeed under this doctrine, they must show that there was a procedural defect in the contract formation process, or that the contract is substantially unfair.

# International Filter Co. v. Conroe Gin, Ice & Light Co.

(Filter Manufacturer) v. (Ice Manufacturer)

277 S.W. 631 (Tex. Com. App. 1925).

TEXAS APPEALS COURT AFFIRMS OFFEROR'S RIGHT TO CONTROL THE METHOD OF ACCEPTANCE

■ **INSTANT FACTS** A water filter manufacturer refuses to cancel an ice company's order for a filter.

■ **BLACK LETTER RULE** The offeror controls the method and means of acceptance by the language of the offer.

■ **PROCEDURAL BASIS**

Appeal from an affirmance of a trial court judgement for the defendant in a breach of contract action.

■ **FACTS**

On February 10, 1920, the International Filter Co. (IFC) (P) made a written offer to sell a water filter to the Conroe Gin, Ice & Light Co. (Conroe) (D). The offer was subject to certain conditions including a set price. The offer also stated that it would become a contract upon acceptance by Conroe (D) and approval by IFC's (P) executive officer in Chicago. Finally, the offer stated that It was "submitted for prompt acceptance." Conroe (D) accepted the offer the same day, in writing, including a request for delivery by March 10th. This acceptance was approved by IFC's (P) president and vice-president [the same person] in Chicago. He wrote, "O.K." on Conroe's (D) order and dated it. IFC (P) then sent an acknowledgment of the order to Conroe (D) by mail, on February 14th. Conroe (D) subsequently sent two letters to IFC (P) in an attempt to cancel the order. IFC (P) responded to the first letter, refusing to do so. They then sued Conroe (D) for breach of contract. The trial court found for Conroe (D). The Court of Civil Appeals affirmed and, as a result, IFC (P) appeals.

■ **ISSUE**

Can the offeror control the method of acceptance with the language of the offer?

■ **DECISION AND RATIONALE**

(Nickels) Yes. For instance, the offeror can dispense with the obligation to notify the offeree that their acceptance has been approved. Whether this has been done can be determined by the language of the offer. Conroe (D) argues that no contract was created with IFC (P) for two reasons. First, they claim that their order was not approved by IFC's (P) executive officer in Chicago. They argue that the president's "O.K." and the resulting acknowledgment letter do not constitute the required approval. Alternately, Conroe (D) claims that IFC (P) took too long to notify them that the order had been approved. They claim that a prompt response was required by the terms of the offer and by a verbal agreement made between their respective agents when the written order was placed. However, the offer explicitly states that a contract will be formed when Conroe (D) accepts the offer and when IFC's (P) executive officer approves the acceptance. The offer would contradict itself if the phrase "[t]his proposal is submitted for prompt acceptance" was interpreted as a requirement for notification to Conroe (D) after IFC's (P) acceptance. This phrase simply puts the offeree on notice that IFC's (P) approval will follow promptly after Conroe's (D) acceptance. It is not a further requirement to the formation of a valid contract. As a result, a valid contract was formed when Conroe (D) accepted the offer and IFC (P) approved. However, even if notice were required, then IFC's (P) acknowledgment letter was sufficient. There are no requirements governing notification unless the parties agree to them. In this case, that was not done. The contract is valid. Reversed and remanded.

## Analysis:

The offeror can dictate the terms of the offer, the method and means of acceptance, and the method and means of notification. Most cases deal with the method of acceptance. There is no legal requirement that the offeror follow up with notification that this acceptance has been approved. However, as the case indicates, this requirement could have been written into the offer at IFC's (P) discretion. At times, it is possible for courts to resolve a contract dispute by relying solely on the language of the contract. This is generally referred to as staying within the "four corners" of the contract. However, it is not unusual for courts to arrive at different legal conclusions while analyzing and re-analyzing the same contract language.

# White v. Corlies & Tift

(Builder) v. (Prospective Client)

46 N.Y. 467 (1871)

**NEW YORK COURT OF APPEALS REQUIRES ONLY A REASONABLE MEANS OF ACCEPTANCE OF AN OFFER ABSENT SPECIFICATION OF MANNER OF ACCEPTANCE BY THE OFFEROR**

■ **INSTANT FACTS** A builder accepts a construction contract by beginning to purchase lumber for the job.

■ **BLACK LETTER RULE** In the absence of express provisions in the offer, an acceptance must be by reasonable means given the circumstances surrounding the offer.

■ **PROCEDURAL BASIS**

Appeal from an affirmance of the trial court's judgement for the plaintiff in a breach of contract action.

■ **FACTS**

Corlies & Tift (D) (Corlies) asked White (P), a builder, for an estimate on renovating a suite of offices for them. White (P) gave them an estimate, which he later signed and returned to Corlies (D) after approving some changes in their specifications. Corlies (D) sent White (P) a note telling him to start the job and giving him two weeks to finish it. White (P) never responded to this note. The next day, it was countermanded by a second note from Corlies (D) canceling White's (P) participation in the job. White (P) had already begun work, however, buying lumber for the job. When White (P) received the cancellation letter he sued Corlies (D) for breach of contract. The trial court instructed the jury that, in the judge's opinion, White (P) was not obligated to make a formal acceptance of Corlies' (D) first note in order for there to be an enforceable contract between them. According to the trial judge, the contract became binding as soon as White (P) began working on the job. The jury found for White (D). The intermediate appellate court affirmed and, as a result, Corlies (D) appeals.

■ **ISSUE**

Is performance a sufficient means of acceptance if the offer is not specific on the issue?

■ **DECISION AND RATIONALE**

(Folger) That depends. After an offer is made, the offeree can only accept by some affirmative act. This act need not be immediately communicated to the offeror. It must, however, be a proper response, given the usual course of events, and be communicated to the offeror within a reasonable amount of time. For instance, an offer which is made by mail becomes binding when an acceptance is mailed, even though the offeror will not learn of the acceptance until it is received [the mailbox rule]. The importance lies in an affirmative act which is recognizable as an acceptance of the offer. As a result, an offeree's subjective desire to accept an offer will not be binding. In this case, White (P) received a communication from Corlies (D) which was an offer. This offer took the form of an acceptance of his bid and a request that the work start immediately and be completed within two weeks. White (P) had to accept this offer in order to create a binding contract. Indeed, he did accept the offer in his mind [perhaps the voices in his head weren't speaking loud enough for anyone else to hear]. He also began working on the job. However, Corlies (D) could not distinguish White's (P) preparations for their job from any other job for which he might be getting ready. As a result, his acceptance was never communicated to them and they had a right to cancel the offer. In contrast, the trial court instructed the jury that White (P) had accepted Corlies' (D) offer by starting work on the job. This instruction misled the jury and constitutes error. Reversed and remanded for a new trial.

**Analysis:**

The old rule was that acceptance had to be made by the same method as the offer. For instance, an offer made by mail could not be accepted by telegram. The impracticality of this rule gave rise to the new rule, which is that, unless otherwise specified, acceptance must be made by a reasonable means. Justice Folger hints at this approach when he writes that an acceptance must be by a proper means, given the circumstances, and communicated within a reasonable time. The circumstances will determine the reasonableness of the method. Remember, however, that the offeror can restrict the means of acceptance in the terms of the offer. If the offeror states that acceptance will only be valid if received by carrier pigeon, then that is the only permissible means of acceptance.

■ **CASE VOCABULARY**

THE MAILBOX RULE: A rule which makes the acceptance of an offer effective as soon as it is placed in the mail.

# Ever-Tite Roofing Corporation v. Green

(Roofer) v. (Prospective Client)

83 So.2d 449 (La.App. 1955)

LOUISIANA COURT OF APPEALS ENFORCES A REASONABLE RESPONSE TIME FOR AN OTHER-WISE UNSPECIFIED OFFER

■ **INSTANT FACTS** A roofing company arrives to start a job only to discover that their prospective client has hired someone else.

■ **BLACK LETTER RULE** In the absence of specific language in an offer, the offeror must allow a reasonable amount of time for acceptance.

■ **PROCEDURAL BASIS**

Appeal from a trial court judgement for the defendant in a breach of contract action.

■ **FACTS**

The Greens (D) wanted the Ever-Tite Roofing Corporation (Ever-Tite) (P) to do some work on their house. They signed a document which detailed the work desired and the price to be paid. An agent from Ever-Tite (P) also signed the document, even though he had no authority to bind them to a contract. In fact, the document contained a provision which stated that it became binding only upon acceptance by an authorized agent of Ever-Tite (P) or upon commencement of the work requested. The Greens (D) knew that the work could not start until a lender approved their credit. This approval came nine days later. When Ever-Tite (P) arrived to start the job, however, there was another company there which had already been working for two days. Ever-Tite (D) was not permitted to do any work, and, as a result, they sued the Greens (D) for breach of contract. The trial court found for the Greens (D). Ever-Tite (P) appeals.

■ **ISSUE**

In the absence of specific provisions in an offer, must the offeror provide a reasonable amount of time for acceptance?

■ **DECISION AND RATIONALE**

(Ayres) Yes. An offeree has a reasonable amount of time to accept if the offer does not specify a time by which it must be accepted. A reasonable amount of time can be inferred from the circumstances surrounding the offer and the intent of the parties. In this case, the trial court found that the Greens (D) had given Ever-Tite (P) sufficient notice that they no longer wanted them to work on the house. However, this notice did not come until Ever-Tite (P) was actually at the house. This is not a reasonable amount of time based on the language of the contract and the knowledge of the parties. The contract stated that it would become binding upon acceptance by Ever-Tite's (P) authorized agent or by commencement of the work requested. In this case, the work began when Ever-Tite (P) loaded its trucks before driving to the job site. In addition, the Greens (D) knew that it might take some time for financing to come through. Given that this did not take an unreasonably long time, the contract became binding when Ever-Tite (P) commenced performance. Reversed and remanded.

**Analysis:**

In this case, the contract specifically provided that performance by Ever-Tite would bind both parties. As a result, the Greens (D) were on notice that Ever-Tite's (P) acceptance might be unknown to them until the workers actually arrived. As in *White v. Corlies & Tift*, Justice Ayres considers the amount of time it took for Ever-Tite (P) to notify the Greens (D) of its acceptance. In this case, he found that the amount of time was reasonable given the circumstances. Consider also that in *White v. Corlies & Tift*, the unspecified contract term was the means of acceptance. In this case, the unspecified term was the time allotted for acceptance. In both cases, the courts fill in the blanks by looking at the language of the contracts and the relationship of the parties. The yardstick for implied terms is, as always, a reasonableness standard.

# Allied Steel and Conveyors, Inc. v. Ford Motor Co.

(Machinery Provider) v. (Auto Manufacturer)

277 F.2d 907 (6th Cir. 1960)

CIRCUIT COURT OF APPEALS ENFORCES PERFORMANCE AS AN ALTERNATIVE MEANS OF ACCEPTING AN OFFER EVEN THOUGH THE OFFER SUGGESTS OTHER MEANS

■ **INSTANT FACTS** Ford sought to hold Allied to an indemnification agreement when an Allied employee was injured at the Ford plant.

■ **BLACK LETTER RULE** An offer which suggests a means of acceptance may become binding by performance by the offeree.

■ **PROCEDURAL BASIS**

Appeal from a trial court judgement against an impleader defendant requiring indemnification of the original defendant in a negligence action.

■ **FACTS**

The Ford Motor Co. (Ford) (3dP) [third party plaintiff—see vocabulary] ordered machinery from Allied Steel and Conveyors, Inc. (Allied) (3dD) [third party defendant—see vocabulary]. Ford (3dP) placed the order with their own purchase order as well as another attached form. Both of these forms Included indemnity provisions which made Allied (3dD) responsible for the negligence of their employees while installing Allied (3dD) equipment on Ford (3dP) premises. In addition, the attached form made Allied (3dD) responsible for the negligence of Ford (3dP) employees in connection with Allied's (3dD) work. This provision was marked "VOID." Allied (3dD) accepted the equipment order and the work was performed. Subsequently, Ford (3dP) submitted an amendment to the original purchase order, requesting additional machinery. The amendment stated that it was not binding until it was accepted. It also stated that acceptance should be executed on the acknowledgment copy and then returned to Ford (3dP). Finally, there was another attached form, like the one attached to the original purchase order. However, on this copy, the extended Indemnification provision was not marked "VOID." Allied (3dD) began Installation on the amended purchase order just over a month later. They did not execute and return the acknowledgment copy of the order until two months after that. During this time, between the beginning of the work and the return of their formal acceptance, an Allied (3dD) employee was injured as the result of a Ford (3dP) employee's negligence. The employee sued Ford (3dP) and Ford (3dP) subsequently Impleaded Allied (3dD) on the strength of their indemnification agreement. The trial court ruled in favor of the injured employee, and in favor of Ford (3dP) with regard to their indemnification claim against Allied (3dD). Allied (3dD) appeals.

■ **ISSUE**

Does an offer which specifies a particular means of acceptance preclude other possible methods of acceptance?

■ **DECISION AND RATIONALE**

(Miller) No. Allied (3dD) argues that they were not bound by the indemnification agreement at the time of the injury because they had not yet executed and returned the acknowledgment copy of the amended purchase order. In support of this argument, they claim that this was the only method of acceptance which was approved by the amendment. This is not entirely correct. It is true that the offeror controls the means of acceptance through the language of his offer. In addition, it is true that the offeror, within this control, can prescribe a specific and exclusive means of acceptance which cannot be circumvented by the offeree. However, if the offeror merely suggests a means of acceptance, other methods of acceptance are not precluded. More particularly, the offeror may request a promise in return for the offer. Under these circumstances, the offeree may either make the return promise or begin performance on whatever the return promise entailed. A binding contract results if the offeree begins or completes performance during the period allotted for the return promise. In this case, the purchase order amendment merely suggested a means of accepting the order. This was for Allied's protection. It was a way of insuring that Allied (3dD) fully acknowledged their responsibilities before they began working since the extended indemnification provision itself was clearly for Ford's (3dP) protection. Allied (3dD) chose to begin the installation of the additional machinery before they returned the acknowledgment form. They did so with Ford's (3dP) acquiescence. Since Allied (3dD) was acting in accordance with the terms of the equipment order, they cannot now claim that their subjective intent was otherwise. Curiously, Allied (3dD) argues that despite the commencement of performance, Ford (3dP) could have canceled their order with no recourse left to Allied (3dD). This is also incorrect. Ford (3dP) would be estopped from claiming that there was no contract if they had acquiesced in the face of Allied's (3dD) performance and accepted its benefit. Looking at the relationship of the parties from both of their perspectives only serves to compel the conclusion that a binding contract existed between Ford (3dP) and Allied (3dD). Judgement affirmed.

**Analysis:**

Judge Miller relied on the first Restatement of Contracts in his enunciation of the law regarding performance as acceptance. His interpretation is still valid according to Restatement (Second) of Contracts § 62. More importantly, his opinion introduces the two most basic forms of acceptance: promise and performance. An offeror can specify that acceptance come in the form of a return promise or in the form of performance. The first exchange, a promise made in return for another promise, gives rise to a bilateral contract. The second exchange, a promise made in return for performance, gives rise to a unilateral contract. The reasons why an offeror might prefer one type of contract over another vary from business to business. Frequently, courts will blur the lines between bilateral and unilateral contacts in order to avoid unfairness to a party. In this case, for instance, the court permits what appears to be an ongoing business relationship to obliterate a fairly clear acceptance requirement in the amended purchase order.

## ■ CASE VOCABULARY

ESTOPPEL: A doctrine which precludes a party from asserting a particular claim or right due to some prior, disqualifying act on their part.

IMPLEAD: A measure under Federal Rule of Civil Procedure 14 by which a third party can be brought into a civil action because, among other possibilities, they are liable to the defendant for part or all of the damages which the defendant may be required to pay the plaintiff.

INDEMNIFICATION: A defendant in a civil action is entitled to seek compensation from a third party who is responsible to them for any damages the defendant is required to pay. A claim for Indemnification can be predicated, as in this case, on a prior agreement between the defendant and the third party.

THIRD PARTY DEFENDANT: A third party who is successfully brought into a civil action by impleader is deemed a third party defendant with respect to the original defendant.

THIRD PARTY PLAINTIFF: A defendant in a civil action who successfully impleads a third party will be deemed a third party *plaintiff* with respect to the impleaded party.

# Corinthian Pharmaceutical Systems, Inc. v. Lederle Laboratories

(Drug Distributor) v. (Drug Manufacturer)

724 F.Supp. 605 (S.D. Ind. 1989)

SHIPPING NON-CONFORMING GOODS MAY BE AN ACCOMMODATION, NOT COUNTER-OFFER

■ **INSTANT FACTS** A drug distributor sought to force a drug manufacturer to sell it a vaccine at a certain price.

■ **BLACK LETTER RULE** If a seller ships to the buyer non-conforming goods and gives notice that the shipment is an accommodation, the seller is not in breach of contract and is not obligated to deliver goods that conform to the buyer's order.

■ **PROCEDURAL BASIS**

Motion for summary judgment in breach of contract action seeking specific performance.

■ **FACTS**

Lederle Laboratories ("Lederle") (D) manufactures the DTP vaccine. Corinthian Pharmaceutical Systems, Inc. ("Corinthian") (P) is a drug distributor that purchases the vaccine from manufacturers and resells it to physicians and other providers. Lederle (D) periodically sent a price list to its customers stating that the prices shown were in effect at the time of publication but were subject to change without notice. The price list also stated that changes in price take immediate effect and are applied to unfilled orders. In 1985 and 1986, Corinthian (P) purchased often from Lederle (D); the largest purchase was for 100 vials. In early 1986, product liability lawsuits concerning DTP increased and insurance became difficult to procure. Lederle (D) decided to self-insure and substantially increase the cost of DTP to cover the cost of self-insurance. To communicate the price change to its sales people, Lederle (D) prepared "Price Letter No. E-48." The price letter was dated May 19, 1986 and stated that effective May 20, 1986 the price of DTP would be raised from $51 to $171 per vial. Corinthian (P) did not know of this internal price letter until several weeks after May 20, 1986. Lederle (D) wrote a letter dated May 20, 1986 to its customers announcing the price increase. Corinthian (P) somehow became aware of the letter on May 19, 1986, the day before the price increase was to take effect. On May 19, Corinthian (P) ordered 1000 vials of DTP from Lederle (P) through Lederle's (P) telephone computer ordering system, "Telgo," and received a tracking number. Also on May 19, Corinthian (P) sent Lederle (D) two written confirmations of its order stating that the order is to "receive the $64.32 per vial price." On June 3, 1986. Lederle (D) sent an invoice to Corinthian (P) for 50 vials of DTP vaccine at $64.32 per vial. Lederle (D) sent the 50 vials to Corinthian (P) and Corinthian (P) accepted them. At the same time, Lederle (D) sent a letter to Corinthian (P) stating that the enclosed is a partial shipment of DTP and that Lederle's (D) normal policy would be to invoice the order at the price in effect when the shipment was made. However, because of the magnitude of the price increase, Lederle (D) decided to ship a portion at the lower price. The letter stated that the balance of the order would be priced at $171 per vial. The letter concluded that if Corinthian (P) wished to cancel the balance of the order it should contact Lederle (D) on or before June 13. Corinthian (P) sued Lederle (D) for specific performance for the 950 vials of DTP that Lederle (D) did not deliver. Lederle (D) moved for summary judgment arguing that no contract for the sale of 1000 vials was formed. In the alternative, Lederle (D) argued that if a contract was formed, it was governed by Lederle's (D) terms and conditions, and that it sent Corinthian the 50 vials as an accommodation.

## ■ ISSUE

If a seller ships non-conforming goods to the buyer, is the seller obligated to deliver goods that conform to the buyer's order?

## ■ DECISION AND RATIONALE

(McKinney, J.)   No, not if the seller sends notice to the buyer that the shipment is an accommodation. This action involves a sale of goods by merchants and is governed by the Uniform Commercial Code [model approach to commercial law which has been adopted, in whole or in part, by every state].   The first step here is to determine where the first offer originated.   An offer is the manifestation of willingness to enter into a bargain, so made as to justify another person in understanding that his assent to that bargain is invited and will conclude it.   Lederle's (D) price lists were not offers.   Quotations are merely Invitations to make an offer.   Lederle's (D) internal price memorandum and its May 20 letter to customers were not offers to sell the 1000 vials at the lower price.   The letter was a mere quotation, and there is no evidence that Lederle (D) intended Corinthian (P) to receive the internal price memorandum. As a matter of law, Corinthian's (P) May 19 order for 1000 vials at $64.32 was the first offer.   The next question is whether Lederle (D) accepted the offer.   Lederle (D) did not communicate with Corinthian (P) before shipping the 50 vials.   When Corinthian (P) placed its order, it merely received a tracking number from Telgo.   An automated, ministerial act like that does not constitute an acceptance.   Thus, Lederle (D) did not accept Corinthian's (P) offer before shipping the 50 vials.   Under UCC § 2-206(1)(b), a seller accepts the offer by shipping goods, whether they are conforming or not, but if the seller ships non-conforming goods and seasonably notifies the buyer that the shipment is a mere accommodation, then the seller has not accepted the buyer's offer.   Lederle's (D) shipment to Corinthian (P) was non-conforming because it was only 1/20 of the quantity Corinthian (P) requested. An accommodation is an arrangement or engagement made as a favor to another.   Consideration is not required.   Lederle's (D) shipment of 50 vials was an accommodation because Lederle (D) had no obligation to make the partial shipment and did so only as a favor to Corinthian (P).   Lederle (D) clearly informed Corinthian (P) that the 50 vials were being sent as an exception to Lederle's (D) general policy, that the balance of the offer would be at the higher price, and that Corinthian (P) could cancel the rest of the order.   Therefore UCC § 2-206(1)(b) was satisfied.   Where the notification is properly made, the shipment of nonconforming goods is treated as a counter-offer, and the buyer may accept or reject the counter-offer.   Thus, there is no genuine issue of material fact, and summary judgment is granted to Lederle (D).

---

**Analysis:**

UCC has made to the common law of offer and acceptance.   UCC § 2-206(1)(b) provides that "an order or other offer to buy goods for prompt or current shipment shall be construed as inviting acceptance either by a prompt promise to ship or by the prompt or current shipment of conforming or non-conforming goods, but such a shipment of non-conforming goods does not constitute an acceptance if the seller seasonably notifies the buyer that the shipment is offered only as an accommodation to the buyer."   Thus, under the UCC, even if the seller sends non-conforming goods, there is a contract.   The non-conforming shipment is an acceptance of the offer and a breach. However, if the seller "seasonably notifies the buyer that the shipment is offered only as an accommodation to the buyer," there is no contract and the shipment is treated as a counter-offer. Here, Lederle (D) sent non-conforming goods and notified Corinthian (P) that the shipment was an accommodation in light of the magnitude of the price increase.   Had Lederle (D) not sent that notice, Corinthian (P) likely would have won the case.

---

## ■ CASE VOCABULARY

SELF-INSURANCE: The assumption of the risk of one's own loss by one having an insurable interest. However, in reality, a self-insurer does not provide any insurance.   That a company is "self-insured" merely shows that it has the financial ability to satisfy a judgment against it within statutory liability minimums.

# Dickinson v. Dodds

(Offeree) v. (Offeror)
2 Ch. Div. 463 (1876)

DON'T WAIT UNTIL THE LAST MINUTE TO ACCEPT AN OFFER

■ **INSTANT FACTS** An offeror gave an offeree until Friday to accept an offer to sell property, but sold the property to someone else on Thursday.

■ **BLACK LETTER RULE** Without separate consideration, an offeror may revoke an offer anytime before the offeree's deadline to accept the offer.

■ **PROCEDURAL BASIS**

Appeal of Vice Chancellor's decision granting specific performance in breach of contract action.

■ **FACTS**

On June 10, 1874, Dodds (D) delivered a memo to Dickinson (P) stating that Dodds (D) would sell certain real estate to Dickinson for £800. In a postscript, the memo stated that the offer would be open until Friday, June 12, 1874 at 9:00 a.m. Dickinson (P) alleged that he decided to accept the offer on the morning of June 11, but did not communicate this to Dodds (D) because he believed he had the power to accept until 9:00 a.m. the next day. In the afternoon of June 11, Dickinson (P) was informed that Dodds (D) had been negotiating with Allan (D) to sell the property. At about 7:30 that evening, Dickinson (P) went to Dodds' (D) mother-in-law's house, where Dodds (D) was staying, and left her a written acceptance of the offer. The mother-in-law forgot to give the note to Dodds (D). On Friday morning at 7:00, Dickinson's (P) agent found Dodds (D) and gave him a duplicate of Dickinson's (P) written acceptance. Dodds (D) replied that he had already sold the property. Soon thereafter, Dickinson (P) found Dodds (D) and handed him another duplicate of the acceptance [enough already!]. Dodds (D) told Dickinson (P) that it wastoo late, that he already sold the property. Dodds (D) had sold the property to Allan (D) on June 11 for £800. Dickinson (P) sued for specific performance of the sale of the property and for damages. The Vice Chancellor held for Dickinson (P).

■ **ISSUE**

If an offeror states that an offer will be open for a certain period of time, may the offeror accept another offer within that period?

■ **DECISION AND RATIONALE**

(James, L J.) Yes, if no consideration is paid to keep the offer open. Dodds' (D) memo was only an offer, not a contract. Dickinson (P) did not give Dodds (D) any consideration to keep the property unsold until June 12. Therefore, the promise to keep the offer open until June 12 was not binding on Dodds (D). Furthermore, before Dickinson (P) accepted the offer, he learned that Dodds (D) had changed his mind about selling to Dickinson (P) and was going to sell the property to Allan (D). Therefore, there was never a point in time where there was a meeting of Dodds' (D) and Dickinson's (P) minds. Thus, there was no binding contract between Dodds (D) and Dickinson (P). Reversed.

■ **CONCURRENCE**

(Mellish, L J.) I am of the same opinion. Dodds' (D) offer to keep the offer open was not binding. Even if Allan (D) knew about Dodds' (D) offer to Dickinson (P), Allan (D) was not prevented from making a more favorable offer and entering into an agreement with Dodds (D). Moreover, it would be absurd to allow an offeree to accept an offer after learning that the offeror already sold the property to someone else.

**Analysis:**

An offeror's promise to keep an offer open is called an "option." One way to create an enforceable option is by giving consideration. Here, Dodds (D) terminated Dickinson's (P) ability to accept the offer to buy the property by revoking the offer. Revocation is the manifestation of an intent not to enter into a proposed offer, Dodds (D) manifested his intent not to enter into a contract with Dickinson (P) by entering into an agreement with Allan (D). Dodds (D) revoked the offer indirectly. He did not communicate the revocation directly to Dickinson (P), but the offer was deemed revoked when Dickinson (P) received reliable information that Dodds (D) had sold the property to Allan (D). This rule is set forth in Restatement (Second) § 43. Case law holds that to be reliable, information must be true and come from a reliable source. The offeree may ignore the information. If the source is reliable, the offeree has a duty to reasonably inquire about the accuracy of the information. Here, Dickinson (P) heard that Allan (D) had accepted Dodds' (D) offer. Dickinson (P) should have thus concluded that Dodds (D) revoked the offer to Dickinson (P). If Dickinson (P) had heard only that Dodds (D) made an offer to Allan (D). Dickinson (P) could reasonably have reached two different conclusions. He could have concluded that Dodds (D) would not want to make two offers to sell the same property and, therefore, intended to revoke the offer to Dickinson (P). He could also conclude that Dodds (D) was willing to run the risk of making two offers, and that the offer to Dickinson (P) remained open. According to Corbin, a leading contracts law scholar, the second conclusion is preferable.

■ **CASE VOCABULARY**

NUDUM PACTUM: A contract made without a consideration; it is called a nude or naked contract because it is not clothed with the consideration required by law in order to give an action.

# Ragosta v. Wilder

(Prospective Buyer) v. (Shop Owner)

156 Vt. 390, 592 A.2d 367 (1991)

VERMONT SUPREME COURT EXPLORES THE REVOCABILITY OF OFFERS AND PART PERFORMANCE

■ **INSTANT FACTS** A shop owner and a prospective buyer dispute the meaning of a cash-in-hand offer that the owner made for the sale of the shop.

■ **BLACK LETTER RULE** An offer is freely revocable until the offeror is bound by a valid acceptance.

■ **PROCEDURAL BASIS**

Appeal from a trial court judgement and order of specific performance against the defendant in a breach of contract action.

■ **FACTS**

Ragosta (P) [representing more than one party] was interested in buying a piece of property called "The Fork Shop" from its owner, Wilder (D). Ragosta (P) and Wilder (D) discussed the purchase but were unable to reach an agreement. Two years later, the property went up for sale again. Ragosta (P) sent Wilder (D) a check for $2,000 along with an offer for the property, and began arranging financing for the purchase. Wilder (D) sent the check back without approving the sale. He did, however, include a counter-offer in his response. Wilder (D) offered to sell Ragosta (P) the property for $88,000 anytime up until November 1, 1987. Ragosta (P) was required to pay the entire sum at a specified bank at the time of purchase. In addition, the sale could only go forward if the property had not already been sold. Ragosta (P) called Wilder (D) on October 1st and told him that he was prepared to accept the offer. Wilder (D) stated that no one else was currently interested in the property. Ragosta (P) subsequently called to say that he would be able to complete the transaction on October 10th. However, before that day arrived, Wilder (D) told Ragosta (P) that he was no longer interested in selling the property. Despite this, Ragosta (P) said that he would be at the bank on October 15th. Ragosta (P) arrived at the bank with $88,000 but Wilder (D) never showed up. Ragosta (P) sued for breach of contract, asking for damages for his closing costs. He also requested specific performance for the sale of the property. The trial court ruled for Ragosta (P). Wilder (D) appeals.

■ **ISSUE**

Is an offer freely revocable before acceptance is tendered?

■ **DECISION AND RATIONALE**

(Peck) Yes. Ordinarily, an option is an offer which cannot be revoked before the time limit if it is supported by consideration. Ragosta (P) argues that consideration for the option was satisfied by his efforts to obtain financing for the purchase. However, the Restatement (Second) of Contracts notes that, in order to qualify as consideration, a return promise or performance must be bargained for. In other words, the consideration must be something that Wilder (D) sought in making the offer. In this case, Ragosta (P) began arranging financing before Wilder (D) made his offer. Therefore, it cannot be consideration for the option to buy the shop. Since there was no consideration for the option, the offer was freely revocable until Ragosta (P) tendered his acceptance. The trial court found that Ragosta (P) accepted the offer by part performance. Specifically, his efforts to obtain financing were the beginnings of performance. According to the Restatement (Second) of Contracts, when an offer invites the offeree to accept by performance, an option contract is created when the offeree either performs or begins performance. However, the performance must be that which was invited by the offer. Wilder's (D) offer requested payment in full for the purchase of the shop. When he revoked his offer, Ragosta (P) was still in the process of obtaining financing. This was preparation for performance but not a portion of the performance itself. As a result, Ragosta (P) never actually accepted Wilder's (D) offer. The trial court also found for Ragosta (P) under a theory of equitable estoppel. The judge reasoned that Wilder (D) should be estopped from claiming that there was no contract with Ragosta (P) because Ragosta (P) was already performing in reliance on the offer. There are four requirements for this claim: 1) the party to be estopped knows the facts, 2) the party being estopped must have intended for his conduct to be acted upon, or have given the other party the right to believe that he intended it to be acted upon, 3) the party seeking estoppel must be ignorant of the true facts, and 4) the party seeking estoppel must rely on the conduct of the other party to their detriment. Ragosta (P) was not ignorant of the facts here. He knew that Wilder (D) did not have to sell him the shop if it was purchased by someone else first. Also, Ragosta (P) did not act in reliance on Wilder's (D) offer. As discussed above, he began seeking financing before Wilder (D) ever made his offer. Since Ragosta's (P) arguments fail under both contract theory and equitable estoppel, Wilder's (D) offer was freely revocable. Reversed.

## Analysis:

Many basic contracts issues contribute to the resolution of this case. These issues include consideration, the bargain theory of contracts, offer and acceptance, option contracts, equitable estoppel, and now, revocation. The case is a good review of these doctrines and is instructive with regard to their interrelation and interdependence. In addition, policy concerns play a significant role in Justice Peck's decision. At one point, he suggests that Ragosta (P) assumed the risk that the purchase would fall through when he sought financing even though the property might have been sold before he obtained the necessary funds. Many contracts cases are similarly decided, based on the distribution of information, control, and risk between the parties. Pay attention to the policies that courts seek to further, along with the legal rules they enforce.

## ■ CASE VOCABULARY

EQUITABLE ESTOPPEL: Equitable estoppel precludes a person from asserting a right or defense due to an affirmative act on their part. Generally, a person makes a representation which induces reliance in another party and is then estopped from disclaiming any obligations to that party. Also see ESTOPPEL in *Allied Steel and Conveyors, Inc. v. Ford Motor Co.* [indemnification clause accepted by means of performance on the contract by the offeree].

# Dorton v. Collins & Aikman Corp.

(Carpet Seller) v. (Carpet Manufacturer)

453 F.2d 1161 (6th Cir. 1972)

COURT OF APPEALS APPLIES UCC § 2–207 TO ARBITRATION PROVISIONS IN A BATTLE OF FORMS

■ **INSTANT FACTS** A carpet manufacturer wants to hold a dissatisfied retailer to an arbitration agreement pre-printed on the manufacturer's sales forms.

■ **BLACK LETTER RULE** Under UCC § 2–207, if an arbitration provision materially alters an existing agreement, it will not be incorporated into the contract unless expressly agreed to by both parties.

## ■ PROCEDURAL BASIS

Appeal from the district court's denial of a defense motion for a stay of proceedings in a fraud action.

## ■ FACTS

Dorton, otherwise known as The Carpet Mart (TCM) (P), purchased carpets from Collins & Aikman Corp. (C&A) (D) fifty-five times over a period of three years. TCM (P) placed their orders buy phone with C&A (D). C&A (D) checked with their credit department and then returned a pre-printed acknowledgment form with the details of the order. Depending upon the form that was used, it stated that a contract was created when it was signed and delivered by the buyer and accepted in writing by the seller, or when the buyer received and retained the order for ten days without objection, or when the buyer accepted delivery of any part of the order or otherwise indicated acceptance of the terms of the acknowledgment form. In addition, all of the forms stated that acceptance of the order was subject to the terms and conditions on the face and reverse of the form. The reverse side of every form contained a provision which obligated the buyer to submit to arbitration for any claims arising out of the agreement. TCM (P) usually received one of these forms before they received their carpets. They always took delivery and paid for the carpets without objecting to the terms in the acknowledgment form. As it turned out, TCM (P) discovered that some of C&A's (D) carpets were made out of inferior materials. They sued C&A (D) for fraud and misrepresentation regarding the quality of the carpets. C&A (D) argued that they were entitled to a stay of proceedings until TCM (P) submitted to arbitration. The district court denied the stay and C&A (D) appeals.

## ■ ISSUE

Are the parties to an agreement bound by an arbitration clause which is not present in both of their contracts?

## ■ DECISION AND RATIONALE

(Celebrezze) Maybe. Article 2 of the Uniform Commercial Code [a model approach to commercial law which has been adopted, in whole or in part, by every state] applies to the sale of goods. In particular, UCC § 2–207, governs transactions in which the parties have not expressly agreed to a particular written contract, and the existing writings exchanged by the parties do not agree. It is not clear, however, that UCC § 2–207 governs this case for two reasons. First the district court will have to determine whether C&A's (D) acknowledgment forms were acceptances or confirmations. This will depend on whether TCM (P) and C&A (D) reached an oral agreement before the acknowledgment forms were sent. In either case, it is possible that an oral agreement between the parties included an implied arbitration provision. In that case, the arbitration terms in the acknowledgment forms would not be "additional" for the purposes of UCC § 2–207. That said, if the arbitration provisions are found to be additional, UCC § 2–207 would govern unless acceptance of the pre-printed form was expressly conditioned on assent to the arbitration provision. It is difficult to see how this could be the case. C&A's (D) forms contained a wide range of approved methods of acceptance. The methods requiring action by the buyer would create a valid contract. The methods requiring *inaction* by the buyer, like retaining the carpets for ten days without objection, would not constitute a valid acceptance. As a result, the forms did not make it clear that their acceptance was expressly conditional on assent to the arbitration terms. However, under § 2–207 (2), the terms may be considered proposals for additional terms unless they materially alter the agreement. This question can be answered by the district court when, after a full trial, all of the facts of the case have been examined. Reversed and remanded.

### Analysis:

Article 2 of the UCC governs the sale of goods. The section of the UCC that is discussed in this case is a significant modification of the common law "mirror image" rule. The mirror image rule states that in order for an acceptance to be valid, it must exactly minor each of the terms of the offer. This rule was decidedly unwieldy for commercial transactions, which frequently give rise to a battle of forms. It was necessary to modify the rule in order to provide some stability in transactions involving the sale of goods. By recognizing those terms on which the parties agree, transactions can be facilitated rather than thwarted, contracts can be recognized rather than disclaimed, and additional terms can be implied by the UCC or struck out. Also, since the UCC recognizes that certain terms are common in commercial contracts, its application prevents the recognition of highly unusual or exploitative terms. In addition, § 207(3) will imply a contract between the parties if their conduct recognizes one. In that event, the contract is comprised of the terms to which the parties agree. The only other terms are those that other sections of the UCC would imply.

### ■ CASE VOCABULARY

ARBITRATION: A form of alternative dispute resolution which may be court-ordered or agreed to by the parties. Arbitration is done outside the courtroom and without a jury.

STAY OF PROCEEDING: A court can grant a stay of proceedings in order to await a decision or to enforce a rule which may affect the rights or duties of the parties. The proceedings will usually resume without any change in procedural status at the point where they left off.

# Step-Saver Data Systems, Inc. v. Wyse Technology [and The Software Link, Inc.]

(Software Dealer) v. (Software Producer)

939 F.2d 91 (3rd Cir. 1991)

---

COURT OF APPEALS APPLIES THE UCC TO MULTIPLE SALES AGREEMENTS WITH DIFFERENT TERMS

---

■ **INSTANT FACTS** A software dealer used a defective program in one of its commercial systems and sought to enforce a warranty against the producer of the program.

■ **BLACK LETTER RULE** UCC § 2–207 governs contracts for the sale of goods where the parties have multiple agreements with additional or different terms.

---

■ **PROCEDURAL BASIS**

Appeal from a trial court directed verdict for the defendant in a breach of warranty [breach of contract] action.

■ **FACTS**

Step-Saver Data Systems, Inc. (Step-Saver) (P) purchased 142 copies of a computer program called Multilink Advanced [also referred to as Advanced Multilink] from an intermediate dealer, The Software Link, Inc. (TSL) (D2) over a period of eight months. The program was produced by a company called Wyse Technology (D1). Normally, Step-Saver (P) would place an order for twenty copies of the program with TSL (D2) over the phone. TSL (D2) would accept the order and promise to ship the goods promptly. Step-Saver (P) would follow up with a purchase order detailing the goods ordered, along with the price, shipping, and payment terms. TSL (D2) would then ship the order with an invoice which essentially duplicated the terms of Step-Saver's (P) purchase order. None of these documents contained any provisions limiting the liability of Wyse Technology (D1) or TSL (D2) for program defects. The program packaging did, however. The box-top contained a licensing agreement which was alleged to be the complete agreement between the parties. Among other provisions, it disclaimed all warranties except for a warranty against defective program disks. In addition, the license agreement stated that opening the package constituted acceptance of the agreement. Otherwise, it stated, the package should be returned unopened. Step-Saver (P) purchased and incorporated the program into a larger system which it sold to law and medical offices. However, at least twelve of these purchasers had problems with the system and sued Step-Saver (P). Step-Saver, in turn, sued Wyse Technology (D1) and TSL (D2) for breach of warranty and for indemnification against the claims of their customers. The district court exonerated Wyse Technology (D1) and granted TSL (D2) a directed verdict against Step-Saver (P). Step-Saver (P) appeals.

■ **ISSUE**

Can the parties to a contractual relationship be bound by the terms of differing agreements between them?

■ **DECISION AND RATIONALE**

(Wisdom) Maybe. This case involves the sale of goods. As a result, Article 2 of the Uniform Commercial Code [a model approach to commercial law which has been adopted, in whole or in part, by every state] applies. UCC § 2–207, in particular, governs transactions in which the parties have not expressly agreed to a particular written contract, and the existing writings exchanged by the parties do not agree. While there is no question that there is a contract between Step-Saver (P) and TSL (D2), it is necessary to determine by what terms that contract will be enforced. Under the common law, and certain agreements not governed by the UCC, courts have followed the "last shot rule." This meant that parties to a sales transaction were bound by the terms of the last form sent by one of the parties. The UCC rejected this approach, recognizing that most parties to sales transactions are more concerned with the completion of their transactions than the enforcement of specific provisions of their pre-printed forms. The drafters of the UCC felt that it was unfair and arbitrary to bind both parties to the last form sent. Consequently, UCC § 2–207 enforces those terms which are in agreement, as well as any other terms implied by the UCC. TSL (D2) begins by arguing that certain terms, particularly the warranty requirements, can only be determined by the parties. TSL (D2) claims that the contract would be insufficiently definite without these terms. However, the UCC would supply the appropriate warranty in the absence of any agreement between the parties. As a result, it is not necessary to enforce TSL's (D2) limited box-top warranty in order to create a binding contract. TSL (D2) also draws attention to the language of the box-top license itself. The license warns that opening the package indicates acceptance of its terms. Consequently, TSL (D2) argues that the warranty provisions were conditional terms—essentially counter-offers the acceptance of which was necessary to the formation of a contract. TSL (D2) supports this argument with the license's refund offer which states that the purchaser can return the product if they do not accept its terms. However, the facts of the case do not bear out TSL's analysis [the court's discussion of these facts is omitted from the case—however, it is quite likely that the repeated dealings between the parties, free of the constraints of the box-top license, indicated an implied waiver of the "conditional" warranty provisions]. Finally, TSL (D2) argues that Step-Saver (P) made successive orders for copies of Multilink Advanced when they were already on notice of the warranty provisions. TSL (D2) argues that the repeated expression of the provisions incorporates them into the agreement. This is not a generally accepted approach. However, the behavior of the parties may be informative on this issue. Step-Saver (P) repeatedly refused to sign the box-top license agreement, and TSL (D2) spent a great deal of time trying to solve the problems with Multilink Advanced. It seems that the parties continued to deal with each other regardless of the warranty provisions. Consequently, there is no pattern of behavior which would call for incorporating the provisions. This does not end the analysis, however. UCC § 2–207 also states that an additional term will not be incorporated if it would materially alter the agreement. Step-Saver (P) claims that the parties agreed to certain express warranties and that certain implied warranties were also part of their contract with TSL (D2). These claims were never considered by the district court. However, if they were proven to be true, then the addition of the limited warranty provisions would materially alter the agreement between the parties. As a result, the warranty provisions cannot be incorporated into the agreement. Further, the district court must consider Step-Saver's (P) claims in order to determine the status of any express or implied warranties existing between the parties. Reversed and remanded.

## Analysis:

Note that if a new term is material, the party who proposed it must present additional evidence, usually evidence of prior dealings between the parties, to show that it was reasonable to infer that the other party consented to the new term. If a new term is not material, the other party's silence may constitute consent to the term. In addition, the fact that a term is commonly used in a particular industry may suggest that the other party consented to it. On the other hand, if a term diverges from trade usage, there may be reason to doubt that the other party consented to it. Justice Wisdom's opinion deals with the most important elements of § 2-207. The actual text and the commentary following the rule will help you appreciate the sheer complexity of this particular UCC section.

## ■ CASE VOCABULARY

DIRECTED VERDICT: Governed by Federal Rule of Civil Procedure 50, a motion for directed verdict, now referred to as a motion for judgement as a matter of law, can be made at the end of a party's presentation of their evidence. The moving party asks the court to rule that their opponent has not met their burden of production. In other words, the judge is asked to rule—without consulting the jury—that the moving party is entitled to a judgement in their favor. A renewed motion for judgement as a matter of law, formerly known as a judgement notwithstanding the verdict, can be made after the jury has already reached a verdict and involves the same analysis.

MIRROR IMAGE RULE: A common law rule which requires the terms of an acceptance to match the terms of the offer in order to create a binding contract.

WARRANTY: Warranty doctrine covers a broad range of provisions by which, for instance, a party guarantees the fitness of an article or indemnifies a party against an undesirable event. Under the UCC, goods are subject to an implied warranty of merchantability. This means, among other requirements, that the goods are fit for the general purpose for which such goods are ordinarily used.

terms of the license on the outside of the box. However, providing notice of the license on the outside of the box, the terms of the license inside the box, and the right to return the software for a refund if the terms are unacceptable is an acceptable way to do business. Standardized agreements save time and are essential to a system of mass production and distribution. Transactions in which the exchange of money precedes the communication of the details of the contract are common. Examples include the sale of insurance, airline tickets, concert tickets, warranties on consumer goods, and drugs. Purchases of software are often made by phone or on the internet, where there is no box setting forth the terms. On Zeidenberg's (D) argument, the seller has made a broad warranty and must pay consequential damages for any shortfalls in performance. This would drive the price of software through the ceiling. UCC § 2–204(1) provides that "A contract for sale of goods may be made in any manner sufficient to show agreement, including conduct by both parties which recognizes the existence of such a contract." Here, ProCD (P) proposed a contract that a buyer accepts by using the software after having an opportunity to read the license. Zeidenberg (D) agreed to the terms by using the software. UCC § 2–606 reinforces our opinion. It states that a buyer accepts goods when, after an opportunity to inspect, the buyer fails to reject the goods. Here, Zeidenberg (D) inspected the license and the software, and did not reject the goods. Reversed and remanded.

## Analysis:

The court here distinguished *Step-Saver Data Systems, Inc. v. Wyse Technology*. *Step-Saver* was a "battle-of-the-forms" case where the buyer and the seller sent each other conflicting invoices and purchase orders and the court was left to sort out the terms of the contract. In *Step-Saver*, the court applied UCC § 2–207, which enforces those terms to which both parties agree. Here, there were not two forms. ProCD (P) offered its license as part of the sales contract and Zeidenberg (D) chose not to abide by its terms. Zeidenberg (D) never communicated his rejection of the license agreement, unless breach is the same as rejection. *Step-Saver* also involved a "box-top license" disclaiming certain warranties. The box-top license stated that opening the package constituted acceptance of the agreement. Here, on the other hand, a purchaser of the SelectPhone software was able to open the package, review the license agreement, and choose whether to abide by it. By using the software, Zeidenberg (D) was held to have accepted the license terms. Here the court relied on UCC § 2–204(1) rather than § 2–207. Section § 2–204 provides that "[a] contract for sale of goods may be made in any manner sufficient to show agreement, including conduct by both parties which recognizes the existence of such a contract." This is also the rule at common law. It provides that a contract is implied where the parties' intention to contract is not manifested by explicit words but by their conduct.

## ■ CASE VOCABULARY

LICENSE: Permission to do or omit an act, such as permission to use a copyrighted work for specific purposes.

# Hill v. Gateway 2000, Inc.

(Computer Buyer) v. (Computer Seller)

105 F.3d 1147 (7th Cir. 1997)

---

TERMS CONTAINED INSIDE A PACKAGE MAY BECOME PART OF THE CONTRACT

---

Don't forget to include the "approve-or-return" arbitration agreement in every box. No scrooge is going to litigate us out of a good Christmas!

stus.com

■ **INSTANT FACTS** Hill (P) purchased a computer from Gateway (D) and claimed that the arbitration agreement included in materials enclosed inside the box, which purported to govern unless the computer was returned within thirty days, was unenforceable.

■ **BLACK LETTER RULE** A seller may provide that acceptance of an offer will be by conduct, and the buyer accepts by performing the acts that the seller proposes to treat as acceptance.

---

■ **PROCEDURAL BASIS**

Appeal from an order denying a motion to enforce an arbitration clause.

■ **FACTS**

Hill (P) purchased a computer from Gateway (D). The computer was ordered over the telephone and delivered to Hill (P). The box in which the computer was shipped contained a list of contractual terms that would be effective unless Hill (P) returned the computer to Gateway (D) within thirty days. One of those terms was an arbitration agreement. Hill (P) kept the computer for more than thirty days, and then began complaining about its components and performance. Hill (P) brought a RICO suit against Gateway (D), and Gateway (D) moved for enforcement of the arbitration clause. The district court refused to enforce the clause, finding that there was no evidence of a valid arbitration clause or that Hill (P) had adequate notice of the arbitration clause.

■ **ISSUE**

Was the arbitration clause part of the contract between Hill (P) and Gateway (D)?

■ **DECISION AND RATIONALE**

(Easterbrook, J.) Yes. A seller may provide that acceptance of an offer will be by conduct, and the buyer accepts by performing the acts that the seller proposes to treat as acceptance. This case is governed by the rule in *ProCD, Inc. v. Zeidenberg*, 86 F. 3d 1447 (7th Cir. 1996), in which the court held that contractual terms inside a box containing software bind consumers who use the software after an opportunity to read the terms and to reject them by returning the product. Hill (P) argues that the holding in *ProCD* should be limited to software. There is no logical reason to do so. Payment before the full terms of a contract are revealed is common in many industries, and practical considerations support allowing vendors to enclose the full terms with their products. Cashiers cannot be expected to read the full terms to customers before ringing up a sale, and customers cannot be expected to listen to all of the terms as they are read to them. The approve-or-return device is simple and benefits both parties. In addition, the computer box sent to Hill (P) contained a lot of software. Limitation of the *ProCD* rule to software would not help Hill (P).

Hill (P) also argues that *ProCD* should be limited to executory contracts, such as licenses, and therefore does not apply because performance of the contract in this case was complete when the computer

---

arrived at his home. The question in this case relates to contract formation, not performance. *ProCD* was characterized as a case involving a sale of goods, not a license. In addition, Gateway (D) did not complete performance with delivery. Part of the agreement was the warranty for future service, which Hill (P) invoked. Gateway (D) offered "lifetime service," and the promises of future performance bind Gateway (D) just as the arbitration clause binds Hill (P).

Hill (P) further claims that *ProCD* does not apply because Zeidenberg was a merchant and Hill (P) is not. Section 2–207(2) of the UCC provides that, in a transaction between merchants, additional terms after the acceptance of an offer are construed as proposals for additions to a contract, and such terms become a part of the contract unless the offer expressly limits acceptance to the terms of the offer, the additional terms materially alter the contract, or notification of objection to the terms has been given or is given within a reasonable time. Hill's (P) argument is that the result in *ProCD* was dictated by the fact that Zeidenberg was a merchant and the additional terms were not excluded by § 2–207. The opinion in *ProCD* concluded that § 2–207 was irrelevant, because there was only one set of terms. The question was not whether additional terms were added after the contract was formed, but how and when the contract was formed in the first place. In addition, Zeidenberg in *ProCD* was not acting as a merchant: he bought the software at a retail store and put it on the Internet for anyone to use.

Finally, Hill (P) attempted to distinguish *ProCD* by stating that the software box in that case displayed a notice that there were additional terms inside, but the box from Gateway (D) did not. This is a functional distinction, not a legal one. Gateway's (D) box is a shipping carton and has no information for the consumer. Hill (P) may have had a better argument if he first knew of the additional terms after opening the box but was dissuaded from returning it by the high cost of shipping. In any event, Gateway's (D) advertisements state that their products come with limited warranties and lifetime support, but that does not describe the warranties or support fully. Buyers have several methods for learning about the terms, including inspecting the relevant documents after delivery of the product. This is the option Hill (P) chose, and by keeping the computer more than thirty days, Gateway's (D) offer was accepted. Vacated and remanded, with directions to compel Hill (P) to submit to arbitration.

## Analysis:

The court emphasizes that this case is about contract formation, and the question being addressed is, when was the contract formed? The court holds that the contract is not formed until thirty days after delivery of the computer, but does that agree with the expectations of most buyers? Critics of this case and the *ProCD* case have posed the question of whether Gateway (D), after taking Hill's (P) order, could say that the price has gone up and the computer will not be delivered until Hill (P) pays more. If the contract is not formed until a considerable time after delivery, it would appear that there would be no reason why Gateway (D) could not change its terms any time within thirty days.

## ■ CASE VOCABULARY

ARBITRATION: A method of dispute resolution involving one or more neutral third parties who are usu. agreed to by the disputing parties and whose decision is binding.

EXECUTORY: Taking full effect at a future time; to be performed at a future time; yet to be completed.

RICO: Racketeer Influenced and Corrupt Organizations Act. A law designed to attack organized criminal activity and preserve marketplace integrity by investigating, controlling, and prosecuting persons who participate or conspire to participate in racketeering. Enacted in 1970, the federal RICO statute applies only to activity involving interstate or foreign commerce. 18 USCA §§ 1961–1968.

# Drennan v. Star Paving Co.

(General Contractor) v. (Paving Subcontractor)

51 Cal.2d 409, 333 P.2d 757 (1958)

CALIFORNIA SUPREME COURT PERMITS GENERAL CONTRACTOR'S RELIANCE TO BIND SUBCONTRACTOR TO THEIR BID

■ **INSTANT FACTS** A general contractor wants to enforce a subcontractor's bid on a construction job.

■ **BLACK LETTER RULE** An offer may not be freely revocable if the offeree has substantially relied on the offer.

■ **PROCEDURAL BASIS**

Appeal from a trial court judgement for the plaintiff in a breach of contract action.

■ **FACTS**

Drennan (P), a general contractor, was bidding on a construction job for the Monte Vista School. As usual, he received the bids of his subcontractors by telephone on the day before his bid was due. Star Paving Co. (Star Paving) (D) was one of those subcontractors. Their estimator called Drennan (P) and submitted a $7131.60 bid for the paving work on the contract. This bid was included in Drennan's (P) successful bid for the job. Drennan (P) was required to guarantee his bid with a 10% bond—over $30,000. When he stopped by Star Paving's (D) offices after his bid was accepted, their engineer told him that there had been a mistake. In fact, they refused to do the job for less than $15,000. Drennan (P) had no alternative but to find another paving company. After accepting new bids, he hired the lowest bidder at $10,948.60. He also sued Star Paving (D) for breach of contract. The trial court found that Star Paving (D) made a definite offer to do the paving work for $7131.60. The court also found that Drennan (P) relied on this offer when he calculated his own bid and when he listed Star Paving (D) as the subcontractor. As a result, the trial court found for Drennan (P) and awarded him $3817 in damages—the difference between Star Paving's (D) bid and the price charged by their replacement. Star Paving (D) appeals.

■ **ISSUE**

Is an offer freely revocable after the offeree has relied on it?

■ **DECISION AND RATIONALE**

(Traynor) No. Star Paving (D) makes three claims in this case. The first is that their offer was freely revocable, and was in fact revoked by the time Drennan (P) communicated his acceptance. However, according to section 90 of the Restatement [First] of Contracts, a binding agreement can be created under the following circumstances: 1) a promise is made which should reasonably be expected to induce action or forbearance of a definite and substantial character on the part of the promisee, 2) such action or forbearance is induced, and 3) injustice can be avoided only by enforcing the promise. Star Paving (D) could not justifiably revoke their offer if these elements were satisfied. Star Paving's (D) bid was reasonably expected to induce action of a definite and substantial character on the part of Drennan (P). Specifically, Star Paving (D) submitted its bid in the hopes that they would be offered the job as the low bidder. They knew that Drennan (P) would have to submit their bid along with the others for this to happen. In addition, they knew that Drennan (P) was bound by the overall bid that *he* submitted. Finally, their bid was not submitted with any language suggesting that it was freely revocable before acceptance. Despite this, there remains the question of whether consideration was required to keep Star Paving's (D) offer open. Section 45 of the Restatement [First] of Contracts notes that consideration, in the form of part performance, can bind the offeror to a unilateral contract [an offer which requests performance as acceptance]. However, section 45 also suggests that justifiable reliance on an offer may be sufficient to bind the offeror. Implicit in this suggestion is that reliance can substitute for consideration in cases where injustice would result from a strict application of the rule. As a result, Star Paving (D) should be bound by their offer. They claim, however, that their bid was the result of a mistake. They argue that contractors have been released from their bids in similar cases. In those cases, though, the mistake was always known to the party receiving the bid. In this case, Drennan (P) had no way of knowing that there was an error in the bid, particularly since it fell within the range of expected bids. In addition, Star Paving (D) had a lot to gain from a successful bid. They should also have recognized the harm that a mistaken bid could cause Drennan (P). While these are not reasons to grant recovery, they certainly militate against denying recovery. Finally, Star Paving (D) argues that Drennan (P) failed to state a claim for which relief can be granted because he did not allege that he did anything to mitigate his damages. This argument is without merit. Drennan (P) alleged that he was required to hire a new, low-bidding paving subcontractor and that it took several months to do so. For the reasons stated above, the judgement is affirmed.

## Analysis

In this case, Justice Traynor finds that the offer was accepted prior to revocation by permitting Drennan's (P) reliance on the subcontractor's bid to substitute as consideration for keeping the offer open. Normally, the bargain theory states that consideration is something of value that the offeror sought when he made the offer. However, Star Paving (D) knew full well that Drennan (P) would rely on its bid. In addition, it stood to benefit from his reliance. As a result, it would not be fair to let Star Paving (D) revoke its offer after Drennan (P) relied to his detriment. Justice Traynor uses existing doctrine to circumvent the normal rule in order to achieve a desirable result.

## ■ CASE VOCABULARY

PROMISSORY ESTOPPEL: Justice Traynor does not identify it as such, but the rule which he cites from section 90 of the Restatement [First] of Contracts is also known as the doctrine of promissory estoppel. As with other estoppel doctrine, the promisor is precluded from claiming that their promise is not binding if the elements apply.

# Hoffman v. Red Owl Stores

(Prospective Franchise) v. (Supermarket Chain)

26 Wis.2d 683, 133 N.W.2d 267 (1965)

WISCONSIN SUPREME COURT DISTINGUISHES PROMISSORY ESTOPPEL FROM BREACH OF CONTRACT

■ **INSTANT FACTS** A bakery owner wants to open a supermarket franchise but is rejected by the franchiser after making preparations at their request.

■ **BLACK LETTER RULE** It is not necessary for an offer to address every detail of an agreement in order to support a promissory estoppel claim.

■ **FACTS**

Hoffman (P) was a bakery owner in Wisconsin who wanted to obtain a franchise for a supermarket in the Red Owl Stores (Red Owl) (D) chain. He contacted Red Owl (D) and, after a year and a half, they began working toward that goal. Red Owl's (D) representative, Lukowitz, advised Hoffman (P) to buy and operate a small grocery store in order to get some experience. After three months, Lukowitz advised him to sell the store, assuring him that Red Owl (D) would find him a bigger store. Then Lukowitz advised him to put a security deposit down on a lot for the proposed franchise. Soon after, Lukowitz told him that everything was ready to go. In fact, he told Hoffman (P), "Get your money together and we are set." He also told Hoffman (P) to sell his bakery. Hoffman (P) sold the bakery and then moved his family closer to the proposed store location. Red Owl (D) also asked him to work at their nearest franchise but the job never came through. Hoffman (P) and Red Owl (D) then began a complicated series of negotiations over the leasing of the franchise site and Hoffman's (P) financial contribution. They could not agree on certain terms, however, including the status of a substantial loan which Hoffman (P) arranged with his father-in-law. Finally, the negotiations fell through and Hoffman (P) sued Red Owl (D) under a theory of promissory estoppel. Red Owl (D) argued that the parties never reached an agreement on many of the specifics necessary to establish a contract. Nonetheless, Hoffman (P) was awarded damages equal to the value of the grocery store he sold, the loss he incurred in selling his bakery, the costs of moving his family and renting a house near the new location, and the cost of securing a lot for the new store. The trial court confirmed the verdict, with the exception of the damages for selling the grocery store for which it ordered a new trial. Red Owl (D) appeals.

■ **ISSUE**

Is it necessary for an offer to be specific enough to create a contract in order to support a claim of promissory estoppel?

■ **DECISION AND RATIONALE**

(Currie) No. Promissory estoppel was originally envisioned as a substitute for consideration. In other words, the offeree's reliance on the offeror's promise satisfied the need for consideration. However, a claim for promissory estoppel need not meet the other requirements of a binding contract, for instance, the need for an offer which is definite with respect to the details of the contract. As a result, a claim under promissory estoppel is not equivalent to a breach of contract claim. This interpretation is supported by the Restatement [First] of Contracts § 90. The Restatement requires a promise which the promisor should reasonably expect to induce action or forbearance of a definite and substantial character on the part of the promisee. The Restatement also requires that the promise actually induce such reliance. Finally, § 90 places the responsibility on the court to determine whether injustice would result if the promise were not enforced. This is more discretion than a court has in an ordinary breach of contract case. Accordingly, injustice cannot be avoided in this case unless the court enforces the promises that Red Owl (D) made to Hoffman (P). That said, the trial court correctly ordered a retrial on the issue of damages associated with the sale of the grocery store which Hoffman (P) bought at Red Owl's urging. Since this is not a breach of contract action, it is not appropriate to apply strict measures of contract damages, like lost profits, in order to adequately compensate Hoffman (P) for this sale. He is only entitled to an amount necessary to avoid injustice. Judgment is affirmed

## Analysis:

Promissory estoppel is a purely equitable doctrine that entitles courts to ignore most of the rules of contract formation in order to do justice in a particular case. This approach seems antithetical to the notion of freedom of contract, which is thought to be the bedrock of contract theory. However, as in the above case, there ought to be a way of compensating parties like Hoffman (P) who are taken in by offers that skirt the requirements for contracts but are nonetheless enough like offers to induce reliance. This is the situation in which promissory estoppel functions most effectively and in which the courts are in the greatest need of the discretion it affords. Note, however, that along with that discretion comes the discretion to vary the damages as justice demands. Some commentators argue that courts are granting reliance damages in these cases, but doing so based on a measure of damages equal to the plaintiff's expectation interest. Other commentators argue that courts are simply granting reliance damages based on the plaintiff's reliance interest. Either way, it appears that courts are able to arrive at a just resolution despite the legal confines of contract damages.

# Cyberchron Corp. v. Calldata Systems Development, Inc.

(Manufacturer) v. (Buyer)

47 F.3d 39 (2nd Cir. 1995)

PROMISSORY ESTOPPEL COVERS WORK DONE IN RELIANCE ON PROMISES THAT THE PARTIES WILL ENTER INTO A CONTRACT

■ **INSTANT FACTS** A computer hardware manufacturer produced equipment for a buyer without entering into a contract, and sued for promissory estoppel.

■ **BLACK LETTER RULE** A party who relies on a promise that a contract is forthcoming may recover under a promissory estoppel theory.

■ **PROCEDURAL BASIS**

Appeal of district court judgment on a claim for damages based on promissory estoppel.

■ **FACTS**

Cyberchron Corp. (Cyberchron) (P) provides customized computer hardware. Calldata Systems Development, Inc. (Calldata) (D) is a subsidiary of Grumman Data Systems Corp. (Grumman) (D). Grumman (D) had a contract with the U.S. Marine Corps to provide a computer system called ATACC, which consisted of a video processor, a work station, and a monitor (the "Equipment"). In 1989 and 1990, the parties were involved in extensive negotiations for Cyberchron (P) to produce the Equipment. The parties were never able to agree on the weight of the Equipment and the penalties to be assessed against Cyberchron (P) for delivering Equipment that exceeded the agreed weight. After preliminary negotiations, Grumman (D) delivered a purchase order dated May 15, 1990 to Cyberchron (P) that set forth a total weight per unit of 145 pounds and provided for severe penalties for exceeding that weight. Cyberchron (P) did not agree to those terms. Cyberchron (P) had begun producing the Equipment, despite the absence of an agreement. In a June 26, 1990 letter, Grumman (D) and Calldata (D) encouraged Cyberchron (P) to continue to perform its "contractually binding obligations" under the purchase order. Beginning in mid-July 1990, Grumman (D) directed Cyberchron (P) to continue producing the Equipment, assuring Cyberchron (P) that the details of the agreement would be resolved later. On July 30, Cyberchron (P) submitted a payment request to Grumman (D). Grumman's (D) business manager testified that Grumman (D) would have paid the request but for a court order in another case barring Grumman (D) from paying Cyberchron (P). That order was subsequently vacated. On September 6, 1990, Calldata (D) directed Cyberchron (P) to show cause why the purchase order should not be terminated. On September 25, 1990, Calldata (D) rejected Cyberchron's (P) detailed response and terminated the purchase order effective immediately. In August 1990, Grumman (D) commenced negotiations with other suppliers of Equipment. On September 26, Grumman (D) entered into a contract with another supplier for inferior equipment that weighed more. Cyberchron (P) sued for breach of contract, quantum meruit, and promissory estoppel. The district court found that no enforceable contract existed, and dismissed Cyberchron's (P) breach of contract claim and Calldata's (D) contract-based counterclaim. The court dismissed the quantum meruit claim on the ground that Calldata (D) did not receive any benefit. The court found for Cyberchron (P) on its promissory estoppel claim and awarded $162,824.10 for labor and materials incurred after July 15, 1990 and before September 25, 1990. The court denied recovery for lost profits and for administrative and general overhead. Cyberchron (P) appealed, claiming it should recover damages incurred before July 15, 1990 and for overhead. Calldata (D) appealed the promissory estoppel judgment.

## ■ ISSUE

May a party who relies on a promise that a contract is forthcoming recover under a promissory estoppel theory?

## ■ DECISION AND RATIONALE

(Mahoney, J.) Yes. Promissory estoppel has three elements: (1) a clear and unambiguous promise; (2) reasonable and foreseeable reliance by the party to whom the promise is made; and (3) an injury sustained by the party asserting the estoppel by reason of the reliance. Sometimes an unconscionable injury is required to fulfil the third requirement. Calldata (D) pressured Cyberchron (P) to produce the Equipment and assured Cyberchron (P) that if it did the work, the negotiation problems would be resolved. Therefore, we agree with the district court that Cyberchron (P) reasonably relied on this promise and that Grumman's (D) pressure on Cyberchron (P) and abrupt termination of the transaction to buy inferior Equipment from another company was unconscionable. However, we reject Cyberchron's (P) argument that its recovery should extend prior to July 15, 1990, when Calldata (D) made the promises. Cyberchron (P) argues that it should have been awarded overhead and "shutdown" expenses. We believe that recovery of reasonable overhead costs is allowed when there is a demonstrable past history of ongoing business operations. We do not believe proof that a specific alternative project would have absorbed the overhead costs at issue is necessary. Recovery is allowed as long as Cyberchron (P) normally allocates such expenses to specific projects in accordance with its standard cost accounting practices. Affirmed, but remanded for a redetermination of damages.

---

## Analysis:

As an equitable doctrine, promissory estoppel can be used by courts to award what seems like contract damages, even if no contract exists. Ordinarily, negotiations do not constitute an offer. Here, however, Calldata (D) went beyond mere negotiations. It made express promises to Cyberchron (P) that the parties would enter into an agreement, presumably with terms acceptable to Cyberchron (P), if Cyberchron (P) produced the Equipment. The key promise at issue here is Calldata's (D) promise to Cyberchron (P) that if Cyberchron (P) continued to produce the Equipment, the parties could resolve the weight issue and enter into an enforceable contract. Cyberchron (P) relied on this promise and expended considerable funds to build the Equipment, only to have the rug pulled out from under it when Calldata (D) contracted with someone else. While, as a legal matter, Cyberchron (P) did not have to prove that Calldata (D) was negotiating in bad faith, Calldata's (D) bad faith certainly helped Cyberchron's (P) case.

---

## ■ CASE VOCABULARY

PROMISSORY ESTOPPEL: A cause of action available when no contract exists between the parties, but one party has made a promise to the other party on which the other party reasonably relied to its detriment.

QUANTUM MERUIT: A cause of action available when no express contract exists between the parties, but one party confers a benefit on the other party; the courts may imply a contract and impose a duty on the recipient of the benefit to pay for it to prevent unjust enrichment.

# Channel Home Centers, Division of Grace Retail Corp. v. Grossman

(Prospective Lessee) v. (Mall Developer)

795 F.2d 291 (3rd Cir. 1986)

___

## COURT OF APPEALS APPROVES A CONTRACT TO NEGOTIATE TOWARDS AN AGREEMENT

___

■ **INSTANT FACTS** A mall developer abruptly cancels lease negotiations with a prospective tenant.

■ **BLACK LETTER RULE** An agreement to negotiate in good faith toward a prospective contract may be binding if it satisfies the conditions to a binding contract.

___

■ **PROCEDURAL BASIS**

Appeal from a district court judgment for the defendant in a breach of contract action.

■ **FACTS**

Frank Grossman (Grossman) (D) is a real estate developer with ownership or controlling interests in a number of firms. He was in the process of revitalizing a mall in Pennsylvania when he contacted Channel Home Centers (Channel) (P) through one of his firms, Tri-Star Associates (Tri-Star). Tri-Star wrote to Channel's (P) Director of Real Estate, Richard Perkowski, to see if Channel (P) would be interested in leasing a site at the mall. Channel (P) ultimately expressed a desire to lease the site after a preliminary tour and a meeting with Grossman (D) in which some of the lease terms were discussed. Grossman (D), in turn, asked Channel (P) to draft a letter of intent which might help him obtain financing for the project. Channel (P) drafted the letter and Grossman (D) signed it. The letter contained a number of lease terms including a provision requiring Grossman (D) to take the site off the rental market and to negotiate with Channel (P) to completion. In addition, Grossman (D) claims that Channel's (P) president and vice-president agreed orally that Channel (P) would submit a draft lease within thirty days. This agreement is disputed by Channel (P). However, subsequent to the letter of intent, both parties began making the necessary arrangements and acquiring the necessary approvals to facilitate an agreement between the parties. Channel (P) also submitted a draft lease about a month after signing the letter of intent. After some further communications between the parties, Grossman (D) and Channel's (P) lawyer planned a conference call to discuss some of the issues concerning the lease. Both parties thought that the other party was responsible for reinitiating contact between them. [Here's where it gets interesting] During this time, another retail chain, Mr. Good Buys, contacted Grossman (D) about leasing a space at the mall. In fact, Grossman (D) gave them a tour of the proposed Channel (P) site and discussed the terms of a prospective lease with them. Soon after, Grossman (D) terminated their negotiations with Channel (P), claiming that Channel (P) had failed to submit a signed and mutually acceptable lease within the thirty day limit. The next day, Grossman (D) executed a lease with Mr. Good Buys at a much higher rate than that to which Channel (P) had agreed. Channel (P) subsequently sued Grossman (D) for breach of contract. They claimed that the letter of intent was a binding agreement between the parties to negotiate in good faith. The district court found for Grossman (D), holding that there was no binding agreement between the parties. Channel (P) appeals.

■ **ISSUE**

Can a letter of intent bind the parties to a contract if an agreement has not yet been reached?

## ■ DECISION AND RATIONALE

(Becker) Yes. Channel (P) claims that the letter, along with the surrounding circumstances, constituted an agreement to negotiate in good faith. Grossman (D) claims that the letter is not binding since it was not backed by an agreement to the underlying lease transaction. He claims that the letter is unenforceable evidence of preliminary negotiations between the parties. In addition, Grossman (D) argues that the letter would be unenforceable even if it was considered a contract because it was not supported by consideration. Grossman's (D) first argument misconstrues Channel's (P) claim, however. Channel (P) does not claim that Grossman (D) breached an agreement to lease the mall site. They claim that Grossman (D) breached an agreement to negotiate in good faith toward the desired goal of a binding lease. Pennsylvania law sets the following requirements for an enforceable contract: 1) both parties must manifest an intention to be bound by the terms of the contract [offer and acceptance], 2) the terms of the contract must be sufficiently definite, and 3) the contract must be supported by consideration. Consideration may be a benefit granted to the promisor or a detriment suffered by the promisee. In either case, consideration must be bargained for and granted in exchange for the original promise. No Pennsylvania court has decided whether an agreement to negotiate in good faith can be valid. However, other jurisdictions have approved such agreements. As a result, we will consider whether this particular agreement meets the requirements for a binding contract. First, the letter contains a promise by Grossman (D) to take the property off the rental market and to negotiate in good faith. After agreeing to the letter, both parties endeavored to satisfy the contingencies which would enable them to sign a lease agreement. Channel (P) began making the necessary administrative, architectural, and marketing arrangements while Grossman (D) applied for the necessary zoning approvals. As a result, both parties acted on the letter as if it were a serious manifestation of their desire to enter into an agreement. Second, the letter itself-is-sufficiently definite to constitute an agreement since it calls for the removal of the property from the rental market and for the negotiations to continue to completion. However, the letter must still be supported by consideration. In this case, Grossman (D) asked Channel (P) to draft the letter so that he could show it to potential lenders. Grossman (D) was hoping that a commitment from a large store like Channel (P) would help it to get financing. Consequently, the execution and tender of the letter was of substantial value to Grossman (D). Similarly, Channel (P) executed and tendered the letter in order to garner Grossman's (D) commitment to the terms of the negotiation. It was of substantial value to Channel (P) to have a preliminary commitment, at the very least, to a good faith negotiation over the lease agreement. As a result, each party received a benefit which counted as consideration for their respective obligations. With this in mind, there are two issues for the trial court to resolve on remand. First, while the evidence permits the conclusion that there was a binding contract between the parties, it does not require it. There must be a full trial on the merits in order to-make this determination. Second, the issue of whether there was a time limit on the parties' negotiations is as yet unresolved since the district court never reached the factual issues in the case. This issue must also be resolved at trial. Reversed and remanded for further proceedings consistent with this opinion.

## Analysis:

This opinion is another excellent review of many of the principles of contract formation. The court notes early on that negotiations between parties or an agreement to enter into a contract in the future are not contracts in themselves. However, in this case, we see that while agreements to agree will generally not be enforced, if they can be characterized as agreements to negotiate in good faith, and the three requirements for a valid contract are present, the agreement will be enforced. An agreement to negotiate in good faith is an important tool in business, where most contracts are skeletal in nature because of the fast-paced world within which transactions are completed. Even though a formal agreement on all essential terms is not reached, the parties are able to go forward with the overall transaction confident in the knowledge that they have agreed to negotiate in good faith a full-fledged agreement.

■ **CASE VOCABULARY**

LETTER OF INTENT: A letter of intent is exactly what it sounds like—it is a preliminary communication between parties to a prospective agreement which demonstrates their desire to do business with each other.

# Toys, Inc. v. F.M. Burlington Company

(Lessee) v. (Lessor)

155 Vt. 44, 582 A.2d 123 (1990)

VERMONT SUPREME COURT FINDS AN OPTION AGREEMENT SUFFICIENTLY DEFINITE TO BIND THE CONTRACTING PARTIES

■ **INSTANT FACTS** A lessor and lessee cannot reach an agreement when the lessee attempts to exercise a renewal option.

■ **BLACK LETTER RULE** An option provision may be sufficiently definite to be binding if it contains terms which enable the parties to satisfy their subsequent agreement.

■ **PROCEDURAL BASIS**

Appeal from a trial court grant of summary judgement for the plaintiff in a breach of contract action.

■ **FACTS**

Toys, Inc. (Toys) (P) leased a space in a shopping mall from F.M. Burlington Company (Burlington) (D). Toys (P) had a five-year lease with an option to renew for another five years. If they chose to exercise the option, Toys (P) had to give Burlington (D) one year's notice. In addition, the option stated that the rental price for the second five-year period would be renegotiated at the prevailing rate within the mall when the option was exercised. Toys (P) notified Burlington (D), with one year's notice, that they wanted to renew their lease. Burlington (D) acknowledged the renewal and quoted Toys (P) the prevailing lease rate at the mall. Toys (P) responded with a letter which recounted a conversation they had with Burlington's (D) leasing agent. The leasing agent suggested that Toys (P) would be able to negotiate their lease rate, regardless of the prevailing rate. This suggestion was affirmed by Burlington (D) in their response. They sent Toys (P) a letter inviting them to renegotiate their rate even though the prevailing rate was still binding. In the ensuing negotiation, Toys (P) and Burlington (D) agreed on a rate and Burlington (D) sent Toys (P) a letter describing the terms of the agreement and giving them two weeks to accept. From this point on, the parties failed to come to an agreement and Toys (P) ultimately moved out of the mall and sued Burlington (D) for breach of contract. Burlington (D) claims, among other things, that the option agreement was not sufficiently definite to be enforceable. He claims that it was simply an agreement to agree. The trial court granted Toys' (P) motion for summary judgement on this issue. Burlington (D) appeals.

■ **ISSUE**

Can an option agreement be sufficiently definite as to bind the parties to its terms?

■ **DECISION AND RATIONALE**

(Dooley) Yes. An option agreement can be binding if it contains all of the material and essential terms to be incorporated in the subsequent agreement. At the very least, it must contain provisions which will help the parties to arrive at these terms. This is consistent with the Restatement (Second) of Contracts approach. The Restatement notes that the terms of a contract may be sufficiently definite even if they permit the parties to arrive at certain terms during the course of performance. In addition, courts will interpret these provisions toward the goal of preserving an enforceable agreement if possible. In this case, the option agreement provided for a negotiation to take place over the new lease rate. Burlington (D) claims that this provision is unenforceable because there was no boundary to the parties' negotiations. However, the agreement states that negotiations will take place at the then prevailing market rate. This is the premise upon which the parties actually negotiated when the time came. In addition, neither party claims that the prevailing rate was miscalculated. If nothing else, any ambiguities which the agreement did give rise to should be interpreted against Burlington (D) since they drafted the document. The trial court judgement is affirmed on this issue.

**Analysis:**

Note that this case was remanded for a determination as to whether Toys (P) actually exercised the option and whether it later waived the right of renewal. However, in this portion of the opinion, Justice Dooley applies the standard methods of contract interpretation to an option agreement. He examines the terms of the agreement as well as the behavior of the parties in order to determine whether they had a binding contract. His subsequent interpretation stays true to his announced goal of preserving the agreement despite its inherent defects. This goal is also evident in the promissory estoppel cases, which look very much like the court is finding a tacit agreement between the parties in order to compensate the party who was wronged.

# Oglebay Norton Co. v. Armco, Inc.

(Shipping Company) v. (Iron Ore Producer)

52 Ohio St.3d 232, 556 N.E.2d 515 (1990)

## COURT CAN DETERMINE CONTRACT PRICE WHEN PARTIES CAN'T AGREE

■ **INSTANT FACTS** After about 25 years of doing business pursuant to a contract, the parties could no longer agree on a price to be used.

■ **BLACK LETTER RULE** If parties to a contract have not agreed on the price, the court can set a price so long as the parties intend to be bound by the contract.

## ■ PROCEDURAL BASIS

Appeal of action for declaratory judgment setting a shipping rate.

## ■ FACTS

Oglebay Norton Co. (Oglebay) (P) was a shipping company. In 1957, Oglebay and Armco, Inc. (Armco) (D) entered into a contact requiring Oglebay to have adequate shipping capacity and requiring Armco (D) to use that capacity to transport iron ore on the Great Lakes. The contract provided for two price mechanisms. The primary price mechanism was for Armco (D) to pay the regular net contract rates as recognized by the leading iron ore shippers in that season. If there were no regular net contract, under the secondary price mechanism, the parties were required to mutually agree upon a rate, taking into consideration the rate being charged by the leading independent vessel operators. During the next 23 years, the parties modified the contract four times, requiring substantial capital investment by Oglebay (P) to meet Armco's (D) requirements. Until 1983, the parties established the shipping rate by referring to a rate published in Skillings Mining Review. In 1984, after a downturn in the iron ore industry, the parties negotiated a mutually satisfactory rate. However, after that the parties could not agree on a rate. Oglebay (P) filed an action for declaratory relief asking the court to declare the contract rate to be the correct rate or, in the absence of a contract rate, to declare a reasonable rate. Armco (D) denied that the rate sought by Oglebay (P) was the contract rate and denied that the court had jurisdiction to declare a rate. The parties continued to perform. In 1987, Armco (D) filed a counterclaim seeking a declaration that the contract was no longer enforceable because both the primary and the secondary pricing mechanisms broke down. After 1985, Skillings Mining Review no longer published a new rate and the rate charged by the leading independent vessel operators was no longer publicly available. In 1987, the trial court issued a declaratory judgment, ruling that $6.25 per gross ton was the rate for the 1986 season. The court further held that if the parties could not agree on a rate for upcoming seasons, the court would appoint a mediator to help the parties agree. The court of appeals affirmed.

## ■ ISSUE

(1) If parties to a contract have not agreed on the price, is the contract still binding? (2) If so, can the court set a price?

## ■ DECISION AND RATIONALE

(Per curiam) (1) Yes, if there is evidence that the parties intended to be bound by the contract. Here, the district court properly concluded that the parties intended to be bound by the 1957 contract even though the two pricing mechanisms were no longer available. This is based on the parties' long-standing close business relationship, including joint ventures, interlocking directorates, and Armco's (D) ownership of Oglebay (P) stock. (2) Yes, the court may set the price if the parties intended to be bound by the contract Restatement (Second) § 33, comment e provides that where the parties intend to conclude a contract for the sale of goods and the price is not settled, the price is a reasonable price at the time of delivery if the price is to be fixed by some standard as set or recorded by a third person or agency and it is not so set or recorded. Ordering specific performance of the contract here was necessary because the dramatic changes in the shipping rates and the length of the contract would make it impossible to award Oglebay (P) accurate damages. Appointing a mediator neither added to nor detracted from the parties' obligations under the contract and was within the court's equitable jurisdiction. Affirmed.

**Analysis:**

The court notes here that equity is available when legal damages are too speculative, recovery of monetary damages is inadequate to compensate the aggrieved party, and the parties intend to be bound by the contract. While ordinarily price is a material term that would make a contract void if it is missing, here the parties had been doing business pursuant to their contract for about twenty-five years. If the two pricing mechanisms had failed back in 1957, the court likely would not have ordered specific performance, but would have awarded damages for breach of contract and declared that the contract was no longer enforceable. The parties knew they left the price out of the contract, but formulated two ways in which they would determine the price. Thus, they agreed to agree later about the price. The common law rule is that an agreement to agree does not result in a binding contract. Generally, because the parties intend to fill the gap themselves, the court may not use a gap-filler. A gap-filler is a term courts supply either because the parties would have agreed on the term or because the term seems fair and reasonable. Here, the court used a gap-filler, a reasonable price, and ordered the parties to negotiate further prices in good faith. UCC § 2–204(3) provides that even if one or more terms are left open, a contract for the sale of goods does not fail for indefiniteness if the parties have intended to make a contract and there is a reasonably certain basis for giving an appropriate remedy.

## ■ CASE VOCABULARY

SPECIFIC PERFORMANCE: An equitable remedy that compels a party who has failed or refused to perform a valid contractual obligation to fulfill that obligation by performing the contract.

# CHAPTER THREE

## Statutes of Frauds

### C.R. Klewin, Inc. v. Flagship Properties, Inc.

**Instant Facts:** Klewin (P) entered into an oral agreement with Flagship (D) to act as construction manager on a project, and Flagship (D) claimed that enforcement of that agreement was barred by the Statute of Frauds.

**Black Letter Rule:** An oral contract that does not contain an express term stating that performance is to have a specific duration beyond one year is the functional equivalent of a contract of an indefinite duration and is enforceable because it is outside of the Statute of Frauds.

### Richard v. Richard

**Instant Facts:** The family court ordered Norman (D) to convey property to Gregory (P) and Jennifer (P) pursuant to an oral agreement, and Norman (D) claimed that the Statute of Frauds barred enforcement of the agreement.

**Black Letter Rule:** The Statute of Frauds will not bar enforcement of an oral contract to convey real estate if the party seeking performance can demonstrate part performance, including possession of the property, making improvements, or payment of a substantial part of the purchase price, done in reliance on the agreement.

### St. Ansgar Mills, Inc. v. Streit

**Instant Facts:** St. Ansgar (P) failed to obtain written confirmation of an oral agreement to buy grain, and then Streit (D) refused to accept delivery of the grain.

**Black Letter Rule:** The question of whether the written confirmation of an oral contract was received in a reasonable time is a question of fact for the jury.

### Langman v. Alumni Association of the University of Virginia

**Instant Facts:** Langman and Stowe gave some land to the Alumni Association through a deed that provided for the Association to assume any debts on the property.

**Black Letter Rule:** A grantee of a deed who assumes an existing mortgage is not a surety because he or she does not make a promise to the mortgagee to pay the debt of another, but instead promises the grantor to pay to the mortgagee the debt the grantee owes to the grantor.

### Central Ceilings, Inc. v. National Amusements, Inc.

**Instant Facts:** Central Ceilings (P) obtained a promise from National Amusements (D) that National (D) would pay Central (P) the amounts due from a contractor, and National (D) claimed that the agreement was barred by the Statute of Frauds as a promise to answer for the debt of another.

**Black Letter Rule:** A promise to pay a debt owed by another is not within the Statute of Frauds if the leading object of the promise is to confer some benefit on the promisor.

### Monarco v. Lo Greco

**Instant Facts:** Christie orally agreed to work his parents' farm in exchange for having it passed on to him, but the father passed it to his grandson.

**Black Letter Rule:** The doctrine of estoppel can be applied to keep a party from relying on the Statute of Frauds to block an oral contract when refusal to enforce a given oral contract will result in fraud, as demonstrated by either unconscionable injury after one party has been induced by the other to seriously change his or her position in reliance on the contract, or by one party receiving unjust enrichment out of reliance on the statute.

# C.R. Klewin, Inc. v. Flagship Properties, Inc.

(Construction Manager) v. (Developer)

220 Conn. 569, 600 A.2d 772 (1991)

IF AN AGREEMENT *COULD* BE PERFORMED WITHIN A YEAR, IT DOES NOT HAVE TO BE IN WRITING

It's technically possible that you could finish this deal within a year, so let's just shake on it.

stus.com

■ **INSTANT FACTS** Klewin (P) entered into an oral agreement with Flagship (D) to act as construction manager on a project, and Flagship (D) claimed that enforcement of that agreement was barred by the Statute of Frauds.

■ **BLACK LETTER RULE** An oral contract that does not contain an express term stating that performance is to have a specific duration beyond one year is the functional equivalent of a contract of an indefinite duration and is enforceable because it is outside of the Statute of Frauds.

■ **PROCEDURAL BASIS**

Certified question from the Second Circuit Court of Appeals.

■ **FACTS**

Flagship (D) was the developer of a large building project. At a meeting, Klewin (P) quoted a percentage fee for acting as construction manager on the project, and the meeting was concluded with a handshake and the words "we've got a deal." Flagship (D) and Klewin (P) made a written agreement for Klewin's (P) services for the first phase of construction, which began in May 1987. Flagship (D) became dissatisfied with Klewin's (P) services, and in March 1988 engaged another firm to act as construction manager. Klewin (P) sued Flagship (D) for breach of contract. Flagship (D) moved for summary judgment, alleging that enforcement of the agreement with Klewin (P) was barred by the Statute of Frauds. The district court granted summary judgment on the ground that the contract was not of indefinite duration or open-ended, because full performance would take place when all the phases of the project were completed. The court also held that, as a matter of law, the contract could not possibly have been performed within one year. In making that conclusion, the court focused on the size of the project and on Klewin's (P) admission that the entire project was intended to be constructed in three to ten years.

■ **ISSUE**

Was enforcement of the contract barred by the Statute of Frauds?

■ **DECISION AND RATIONALE**

(Peters, C.J.) No. An oral contract that does not contain an express term stating that performance is to have a specific duration beyond one year is the functional equivalent of a contract of an indefinite duration, and is enforceable because it is outside of the Statute of Frauds. The Statute applies to contracts that have a time for performance definitely fixed at more than one year. If no time is definitely fixed, but full performance *could* occur within one year, the contract is not within the Statute.

The one-year provision has been much criticized. The rationale for the provision is unclear. Some historians have suggested that the provision's original inclusion was to prevent the court from having to rely on the memory of witnesses. Others have suggested that the provision is intended to provide evidence of a continuing contract, or to prevent perjury by witnesses who have forgotten the details of the contract. Whatever the purpose, the one-year provision no longer serves any purpose well, and courts have regarded it with disfavor. It is read narrowly and literally.

Connecticut courts have long held that the one-year provision does not apply unless it appears from the agreement itself that it is not to be performed within one year. The limitation does not apply to contracts that *may* be performed within the year. The limitation does not turn on how subsequent events happen, or on the expectations of the parties as to the probabilities. Contracts of an uncertain duration are excluded, and only those contracts whose performance cannot possibly be completed within one year are included. The Legislature's repeated re-enactment of the Statute of Frauds in substantially the same form suggests legislative approval of this line of precedent and the restrictive interpretation of the one-year provision.

In the case at bar, the only question is what meaning to give the term "possibly" in the application of the Statute of Frauds to contracts "whose contracts cannot possibly be performed within a year." The district court held that the term includes contracts such as the one involved here, in which no definite time period is specified, but it is realistically impossible for performance to be completed within one year. The correct interpretation, however, is that "possibly" includes only those contracts whose completion within a year would be inconsistent with the express terms of the contract. Flagship (D) argues that this possibility must be a "reasonable" one, but no case law has established a "reasonable possibility" requirement. The one-year provision is an anachronism, and should not be expanded. A collateral inquiry into the reasonable possibility of completion within a year would be such an expansion, and would waste judicial time on an inquiry that has nothing to do with the merits of the case. The answer to the certified question is that the contract at issue is not within the Statute of Frauds.

**Analysis:**

The court dismisses a reading of the Statute that would require some reasonable probability that performance could be completed within a year before the one-year limitation would not apply. In this case, such a reasonableness requirement probably would have put the contract within the Statute, since even Klewin (P) acknowledged that the full project would take between three and ten years. The court clearly does not approve of the one-year limitation, and that disapproval may be what prevents it from recognizing a time limitation that clearly is implicit in the agreement.

**■ CASE VOCABULARY**

CERTIFIED QUESTION: A point of law on which a federal appellate court seeks guidance from wither the U.S. Supreme Court or the highest state court by the procedure of certification.

# Richard v. Richard

(Divorcing Spouses) v. (Husband's Father)
900 A.2d 1170 (R.I. 2006)

---

## MOST CONTRACTS FOR THE SALE OF REAL PROPERTY MUST BE IN WRITING

---

Even if you don't like the show, you can't leave after a partial performance. You're stuck until the end.

stus.com

■ **INSTANT FACTS** The family court ordered Norman (D) to convey property to Gregory (P) and Jennifer (P) pursuant to an oral agreement, and Norman (D) claimed that the Statute of Frauds barred enforcement of the agreement.

■ **BLACK LETTER RULE** The Statute of Frauds will not bar enforcement of an oral contract to convey real estate if the party seeking performance can demonstrate part performance, including possession of the property, making improvements, or payment of a substantial part of the purchase price, done in reliance on the agreement.

---

■ **PROCEDURAL BASIS**

Appeal from a family court order directing conveyance of real estate.

■ **FACTS**

Norman (D) agreed to sell real property to his son Gregory (P) and Gregory's (P) wife, Jennifer (P). Gregory (P) and Jennifer (P) occupied the property as tenants before making the agreement. The terms of the sale were not recorded. Gregory (P) and Jennifer (P) claimed that the agreed-upon price was to be $70,000, or approximately one-third of the value of the property, the difference being a result of "family affection." Norman's (D) testimony that the price was actually much higher was deemed not credible by the family court.

After the agreement to sell the property was made, Gregory (P) and Jennifer (P) began making monthly payments in addition to their rent payments to Norman (D). The parties agreed that these payments were to be applied to the purchase price. They were recorded in a ledger and deducted from a $70,000 figure. The purchase price was later reduced by $22,000 to account for a home equity loan taken out by Norman (D), and a private loan from Norman (D) to Gregory (P) and Jennifer (P). In addition to making the regular payments, Gregory (P) and Jennifer (P) made improvements to the property, including replacement of a front door and a banister, replacement of a floor, and renovation of the bedrooms.

Gregory (P) and Jenifer (P) ultimately divorced. As a part of the divorce decree, Norman (D) was ordered to convey the property to Gregory (P) and Jennifer (P). Norman (D) claimed that the Statute of Frauds barred enforcement of the agreement to sell the property. The family court disagreed, and ordered the property sold to Gregory (P) and Jennifer (P).

■ **ISSUE**

Does the Statute of Frauds bar enforcement of the agreement to convey the property?

■ **DECISION AND RATIONALE**

(Williams, C.J.) No. The Statute of Frauds will not bar enforcement of an oral contract to convey real estate if the party seeking performance can demonstrate part performance, including possession of the property, making improvements, or payment of a substantial part of the purchase price, done in reliance

---

on the agreement. Part performance is not by itself sufficient to avoid the bar of the Statute of Frauds; it must be done in reference to, and in reliance upon, the oral agreement. Partial payment, possession, or making improvements alone may not suffice to remove the case from the operation of the Statute, but a combination of all three might be sufficient.

In order to constitute part performance, possession of the property may be continued or existing possession that began before the agreement to convey the property. The fact that possession came before the agreement does not preclude a finding of part performance. The important inquiry is whether the possession indicates an oral agreement. In this case, ledger entries show that payments were deducted from the $70,000 purchase price, and that part of the payments were applied to property taxes and insurance. In addition, the improvements were made to the property after the agreement, with Norman's (D) permission. This evidence satisfies the possession element of the part performance doctrine.

In order for improvements to the property to constitute part performance, they must be permanent and must be the kind of improvements that would be "improvident" in the absence of a contract; as such, they are strong circumstantial evidence of a contract. Determining whether the improvements are "substantial" does not depend on the relative value of the improvements, but more upon whether the improvements are easily removable. The improvements in the case at bar are not easily removable, and so are "substantial." Even if the improvements are not enough to constitute part performance, the combination of the improvements, possession, and payments towards the purchase price are sufficient to constitute part performance of the agreement.

This is a close case, and the court will continue to look with skepticism on the claims of any party who seeks to avoid the bar of the Statute of Frauds. Order directing the conveyance affirmed; remanded for consideration of other issues.

**Analysis:**

The court emphasizes that the part performance of Gregory (P) and Jennifer (P) is evidence of an agreement with Norman (D). The court does not spend much time discussing the issue of fraud, or whether allowing Norman (D) to use the Statute of Frauds to avoid an agreement would be unjust. If Norman (D) had prevailed, he would have reaped a substantial benefit from Gregory (P) and Jennifer (P), who probably would not have conferred that benefit if they didn't think they were buying the property. The court refers to this situation as "circumstantial evidence" of the agreement, and does not rely much on the unjust enrichment or fraud aspect of the case.

# St. Ansgar Mills, Inc. v. Streit

(Grain Dealer) v. (Farmer)

613 N.W.2d 289 (Iowa 2000)

## WHAT IS "REASONABLE" IS GENERALLY NOT A QUESTION OF LAW

The question is "what is reasonable?"

I know what's NOT reasonable... $5 a day to sit through this drudgery.

stus.com

■ **INSTANT FACTS** St. Ansgar (P) failed to obtain written confirmation of an oral agreement to buy grain, and then Streit (D) refused to accept delivery of the grain.

■ **BLACK LETTER RULE** The question of whether the written confirmation of an oral contract was received in a reasonable time is a question of fact for the jury.

## ■ PROCEDURAL BASIS

Appeal from an order granting summary judgment in favor of Streit (D).

## ■ FACTS

St. Ansgar (P) was engaged in the business of selling corn to farmers for animal feed. A normal transaction involved a farmer contacting St. Ansgar (P) and requesting a quote for a cash price for grain for future delivery based on the Chicago Board of Trade price. If the farmer accepted the price, St. Ansgar (P) would obtain a hedge position, which obligated St. Ansgar (P) to purchase the grain at the stated price at the time of the delivery.

Streit (D) and his father (D) were long-time customers of St. Ansgar (P). Streit (D) frequently purchased grain by making an oral request; if he accepted the price, St. Ansgar (P) would prepare a written confirmation. The confirmation was either mailed to Streit (D) to sign and return, or was given to Streit (D) personally when he stopped by the business. Streit's (D) father regularly stopped by St. Ansgar (P) during the first ten days of the month to pay the open account Streit (D) maintained. If St. Ansgar (P) mailed the written confirmation, it was not unusual for Streit to fail to sign the confirmation for a long period, or to fail to return contracts sent to him.

On July 1, 1996, Streit's (D) father telephoned St. Ansgar (P) and placed two orders for 60,000 bushels of corn, one to be delivered in December 1996 (for $3.53 per bushel), and the other to be delivered in May 1997 (for $3.73 per bushel). The order confirmed an earlier conversation with Streit (D). St. Ansgar (P) prepared a written confirmation for Streit's (D) father to sign when he came in to pay the open account. Streit's (D) father did not come by St. Ansgar (P) in July, and St. Ansgar (P) asked a local banker to have Streit's (D) father stop in. Streit's (D) father did not go to St. Ansgar (P) until August 10, 1996, and the written confirmation was given to him at that time. Streit (D) later refused delivery of the corn. The price of corn had dropped drastically since July 1, and Streit (D) was able to purchase corn much more cheaply on the open market. Streit (D) told St. Ansgar (P) it should have followed up earlier with the written confirmation, and that it had no excuse for not doing so.

St. Ansgar (P) brought suit against Streit (D) for breach of contract. Streit (D) moved for summary judgment, claiming that the Statute of Frauds barred enforcement of the agreement. Streit (D) argued that the written confirmation did not meet the requirements of U.C.C. § 2–201 because Streit (D) was not a merchant, and because the written confirmation was not delivered in a reasonable time after the oral agreement. The trial court held that the question of whether Streit (D) was a merchant was a jury question, but also held that the delivery of the written confirmation did not occur within a reasonable time as a matter of law. The court found that the size of the order, the volatility of the grain market, and the lack of an explanation for St. Ansgar's (P) failure to send the written confirmation made the delay unreasonable as a matter of law.

### ■ ISSUE

Was the delay in delivering the confirmation unreasonable as a matter of law, so that Streit (D) was entitled to summary judgment?

### ■ DECISION AND RATIONALE

(Cady, J.) No. The question of whether the written confirmation of an oral contract was received in a reasonable time is a question of fact for the jury. The reasonableness of a party's conduct must be determined according to all of the circumstances of the case. Numerous cases from other jurisdictions have held that the reasonableness of the time of the delivery of a confirmation is a jury question. While some courts have ruled on the reasonableness question as a matter of law, summary judgment on this issue is appropriate only when the evidence is so one-sided that only one party must prevail at trial.

The Statute of Frauds is deeply engrained in the law, but many of the forces that gave rise to the rule no longer prevail. Some of the rigid requirements of the Statute have been modified. One of those modifications is the provision at issue in the case at bar, which deems the writing requirement satisfied in a contract between merchants if a confirmation of the contract is received and the merchant-recipient knows of the contents of the confirmation, unless written notice of objection to the confirmation is given within ten days. While the U.C.C. imposes a specific ten-day requirement for objections, there is a flexible standard of reasonableness. Section 1–204 (2) of the Code [cited in the text as § 2–201 (2)] specifically states that a reasonable time for taking action depends on "the nature, purpose and circumstances" of the action. Thus, all relevant circumstances are to be considered.

The factors cited by the trial court—the volatility of the market conditions and the high sale price—would normally narrow the amount of time considered reasonable. There are other factors to consider, such as the custom or practice of the parties to delay delivery of the confirmation, the long-standing amicable business relationship between the parties, the numerous similar transactions that were completed without incident, and the fact that St. Ansgar (P) did not suspect the failure of Streit's (D) father to stop by was a matter of concern. These factors show a genuine dispute over the reasonableness of the delay. In addition, conduct is not rendered unreasonable solely because there is no particular explanation for the conduct. The reasonableness of conduct must be determined by the facts and circumstances existing at the time the conduct occurred. Reversed and remanded.

---

### Analysis:

Streit's (D) claim that he should not be bound to the contract with St. Ansgar (P) is based on St. Ansgar's (P) failure to send written confirmation. Given the course of dealing of the parties, particularly his occasional failure to send back the written confirmations he did receive, this argument seems like a bit of a stretch. In effect, Streit (D) is opting out of an agreement he does not deny making and relying on his, or his father's, inactions as justification. Even so, the outcome is not so clearly one-sided that the case should be taken from the jury.

---

# Langman v. Alumni Association of the University of Virginia

(Previous Owner) v. (New Owner)

247 Va. 491, 442 S.E.2d 669 (1994)

---

A GRANTEE OF A DEED WHO ASSUMES AN EXISTING MORTGAGE IS NOT A SURETY

---

■ **INSTANT FACTS** Langman and Stowe gave some land to the Alumni Association through a deed that provided for the Association to assume any debts on the property.

■ **BLACK LETTER RULE** A grantee of a deed who assumes an existing mortgage is not a surety because he or she does not make a promise to the mortgagee to pay the debt of another, but instead promises the grantor to pay to the mortgagee the debt the grantee owes to the grantor.

---

■ **PROCEDURAL BASIS**

Appeal from judgment in action for damages.

■ **FACTS**

Dr. M.W. Langman (P) and Caleb Stowe were owners, in common, of a commercial property in Maryland. Wanting to make a gift to the University of Virginia, Langman (P) and Stowe conveyed the property to the Alumni Association (D) in 1986. Earlier that year, the property had been appraised at $775,000. The deed to the Association (D) stated that the property was subject to a lien. This lien resulted from a $600,000 debt that Langman (P) and Stowe incurred in purchasing the property. The deed also stated that "[t]he Grantee [namely, the Association (D)] does hereby assume payment of such obligation and agrees to hold the Grantors [Langman (P) and Stowe] harmless from further liability on such obligation." While the Association (D) did not sign this deed, it (D) did acknowledge the gift and have the deed recorded. In a short time, the cost of operating the property exceeded the income it generated. Stowe continued to manage the property, but only continued payments on the outstanding loan until the summer of 1989. The lender then demanded payments from Langman (P). She (P) cured this default and then sued the Association (D), claiming that it was its (D) responsibility to reimburse her (P) under the deed. The trial court held that the Association (D) "did not knowingly accept the gift with contractual conditions." Also, the court found that the assumption clause was placed in the deed by mistake, and that the Association had "sufficiently rejected the gift to require a finding by the court that the conveyance is ineffective." Thus, the assumption clause was unenforceable and the attempted conveyance was a nullity. Langman (P) appealed.

■ **ISSUE**

Does a grantee who assumes an existing mortgage through a deed become a surety falling under the suretyship clause of the Statute of Frauds?

■ **DECISION AND RATIONALE**

(Keenan) No. A grantee of a deed who assumes an existing mortgage is not a surety because he or she does not make a promise to the mortgagee to pay the debt of another, but rather promises the grantor to pay to the mortgagee the debt the grantee owes to the grantor. The trial court erred in

---

holding that the Statute of Frauds does not bar enforcement of an unsigned mortgage assumption clause. The Association (D) claims that the "suretyship" provision of the Statute requires that it (D) sign the agreement before assuming any debts. Further, the Association (D) claims that Langman (P) would still remain secondarily liable to the lender for the mortgage debt, even if there were an effective assumption by someone else. Because of this, the Association (D) claims that its (D) agreement to assume the mortgage was a "collateral" agreement falling within the Statute of Frauds. Specifically, the state code equivalent of the Statute provides that "unless a promise, contract, [or] agreement . . . is in writing and signed by the party to be charged or his agent, no action shall be brought . . . [t]o charge any person upon a promise to answer for the debt, default, or misdoings of another." The Association (D) is incorrect. A grantee that assumes an existing mortgage is not a surety. The Association (D) did not promise the lender that it (D) would pay Langman's (P) debt. Instead, the Association (D) promised Langman (P) that it (D) would pay to the lender whatever it owed to Langman (P). This is an original, not collateral, undertaking. The Association (D) received a direct benefit and did not merely serve as a surety for Langman (P) and Stowe. Thus, the Statute of Frauds did not bar enforcement of the mortgage assumption clause, and the Association is responsible for paying the debt. Trial court judgment affirmed.

---

## Analysis:

There are two main, recurring situations in which courts have held that no suretyship relationship exists. In both cases, the courts make their decisions on the basis of a lack of a duty owed by a principal debtor. One situation involves the circumstances found here, where the primary debtor (Langman (P)) renders performance while relying on the promisor's (Association's (D)) credit. The other situation involves a novation, or the adding of a new party to an earlier contract. In both situations, the promisor is not a surety, so the promise in question falls outside the Statute. There are, however, several more exceptions by which a promise falls outside the suretyship provision, even though the promisor is a surety. One example is where the debtor had no actual or constructive notice that the promisor was a surety. Other examples include when the surety makes the promise to the principal and not to the debtor, and when the promisor agrees to render performance that has nothing to do with the promise he or she has just made.

---

## ■ CASE VOCABULARY

GUARANTOR: One who makes a promise or guarantee to become liable for the debt of another.

NULLITY: That which is legally invalid.

PAROL: Oral or verbal.

SURETY: One who at another person's request becomes responsible for the performance by that other person of some act for the benefit of a third person; also, a person who is primarily liable for the performance of another's obligation or the payment of another's debt.

# Central Ceilings, Inc. v. National Amusements, Inc.

(Subcontractor) v. (Theater Owner)

70 Mass.App.Ct. 172, 873 N.E.2d 754 (2007)

■ **INSTANT FACTS** Central Ceilings (P) obtained a promise from National Amusements (D) that National (D) would pay Central (P) the amounts due from a contractor, and National (D) claimed that the agreement was barred by the Statute of Frauds as a promise to answer for the debt of another.

■ **BLACK LETTER RULE** A promise to pay a debt owed by another is not within the Statute of Frauds if the leading object of the promise is to confer some benefit on the promisor.

## ■ PROCEDURAL BASIS

Appeal from a judgment for Central Ceilings (P).

## ■ FACTS

Old Colony Construction was the prime contractor on a theater complex project owned by National Amusements (D). Old Colony subcontracted with Central Ceilings (P) to perform carpentry work on the project. The project began to have problems; there were delays project, and the deadline for completion passed. Old Colony also had financial problems, and Central (P) became concerned about whether it would receive payment. At a meeting of the three parties, Central's (P) representative said to National's (D) representative, "You've got to guarantee me the payment. You've got to guarantee me that I will get funded for this project." National's (D) representative said that he would guarantee Central's (P) payment.

Central (P) continued to work on the project. Some months later, National (D) learned that it owed nothing more to Old Colony. National (D) resisted making any payment to Central (P). Central (P) brought suit for breach of contract, and National (D) claimed that enforcement of the guarantee promise was barred by the Statute of Frauds.

## ■ ISSUE

Was enforcement of the promise to pay Central (P) barred by the Statute of Frauds?

## ■ DECISION AND RATIONALE

(Peretta, J.) No. A promise to pay a debt owed by another is not within the Statute of Frauds if the leading object of the promise is to confer some benefit on the promisor. In such a case, the debt could be considered to be the debt of the promisor. National (D) argues that the agreement is outside the Statute of Frauds only if there was a novation; that is, if the agreement had released Old Colony from its debt and substituted National (D). A novation is not required, however. The "leading object" exception to the Statute of Frauds applies when there is a debt of a third party, there is no novation, and the debt will be terminated by the performance of the promise. An agreement made under those circumstances may be enforceable if the facts and circumstances of the transaction show that the promise was given primarily or solely to serve the promisor's own interests. It has been recognized that a property owner's promise to pay subcontractors may, in the appropriate circumstances, fall within the "leading object" exception.

There was evidence in this case that National (D) wanted to complete the theater complex in time for it to be open on Labor Day; that the project was on a tight schedule; and that Central (P) was one of the main subcontractors on the project and had already started the work, and was one of the few, if not the only, subcontractors capable of finishing the work on time. Under these circumstances, the evidence was sufficient to conclude that National's (D) promise was given to secure Central's (P) continued performance, and that satisfaction of Old Colony's obligation was incidental to the promise. Affirmed.

### Analysis:

The court refers to the "leading object" rule as an "exception" to the Statute of Frauds. It is probably more accurate to say that a promise that falls within the leading object rule is not a "promise to answer for the debt of another," and so not subject to the Statute at all. In this case, Old Colony was essentially little more than an intermediary between Central (P) and National (D). Central (P) did the work that National (D) wanted, and National's (D) payments to Old Colony were meant, at least in part, to pay Central (P).

### ■ CASE VOCABULARY

NOVATION: The act of substituting for an old obligation a new one that either replaces an existing obligation with a new obligation or replaces an original party with a new party. A novation may substitute (1) a new obligation between the same parties, (2) a new debtor, or (3) a new creditor.

# Monarco v. Lo Greco

(Owners' Grandson) v. (Owners' Son)

35 Cal.2d 621, 220 P.2d 737 (1950)

ONE CAN BE ESTOPPED FROM RELYING ON THE STATUTE OF FRAUDS IF FAILING TO ENFORCE AN ORAL CONTRACT WILL RESULT IN FRAUD, AS SHOWN BY UNCONSCIONABLE INJURY OR UNJUST ENRICHMENT

■ **INSTANT FACTS** Christie orally agreed to work his parents' farm in exchange for having it passed on to him, but the father passed it to his grandson.

■ **BLACK LETTER RULE** The doctrine of estoppel can be applied to keep a party from relying on the Statute of Frauds to block an oral contract when refusal to enforce a given oral contract will result in fraud, as demonstrated by either unconscionable injury after one party has been induced by the other to seriously change his or her position in reliance on the contract, or by one party receiving unjust enrichment out of reliance on the statute.

■ **PROCEDURAL BASIS**

Appeal from judgment in action for partition and accounting after probate.

■ **FACTS**

Natale and Carmela Castiglia were married and lived in Colorado. Natale had a grandson, Carmen Monarco (P). Carmela also had three children by a previous marriage named John, Rosie and Christie (D). Rosie was married to Nick Norcia. Mr. and Mrs. Castiglia moved to California and invested their assets, worth roughly $4,000, in a half interest in agricultural property. Rosie and Nick Norcia acquired the other half interest. Christie (D), a teenager at this time, moved with the family to California. Monarco (P) stayed in Colorado. In 1926, Christie (D), then 18 years old, decided to live on his own. Mr. and Mrs. Castiglia orally proposed to him that if he stayed home and worked, then they would keep their property in joint tenancy so that it would pass to the survivor. The survivor would then leave the property to Christie (D) by will, only with some small devise to be made to John and Rosie. Persuaded by this promise, Christie (D) stayed home and worked in the family business, in exchange for room and board and some spending money. By doing this, Christie (D) gave up any opportunity for further education or any chance of accumulating property of his (D) own. After Christie (D) got married, Natale told him (D) that he (D) would receive all the property when Mr. and Mrs. Castiglia died. Mr. and Mrs. Castiglia placed all of their property in joint tenancy, and in 1941 they both executed wills according to their earlier agreement, with an additional $500 to Monarco (P). While these wills did not refer to the earlier agreement, Mr. and Mrs. Castiglia and Christie (D) all agreed to the terms. Natale Castiglia eventually decided, however, to leave his half of the joint property to his grandson, Monarco (P). Shortly before his death, Natale terminated the joint tenancies and executed a will leaving all of his property to Monarco (P). Natale died soon thereafter, with his and Carmela's interest worth roughly $100,000. The will was probated and the court distributed the property to Monarco (P). Monarco (P) then filed for partition of the properties and an accounting. The trial court then ordered a judgment for Christie (D), and Monarco (P) appealed.

■ **ISSUE**

Can a party be estopped from relying on the Statute of Frauds to block an oral contract?

### Odorizzi v. Bloomfield School District

**Instant Facts:** After a schoolteacher was arrested for homosexuality, the school forced his resignation and threatened to fire him publicly.

**Black Letter Rule:** Contracts secured by excessively coercive persuasion are voidable at the victim's option, even if the victim was sane and independent, and even if the threat was legal.

### Swinton v. Whitinsville Sav. Bank

**Instant Facts:** Whitinsville Bank knew the house it sold to Swinton was infested with termites, but did not tell him about it when making the sale.

**Black Letter Rule:** A party cannot be held liable for failing to disclose information when there is no evidence of any special duty to disclose anything.

### Kannavos v. Annino

**Instant Facts:** Mrs. Annino sold her apartment building to Kannavos without telling him that the building was in violation of the local zoning ordinances.

**Black Letter Rule:** Although a party may be under no duty to disclose information to another, if that party does speak with reference to a given point of information, then that party is bound to speak honestly and to divulge all the material facts bearing upon that point within that party's knowledge.

### Vokes v. Arthur Murray, Inc.

**Instant Facts:** After a dance instructor induces a widow to buy numerous dance lessons by overpraising her skill, she sues for misrepresentation.

**Black Letter Rule:** False statements of opinion by experts with superior knowledge are actionable as misrepresentations.

# Kiefer v. Fred Howe Motors, Inc.

(Minor) v. (Car Dealer)

39 Wis.2d 20, 158 N.W.2d 288 (1968)

---

EVEN THE CONTRACT OF A MINOR WHO IS EMANCIPATED THROUGH MARRIAGE WILL BE CONSIDERED VOID OR VOIDABLE UNLESS IT IS FOR A NECESSARY ITEM

---

■ **INSTANT FACTS** Kiefer bought a car before he was 21 years old, but after seeing the car was damaged, tried to return it after turning 21.

■ **BLACK LETTER RULE** The contract of a minor, whether emancipated or unemancipated, is either void or voidable at the option of the minor, unless it is a contract for necessaries.

---

■ **PROCEDURAL BASIS**

Appeal from judgment.

■ **FACTS**

Steven Kiefer (P) bought a five-year-old station wagon from Fred Howe Motors, Inc. (Howe) (D). At the time of purchase, Kiefer (P) was only twenty years old, but already had a wife and child, and was working to support them. Kiefer (P) had signed a purchase contract which stated: "I represent that I am 21 years of age and over and recognize that the dealer sells the above vehicle upon this representation." He (P) eventually had trouble with the car, and claimed it had a cracked engine block. After turning twenty-one, Kiefer (P) unsuccessfully tried to return the car to Howe (D). He (P) then sued to recover the price. The court found for Kiefer (P), and Howe (D) appealed.

■ **ISSUE**

Can a contract entered into by a person while he or she was a minor be voided after the person is no longer a minor?

■ **DECISION AND RATIONALE**

(Wilkie) Yes. The contract of a minor, whether emancipated or unemancipated, is either void or voidable at the option of the minor, unless it is a contract for necessaries. Howe (D) urges that a rule be adopted, as a matter of public policy, that allows an emancipated minor over eighteen years of age to be made legally responsible for his contracts. The rule of the voidability of minors' contracts was established as a just and commendable rule designed to protect minors. Historically, minors were considered immature in both mind and experience, and as such required protection from their own bad choices and from adults who would try to take advantage of them. Today, the rule seems to have lost some of its appeal, as minors are allowed to join the military or get married, but are not allowed to assume contractual burdens. More relevantly, this state allows a minor to drive a car legally at sixteen, but forces that same minor to wait until he or she is twenty-one before purchasing one. Clearly, a line must be drawn. That line, however, should be drawn by the legislature, and not by the courts. Minors still require some protection from the pitfalls of the market place. A rule allowing an emancipated minor to be without this protection would suggest that the married minor is somehow wiser and more mature than the unmarried minor. This kind of rule would not make sense, particularly as a marriage between two minors is often considered to be an unwise course of action. Judgment affirmed.

---

## ■ DISSENT

(Hallows, C.J.)  The magical age limit of 21 years for contractual maturity no longer has a basis in fact or in public policy.  Moreover, an automobile was a necessity in this case, and may very well be a necessity for other parents under 21 years of age who use it to go to and from work.  Because of this, the contract should not be affirmed.

## Analysis:

There are three main exceptions to the rule that a minor can void a contract he or she enters into.  One is that minors are accountable for the reasonable value of necessaries they may receive through contracts.  Another exception used in many states allows a minor to fill the role of plaintiff and recover money he or she paid to someone else, with the exception, however, that minors are not allowed to hide behind a minority status simply to prevent others from recovering money from them.  This bears some resemblance to Kiefer's (P) situation.  A third exception seems to fit this case, though it is not expressly mentioned in the opinion.  That exception allows a minor to be held liable for fraudulent misrepresentation of his or her age if it somehow resulted in reliance by another party.  Though this exception is employed in several states, including Texas, Iowa, *and* Wisconsin (where *Kiefer* was decided), the courts there have also decided against applying it when the misrepresentation took the form of a signed affirmation of age on a standard form presented by the other party.  Here, as no intent to defraud was shown the exception was not applicable.

## ■ CASE VOCABULARY

EMANCIPATED:  Term used to describe a minor who has been released from parental care and custody and is able to care for himself financially.

VOID:  Term used to describe a contract which has no legal effect.

VOIDABLE:  Capable of being declared void or disaffirmed, though not used to describe something that is void in and of itself.

# Ortelere v. Teachers' Retirement Bd.

(Schoolteacher) v. (Retirement Board)

25 N.Y.2d 196, 303 N.Y.S.2d 362, 250 N.E.2d 460 (1969)

A PERSON IS MENTALLY INCOMPETENT TO ENTER A CONTRACT ONLY IF A MENTAL ILLNESS OR DEFECT MAKES THE PERSON UNABLE TO ACT IN A REASONABLE MANNER AND THE OTHER PARTY HAS REASON TO KNOW OF SUCH A CONDITION

■ **INSTANT FACTS** Ortelere was on leave for mental illness when she maximized her retirement benefits during her lifetime, and left her family with nothing when she died.

■ **BLACK LETTER RULE** A person's contractual duties will be voidable if, by reason of mental illness or defect, he or she is unable to act in a reasonable manner in relation to the transaction, and the other party has reason to know of his or her condition.

■ **PROCEDURAL BASIS**

Appeal from judgment.

■ **FACTS**

Grace Ortelere was a sixty-year-old New York City schoolteacher who went on leave for mental illness after suffering a nervous breakdown. Specifically, she was diagnosed by her psychiatrist as having "involutional psychosis, melancholia type," and possibly cerebral arteriosclerosis. Her husband of thirty-eight years, Mr. Ortelere (P) quit his (P) job to take care of her. Mrs. Ortelere had participated in a public retirement plan administered by the Teachers' Retirement Board (Board) (D) for over forty years. As a result, she had accumulated a $70,925 reserve. In 1965, she wrote a letter to the Board (D) asking several questions. One example of these questions was an inquiry into what her monthly allowance would be if she were to "take a loan of $5,000 before retiring and select option four-a on both the pension and annuity..." Soon afterwards, she borrowed the maximum amount possible from the fund, $8,760. She also made an irrevocable election to receive the maximum benefits of $450 per month during her lifetime. She made these changes without informing her husband (P). As a result, an earlier plan by which Mrs. Ortelere would have received $375 per month, and her husband (P) would have taken the remaining fund when she died, was revoked. This new plan left Mr. Ortelere (P) and their two grown children with no benefits upon her death. Mrs. Ortelere died of cerebral arteriosclerosis two months later. Mr. Ortelere (P) sued to set aside his (P) wife's modification of the retirement plan, claiming she was mentally incompetent. Her psychiatrist testified that victims of involutional melancholia "can't think rationally..." and that "[e]verything is impossible [for them] to decide." The trial court judged for Mr. Ortelere (P), and the Board (D) appealed. The Appellate Division reversed and dismissed the complaint, and Mr. Ortelere appealed.

■ **ISSUE**

Is a person automatically considered mentally incompetent to enter contracts if he or she has a mental illness and is incapable of making decisions?

■ **DECISION AND RATIONALE**

(Breitel) No. A person's contractual duties will be voidable if, by reason of mental illness or defect, he or she is unable to act in a reasonable manner in relation to the transaction, *and* the other party has reason to know of his or her condition. Traditionally, this State and others have measured a person's mental capacity to enter contracts by a primarily "cognitive" test. With such a test, the question is whether a person's mind was "so affected as to render [the person] wholly and absolutely incompetent to comprehend and understand the nature of the transaction." This test also required that the person be capable of making a rational judgment regarding the particular transaction. These standards were set when psychiatric knowledge was relatively primitive, and when it was believed that all mental abilities were affected at the same time by a mental illness. This belief no longer carries weight today. Accordingly, the Restatement Second of Contracts states that: "(1) A person incurs only voidable contractual duties by entering into a transaction if by reason of mental illness or defect . . . (b) he is unable to act in a reasonable manner in relation to the transaction and the other party has reason to know of his condition." The Board (D) knew, or should have known, of Mrs. Ortelere's condition by virtue of her leave of absence for medical reasons related to mental illness. It would not be wise to allow a retirement fund that was accumulated over the course of forty years to be completely emptied by a single act committed by a person known to be mentally ill. New trial ordered, and judgment reversed.

### ■ DISSENT

(Jasen) The kind of detailed, explicit, and extremely pertinent questions posed by Mrs. Ortelere in her letter to the Board (D) reveal a mind fully in command of the more prominent features of the Retirement System. Certainly it could not be said that she possessed sufficient capacity to write this letter, yet lacked the capacity to understand the answers to her questions. The evidence shows that Mrs. Ortelere made this decision to increase her monthly benefit payments was based on a need for a higher income to support two people, namely her husband (P) and herself. Her decision was both a rational and necessary one. Further, there is no evidence to indicate that Mrs. Ortelere had any indication or warning that her life expectancy would be reduced by her condition.

### Analysis:

The court here describes the two main tests for mental capacity. The first, known as the cognitive test, is the traditional one. This test focuses on the question of whether the party in question lacked the capacity to understand the nature and consequences of the particular contract. This test, though criticized as unscientific and too ambiguous to be accurately defined, is nonetheless almost universally accepted by the courts. The second test, known as the volitional test, weighs the question of whether a mentally Ill person has effective control of his or her actions. The *Ortelere* court adopted the Restatement Second's compromise position. This test combines a qualified volitional test with the traditional cognitive test. This modern standard has met with increasing acceptance, but the cognitive test is still prevalent.

### ■ CASE VOCABULARY

ARTERIOSCLEROSIS: A chronic disease resulting in the abnormal hardening and thickening of the arteries.

INVOLUTIONAL: Having to do with regression or decline characteristic of the aging process.

MELANCHOLIA: A mental condition characterized by severe depression , and often by hallucinations and delusions.

RUBRIC: An authoritative rule or doctrine.

# Watkins & Son v. Carrig

(Excavation Company) v. (Client)

91 N.H. 459, 21 A.2d 591, 138 A.L.R. 131 (1941)

A NEW PROMISE BY PARTIES TO AN EXISTING CONTRACT RESULTS IN A MUTUAL RESCISSION OF THE INITIAL CONTRACT AND THE CREATION OF A NEW CONTRACT

■ **INSTANT FACTS** Carrig hired Watkins & Son to dig a cellar, and agreed to pay nine times more after learning they had to dig through solid rock.

■ **BLACK LETTER RULE** A new promise by the parties to an existing contract constitutes a mutual rescission of the existing contract and the formation of a new one.

■ **PROCEDURAL BASIS**

Assumpsit for work done.

■ **FACTS**

Watkins & Son (P) agreed through a written contract to excavate a cellar for Carrig (P) for a particular price. The contract provided that "all material" was to be removed from the site, and there was no qualification as to the term "to excavate." After work began, the workers discovered solid rock at the digging site. The manager for Watkins & Son (P) informed Carrig (D) of this. A meeting between the manager and Carrig (D) followed, and, at Watkins & Son's (P's) Insistence, it was orally agreed that Watkins & Son (P) would remove the rock at a higher unit price. This new price would be about nine times greater than the unit price which served as the basis for the gross amount to be paid under the original written contract. The rock eventually amounted to two-thirds of the material that had to be excavated. A referee found that the oral agreement "superseded" the written contract, and thus reported a verdict for Watkins & Son (P). Carrig (D) took exception to the acceptance of this report and a subsequent order of judgment.

■ **ISSUE**

Does a new promise by parties to an existing contract rescind the old contract?

■ **DECISION AND RATIONALE**

(Allen) Yes. A new promise by the parties to an existing contract constitutes a mutual rescission of the existing contract and the formation of a new one. The referee's finding that the written contract was "superseded" by a subsequent oral contract apparently means that the parties (P and D) agreed to treat the written contract as though it never existed, and the oral contract was the only one made. Carrig (D) agreed to the new price for excavating the rock, and Watkins & Son (P) proceeded on the strength of that promise. Carrig (D) granted relief for Watkins & Son (P) from an unforeseen burden tied to the contract, and received reasonable value for the higher price he (D) paid. The problem is whether this grant of relief constituted a valid contract. The basic rule is that a promise without consideration is invalid. From that rule comes the idea that a promise to pay for what the promisor already has a right to receive is invalid. Watkins & Son (P) claims that the original contract was rescinded by mutual consent, and that the idea that Carrig (P) promised to pay for performance of a pre-existing duty is unfounded. Granted, an agreement for rescission is still an agreement, and as such requires consideration. There is, however, an important distinction between a regular promise and a promise in adjustment of an outstanding contractual promise. Parties to a valid contract generally understand that their contract is subject to any mutual action they may take in its performance. A rescission made interdependently with the formation of a new contract is not invalid for lack of consideration. All Carrig (D) has done here is intentionally and voluntarily yield to a demand for a special price for excavating rock. In doing this, he (D) yielded his contractual right to the earlier price. If the essence of this later transaction was Carrig's (D) promise to pay more for the excavation, then there was also, in its inherent makeup, a valid discharge of an obligation by Carrig (D). Because Carrig (D) relinquished this right of price, he (D) should, in fairness, be held to the new agreement. Exceptions overruled.

## Analysis:

This case demonstrates an exception to the pre-existing duty rule. The Restatement Second has taken on the spirit of this exception, having been influenced by the terms of UCC § 2–209(1). The Restatement treats this exception as a fair and useful device, because a modification is "ancillary" to the original contract. It goes on to provide that an agreement to modify an existing contract that is not yet fully performed by either side will be valid and binding if the proposed modification is a fair and equitable one. The question of whether the modification is fair and equitable will depend upon several factors, including circumstances not anticipated when the contract was formed.

## ■ CASE VOCABULARY

ASSUMPSIT: Latin for "he promised"; a promise by which a person assumes the responsibility of doing some act or paying some amount to another.

IMPROVIDENT: Not foreseeing and planning for the future.

# Austin Instrument, Inc. v. Loral Corporation

(Parts Supplier) v. (Radar Set Manufacturer)

29 N.Y.2d 124, 324 N.Y.S.2d 22, 272 N.E.2d 533 (1971)

## A PARTY WHO ENTERED A CONTRACT UNDER ECONOMIC DURESS CAN VOID THAT CONTRACT

■ **INSTANT FACTS** Austin began delivering parts to Loral for one government contract, but stopped delivery until Loral paid Austin for all the parts for a second contract.

■ **BLACK LETTER RULE** A contract is voidable on the ground of duress when it is established that the party making the claim was forced to agree to it by means of a wrongful threat precluding the exercise of his free will; economic duress is demonstrated by proof that one party to a contract has threatened to breach the agreement by withholding needed goods unless the other party agrees to some further demand, that the threatened party could not obtain the goods from another source, and that the ordinary remedy for breach of contract would be inadequate.

## ■ PROCEDURAL BASIS

Appeal from judgment in action for economic duress for damages.

## ■ FACTS

In July 1965, the Navy awarded Loral Corporation (Loral) (D) a $6,000,000 contract for the production of radar sets. This contract included a schedule of deliveries in the second half of 1966, a liquidated damages clause applicable to late deliveries, and a cancellation clause in case Loral (D) defaulted. Loral (D) then solicited bids for the roughly 40 precision gear components it (D) needed to produce the radar sets. Austin Instrument, Inc. (Austin) (P) was awarded a subcontract by Loral (D) to supply 23 of those parts. Austin (P) began delivery in early 1966. In May 1966, Loral (D) was awarded a second Navy contract for the production of more radar sets. Again, Loral (D) solicited bids for the needed components. Austin (P) bid to produce all 40 components, but, on July 15, a Loral (D) representative informed Austin's (P) president that Austin (P) would only receive the subcontract for parts that it (P) was the lowest bidder for. Austin (P) refused to accept an order for less than the 40 parts. The next day, Austin (P) informed Loral (D) that it (P) would cease delivery of the parts from the first subcontract unless Loral (D) agreed to increase the amount paid for those parts, and order all 40 parts needed under the second contract from Austin (P). Soon thereafter, Austin (P) did stop delivery. Loral (D) then contacted ten different manufacturers, but could find none who could produce the parts in time for it (D) to meet its (D) commitments to the Navy. In a letter dated July 22, Loral (D) accepted Austin's terms, saying that it (D) was "left with no choice or alternative but to meet [Austin's] conditions." After the last delivery under the second subcontract in July 1967, Loral (D) notified Austin (P) of its (D) intention to seek recovery of the price increases. On September 15, 1967, Austin (P) filed an action against Loral (D) to recover over $17,750 which was still due on the second subcontract. That same day, Loral (D) filed an action against Austin (P) for roughly $22,250, or the amount of the price increases under the first subcontract, on the ground of economic duress. Austin (P) was awarded its (P) requested sum, while Loral's (D) complaint was dismissed. The Appellate Division affirmed.

# ■ ISSUE

Can a party who is threatened by another party's withholding of required goods into agreeing to a contract, later void that contract on duress grounds?

# ■ DECISION AND RATIONALE

(Fuld) Yes. A contract is voidable on the ground of duress when it is established that the party making the claim was forced to agree to it by means of a wrongful threat precluding the exercise of his free will; economic duress is demonstrated by proof that one party to a contract has threatened to breach the agreement by withholding needed goods unless the other party agrees to some further demand, that the threatened party could not obtain the goods from another source, and that the ordinary remedy for breach of contract would be inadequate. The evidence here makes out a classic case of duress. In July 1966, Loral (D) was concerned with meeting deadlines for radar sets due later that year. For Loral (D), the threat of paying the liquidated damages, as well as defaulting, were very real possibilities. In addition, Loral (D) could not risk losing future contracts as a result of failure to deliver for this first radar set contract. These factors made it perfectly reasonable for Loral (D) to consider itself in an emergency, duress situation. While Austin (P) argues that Loral (D) should have asked the Government for an extension, Loral (D) had no way of knowing when substitute suppliers could have supplied it (D) with the parts needed to complete its (D) orders. Loral (D) also had the burden of demonstrating it (D) could not obtain the needed parts from other sources within a reasonable time. In contacting ten different manufacturers of precision gears and receiving no assurances that the parts could be delivered on time, Loral (D) met this burden. Loral (D), having contracted to produce a sophisticated piece of military equipment, did not need to contact suppliers that it did not believe to be capable of making the required parts. These factors clearly demonstrate that Loral (D) had no reasonable choice other than to accept Austin's (P) demands and sue to recover the excess price later. Loral (D) also had sufficient reason to wait until after Austin (P) completed delivery before raising a complaint, considering Austin's (P) previous threats and behavior. Order modified so that dismissal of Loral's (D) claim is reversed, and, except as so modified, affirmed.

## Analysis:

The test for whether a threat is serious enough to justify a party's acceptance of another party's terms has changed over the years. The early common law imposed a strict objective requirement that the threat be enough to "overcome mind and will of a person of ordinary firmness." After this period of strict objectivity, the courts went to a more subjective standard, which required only that the alleged threat had deprived the victim of his or her free will. As the Eighth Circuit described it in *Winget v. Rockwood*, "the ultimate fact in issue is whether such person was bereft of the free exercise of his will power." The ambiguousness of the term "free will," however, caused judicial opinion to swing to another new standard. The alleged threat must have left the victim with "no reasonable alternative." This standard is hinted at in the *Austin* opinion. Also, the Restatement (Second) adopted this standard as § 175(1), providing that duress must leave "the victim no reasonable alternative."

# ■ CASE VOCABULARY

DURESS: Any unlawful threat or coercion made by one person to induce another person to act in a manner against his or her free will.

LIQUIDATED DAMAGES: An expressly stipulated amount of damages to be received by either party to a contract in the event of breach by the other.

# Odorizzi v. Bloomfield School District

(Employee) v. (Employer)

246 Cal.App.2d 123, 54 Cal.Rptr. 533 (1966)

---

CONTRACTS OBTAINED THROUGH UNDUE INFLUENCE ARE VOIDABLE

---

■ **INSTANT FACTS** After a schoolteacher was arrested for homosexuality, the school forced his resignation and threatened to fire him publicly.

■ **BLACK LETTER RULE** Contracts secured by excessively coercive persuasion are voidable at the victim's option, even if the victim was sane and independent, and even if the threat was legal.

---

■ **PROCEDURAL BASIS**

In contract action seeking rescission, appeal from summary judgement for defendant.

■ **FACTS**

Mr. Odorizzi (P), an elementary school teacher for the Bloomfield School District ("School") (D), was arrested for homosexual acts. The next day, School's (D) principal and superintendent told him that, unless he resigned, he would be fired and the charges against him would be publicized. Odorizzi (P) resigned. Later, the criminal charges against Odorizzi (P) were dropped. Odorizzi (P) sued to rescind his resignation, contending it was obtained by duress and undue influence. At trial, School demurred [moved to dismiss], and the judge dismissed Odorizzi's (P) complaint. Odorizzi (P) appeals.

■ **ISSUE**

Is a resignation secured by threat of firing and adverse publicity voidable for undue influence?

■ **DECISION AND RATIONALE**

(Fleming) Yes. Contracts secured by excessively coercive persuasion are voidable at the victim's option, even if the victim was sane and independent, and even if the threat was legal. There was no duress here, since School's (D) threat to fire Odorizzi (P) was not just its legal right, but its positive duty, even if it would damage his reputation. Undue influence is a legal phrase describing persuasion which tends to be coercive in nature, which overcomes the will without convincing the judgement. Its hallmark is high pressure which works on mental, moral, or emotional weakness to such an extent it approaches coercion. It does not require proving misrepresentations of law or fact, since a person's will may be overborne without misrepresentation. By California's statutory definition, undue influence includes "taking . . . unfair advantage of another's weakness of mind, or . . . taking a grossly oppressive and unfair advantage or another's necessities or distress." While most decided cases of undue influence involve persons in a confidential or authoritative relationship, this is unnecessary when the complaint alleges preying on weakness or distress. All that is required is that the plaintiff have a lessened capacity to make a free contract, or that the defendant used extraordinary force. If will was overcome against judgement, consent may be rescinded. Undue influence usually involves several of these elements: discussing the transaction at an unusual/inappropriate time, executing it at an unusual place, insistent demands it be executed immediately, extreme emphasis on the consequences of delaying, using multiple persuaders against the victim, absence of advisors, and/or statements that there is no time to consult financial advisors or attorneys. Here, School (D) used undue influence to

---

secure Odorizzi's (P) signature, assuring him he should trust them and rely on their advice, that there wasn't time to consult an attorney, and that failing to resign would generate publicity which would jeopardize his career elsewhere. Thus, Odorizzi (P) stated facts sufficient to raise a triable issue of fact and survive summary judgement. We express no opinion on the merits of Odorizzl's (P) case, the propriety of his continued teaching, or the timeliness of his rescission. Reversed.

## Analysis:

Courts will sometimes allow contractual parties to void agreements that were secured by "excessive" pressure. However, the decision on whether any given persuasion was "excessive" is a highly individualistic one, and courts use a fact-specific case-by-case analysis. The court lists scenarios that may indicate undue influence, but the list is neither determinative nor exhaustive. Most undue influence suits involve either a defendant who had a close personal or fiduciary relationship with the victim (e.g., attorney, ward, agent) or a victim whose physical/mental condition made him unusually susceptible to pressure (e.g., old, sick, senile, uneducated). However, undue influence may be present without such relationships or weaknesses. Perfectly rational, independent plaintiffs may claim undue influence if their counter party used extraordinarily coercive persuasion, though they may bear a high burden of proof.

## ■ CASE VOCABULARY

DEMURRER: Archaic term superseded by "motion to dismiss for failure to state a claim." It argues that, even if the complaint's facts are true as alleged, they do not make out an actionable claim. [Here, School (D) effectively claims that, even if it threatened to publicize Odorizzi's (P) arrest, that still doesn't constitute undue influence or duress.]

# Swinton v. Whitinsville Sav. Bank

(Home Buyer) v. (Home Seller)

311 Mass. 677, 42 N.E.2d 808, 141 A.L.R. 965 (1942)

THERE IS NO LIABILITY FOR BARE NONDISCLOSURE

■ **INSTANT FACTS** Whitinsville Bank knew the house it sold to Swinton was infested with termites, but did not tell him about it when making the sale.

■ **BLACK LETTER RULE** A party cannot be held liable for failing to disclose information when there is no evidence of any special duty to disclose anything.

■ **PROCEDURAL BASIS**

Appeal from demurrer in action for damages.

■ **FACTS**

On or about September 12, 1938, Whitinsville Savings Bank (Whitinsville) (D) sold Swinton (P) a house. At the time of sale, the house was infested with termites. Whitinsville (D) knew the house was infested, and did not inform Swinton (P) of this fact. Swinton (P) could not readily observe this condition upon inspection, and had no knowledge of the termites' presence until August 30, 1940. Swinton (P) spent considerable amounts of money in repairing the damage caused by the termites and in installing termite control to prevent the loss and destruction of his (P's) house.

■ **ISSUE**

Can a party be held liable for nondisclosure of information when he or she is not under a duty to disclose the information?

■ **DECISION AND RATIONALE**

(Qua) No. A party cannot be held liable for failing to disclose information when there is no evidence of any special duty to disclose anything. There is no evidence that Whitinsville (D) made any false statements or representations to Swinton (P) regarding termites in the house. Further, Whitinsville (D) did nothing to prevent Swinton (P) from learning this information. Without anything to show a fiduciary relationship between Swinton (P) and Whitinsville (D), characterizing Whitinsville's (D) actions as false and fraudulent does nothing to advance Swinton's (P) claim. If Whitinsville (D) were to be held liable in this matter, then every party in a transaction, whether buyer or seller, could be held liable for failing to disclose any nonapparent fact that he or she is aware of which would materially affect the value of the item or property being sold. The rule of nonliability for bare nondisclosure is binding in this matter. Order sustaining demurrer is affirmed, with judgment for Whitinsville (D).

**Analysis:**

Courts are sometimes willing to hold that failure to disclose facts to remedy a misapprehension, like a buyer's belief that there is no termite problem in a house, amounts to an assertion that the undisclosed fact does not exist. *Swinton* is the leading case against this position, but even the Restatement

(Second) recognizes this growing trend. It provides, in general, that nondisclosure of a particular fact constitutes an assertion that the fact does not exist, if the party knows "that disclosure of the fact would correct a mistake of the other party as to a basic assumption on which the party is making the contract."

# Kannavos v. Annino

(Apartment Buyer) v. (Apartment Owner)

356 Mass. 42, 247 N.E.2d 708 (1969)

---

A PERSON WHO DOES SPEAK IN REFERENCE TO A PARTICULAR PIECE OF INFORMATION MUST SPEAK HONESTLY ABOUT THAT INFORMATION AND DIVULGE ALL MATERIAL FACTS OF WHICH HE OR SHE IS AWARE

---

■ **INSTANT FACTS** Mrs. Annino sold her apartment building to Kannavos without telling him that the building was in violation of the local zoning ordinances.

■ **BLACK LETTER RULE** Although a party may be under no duty to disclose information to another, if that party does speak with reference to a given point of information, then that party is bound to speak honestly and to divulge all the material facts bearing upon that point within that party's knowledge.

■ **PROCEDURAL BASIS**

Appeal from findings by master for bill in equity for rescission.

■ **FACTS**

In the early 1960's, Carrie Annino (P) bought a one-family dwelling. Without obtaining a building permit, and in knowing violation of the local zoning ordinance, Annino (P) converted the eight-apartment, multi-family building. In 1965, she (P) worked with a real estate broker, Foote, to sell the property. The broker placed ads in the newspapers, Including one which read: "income gross $9,600 yr. In lg. single house, converted to 8 lovely, completely furn. (includ. TV and china) apts. 8 baths, ideal for couple to live free with excellent income. By apt. only. Foote Realty." Apostolos Kannavos (P) contacted Foote, who gave him (P) income and expense figures supplied by Annino (D). Kannavos (P) contracted to buy the property. Annino (P) and Foote knew that Kannavos's (P) reason for buying the property was to rent the apartments later. Kannavos (P) was unaware of any zoning or building permit violations, and would not have bought the property if he (P) had known of any such violation. The property was worth substantially more if operated as an apartment building than if kept as a single-family dwelling. Shortly after the sale, the city started legal proceedings to stop the non-conforming use of property. Kannavos (P) brought a bill in equity against Annino (D) to rescind the purchase. The trial court overruled a demurrer, and granted a rescission based on a master's findings. Annino (D) appealed.

■ **ISSUE**

Can a party to a contract be held liable for nondisclosure after partially disclosing material information when that party was under no special duty to disclose in the first place?

■ **DECISION AND RATIONALE**

(Cutter) Yes. Although a party may be under no duty to disclose information to another, if that party does speak with reference to a specific point of information, then he or she is bound to speak honestly and to divulge all the material facts bearing upon that point within his or her knowledge. The court in

*Swinton* applied the longstanding rule of nonliability for bare nondisclosure. The present case, however, differs from *Swinton* in two important respects. The first is that the statements of Annino (D) and Foote went beyond the "bare nondisclosure" that occurred in *Swinton*. Fragmentary Information, such as that provided in the ads for the property, can be as misleading as active misrepresentation, and half-truths can be just as valid causes of actions as total lies. Annino (D) and Foote knew that Kannavos (P) was interested in using the building for apartments. Furnishing Kannavos (P) with income and expense figures demonstrates this knowledge, as does the sale of multiple refrigerators, stoves, and pieces of furniture that were appropriate for use in a multi-apartment building to Kannavos (P). In addition, although Kannavos (P) did not diligently research the public records to learn of the zoning violations, previous cases have not barred recovery for those who did not use due diligence. The ads used in selling the property effectively stated that the property was multi-family housing suitable for investment, and that the housing could continue to be used for that purpose. Because Annino (D) went so far as to say this, she (P) was required to say more about the property. By failing to mention the zoning problems, Annino (D) was responsible for misrepresentation. Decree overruling demurrer affirmed. Final decree reversed to allow further consideration of relief, due to fire that occurred on property.

## Analysis:

In this case, partial disclosure results in misrepresentation, and the court finds an exception to the general rule of no liability for nondisclosure where no duty exists. There are several other exceptions to this rule as well. For example, disclosure may be required by statute or regulation. Also, positive action intended to hamper another party's investigation into the facts of a transaction can result in liability for misrepresentation. Another exception involves a party making a statement in good faith, but then later learning facts that prove the earlier statement was not true, or having that earlier statement rendered false by subsequent events. Such party would have to disclose the new information if he or she knew that the other party was acting in reliance upon that original statement.

# Vokes v. Arthur Murray, Inc.

(Dance Student) v. (Dance School)

212 So.2d 906 (Fla. Distr. Ct. App. 1968)

## EXPERTS' OPINIONS MAY BE ACTIONABLE AS MISREPRESENTATION

■ **INSTANT FACTS** After a dance instructor induces a widow to buy numerous dance lessons by overpraising her skill, she sues for misrepresentation.

■ **BLACK LETTER RULE** False statements of opinion by experts with superior knowledge are actionable as misrepresentations.

## ■ PROCEDURAL BASIS

In contract action seeking rescission, appeal from summary judgement for defendant.

## ■ FACTS

Dance school Arthur Murray, Inc.'s (D) owner Davenport (D) encouraged lonely widow Vokes (P) to take dance classes. Davenport (D) constantly told Vokes (P) she was an excellent dancer, with great potential for learning through additional instruction, and flattered and cajoled her. Over 16 months, Vokes (P) bought 14 dance lesson packages, entitling her to 2302 hours of instruction, for $31K. Later, when Vokes (P) realized she had no talent and could not even hear the rhythm, she sued Arthur Murray (D) for misrepresentation. Davenport (D) and Arthur Murray (D) defended, contending such talk was permissible sales puffery or non-actionable opinion. At trial, the court dismissed for failure to state a claim. Vokes (P) appeals.

## ■ ISSUE

May a contractual party rescind if the contract was induced by an expert's falsely optimistic opinions?

## ■ DECISION AND RATIONALE

(Pierce) Yes. False statements of opinion by experts with superior knowledge are actionable as misrepresentations. Assuming Vokes' (P) complaint's allegations are true, they state a claim for misrepresentation. Vokes' (P) complaint alleges she embarked on an almost endless pursuit of the terpsichorean art, influenced by a continuous barrage of flattery, false praise, panegyric encomiums, overreaching blandishment and cajolery. [See definitions below. And be sure to fill out the attached petition to censure Judge Pierce.] Her purchases of dance lessons were procured by Davenport's (D) and Arthur Murray's (D) false representations that she had excellent potential, and was improving. Vokes (P) alleges their representatives were knowingly false. Vokes (P) also alleges she relied on Davenport's (D) opinion as an expert judge of dancing ability. Generally, misrepresentations must be factual rather than opinion to be actionable. But this rule is inapplicable when a fiduciary relationship exists between the parties, or where the representor employed some artifice or trick, or where the parties do not deal at "arm's length," or where the victim lacks equal opportunity to learn of the represented facts' truth/falsity. Statements by parties having superior knowledge may be regarded as statements of fact, even though they would be considered opinions coming from non-experts. Here, it is conceivable Davenport (D) and Arthur Murray (D) had "superior knowledge" of whether Vokes (P) had "dance potential." Even where a party owes no duty to disclose known information or answer inquiries, if he undertakes to do so, he must disclose the whole truth. Here, it is possible the defendants acquired a duty to tell Vokes (P) her slow and awkward progress did not justify her vast outlay for hundreds of hours of additional instruction. We repeat that, where parties contract at arms' length without inequities or inherently unfair practices, courts generally will leave the parties where they find themselves. But we cannot say as a matter of law that these elements were present here. Reversed.

### Analysis:

*Vokes* provides a rare example of sales "puffery" being actionable as "misrepresentation." Puffery is a salesperson's exaggerated opinion of his or her products' worth or potential, e.g., "This is the hottest stock I've ever seenl It's poised to really take off!" Usually, courts tolerate it on the basis that it involves no false *factual* statements, just unjustified optimism and boundless enthusiasm. *Vokes* takes the unusual position that an opinion, when delivered by an expert as his professional opinion, may be equivalent to a statement of fact. Here, it is likely that Vokes (P) continued her dance training because she believed Davenport's (D) estimation of her skill, though it also seems she was just lonely and likely to believe similar flattery from anyone. *Vokes's* holding is still the exception rather than the rule.

### ■ CASE VOCABULARY

BLANDISHMENT: Praise; flattery.

ENCOMIUM: Praise, especially in an official commendation.

PANEGYRIC: Praise, especially in a eulogy.

PUFFERY: Salesmen's inflated overestimation of their products' worth. Since puffery does not involve factual statements, it is usually not actionable as "misrepresentation."

TERPSICHOREAN: Relating to dancing. In Greek myth, Terpsichore was Muse (angel) of dance.

# CHAPTER FIVE

## Determining the Parties' Obligations Under the Contract: Ascertaining, Interpreting, and Supplementing the Agreement

### Gianni v. R. Russell & Co., Inc.

**Instant Facts:** A store owner tries to hold his landlord to an oral agreement which conflicts with their written lease.

**Black Letter Rule:** An oral agreement cannot be considered a separate, breachable contract if it falls within the scope of a contemporaneous, completely integrated written agreement.

### Masterson v. Sine

**Instant Facts:** A married couple takes possession of their in-laws' ranch, but refuses to honor their in-laws' option to buy it back.

**Black Letter Rule:** A court, when considering a disputed contract, may consider evidence of a collateral agreement if it is of a sort that would naturally be made separately from the disputed contract.

### Bollinger v. Central Pennsylvania Quarry Stripping and Construction Co.

**Instant Facts:** A property owner discovers a missing term in their contract with a construction company.

**Black Letter Rule:** A court of equity is permitted to reform a contract in response to a mutual mistake which rendered the contract's terms incomplete.

### Pacific Gas & Electric Co. v. G.W. Thomas Drayage & Rigging Co.

**Instant Facts:** The parties to a turbine repair contract dispute the interpretation of an indemnification clause in the agreement.

**Black Letter Rule:** Extrinsic evidence of a party's Intent is admissible to assist in the interpretation of a disputed contract term.

### Greenfield v. Philles Records, Inc.

**Instant Facts:** Greenfield (P) signed an agreement that transferred her ownership rights in her singing group's recordings to Philles Records (D), but claimed that relicensing for use by new technologies was not covered by the agreement.

**Black Letter Rule:** The court may not consider extrinsic evidence to interpret a contract or add terms if the agreement on its face is reasonably susceptible of only one meaning.

### W.W.W. Associates, Inc. v. Giancontieri

**Instant Facts:** An Integrated real estate contract gave either party the option to cancel. When the seller unexpectedly cancels, the buyer demands specific performance, contending the option was intended for *his* benefit alone.

**Black Letter Rule:** An unambiguous and final contract may not be reformed based on parol evidence.

### Trident Center v. Connecticut General Life Ins. Co.

**Instant Facts:** A loan document between Trident Center (P) and Connecticut General (D) prohibited prepayment before a certain date, but Trident (P) argued that extrinsic evidence should be admitted to show that prepayment was in fact permitted.

**Black Letter Rule:** Under California law, relevant, extrinsic evidence may be always admitted to show the intent of the parties to a written agreement.

### Frigaliment Importing Co. v. B.N.S. International Sales Corp.

**Instant Facts:** An importer and an exporter dispute the meaning of the word "chicken" in their supply contract.

**Black Letter Rule:** The subjective interpretation of a contract term must be coupled with objective evidence supporting that Interpretation.

### Hurst v. W.J. Lake & Co.

**Instant Facts:** The parties to a transaction involving horse meat scraps dispute the practical interpretation of the terms of their contract.

**Black Letter Rule:** If appropriate, a court may rely on trade usage to inform its interpretation of a seemingly unambiguous contract term.

### Nanakuli Paving & Rock Co. v. Shell Oil Co.

**Instant Facts:** Nanakuli Paving & Rock Co. (P) sued Shell Oil Co. (D) for breach of their 1969 contract based on Shell's (D) failure to protect Nanakuli (P) against increases in asphalt prices.

**Black Letter Rule:** A court may use evidence of standard industry practices and prior performance of parties to the contract to interpret the contract, if such evidence is not inconsistent with the terms of the contract.

### Columbia Nitrogen Corp. v. Royster Co.

**Instant Facts:** Royster (D), seller of phosphate, who had a contract with Columbia Nitrogen Corp. (P) for sale of phosphate, sued the latter for damages for breach of contract when Columbia (P) failed to buy the amount of phosphate agreed upon under their contract.

**Black Letter Rule:** Evidence of custom and usage or course of dealings is not admissible where it contradicts the express, plain, and unambiguous terms of a validly written and fully integrated contract.

### Raffles v. Wichelhaus

**Instant Facts:** Two parties to a cotton transaction disagree as to the exact identity of a ship named in their contract.

**Black Letter Rule:** A contract can be voided if it contains an ambiguous term which was, in fact, interpreted differently by the parties.

### Oswald v. Allen

**Instant Facts:** Two coin collectors each have a different interpretation of a contract for the sale of Swiss coins.

**Black Letter Rule:** A contract should be voided if the parties each held different understandings of an ambiguous term and neither party should have been aware of the other's understanding.

### Colfax Envelope Corp. v. Local No. 458–3M

**Instant Facts:** Colfax (P) signed a collective bargaining agreement that had an erroneous term in it, and when the corrected agreement was sent to it, Colfax (P) tried to renegotiate, saying that it had no contract with Local 458–3M.

**Black Letter Rule:** A party to a contract who agrees to a term knowing that the term is ambiguous may not obtain rescission of the contract based on the ambiguity of that term.

### Koken v. Black & Veatch Construction, Inc.

**Instant Facts:** A fire blanket manufactured by Auburn Manufacturing (D) did not prevent a fire, and Black & Veatch (P) brought a claim for breach of the warranty of merchantability.

**Black Letter Rule:** A breach of the warranty of merchantability is shown when a product does not perform according to the reasonable expectations of an ordinary user or consumer.

### Lewis v. Mobil Oil Corporation

**Instant Facts:** Lewis (P) purchased oil recommended by Mobil (D) for use in hydraulic machinery, but the oil did not function properly and Lewis's (P) machinery was damaged.

**Black Letter Rule:** An implied warranty of fitness arises when the seller has reason to know of the use for which goods are purchased and the buyer relies on the seller's expertise in supplying the proper product.

### South Carolina Electric and Gas Co. v. Combustion Engineering, Inc.

**Instant Facts:** South Carolina Electric and Gas (P) brought a breach of warranty claim against Combustion (D), and Combustion (D) claimed that the warranties of merchantability and fitness had been disclaimed.

**Black Letter Rule:** A disclaimer of warranties will be effective if the circumstances surrounding the sale are sufficient to draw the buyer's attention to the exclusion of warranties.

### Henningsen v. Bloomfield Motors, Inc.

**Instant Facts:** Henningsen sued Bloomfield for breach of warranty after the steering in his new car failed, and Bloomfield countered with a disclaimer written in fine print.

**Black Letter Rule:** Disclaimers and attempted limitations of warranties or liability, whether in a public, quasi-public, or private contract, are not enforceable unless the limitation is fairly and honestly made and understandingly entered into.

# Gianni v. R. Russell & Co., Inc.

(Store owner) v. (Landlord)
281 Pa. 320, 126 A. 791 (1924)

PENNSYLVANIA SUPREME COURT APPLIES THE PAROL EVIDENCE RULE TO AN ORAL AGREE-MENT THAT FALLS WITHIN THE SCOPE OF A CONTEMPORANEOUS WRITTEN CONTRACT

■ **INSTANT FACTS** A store owner tries to hold his landlord to an oral agreement which conflicts with their written lease.

■ **BLACK LETTER RULE** An oral agreement cannot be considered a separate, breachable contract if it falls within the scope of a contemporaneous, completely integrated written agreement.

■ **PROCEDURAL BASIS**

Appeal from a trial court judgement for the plaintiff in a breach of contract action.

■ **FACTS**

Gianni (P) owned a small store inside an office building that was taken over by R. Russell & Co., Inc. (Russell) (D). The parties negotiated a new lease for Gianni (P), agreeing on its terms. Gianni (P) was permitted to sell fruit, candy and soda, among other items, but he was not allowed to sell tobacco. Gianni (P) claims, however, that he and Russell's (D) agent came to a separate oral agreement during the course of lease negotiations. This agreement, he alleges, gave him the exclusive right to sell soft drinks in the building. This provision does not appear in the written agreement. Russell (D) subsequently rented space to a drug company, permitting it to sell soft drinks as well. Gianni (P) then sued Russell (D) for breach of the oral agreement. He presented a witness who heard Russell's (D) agent agree to the exclusivity provision. In addition, Gianni (P) testified that the oral agreement was mentioned again at the signing of the written lease. Indeed, he claims that he signed the new lease in reliance on the oral agreement. Russell (D) denies the existence of any agreement other than the written lease. Nonetheless, the trial court found for Gianni (P). Russell (D) appeals.

■ **ISSUE**

Is an oral agreement which conflicts with a contemporaneous written agreement enforceable?

■ **DECISION AND RATIONALE**

(Schaffer) No. Gianni (P) argues that he and Russell (D) had an oral agreement which was completely independent of their written agreement. This is not the case. Once the parties to a negotiation arrive at a written contract, it is presumed to be the best and only evidence of their obligations. At this point, all of their preliminary negotiations are merged with the written contract. The court will not consider evidence of other agreements which would alter the contract's terms, otherwise known as parol evidence, unless a party alleges fraud, accident or mistake. That said, it is still necessary to examine the contract itself in order to determine whether it constitutes the entire agreement between the parties. If the contract's terms appear to satisfy its goals, without any uncertainty, then the contract is presumed to be the complete agreement between the parties. In that event, the court must determine whether the oral agreement falls within the field of the written contract. If it does, then they cannot be considered separate agreements and the written contract will govern the parties' relationship. However, if the oral agreement does not fall within the field of the written contract, it may be considered a wholly separate contract. In order to make this determination, the court must decide whether the parties would naturally have included the oral agreement within the written lease. In other words, we must decide whether the subject matter of the two agreements is so interrelated that they would normally be contained in a single contract. In this case, the terms of the written contract control Glanni's (P) ability to sell certain items in the store. He is permitted to sell soda, candy and other items, but is not permitted to sell tobacco. These terms would naturally cover an agreement that granted Gianni (P) the exclusive right to sell soft drinks in the building. In fact, Gianni (P) claims that he agreed not to sell tobacco as consideration for this right. This makes it more difficult to interpret the oral agreement as a distinct contract. Normally, the consideration for a promise and the promise itself are contained in a single contract. With that in mind, we find that the subject matter of Glanni's (P) written contract encompasses the alleged oral agreement. That being the case, we cannot recognize an action on the oral contract as a separate agreement. We are also precluded from considering it as evidence of the terms of the written contract since it would alter those terms. The judgement of the trial court will be reversed and entered, Instead, in Russell's (D) favor.

## Analysis:

According to the Restatement, two types of agreements are subject to the parol evidence rule integrated agreements and completely integrated agreements. An integrated agreement discharges prior agreements to the extent that it is inconsistent with them. This rule precludes consideration of prior agreements that would alter the terms of a current agreement. A *completely* integrated agreement, on the other hand, discharges prior agreements to the extent that they fall within its scope. A completely integrated agreement is usually identified as such by a merger clause. A merger clause might read, "This agreement is the complete and final statement of any and all rights and obligations of the parties." Interestingly, judge Schaffer applies the law concerning both types of agreements to Glanni's (D) lease. This should not be surprising since a completely integrated agreement is, necessarily, an integrated agreement. More often than not, though, he treats the lease as a completely integrated agreement. He refers to this agreement as the "entire agreement" or the "complete agreement" between the parties. Judge Schaffer then goes on to determine whether the exclusivity agreement falls within the "field" or scope of the written lease. However, it is more important to keep in mind the policy behind the parol evidence rule. The rule is intended to preserve the integrity of written contracts. Courts do not look favorably on a party's efforts to circumvent a written agreement by alleging other communications that would alter its terms. In fact, the rule is so commonly applied that it exists, in substantially the same form, in the Uniform Commercial Code as in the Restatement (Second) of Contracts.

## ■ CASE VOCABULARY

MERGER: A term which describes the integration of prior agreements into a completed written contract

PAROL EVIDENCE RULE: The simplest version of this rule can be found in the Uniform Commercial Code. The rule renders an earlier or contemporaneous oral agreement unenforceable if it contradicts the terms of a current written agreement. The same rule can be found, albeit in a slightly more complicated form, in the Restatement (Second) of Contracts.

# Masterson v. Sine

(In-Laws) v. (Ranch Owners)

68 Cal.2d 222, 65 Cal.Rptr. 545, 436 P.2d 561 (1968)

CALIFORNIA SUPREME COURT DISTINGUISHES BETWEEN A GRANT DEED OPTION AND A SEPA-RATE CONTRACT LIMITING ITS ASSIGNABILITY

■ **INSTANT FACTS** A married couple takes possession of their in-laws' ranch, but refuses to honor their in-laws' option to buy it back.

■ **BLACK LETTER RULE** A court, when considering a disputed contract, may consider evidence of a collateral agreement if it is of a sort that would naturally be made separately from the disputed contract.

## ■ PROCEDURAL BASIS

Appeal from a trial court judgement in favor of the plaintiff in an action for declaratory relief.

## ■ FACTS

The Mastersons (P) owned a piece of property as tenants in common [the actual plaintiffs in this case were Mrs. Masterson and her husband's trustee in bankruptcy]. They transferred this property to Mr. Masterson's (P) sister and her husband, Lu Sine (D). The Mastersons (P) retained an option in the grant deed to buy back the land within ten years. If they exercised the option, the Mastersons (P) were obligated to pay an amount equal to "the same consideration as paid heretofore," plus the depreciation value of any improvements that the Sines (D) made to the property after two and a half years. These confusing payment terms were part of the subsequent litigation between the parties. The litigation was sparked by the Masterson's (P) desire to repurchase the property. At the time, Mr. Masterson (P) was bankrupt. His trustee in bankruptcy and Mrs. Masterson (P) brought an action for declaratory relief. They sought an interpretation of the agreement which would secure their right to exercise the repurchase option. During the trial, the court admitted extrinsic evidence which resolved the confusing payment terms. The court found that the parties intended "the same consideration as paid heretofore" to equal $50,000. In addition, the parties intended the depreciation value of any improvements to be measured by United States income tax regulations. The Sines (D), however, wanted to present extrinsic evidence that the option provision was nonassignable because it was intended to keep the property in the family. As a result, the Sines (D) argued that the option could not be exercised by Masterson's (P) trustee in bankruptcy. The trial court rejected this evidence as a violation of the parol evidence rule and found for the Mastersons (P). The Sines (D) appeal. Rather than dispute the exclusion of their own evidence, they claim that the trial court erred in admitting extrinsic evidence to clarify the option payment terms.

## ■ ISSUE

Can extrinsic evidence be used to clarify the terms of an agreement which would otherwise remain too uncertain to be enforceable?

## ■ DECISION AND RATIONALE

(Traynor) Yes. The trial court was justified in admitting extrinsic evidence in order to further the goals of the parties by clarifying the terms of their agreement. The trial court erred, however, in refusing to admit any evidence regarding the Mastersons' (P) right to assign the option. The crucial question in this case is whether the agreement between the Mastersons (P) and the Sines (D) was an integration. By this, we mean a contract which the parties intended to be their final and exclusive agreement. There are two ways to determine whether a contract is an integration. First, a court can rely on the language of the contract itself. Frequently, a contract will contain language which identifies it as an integration. If so, the parol evidence rule precludes the consideration of evidence which would alter the contract's terms. Without this language, a court can either find that the contract is not an integration, or it can look at the circumstances surrounding the transaction to make its determination. However, even if the contract states that it is an integration, it may be necessary to look at other agreements between the parties in order to decide whether they fall within its scope or whether they are separate agreements. This is particularly necessary when a contract is silent on a point which is disputed by the parties. As a result, it has proven impossible to rely solely on the language of the contract in order to determine its status. This does not obviate the need for the parol evidence rule, however. Several policies have been advanced for the preservation of the rule. First, the written word may be inherently more reliable than a party's memory of contract negotiations. Second, courts are afraid that witnesses will be encouraged to manufacture contract terms which are favorable to the respective parties. Finally, courts fear that juries may be overly sympathetic to parties who seek the introduction of parol evidence, since they are usually the underdogs in the dispute. All of these policies reflect a desire to ensure the credibility of evidence in contract disputes. The Restatement and the Uniform Commercial Code take two different approaches to this evidence. The Restatement admits evidence of collateral agreements only if the parties would naturally have made them as separate agreements from the contract in question. The UCC excludes this evidence only if the parties would certainly have made the agreements part of the contract. In this case, the contract does not state that it is an integration. It is also silent on the question of assignability. However, a deed, by its very nature, is unlikely to embody all of the rights and obligations of the parties. The Mastersons (P) may have included the option provision to put potential buyers on notice of their reserved rights. There is no evidence to suggest that the parties understood the danger of not including the entire agreement in the deed. As a result, the Restatement-and the UCC tests are both satisfied. The assignment provision would naturally be agreed to in a separate document, calling for its admission under the Restatement. Similarly, under the UCC, it cannot be said that the parties would certainly have included the assignment provision in the grant deed since it was not the proper document in which to place such a provision. The Mastersons (P), on the other hand, claim that option provisions are presumptively assignable regardless of the language of the contract. This does not prevent the court from considering parol evidence which might defeat this presumption, however. As a result, the trial court erred in excluding evidence on the assignment provision and its judgement must be reversed.

### ■ DISSENT

(Burke) I dispute the majority's findings on virtually every issue in this case. First, the majority violates the spirit of the parol evidence rule by permitting evidence of a collateral agreement to obliterate an existing written agreement. This compromises the reliability of many transactions, including conveyances and debtor/creditor relationships. The central problem with the majority's approach is its failure to acknowledge the strength of option agreements in general, and the nature of the option in this case, in particular. Options are, by nature, assignable property rights. The only way to limit an option is by specific language in the agreement. If this rule were otherwise, a party to a contract could always find a way out of an unfavorable option by fabricating an agreement which limited its effect. In this case, the Mastersons' (P) creditor is deprived of a valid property right as a result of this approach. The majority invites this result by characterizing the parol evidence rule as a rule of credibility. The parol evidence rule is specifically designed to exclude *any* extrinsic evidence of a contract's terms, not just evidence which might be unreliable. This is because extrinsic evidence is presumed to be unreliable. In addition, the majority favors the Restatement's approach to the parol evidence rule. California courts must now determine whether an agreement would naturally be arrived at separately from the disputed contract. Courts might easily disagree as to whether an agreement was naturally separate or not, however. Finally, the majority relies on the fact that the agreement is a deed in order to determine that the absence of the assignment provision is to be expected. This is absurd. If the option itself is contained in the deed, why would the parties have shrunk from including one more line, limiting the option's assignability. For all of these reasons, I would affirm the judgement of the trial court.

**Analysis:**

Justice Traynor is willing to look at all aspects of the parties' transaction in order to determine whether the parol evidence rule applies here. Justice Burke is clearly uncomfortable with this approach. He is more likely to favor the "four comers" approach to contract interpretation. This approach limits the court's attention to the language of the contract. However, Justice Burke loses sight of the fact that deeds and contracts are not equivalent documents. Indeed, he berates the majority for resting its interpretation on this distinction. However, parties do not usually put the details of a real estate transaction in the deed. In this case, the Mastersons (P) were obviously concerned with securing their right to repurchase the property. They might have put this provision in the deed in order to avoid fighting a future purchaser for the return of the property after it was already sold. Once they added the provision, however, they invited the difficulties that arose in this case—namely, that any caveats that might limit their repurchase option would normally be in the contract of sale, another legally enforceable document. Think of the deed as a declaration of rights and the contract of sale as an agreement regarding those rights. The majority relies on this distinction as the key to its analysis.

# Bollinger v. Central Pennsylvania Quarry Stripping and Construction Co.

(Property Owner) v. (Construction Company)

425 Pa. 430, 229 A.2d 741 (1967)

PENNSYLVANIA SUPREME COURT AFFIRMS THE EQUITABLE REFORMATION OF A CONTRACT TO CONFORM TO THE PARTIES' INTENT

■ **INSTANT FACTS** A property owner discovers a missing term in their contract with a construction company.

■ **BLACK LETTER RULE** A court of equity is permitted to reform a contract in response to a mutual mistake which rendered the contract's terms incomplete.

■ **PROCEDURAL BASIS**

Appeal from an equity court decree in favor of the plaintiff in an action for contract reformation.

■ **FACTS**

The Central Pennsylvania Quarry Stripping Construction Company (Central) (D) had an agreement permitting it to deposit construction waste on the Bollingers' (P) property. Central (D) was working on the Pennsylvania Turnpike and the Bollingers' (P) property was conveniently nearby. The Bollingers (P) thought the parties had a mutual understanding regarding the disposition of the waste. They were under the impression that Central (D) would remove the topsoil from their property before depositing the construction waste. Central (D) was then supposed to restore the topsoil, covering whatever waste they deposited on the property. In fact, Central (D) followed this plan at the beginning of the job. After a while they stopped removing and replacing the topsoil. When the Bollingers (P) complained, Central (D) told them there was nothing they could do. In fact, the agreement between the Bollingers (P) and Central (D) did not contain any provisions regarding the removal and replacement of topsoil. The Bollingers (P) sued for reformation of the contract to include their original understanding. The equity court granted their request. Central (D) now appeals.

■ **ISSUE**

Can a court of equity add terms to a written contract on the basis of a contemporaneous oral agreement?

■ **DECISION AND RATIONALE**

(Musmanno) Yes. A court of equity has the power to amend a written contract in order to make it conform to the understanding of the parties. The need for reformation might arise from a mistake which led to an incomplete statement of the parties rights. This mistake must have been mutual in order for reformation to be proper. This does not mean that both parties must admit to the mistake. It simply means that the court must determine that a mutual mistake has been made. Normally, a party is bound by the terms of a completed, signed contract. In the case of mutual mistake, though, it is appropriate for an equity court to acknowledge the original intent of the parties. In this case, the Chancellor was satisfied that the parties had agreed to the topsoil provisions. Indeed, Central (D) began performance as if it were bound by those provisions. It removed and replaced the Bollingers'

(P) topsoil as they went along. They also provided a similar service to the Bollingers' (P) neighbors. Despite the Chancellor's findings, Central (D) tried to garner a rehearing based on newly discovered evidence. This evidence is not at odds with the Chancellor's findings, however. As a result, the equity court's decree is affirmed.

**Analysis:**

It is important to recall the special role that courts of equity play in the legal system. They are specifically empowered to resolve disputes according to principles of fairness, as opposed to strict rules of law. Even though most equity courts have been merged with courts of law, a plaintiff may still request equitable relief if the circumstances call for it. In this case, the evidence was sufficient for the Chancellor to determine that it would be unfair to hold the Bollingers (P) to the written contract. This may have been an easy case, considering that Central (D) acted according to the terms of the topsoil provisions despite their absence in the contract. However, the same result would almost certainly have been unavailable in a breach of contract action, because the topsoil provisions were not the sort of terms that would be found anywhere but in the written agreement.

### ■ CASE VOCABULARY

REFORMATION: An equitable remedy which permits the court to reinterpret a contract in conformance with the demonstrated intent of the parties.

# Pacific Gas & Electric Co. v. G.W. Thomas Drayage & Rigging Co.

(Turbine Owner) v. (Turbine Repairmen)

69 Cal.2d 33, 69 Cal.Rptr. 561, 442 P.2d 641 (1968)

---

## CALIFORNIA SUPREME COURT ADMITS EXTRINSIC EVIDENCE TO SETTLE A DISPUTE OVER A CONTRACT TERM

---

■ **INSTANT FACTS** The parties to a turbine repair contract dispute the interpretation of an indemnification clause in the agreement.

■ **BLACK LETTER RULE** Extrinsic evidence of a party's Intent is admissible to assist in the interpretation of a disputed contract term.

---

## ■ FACTS

G.W. Thomas Drayage & Rigging Co. (Thomas) (D) agreed to replace the cover on Pacific Gas & Electric Co.'s (PG&E) (P) steam turbine. The agreement required Thomas (D) to indemnify PG&E (P) against any property damage resulting from Thomas's (D) work. To that end, Thomas (D) was obligated to purchase an insurance policy with more than $50,000 liability coverage for property damage. PG&E (P) was to be listed as an additional insured. In addition, PG&E (P) was supposed to be specifically covered for damage to its property. Thomas (D) subsequently damaged PG&E's (P) engine in the course of its work. PG&E (P) then sued Thomas (D), requesting the cost of repairs under the indemnification clause. Thomas (D) argued that the indemnification clause only covered damage to property owned by third parties. The trial court rejected its proof on this issue, however. The judge acknowledged that the indemnification clause was of a sort which normally covered only the property of third parties. Nonetheless, he decided that the plain language of the contract indemnified against damage to PG&E's (P) property as well. The trial court then found in favor of PG&E (P). Thomas (D) appeals.

## ■ ISSUE

Is a court required to admit extrinsic evidence which may assist in the interpretation of a disputed contract term?

## ■ DECISION AND RATIONALE

(Traynor) Yes. It is not appropriate for a judge to presume that his interpretation of particular contract language is so secure that it could not be swayed by relevant evidence to the contrary. The judge's own linguistic ability is not infallible, nor is the language in the contract likely to be free from any ambiguities. We understand that many judges rely on particular language to give rise to certain contractual obligations. However, California courts should not rely on the magical incantation of special phrases in order to create and destroy contract rights. Contractual obligations are created by the intent of the parties. If a court can determine this intent from the language of the contract, then it need not admit any further evidence. However, language is seldom so clear as to warrant this approach. Ordinarily, the court must admit any evidence which is "relevant to prove a meaning to which the language of the instrument is reasonably susceptible." This rule does not compromise the parol evidence rule, which still precludes the consideration of evidence which would add to or vary the terms of a contract. Instead, the rule protects the parties' intent by using the circumstances

---

surrounding the transaction as a guide to the meaning of their contract. The judge must at least take a preliminary look at the parties' evidence in order to determine if it should be admitted. He should endeavor to place himself in the circumstances in which the parties found themselves at the time of contracting. The judge can do this through the consideration of evidence regarding the contract's object, nature and subject matter, among other things. If the court cannot settle on a single interpretation of the contract's language at this point, then extrinsic evidence should be admissible to further its interpretation. In this case, the trial court erred in two ways. First, the court refused to consider extrinsic evidence which was relevant to the determination of whether the Indemnification clause covered PG&E's (P) property. Second, the court failed to admit this evidence even though the indemnification clause was equivocal on this point. As a result, the trial court's judgement must be reversed.

## Analysis:

Chief Justice Traynor's views are controversial. Some commentators feel that his approach subverts the parol evidence rule to the point where there is little left to enforce. He does walk a fine line between admitting evidence of subjective intent and permitting that intent to govern and change the contract in a way that violates the parol evidence rule. He defends this approach as a means of protecting the intent of the parties. There is validity in this defense. Contracts are supposed to reflect the common intent of the parties. When the language of the contract itself fails to make this intent clear, a court must resort to other evidence of the parties' intent in order to preserve the enforceability of the contract. As shown in *Oswald v. Allen*, there is a point at which this evidence fails to yield a consensus and the contract is unenforceable. Chief Justice Traynor tries to avoid this result rather than surrender to it without a fight.

# Greenfield v. Philles Records, Inc.

(Singer) v. (Record Producer)

98 N.Y.2d 562, 780 N.E.2d 166, 750 N.Y.S.2d 565 (2002)

CALIFORNIA AND NEW YORK LAW DIFFER ON CONTRACT INTERPRETATION

He only wanted me while young, but he wants my music forever and in "any method now or hereafter known".

Divorce Specialist

stus.com

■ **INSTANT FACTS** Greenfield (P) signed an agreement that transferred her ownership rights in her singing group's recordings to Philles Records (D), but claimed that relicensing for use by new technologies was not covered by the agreement.

■ **BLACK LETTER RULE** The court may not consider extrinsic evidence to interpret a contract or add terms if the agreement on its face is reasonably susceptible of only one meaning.

■ **PROCEDURAL BASIS**

Appeal from an order affirming a judgment for Greenfield (P).

■ **FACTS**

Greenfield (P) was a member of a singing group, "The Ronettes." In 1963, Greenfield (P) and the other members of the group signed a recording contract with Philles Records (D). The contract provided that Greenfield (P) and her group would perform exclusively for Philles (D), and that Philles (D) would acquire an ownership right to the recordings of the Ronettes' musical performances. The ownership provision stated that "[a]ll recordings made hereunder ... shall be entirely [Philles's] property_.._.. .. [Philles] shall have the right to make phonograph records, tape recordings or other reproductions of the performances embodied in such recordings by any method now or hereafter known, and to sell and deal in the same...." The agreement also provided for royalties for the Ronettes. Greenfield (P) and the other members of the group shared a $15,000 advance from Philles (D), but received no further payments.

The Ronettes recorded several songs for Philles (D). In 1967, the group disbanded, and Philles (D) eventually went out of business. Greenfield (P) married Phil Spector, the owner of Philles, in 1968, but they separated and ultimately divorced in 1974. As a part of the divorce settlement, Spector and Greenfield (P) executed mutual releases that purported to resolve all claims and obligations between them, including those between Spector's companies and Greenfield (P).

Some years after the Ronettes disbanded, Philles (D) began to license recordings of the Ronettes' performances for use in movie and television productions (a process called "synchronization"). Philles (D) also licensed master recordings to third-parties for production and distribution in the United States, and sold compilation albums containing performances by the Ronettes. Philles (D) paid no royalties to Greenfield (P) or any of the other members of the group. Greenfield (P) brought a breach of contract action against Philles (D), alleging that the 1963 agreement did not grant the right to license recordings for synchronization or domestic redistribution. The trial court entered judgment for Greenfield (P). The appellate court affirmed, holding that the 1963 agreement did not specifically transfer the right to issue synchronization or third-party distribution licenses.

■ **ISSUE**

Did the absence in the contract of a specific reference to new media or markets prohibit the exploitation of the recordings in those new media or markets?

## ■ DECISION AND RATIONALE

(Graffeo, J.) No. The court may not consider extrinsic evidence to interpret a contract or add terms if the agreement on its face is reasonably susceptible of only one meaning. Contracts are to be construed according to the intent of the parties, and the best way of determining that intent is to consider what is said in writing. Extrinsic evidence of the parties' intent may be considered only when a contract is ambiguous, and the existence of an ambiguity is a question of law. Here, the contract's silence on synchronization and domestic licensing does not create an ambiguity. Because there is no ambiguity, Philles (D) is entitled to exercise complete ownership rights, subject to the payment of royalties to Greenfield (P).

Philles (D) also argued that Greenfield's (P) suit is barred by the divorce settlement agreement between her and Spector. The release was executed in California, so California law will be considered to determine the validity of the release. California courts consider all credible evidence of the parties' intent, and do not limit the inquiry to the four corners of the agreement. The trial court in this case ruled that Greenfield's (P) right to compensation under the 1963 agreement was not an intended subject of the release. There is no reason to reverse that determination. The case is affirmed as modified.

### Analysis:

The court's opinion validates the "catch-all" clause ("any method now or hereafter known") used in many licensing agreements. A catch-all clause is a way of expressing the parties' intentions regarding uses of a property that are not envisioned at the time the licensing agreement is made. The absence of such a clause has often cost performers or writers a substantial amount of royalties when entirely new uses are made of their work. For example, the lack of a "catch-all" clause has been held to deprive performers of royalties when a theatrical film is reissued on home video, even when the home video version proves more profitable than the original release.

# W.W.W. Associates, Inc. v. Giancontieri

(Real Estate Buyer) v. (Real Estate Seller)

77 N.Y.2d 157, 565 N.Y.S.2d 440, 566 N.E.2d 639 (1990)

COURTS WILL NOT DISTURB COMPLETE AND UNAMBIGUOUS CONTRACTS FOR PAROL EVIDENCE

■ **INSTANT FACTS** An Integrated real estate contract gave either party the option to cancel. When the seller unexpectedly cancels, the buyer demands specific performance, contending the option was intended for *his* benefit alone.

■ **BLACK LETTER RULE** An unambiguous and final contract may not be reformed based on parol evidence.

■ **PROCEDURAL BASIS**

In real estate contract action seeking specific performance, appeal from reversal of judgment for defendant.

■ **FACTS**

W.W.W. Associates, Inc. ("W.W.W.") (P) contracted to buy real estate from Glancontieri (P). During negotiations, Giancontieri (D) learned that a lawsuit against W.W.W. (P) had resulted in a lis pendens filing against the property. Giancontieri (D) feared the suit might impair his ability to obtain title insurance and construction loans. Thus, the contract included a reciprocal cancellation clause, which read: "Sellers have been served with process instituting an action concerning the real property . . . . In the event the closing of title is delayed by . . . such litigation [then] closing . . . will . . . be adjourned until after the conclusion of such litigation *provided, in the event such litigation is not concluded, by . . . 6–1–87 either party shall have the right to cancel this contract whereupon the down payment shall be returned and there shall be no further rights hereunder.*" Also, the contract had a merger clause disclaiming all prior agreements. The litigation was still pending on that date and the closing was postponed, but Giancontieri (D) later canceled for unrelated reasons (allegedly, it believed it could obtain a better price elsewhere). W.W.W. (P) sued Giancontieri (D) for specific performance, contending the cancellation clause was Intended only to benefit *it* in the event the litigation interfered with its plans to build on the land, and that Giancontieri (D) breached in bad faith in the hope of obtaining a higher price. Giancontieri (D) moved for summary judgment, contending the contract as written allowed both parties to cancel, and that contrary parol evidence is inadmissible. At trial, the court dismissed the complaint, finding the right to cancel was mutual. On appeal, the appellate division reversed and ordered specific performance.

■ **ISSUE**

May a clear and final contract be modified based on 1 party's parol evidence?

■ **DECISION AND RATIONALE**

(Kaye) No. An unambiguous and final contract may not be reformed based on parol evidence. The law's policy is that, when parties record their agreement in a clear, complete document, their writing should generally be enforced according to its terms. Usually, evidence outside the document's four corners, regarding what was really Intended but unstated/misstated, is inadmissible. This rule imparts stability to commercial transactions by preventing fraudulent claims, perjury, mistaken recollections, and jury error. This policy is most compelling in real property transactions, where certainty is paramount. Whether a contract is ambiguous is a question of law for the courts. Here, the contract plainly manifests that *both* parties have the option to cancel. In addition, the merger clause states this contract expresses the parties' full agreement. Further, there is a logical reason why Giancontieri (D) would want to retain the option's protection: a seller taking back a purchase-money mortgage might well wish to reserve its option to sell the property if litigation affecting the property continues past a certain date. Thus, the contract contains no ambiguity. It is settled that extrinsic and parol evidence is inadmissible to create ambiguities in written agreements that are complete, clear, and unambiguous on their face. Here, the written contract is clear and unambiguous, and should be enforced as written. There is no evidence of bad faith. Reversed.

## Analysis:

Under the "plain meaning" approach, courts evaluating whether to admit extrinsic evidence in a completely integrated contract follow a two stage process. First, the court decides whether the contract's language is "ambiguous." Generally, judges will analyze only the "four corners" of the document (i.e., only the document itself, without regard to the circumstances or extrinsic claims). Legally, "ambiguous" means that the words may reasonably be interpreted in more than one way. Next, if the contract is ambiguous; the court will admit extrinsic evidence relevant to the question of what the words mean, or which of several meanings was the intended one. Needless to say, judges are widely divided on how much ambiguity is necessary before extrinsic evidence becomes admissible, and the outcome of any given case is often unpredictable.

## ■ CASE VOCABULARY

LIS PENDENS: "Pending lawsuit." A court-issued notice that some property (personal property or land) is subject to a lawsuit, and may be confiscated if the plaintiff wins. The notice is not itself a lien, but potential purchasers are put on notice, and will be unwilling to buy land which may later be turned over to a plaintiff.

MERGER CLAUSE: A contractual provision stating the contract represents the final agreement reached by the party, intended to preclude parol evidence. It is called a "merger" agreement because it often states that the written agreement "merges" (incorporates and supersedes) all prior agreements.

TITLE INSURANCE: Landowner's policy insurance which reimburses the landowner, or a later purchaser which buys from the landowner, for the cost and loss from another claimant's suit contending another person has title to (true legal ownership of) the land.

# Trident Center v. Connecticut General Life Ins. Co.

(Building Partnership) v. (Lender)

847 F.2d 564 (9th Cir. 1988)

THE PARTIES' INTENT CONTROLS OVER THE WRITTEN WORD

Parole Evidence
Firing Squad

■ **INSTANT FACTS** A loan document between Trident Center (P) and Connecticut General (D) prohibited prepayment before a certain date, but Trident (P) argued that extrinsic evidence should be admitted to show that prepayment was in fact permitted.

■ **BLACK LETTER RULE** Under California law, relevant, extrinsic evidence may be always admitted to show the intent of the parties to a written agreement.

## ■ PROCEDURAL BASIS

Appeal from an order dismissing a complaint and sanctioning Trident (P) for bringing a frivolous lawsuit.

## ■ FACTS

In 1983, Trident Center (P), a partnership made up of an insurance company and two large law firms, negotiated a loan from Connecticut General (D) to finance construction of an office building complex. The written loan agreement provided for an interest rate of 12-¼% for a term of fifteen years. The agreement also provided that the loan could not be prepaid "in whole or in part" for the first twelve years of the agreement. In the event of a default, the agreement gave Connecticut General (D) the option of accelerating the note and adding a ten-percent prepayment fee.

In 1987, interest rates were lower, and Trident (P) sought to refinance the loan to take advantage of the lower interest rates. Connecticut General (D) was unwilling to allow refinancing, insisting that the loan could not be prepaid until 1996. Trident (P) brought suit, seeking a declaration that it was entitled to prepay the loan. Connecticut General (D) moved for dismissal of the suit, claiming that the loan agreement clearly and unambiguously precluded prepayment. The trial court dismissed Trident's (P) complaint, and also sanctioned Trident (P) for filing a frivolous complaint. Trident (P) appealed, arguing that the written agreement was ambiguous. Trident (P) also argued that, under California law, written contracts are subject to modification by parol or extrinsic evidence.

## ■ ISSUE

Is parol evidence admissible to show the parties' intent?

## ■ DECISION AND RATIONALE

(Kozinski, J.) Yes. Under California law, relevant, extrinsic evidence may be always admitted to show the intent of the parties to a written agreement. The traditional rule is that extrinsic evidence may not be used to alter or contradict the terms of a written agreement; however, the California Supreme Court, in the case of *Pacific Gas & Electric Co. v. G.W. Thomas Drayage & Rigging Co.*, 69 Cal. 2d 33, 442 P. 2d 641 (1968), ruled that extrinsic evidence is admissible even if the written contract is not ambiguous. According to the court, contractual obligations flow from the intention of the parties, not from the words of the contract. Words do not have absolute and constant referents, so it is not possible to discern contractual intention in the words or the arrangements of the words themselves. The belief in the possibility of perfect verbal expression is a remnant of the primitive faith in the potency and inherent meaning of words.

*Pacific Gas* casts a long shadow of uncertainty over all agreements negotiated and drafted under California law. No contract is impervious to attack by parol evidence. If one party to a contract is willing to claim that the parties intended something other than what is stated in the contract, the court must consider evidence of possible ambiguity. If the evidence discloses an ambiguity where there was none before, the contract language is displaced and the intention of the parties must be discerned through the testimony of witnesses. The witnesses may have a stake in the litigation, or their memories may be made hazy by the passage of time or colored by their own self-interest. It is questionable whether this approach is more likely to reveal the true intention of the parties than reliance on the written language agreed upon at the time the contract was made.

*Pacific Gas* also chips away at the foundation of the legal system. If courts are unwilling to enforce language arrived at by parties dealing face-to-face, how can courts send anyone to jail for violating statutes that consist of "mere words"? How can courts enforce decrees, or carry out the mandate of higher courts, if "perfect verbal expression" is impossible? But still, that is the law.

Trident (P) also claims that the contract in the instant case is ambiguous because a prepayment penalty is imposed in the event of acceleration due to default. Trident (P) claims that this clause gives it the right to prepay. This argument is rejected out of hand.

The trial court's decision is reversed, and the case remanded to allow Trident (P) to introduce extrinsic evidence as to the intention of the parties in drafting the contract.

---

**Analysis:**

Courts nationwide have moved away from the traditional absolute prohibition against extrinsic evidence, but the California courts have gone farther than most, by imposing virtually no restrictions on the situations in which extrinsic evidence may be introduced. It is perhaps going too far to say that written contracts have no significance in California law, but the legal certainty of a written agreement is unquestionably diminished. While as a matter of linguistic theory there may be no reason to prefer written language over other expressions of intent, the written document does give the parties to a contract a clear, definite statement of their rights and obligations. Such a definite statement makes enforcement of the parties' intent easier, even if less accurate in the abstract.

---

# Frigaliment Importing Co. v. B.N.S. International Sales Corp.

(Chicken Importer) v. (Chicken Exporter)

190 F.Supp. 116 (S.D.N.Y. 1960)

DISTRICT COURT APPLIES THE CANONS OF INTERPRETATION TO A CHICKEN CONTRACT

■ **INSTANT FACTS** An importer and an exporter dispute the meaning of the word "chicken" in their supply contract.

■ **BLACK LETTER RULE** The subjective interpretation of a contract term must be coupled with objective evidence supporting that Interpretation.

■ **PROCEDURAL BASIS**

District court judgement on a breach of warranty action.

■ **FACTS**

B.N.S. International Sales Corp. (B.N.S.) (D) is an exporting firm based in New York. Frigaliment Importing Co. (Frigaliment) (P) is a Swiss import firm represented by its agent, Mr. Stovicek. B.N.S. (D) had two contracts to supply Frigaliment (P) with frozen chickens. The first contract called for 25,000 lbs. of 1½- to 2-pound chickens at $36.50 per 100 lbs. It also listed 75,000 lbs. of 2½- to 3-pound chickens at $33.00 per 100 lbs. The second contract called for different quantities of each weight and listed the 1½- to 2-pound chickens at $37.00 per 100 lbs. The two contracts had delivery dates of May 2, 1957 and May 30, 1957, respectively. The problem arose when the first delivery arrived. Frigaliment (P) was expecting the 2½- to 3-pound chickens to be broiler/fryers. As it turns out, B.N.S (D) shipped 2½- to 3-pound *stewing* chickens, which are older than broiler/fryers. Frigaliment (P) complained about the mix-up but accepted the second shipment. This shipment also contained stewing chickens instead of broiler/fryers. It then sued B.N.S. (D) for breach of warranty, claiming that B.N.S. (D) delivered goods that did not correspond to the description in the contract.

■ **ISSUE**

Can a court resolve a dispute based on differing interpretations of contract vocabulary?

■ **DECISION AND RATIONALE**

(Friendly) Yes. The parties urge different interpretations of the word "chicken". In order to resolve this dispute, the court will look at the contract itself, the actual and trade usage of the word, and the behavior of the parties. In this case, the contract provides some guidance. Frigaliment (P) claims that since 1½- to 2-pound chickens are necessarily young chickens, the 2½- to 3-pound chickens should have been young as well. This argument begs the question, since it has been established that the 2½- 3-pound chickens come in two types. B.N.S. (D), on the other hand, argues that the contract incorporated the Department of Agriculture's regulations because Frigaliment (P) requested "US Fresh Frozen Chicken, Grade A, Government Inspected." The USDA regulations refer to "chickens" as broilers, fryers, and stewing chickens (also known as fowl). As a result, the regulations favor B.N.S.'s (D) interpretation of the contract, permitting the shipment of any type of chicken. Indeed, Stovicek's first communication with B.N.S. (D) also referred, generically, to chickens. Finally, at least one food industry witness for B.N.S. (D) relies on the Department of Agriculture's guidelines in his work. These circumstances, together, suggest that the USDA guidelines were intended to govern the contract definition of "chicken." In actual usage, the parties repeatedly used the word chicken during their negotiations. Frigaliment (P) claims that this was because most of the negotiations were in German and they wanted to avoid any confusion between the German word for chicken, "huhn," and the English word "chicken." They thought that "chicken" meant "young chicken" and avoided using the word "huhn" because it included both broilers and stewing chickens. However, when B.N.S. (D) asked Stovicek to be more specific, he told them that any type of chicken would do. The trade usage of the word chicken" is also at issue in this case. Frigaliment (P) contends that "chicken" means "young chicken" in the poultry trade. Since B.N.S. (D) is new to the poultry trade, it is not charged with this knowledge unless Frigaliment (P) can demonstrate that the definition is so prevalent as to create a "violent" presumption that B.N.S. (D) was aware of it. Frigaliment (P) failed to demonstrate this level of use in the industry. Its own witnesses frequently confirm the types of chicken in business transactions by asking whether the parties are talking about broilers or stewing chickens. Other Frigaliment (P) witnesses were more certain that chicken" refers to "young chickens" in the trade, but they were countered by witnesses for B.N.S. (D) that support the contrary conclusion. As noted above, some of B.N.S.'s (D) witnesses rely on the USDA regulations that categorize many types of poultry under the word "chicken." The conduct of the parties further supports our conclusion in favor of B.N.S. (D). First, the market rate for broilers was higher than the rate that B.N.S. (D) was charging Frigaliment (P) for the 2½- to 3-pound chickens. The market rate for stewing chickens was lower. The only way for B.N.S. (D) to make a profit on this transaction was to supply Frigaliment (P) with stewing chickens. B.N.S (D) claims that Frigallment (P) should have known this and we agree. In addition, Frigaliment (P) accepted the second shipment of chickens even though B.N.S. (D) did not acknowledge their complaint about the first shipment. While it might have a claim for damages due to a nonconforming shipment of chickens, its behavior supports the conclusion that the contract called for the shipment of *any* type of chicken. Taking into account all of the arguments above, one thing is clear. Frigaliment (P) harbored a subjective belief that the contract called for the shipment of 2½- to 3-pound broiler/fryers, but failed to demonstrate an objective meaning of the word "chicken" that supports their interpretation. B.N.S. (D), on the other hand, demonstrated a subjective belief that is consistent with a number of objective circumstances that favor its definition. As a result, the term "chicken" in the contract will be interpreted broadly. Frigaliment's (P) claim is dismissed.

---

**Analysis:**

Judge Friendly's opinion is well known for a variety of reasons, not the least of which is his comprehensive approach to contract interpretation. He uses every trick in the book to resolve a seemingly easy question of interpretation that becomes more complicated at every turn. Much of the opinion implicitly relies on objective intent. In other words, the court asks how a reasonable person would interpret the language and behavior of the parties. This approach should be familiar, since it also used in determining the existence of a contract. Judge Friendly also relies on trade usage to determine the definition of "chicken." Even this approach is fraught with complications, however, since B.N.S. (D) was new to the poultry Industry. Finally, Judge Friendly interprets certain ambiguities in the parties' communications against Frigaliment (P). This is a less common device that is used to allocate the burdens of poor contract drafting. In this case, Stovicek's first cablegram referred ambiguously to "chickens." Judge Friendly's analysis shows the variety of ways that a simple contract term can be interpreted and how difficult the analysis can be when two parties approach a contract from different cultural, professional, and linguistic backgrounds.

---

# Hurst v. W.J. Lake & Co.

(Meat Scrap Seller) v. (Meat Scrap Buyer)

141 Or. 306, 16 P.2d 627 (1932)

## OREGON SUPREME COURT INTERPRETS A SEEMINGLY UNAMBIGUOUS CONTRACT TERM ACCORDING TO THE TRADE USAGE OF THE PARTIES

■ **INSTANT FACTS** The parties to a transaction involving horse meat scraps dispute the practical interpretation of the terms of their contract.

■ **BLACK LETTER RULE** If appropriate, a court may rely on trade usage to inform its interpretation of a seemingly unambiguous contract term.

■ **PROCEDURAL BASIS**

Appeal from a trial court judgement on the pleadings in favor of the defendant in an action to recover payments withheld under a contract.

■ **FACTS**

Hurst (P) was a horse meat trader who agreed to sell W.J. Lake & Co. (Lake) (D) 350 tons of horse meat scraps at $50 per ton. The parties agreed that the scraps would be over 50% protein [doesn't everyone like their horse meat lean?]. If Lake (D) discovered, after testing, that the scraps were less than 50% protein, they could deduct $5 from each ton which did not measure up. Lake (D) ultimately deducted $5 from each of 140 tons that did not meet the 50% protein minimum. The nonconforming scraps measured anywhere from 49.53% to 49.96% protein. Hurst (P) sued to recover the deductions for these scraps. He claimed that both parties were experienced horse meat traders [not to be confused with snake oil salesmen]. Apparently, it was understood in the trade that a contract calling for no less than 50% protein was satisfied by scraps which measured over 49.5% protein. The trial court found for Lake (D), despite Hurst's (P) allegations. Hurst (P) appeals.

■ **ISSUE**

Can trade usage govern the interpretation of a seemingly unambiguous contract term?

■ **DECISION AND RATIONALE**

(Rosman) Yes. A court cannot limit its consideration to the plain language of a contract when the trade usage of the parties is relevant to a determination of their Intent. Lake (D) argues that courts will not admit extrinsic evidence of party intent when the language of a contract is unambiguous. He claims that courts will rely. Instead, on the common meaning of the words in order to determine the parties' intent. This approach has simplicity as its advantage. It protects every contract against the occasional perjurer who would testify to bogus industry custom in order to subvert an unfavorable contract. This rule goes too far, however. Many trades make specific allowances for measurements which would not be understood by outsiders. Bricklayers, lumbermen, and rabbit traders are just a few of the tradespeople who subject commonly understood measurements to an arcane understanding observed only within their industries. In addition, familiar terms may be transformed by statute, local usage, or dialect, among other influences. As a result, the court is not persuaded that it should ignore these influences when they are relevant, despite the seeming clarity of the contract. The judgement of the trial court is reversed.

**Analysis:**

Justice Rosman makes a case against the plain meaning rule with regard to the interpretation of contracts between tradespeople. In fact, this approach is ratified in UCC § 1–205. Section § 1–205 states that custom and trade usage can govern the interpretation of contract terms. This approach may even supplement or qualify the terms of an agreement based on the parties' custom or usage. However, if the custom or usage between the parties is not reasonably consistent with the contract, the Code requires that the contract terms govern their relationship. In this case, the UCC rule would lead to the same result. The members of the meat scrap trade loosely interpret the 50% minimum rule. This custom is not inconsistent with the parties' agreement. In fact, it brings the agreement closer to its likely intent. As a result, the court should defer to the parties' trade over the "obvious" meaning of the terms of their agreement.

# Nanakuli Paving & Rock Co. v. Shell Oil Co.

(Buyer) v. (Seller)

664 F.2d 772 (9th Cir. 1981)

## THE UCC LOOKS AT THE ACTUAL PERFORMANCE OF A CONTRACT IN ORDER TO DETERMINE THE PARTIES' INTERPRETATION OF THE TERMS OF THE CONTRACT

■ **INSTANT FACTS** Nanakuli Paving & Rock Co. (P) sued Shell Oil Co. (D) for breach of their 1969 contract based on Shell's (D) failure to protect Nanakuli (P) against increases in asphalt prices.

■ **BLACK LETTER RULE** A court may use evidence of standard industry practices and prior performance of parties to the contract to interpret the contract, if such evidence is not inconsistent with the terms of the contract.

## ■ PROCEDURAL BASIS

Appeal in action for breach of contract.

## ■ FACTS

Nanakuli Paving and Rock Co. (P), a large asphaltic paving company, had two contracts with Shell Oil Co. (D) under which it bought all its asphalt requirements from Shell (D). In 1974, Nanakuli (P) sued Shell (D) for breach of its 1969 contract on the ground that Shell (D) had failed to price-protect Nanakuli (P) against price increases for asphalt. Nanakuli (P) claimed that price protection was included in its 1969 agreement with Shell (D), and that this was demonstrated by the routine use of price protection by suppliers in the trade and by Shell's (D) actual performance of the contract from 1969 until 1974. At the trial level, the jury returned a verdict in favor of Nanakuli (P). The trial court set aside the verdict and granted Shell's motion for judgment n.o.v. Nanakuli (P) appeals.

## ■ ISSUE

May a court use evidence of the routine use of price protection in a trade, and prior performance of parties to the contract, in order to interpret the price terms of a contract, if such evidence is not inconsistent with the terms of the contract?

## ■ DECISION AND RATIONALE

(Hoffman, J.) Yes. A court may use evidence of standard industry practices and prior performance of parties to the contract to interpret the contract, if such evidence is not inconsistent with the terms of the contract. In this case, Nanakuli (P) argues that all material suppliers in the paving industry followed the trade usage of price protection, and that as such, under the U.C.C., it should be assumed that the parties intended to Incorporate price protection into their contract. Additionally, Nanakuli (P) argues that Shell (D) had price-protected it on two prior occasions; thus price protection was a commercially reasonable standard for fair dealing between the parties. Shell (D), on the other hand, argues that 1) "trade," for the purposes of trade usage, should be limited to the buying and selling of asphalt, rather than to the whole asphaltic and paving industry, 2) the two prior occasions on which Shell (D) price-protected Nanakuli (P) constituted waivers of terms of the contract rather than a course of performance between the parties, and 3) price protection, even if used in the industry, is not consistent with the express price term in the contract. It is this court's opinion that the "trade" applicable to the parties in this case is the whole paving industry. Under the UCC, "trade" need not necessarily be one practiced by members of a party's own trade to be binding if it is so commonly practiced in a locality that a party should be aware of it. In this case, while Shell (D) did not regularly deal with aggregate supplies in the business, it had dealt constantly with one asphalt paver, and thus should have been aware of the asphaltic pavers' need for price protection. Nanakuli (P), in this case, has proven that price protection is probably universal in the asphaltic paving industry, and that it has therefore reached the regularity necessary for trade usage. Additionally, Shell's (D) price protection on prior occasions could reasonably be construed by a jury as a course of performance and not a waiver of the express terms of the contract between the parties. Under the UCC, the preference for waiver only applies where the terms of the contract are ambiguous. Whether terms of a contract are ambiguous or not is a question for the jury, and it was not unreasonable for the jury in this case to find that Shell's (D) price protection on the two prior occasions constituted a course of performance and not a waiver. This is true especially in light of the fact that Shell (D) also price-protected Nanakuli (P) on two other occasions after 1974. Further, although at first glance, the express price terms of the contact seem inconsistent with the trade usage of price protection, a jury could have reasonably construed price protection as consistent with the terms of the contract. A commercial agreement is broader than the express terms of the agreement and it should be interpreted in light of commercial practices and other surrounding circumstances. Performance by the parties, trade usages and prior dealings are very important and can be used to supplement the contract. They should be excluded, only if they can not be reasonably reconciled with the express terms of a contract. In this case, there is overwhelming evidence that suppliers in the industry price protected customers under circumstances and contracts similar to the one in this case. Here, the express price term of the contract makes no mention of price protection, including an express negation of price protection. Based on these facts, this court holds that it was reasonable for a jury to find that price protection, being of such wide and broad usage, was included in the parties contract and that it was not inconsistent with the express price terms of the contract. Additionally, in setting its price Shell (D) should have acted with good faith. That is not to say that it could not increase its price with the increase in the market price. However, it should have given prior notice of the increase, which was a long-time trade usage in the industry. In this case, Shell (D) gave no notice. Thus, a jury could reasonably find that its conduct did not conform with commercially reasonable standards in the industry. Further, Shell (D) failed to protect Nanakuli (P) for work which the latter had already bid at the old price. (Judgment of District Court reversed and jury verdict reinstated.)

### Analysis:

Usage of trade only applies to any practice or method of dealing that has a regularity of observance in a place, or trade, as to justify an expectation that it will be observed with respect to the contract and parties in question. Note that this court indicates that the "trade" need not be a party's exact vocation. It is enough that the party deals with the trade in question constantly enough to be aware of its practices. Evidence of usage in trade can be admitted to supplement the terms of a contract even though the contract is fully integrated. Determination of trade usage and course of performance are questions of fact for the jury.

# Columbia Nitrogen Corp. v. Royster Co.

(Nitrogen Producer) v. (Nitrogen Buyer)

451 F.2d 3 (4th Cir. 1971)

UNDER THE UCC, EVIDENCE OF USAGE OF TRADE AND COURSE OF DEALING SHOULD BE EXCLUDED WHENEVER IT CANNOT BE REASONABLY CONSTRUED AS CONSISTENT WITH THE TERMS OF THE CONTRACT

■ **INSTANT FACTS** Royster (D), seller of phosphate, who had a contract with Columbia Nitrogen Corp. (P) for sale of phosphate, sued the latter for damages for breach of contract when Columbia (P) failed to buy the amount of phosphate agreed upon under their contract.

■ **BLACK LETTER RULE** Evidence of custom and usage or course of dealings is not admissible where it contradicts the express, plain, and unambiguous terms of a validly written and fully integrated contract.

■ **PROCEDURAL BASIS**

Appeal from action for damages for breach of contract.

■ **FACTS**

In 1966, Royster (D) negotiated with Columbia Nitrogen Corp. (P) to sell to Columbia (P) a minimum of 31,000 tons of phosphate per year for three years, with an option to extend the contract. The price of phosphate per ton was stated in the contract and was subject to an escalation clause dependent on the cost of producing the phosphate. The contract also contained a merger clause. Due to a plunge in phosphate prices, Columbia (P) was unable to resell phosphate competitively and ordered less than one tenth of the tonnage required under its contract with Royster (D). Royster (D), having sold the phosphate below contract price, sued Columbia (P) for damages. At trial, Columbia (P) sought to show that due to the uncertainty in crop and weather conditions, and other factors, price and quantity terms in contracts in the industry were mere speculations, subject to change based on market conditions. Additionally, Columbia offered evidence to show that in its prior dealings with Royster (D), where Columbia (P) sold nitrogen to Royster (D), there was always substantial deviation from price terms stated in contracts. The trial court excluded this evidence on the ground that it was in contradiction to the express terms of the contract. Columbia (P) appeals the ruling of the trial court.

■ **ISSUE**

Is evidence of custom and usage or course of dealings admissible where it contradicts the express, plain, and unambiguous terms of a validly written and fully integrated contract?

■ **DECISION AND RATIONALE**

(Butzner, J.) Yes. Evidence of custom and usage or course of dealings is not admissible where it contradicts the express, plain, and unambiguous terms of a validly written and fully integrated contract. In this case, Royster (D) contends that the evidence offered by Columbia (P) should be excluded as inconsistent with the terms of the contract because the contract itself has detailed provisions regarding price, its escalation, and quantity of the phosphate to be bought by Columbia (P). This court believes that such a broad exclusionary rule is not within the language of the UCC rule. The test of admissibility is not whether the contract appears on its face to be complete in every detail, but whether the proffered evidence of course of dealing and trade usage reasonably can be construed consistent with the express terms of the agreement. In this case, it is reasonable to construe the terms of the contract with evidence of usage and course of dealings. In the first place, the contract does not expressly state that course of dealings and usage of trade can not be used to explain or supplement the written contract. Additionally, the contract is silent about adjusting prices and quantities to reflect a declining market. Thus, in such a situation it is reasonable to rely on course of dealing and usage to supplement the contract and explain its terms. Finally, the default clause of the contract refers only to the failure of the buyer to pay for delivered phosphate. Both parties during the contract negotiations failed to state any consequences for Columbia's (P) refusal to take phosphate deliveries, for which Royster (D) is now suing. However, unlike what Royster (D) contends, before allowing damages for Columbia's (P) failure to accept the phosphate deliveries, this court must determine that Columbia (P) has in fact defaulted on its contract. This must be done by reliance on evidence of custom and usage and course of dealing that is consistent with the contract's express terms. The contract also states that verbal agreements of the parties will not be recognized because the contract expresses all the terms and conditions of their contract completely. However, evidence of custom and usage and course of dealing is not the same as verbal agreements or understandings between the parties. While evidence of additional terms should be excluded where the contract is complete, no such rule applies to evidence of custom and usage and course of dealings. The official comment to the UCC notes that contracts are to be read on the assumption that evidence of custom and usage and course of dealings were taken for granted when the contract was phrased, unless the terms of the contact carefully negate them. Consequently, such evidence can not be conclusively rejected. (Reversed and remanded.)

---

**Analysis:**

Under the UCC, evidence of custom and usage and course of dealings between the parties can be used to supplement and explain the terms of a contract where it is reasonable. In this case, the contract expressly includes price and quantity requirements. However, the court indicated that this still does not allow per se exclusion of such evidence. It appears from this court's broad interpretation of UCC § 2–202 that evidence of custom and usage and course of dealings can be admitted to interpret contracts under all circumstances, except where the contract clearly negates custom and usage and course of dealing. Remember that under the parol evidence rule, where a contract is fully integrated, and it is complete (such as in this case), evidence of prior or contemporaneous oral agreements or understandings of the parties is not admitted into evidence. However, evidence of custom and usage and course of dealings can be admitted whenever it is reasonably consistent with the terms of a contract, regardless of whether the contract is fully integrated.

---

# Raffles v. Wichelhaus

(Cotton Seller) v. (Cotton Buyer)

2 H. & C. 906, 159 Eng.Rep. 375 (Court of Exchequer 1864)

## EXCHEQUER COURT VOIDS A CONTRACT THAT HINGED ON AN AMBIGUOUS TERM

■ **INSTANT FACTS** Two parties to a cotton transaction disagree as to the exact identity of a ship named in their contract.

■ **BLACK LETTER RULE** A contract can be voided if it contains an ambiguous term which was, in fact, interpreted differently by the parties.

## ■ PROCEDURAL BASIS

Decision of the Court of Exchequer on a breach of contract action.

## ■ FACTS

Raffles (P) agreed to sell Wichelhaus (D) 125 bales of cotton which were supposed to arrive in England by ship. Wichelhaus (D) agreed to pay for the cotton after it arrived from Bombay on a ship called Peerless. Neither party to the contract knew it at the time, but there were two ships called Peerless which sailed from Bombay. One ship sailed in October. The second ship sailed in December. Unfortunately, each party had a different ship in mind for the transaction. Raffles (P) thought that the Peerless which sailed in December was the agreed upon ship. When that ship arrived in England, Raffles (P) attempted to complete the transaction. Wichelhaus (D), however, refused to accept delivery or to pay for the cotton since he had expected the other Peerless. Raffles (P) subsequently sued Wichelhaus (D) for breach of contract. Wichelhaus's (D) plea followed and Raffles (P) demurred. The court then rendered its opinion.

## ■ ISSUE

Can a specific contract term be interpreted according to a party's subjective interpretation of that term?

## ■ DECISION AND RATIONALE

(Mellish) Yes. Raffles (P) and Wichelhaus (D) did not make it clear that the Peerless was a particular ship sailing on a particular date. When it turned out that there were actually two different ships named Peerless, a latent ambiguity was exposed in the contract. In that event, the court can hear parol evidence in order to establish that there was an actual subjective disagreement between the parties. Since there was no consensus ad litem, there is no contract. Since there is no contract, Raffles (P) has no right to sue for its breach. The action will be dismissed and judgement entered in favor of Wichelhaus (D).

## ■ DISSENT

(Milward) I dissent for the following reason. A party's subjective intent is irrelevant to the interpretation of a contract term unless that intent is communicated to the other party at the time of contracting. In this case, Wichelhaus's (D) intent is irrelevant. He never made it clear to Raffles (P) that he wanted the cotton to be delivered on the Peerless sailing in October. The contract appears to name the ship only as a convenience in the event that the Peerless was lost at sea. The identity of the exact ship might be important if the parties were contracting for the sale of the ship itself, but they were not. As a result, it should not matter which Peerless delivered the cotton so long as the contract was fulfilled. In fact, Raffles (P) was not shipping any cotton on the other Peerless—the one that Wichelhaus (D) thought was carrying the cotton. For all of these reasons, Raffles's (P) demurrer should be granted [in other words...he should win].

**Analysis:**

Note that the opinions of judges Mellish and Milward appear in the reverse order in your book. Nonetheless, Mellish's opinion is the decision of the court and Milward's opinion is, in essence, the dissent. Second, note that the rule of law announced by the court is meant for the exceptional case. Usually, courts require the objective intent of the parties to govern the interpretation of a contract. Occasionally, though, a crucial term in the contract is subject to differing interpretations. If the parties actually interpreted an ambiguous term in different ways, the contract can be voided. Much of the debate regarding this case centers on the importance of the ship's identity to the contract. It has been argued that Judge Milward's approach was actually contrary to trade practice at the time. He suggests that the identity of the ship was unimportant as long as the cotton arrived as promised. However, it was apparently common practice for parties to identify a particular ship and a particular arrival date in order to secure a favorable market rate for goods during the latter part of the 1800s. More generally, the case is a novelty because of the peculiar circumstances that led to the dispute. The court was forced to test the adequacy of traditional interpretation doctrine, which was unsuited for such an unlikely controversy.

## ■ CASE VOCABULARY

AD LITEM: *Ad litem* means "for the purposes of the suit." However, the majority most probably meant *"ad idem."* A *consensus ad idem* is a meeting of the minds. It is this which the majority claims did not exist between the parties.

COURT OF EXCHEQUER: A trial level court which existed until 1873. Its jurisdiction was subsequently turned over to the Exchequer Division and then the Queen's Bench Division of the High Court of Justice.

DEMURRER: A demurrer is a means of attacking a party's pleading. In essence, the attacker argues that the pleading need not be answered because it is insufficient or defective in some manner. There are a variety of different demurrers, some of which are still recognized. The modem equivalent of a *general* demurrer is a request for dismissal under Federal Rule of Civil Procedure 12 (b) (6). A request under 12 (b) (6) alleges that the opposing party fails to state a claim for which relief can be granted.

# Oswald v. Allen

(Coin Buyer) v. (Coin Seller)
417 F.2d 43 (2d Cir.1969)

COURT OF APPEALS AFFIRMS THE MODERN APPLICATION OF *RAFFLES V. WICHELHAUS*

■ **INSTANT FACTS:** Two coin collectors each have a different interpretation of a contract for the sale of Swiss coins.

■ **BLACK LETTER RULE:** A contract should be voided if the parties each held different understandings of an ambiguous term and neither party should have been aware of the other's understanding.

■ **PROCEDURAL BASIS**

Appeal from a district court post-trial dismissal of the plaintiff's complaint in an action for specific performance.

■ **FACTS**

Oswald (P) was a Swiss coin collector who arranged to view Allen's (D) Swiss coin collection in New York. As it turns out, Allen (D) had two different collections in separate bank vaults, each of which contained Swiss Coins. The two collections were called the Swiss Coin Collection and the Rarity Coin Collection. During his visit, Oswald (P) was inadvertently shown coins from both collections. Oswald (P) did not speak much English, but arranged through his brother to purchase Allen's (D) Swiss coins for $50,000. Allen (D) thought she was selling the Swiss Coin Collection. Oswald (P) thought he was buying all of Allen's (D) Swiss coins. In fact, he sent Allen (D) a letter, confirming the sale of "all of [her] Swiss coins." Allen (D) realized that the parties were each laboring under a misconception when she met with Oswald's (P) agent. At this point, she balked at the coin sale and Oswald (P) brought suit for specific performance. The district court dismissed Oswald's (P) claim after trial.

■ **ISSUE**

Can a contract be enforced despite both parties failure to interpret a term in the same manner?

■ **DECISION AND RATIONALE**

(Moore) No. This case is very much like *Raffles v. Wichelhaus* [a contract can be voided if it contains an ambiguous term which was, in fact, interpreted differently by the parties]. The rule in *Raffles* has since been adopted by the Restatement [First] of Contracts. A contract should not be enforced when each party has interpreted an ambiguous term differently, unless one party should have been aware of the other's understanding. Ordinarily, a contract is enforceable despite the parties failure to come to a subjective understanding over its terms. This is a rare case, however, where there is no reason to enforce one party's interpretation over the other. In this case, neither Oswald (P) nor Allen (D) knew that they were each contemplating a different coin collection. In fact, Oswald (P) never knew that he had seen coins from two separate collections. There is no reason to burden Oswald (P) and Allen (D) with a contract which was in neither party's contemplation. Consequently, the district court's dismissal of Oswald's (P) complaint is affirmed.

**Analysis:**

This case resembles *Raffles v. Wichelhaus* and *Frigaliment Importing Co. v. B.N.S. International Sales Corp.* The parties in both cases suffered from a language barrier that was partly responsible for their confusion. As *Raffles* demonstrates, confusion can result just as easily between parties who speak the same language. This case represents a modern affirmation of the rule recognized in *Raffles.* The rule is still reserved for exceptional cases, however. Here, neither party would get what they bargained for if the contract were enforced according to its terms. On a wholly different note, if the contract had not been voided, this would have been a perfect case for specific performance. The coin collection is just the sort of unique item for which specific performance would be the appropriate remedy.

# Colfax Envelope Corp. v. Local No. 458–3M

(Employer) v. (Union)

20 F.3d 750 (7th Cir. 1994)

## RESCISSION MAY BE BASED ON MUTUAL MISUNDERSTANDING

I want to return this cat for being lazy and aloof.

Sorry, but you accepted a CAT.

stus.com

HUMANE SOCIETY

■ **INSTANT FACTS** Colfax (P) signed a collective bargaining agreement that had an erroneous term in it, and when the corrected agreement was sent to it, Colfax (P) tried to renegotiate, saying that it had no contract with Local 458–3M.

■ **BLACK LETTER RULE** A party to a contract who agrees to a term knowing that the term is ambiguous may not obtain rescission of the contract based on the ambiguity of that term.

■ **PROCEDURAL BASIS**

Appeal from an order granting summary judgment for Local 458–3M (D).

■ **FACTS**

Colfax Envelope (P) was engaged in the printing business and had seventeen employees who were represented by Local No. 458–3M (D). Because Colfax (P) had so few employees, it did not actively participate in the bargaining between Local 458–3M (D) and the Chicago Lithographers Association, an association that represented other area employers in the printing industry. When a new collective bargaining agreement was reached, Local 458–3M (D) sent a summary of the changes to Colfax (P), and Colfax (P) signed and returned the agreement. If Colfax (P) disagreed with the terms negotiated, it was free to bargain with Local 458–3M (D) on its own.

The collective bargaining agreement in force between 1987 and 1991 set out minimum manning requirements for printing presses. Colfax (P) operated one seventy-eight-inch press that printed in four colors and one that could print in five colors but that was usually used to print in four colors, and it was generally required to man the presses with four employees (five employees were required on the rare occasions that printing was done in five colors). In 1991, Local 458–3M (D) negotiated a new agreement with the Lithographers Association and sent a summary of the changes to Colfax (P). Colfax (P) was asked to indicate whether it agreed to the terms in the summary. The section on manning requirements listed "4C 60 Press–3 Men" and "5C 78 Press–4 Men." Colfax (P) interpreted this language to mean that only three employees would be required to operate all four-color presses, regardless of size. Based on this interpretation, Colfax (P) approved the terms in the summary. A copy of the full agreement was sent to Colfax (P), but it contained a typographical error that supported Colfax's (P) interpretation. A corrected copy of the agreement was sent out, and it set out the manning requirements as requiring four employees on every four-color press over sixty inches. Colfax (P) wanted to renegotiate the agreement, but Local 458–3M (D) took the position that Colfax (P) was bound by its acceptance of the summary.

Colfax (P) brought suit for a declaration that it had no collective bargaining agreement because the parties never agreed on an essential term; namely, the staffing requirements. Local 458–3M (D) counterclaimed for arbitration, claiming that Colfax (P) had accepted the new agreement and was therefore bound by the arbitration clause, which required arbitration of disputes arising out of the interpretation of the contract. The district court granted summary judgment for Local 458–3M (D), holding that the staffing requirements in the summary referred unambiguously to sixty-inch presses and had no application to seventy-eight-inch presses.

# ■ ISSUE

Was Colfax (P) entitled to rescind the collective bargaining agreement?

# ■ DECISION AND RATIONALE

(Posner, C.J.) No. A party to a contract who agrees to a term knowing that the term is ambiguous may not obtain rescission of the contract. A contract should be terminable without liability, however, when there is no sensible basis for choosing between conflicting understandings of the language of the contract. If neither party has the greater blame for the misunderstanding, there is no non-arbitrary basis for deciding which understanding to enforce, and the parties are allowed to abandon the contract without liability.

The clearest cases in favor of rescission are those in which an offer is garbled in transmission. The case at bar is, at least superficially, one such case. Colfax (P) believes that the term "4C 60 Press–3 Men" means four-color presses printing sheets sixty inches and over, while Local 458–3M (D) believes that it means presses sixty inches and under, down to forty-five inches. The previous agreement allowed the use of three-man crews on four-color presses between forty-five and fifty inches, and Local 458–3M (D) interpreted the change as extending the three-man range to sixty inches. In this case, though, Colfax (P) should have realized that the meaning of the contract was unclear. The expression "4C 60 Press" does not, on its face, refer to a seventy-eight-inch press. The interpretation of Local 458–3M (D) may or may not be the correct one. Although the summary is the contract between the parties, the corrected agreement should have made Colfax (P) certain that its interpretation was not the only plausible one.

Colfax (P) could hope that its interpretation was the correct one, but it could not accept the offer in the summary on the premise that, if its interpretation was not correct, it could walk away. When parties agree to a patently ambiguous term they submit to have any dispute over it resolved by interpretation. The possibility of rescission due to a mutual misunderstanding arises only when parties agree to terms that appear clear to each of them. Affirmed.

---

**Analysis:**

In this case, Colfax (P) was put on notice of a crucial omission when the contract summary did not make any reference to four-color seventy-eight-inch presses. Colfax's (P) unreasonable behavior was in assuming that this omission had any substantive meaning. Prudence should have led Colfax (P) to make inquiries as to the staffing requirements for the larger presses. As the court notes, the summary is the contract in this case, and the corrected copy of the agreement is only confirmation of the existence of the mistake. The result here may well have been different if Colfax (P) had made inquiries before signing the summary and was given the copy of the final agreement with the typo in response to those inquiries.

---

# Koken v. Black & Veatch Construction, Inc.

(Insurance Company Liquidator) v. (Contractor)

426 F.3d 39 (1st Cir. 2005)

"REASONABLE EXPECTATIONS" IS AN OBJECTIVE STANDARD

For my next trick, I will melt a fire blanket with only a blow torch.

Trick? Isn't that just physics?

stus.com

■ **INSTANT FACTS** A fire blanket manufactured by Auburn Manufacturing (D) did not prevent a fire, and Black & Veatch (P) brought a claim for breach of the warranty of merchantability.

■ **BLACK LETTER RULE** A breach of the warranty of merchantability is shown when a product does not perform according to the reasonable expectations of an ordinary user or consumer.

■ **PROCEDURAL BASIS**

Appeal from an order granting summary judgment for Auburn (D).

■ **FACTS**

A fire blanket manufactured by Auburn (D) was used to protect the area underneath a torch-cutting welding operation at a construction project. A fire broke out, and the blanket started melting and did not stop the fire. Although the fire was extinguished quickly, the chemicals in the fire extinguisher damaged a generator. The damage to the generator caused approximately $9 million in repair and delay costs.

Black & Veatch (P) brought suit against Auburn (D) and Inpro (D), the distributor, alleging breach of the warranty of merchantability. A witness testified that he was "surprised" that the blanket melted. Other witnesses testified that the blanket performed as expected and that burn-through holes were common. There was no testimony regarding industry standards. The district court granted summary judgment for Auburn (D) and Inpro (D) on the breach of warranty claim.

■ **ISSUE**

Did Black & Veatch (P) establish a claim for breach of the warranty of merchantability?

■ **DECISION AND RATIONALE**

(Dyk, J.) No. A breach of the warranty of merchantability is shown when a product does not perform according to the reasonable expectations of an ordinary user or consumer. The standard is objective rather than subjective. The question thus does not turn on the subjective expectations of a particular user, but the reasonable expectations of an ordinary user or purchaser. Relevant evidence on the question includes testimony regarding customs of the trade, industry standards, and professional literature.

In this case, there was no evidence that an ordinary user of the fire blanket reasonably expected a fire blanket to prevent the type of melting observed here. Black & Veatch (P) produced evidence only regarding the subjective views of one individual. In fact, there was other testimony that the blanket performed as expected. Summary judgment on the breach of warranty claim is affirmed.

**Analysis:**

The excerpt discusses the warranty in terms of the reasonable expectations of consumers. In a portion of the court's opinion not reproduced in the text, it is noted that marketing materials for the type of fire blanket probably involved (the actual blanket was destroyed) cautioned that it should not be used in the horizontal position, as it was in this situation. Auburn (D) manufactured another fire blanket recommended for such applications. While there are some products whose misuse is so common as to be part of the "normal expectations of a consumer (*e.g.* using a screwdriver to open a paint can)," it probably would be considered unreasonable for a user to expect a product to perform in a manner specifically warned against by the manufacturer.

# Lewis v. Mobil Oil Corporation

(Sawmill Operator) v. (Oil Seller)

438 F.2d 500 (8th Cir. 1971)

IF THE SELLER KNOWS HOW THE BUYER WILL USE A PRODUCT, A WARRANTY MAY ARISE THAT THE PRODUCT CAN BE USED IN THAT WAY

■ **INSTANT FACTS** Lewis (P) purchased oil recommended by Mobil (D) for use in hydraulic machinery, but the oil did not function properly and Lewis's (P) machinery was damaged.

■ **BLACK LETTER RULE** An implied warranty of fitness arises when the seller has reason to know of the use for which goods are purchased and the buyer relies on the seller's expertise in supplying the proper product.

■ **PROCEDURAL BASIS**

Appeal from a judgment after a jury verdict for Lewis (P).

■ **FACTS**

In 1964, Lewis (P) installed hydraulic equipment in his sawmill. The system was purchased used but was in good operating condition when Lewis (P) purchased it. After the equipment was installed, Lewis (P) asked Rowe, a local dealer for Mobil (D), for the right hydraulic fluid to operate the machinery. Rowe did not know the proper lubricant, but said he would find out. Rowe may have contacted another Mobil (D) representative, but this point is unclear. Rowe sold Lewis (P) a product known as Ambrex 810, a mineral oil with no additives.

Lewis (P) began having trouble with the operation of the equipment soon after he started to use it. The oil changed color, foamed over, and got hot. The oil was changed several times, but there was no improvement. The system completely broke down approximately six months after it was installed, and there was some suspicion that the oil being used caused the breakdown. Lewis (P) asked Rowe to be sure he was supplying the correct oil, and he continued to supply Ambrex 810.

Lewis (P) had problems with the system from 1965 to 1967. Six new pumps were installed during this time. In April 1967, Lewis (P) began to use a different kind of pump. Ambrex 810 was also recommended by Mobil (D) for this pump, and the pump broke down three weeks after it was installed. Another representative of Mobil (D) and a representative of the pump manufacturer visited Lewis (P). A new pump was installed and, on the recommendations of the manufacturer's representative and the representative from Mobil (D), a different lubricant was used. The new lubricant had additives including a defoamant. The new pump worked satisfactorily.

Lewis (P) brought suit against Mobil (D), alleging a breach of the warranty of fitness. Mobil (D) claimed that there was no warranty of fitness, and that there was no proof of a breach of the warranty of merchantability, because there was no proof that Ambrex 810 was not fit to use in hydraulic systems generally.

■ **ISSUE**

Did Lewis (P) establish a breach of the warranty of fitness?

## DECISION AND RATIONALE

(Gibson, J.) Yes. An implied warranty of fitness arises when the seller has reason to know of the use for which goods are purchased and the buyer relies on the seller's expertise in supplying the proper product. Both of these requirements are met in this case. The existence of a warranty of fitness is a question of fact to be determined by the circumstances of the contract.

Lewis (P) had been a longtime customer of Mobil (D) and dealt exclusively with Rowe. It was common knowledge in the community that Lewis (P) planned to install hydraulic equipment, and Rowe had visited Lewis's (P) business several times during the installation. Lewis (P) asked Rowe for the correct hydraulic fluid, and Rowe knew nothing more specific about Lewis's (P) requirements than the type of pump he had. Rowe did not know what type of oil to use, and referred the question to a superior. The superior recommended Ambrex 810. Lewis (P) also testified that he asked Rowe to make sure that he was using the proper oil when he had problems. Rowe asked a Mobil (D) engineer for a recommendation for oil when the new pump was installed in 1967, and the engineer recommended Ambrex 810. When the new pump failed, the engineer inspected the pump and recommended a different oil.

Mobil (D) argued that there was no warranty of fitness for Lewis's (P) use, because he did not tell them that he needed an oil with particular specifications. The existence of a warranty is a question of fact, to be determined by the circumstances of the contract. Lewis (P) made it clear that he did not know what oil to use, and that he was relying on Mobil (D) to supply the appropriate product. If Mobil (D) needed further information, it was Mobil's (D) obligation to get it before it made its recommendation. The fact that Mobil (D) could easily have obtained the information is demonstrated by the fact that Mobil's (D) engineer visited Lewis's (P) sawmill and changed the previous recommendation. Affirmed on the issue of the existence of a warranty; remanded for a recalculation of damages.

---

### Analysis:

The warranty of fitness comes from the idea that a merchant has some expertise with regard to the goods being sold. Buyers are entitled to rely on this expertise when receiving a recommendation for a particular item. In situations such as the one presented by this case, the assumption of expertise is not an unreasonable one—Rowe had dealt with Lewis (P) for some time, and knew about his business and why he wanted to buy the oil. Most consumer purchases of goods, while governed by the same rule, might cast doubt on that assumption. Is the expertise the same when the sale is of one of thousands of products carried by a "big box" retail chain?

---

# South Carolina Electric and Gas Co. v. Combustion Engineering, Inc.

(Utility Company) v. (Boiler Manufacturer)

283 S.C. 182, 322 S.E.2d 453 (1984)

## BUYERS MUST HAVE NOTICE OF WARRANTY DISCLAIMERS

■ **INSTANT FACTS** South Carolina Electric and Gas (P) brought a breach of warranty claim against Combustion (D), and Combustion (D) claimed that the warranties of merchantability and fitness had been disclaimed.

■ **BLACK LETTER RULE** A disclaimer of warranties will be effective if the circumstances surrounding the sale are sufficient to draw the buyer's attention to the exclusion of warranties.

## ■ PROCEDURAL BASIS

Appeal from an order granting summary judgment to Combustion Engineering (D).

## ■ FACTS

In 1970, South Carolina Electric and Gas (P) purchased a boiler manufactured by Combustion Engineering (D). The boiler was installed in March 1973, and in May 1975, a hose attached to the boiler ruptured and sprayed heated fuel oil on the boiler, allegedly starting a fire that caused South Carolina Electric (P) to sustain damages in excess of $350,000.

The sales contract for the boiler contained an express warranty that the boiler would be free of defects in material and workmanship for one year. The warranty also stated there were no other express or implied warranties, other than the warranty of title. The disclaimer of warranties was on page seventeen of a twenty-two page document, in an item headed "WARRANTY," and it was the last sentence of a two-paragraph section. The disclaimer did not mention "merchantability," and the type face and color of the disclaimer were not different from the rest of the text.

A proposal Combustion (D) sent to South Carolina Electric (P) in August 1968 contained the same disclaimer at issue here. South Carolina Electric (P) replied to that proposal in January 1969. The reply stated that the proposal was unacceptable in certain respects, and that any purchase order would have to meet certain conditions. One of the conditions was that Combustion (P) would agree to be bound by the "warranties implied by the laws of the State of South Carolina." Combustion (D) replied that it would not agree to that condition, and also stated that the agreement must have a limitation on the warranty period and a limitation on the available remedies. South Carolina Electric (P) replied and stated that it agreed that the "warranties implied by [the] laws of South Carolina shall be limited" to the warranty item included in the original proposal.

South Carolina Electric (P) brought suit against Combustion (D) for breach of the warranties of fitness for a particular purpose and merchantability, and for negligent design. Combustion (D) moved for, and was granted, summary judgment.

## ■ ISSUE

Was the language in the sales agreement sufficient to limit the warranty on the boiler?

## ■ DECISION AND RATIONALE

(Goolsby, J.) Yes. A disclaimer of warranties will be effective if the circumstances surrounding the sale are sufficient to draw the buyer's attention to the exclusion of warranties. The warranty language did not meet the requirements for a disclaimer or limitation of warranty set out in U.C.C. § 2–316 (2), in that it did not mention "merchantability," it was not conspicuous, and it was misleading in that it was placed in a section labeled "WARRANTY." However, the U.C.C. provides an exception to the statutory require-ments for disclaimers when the circumstances show that the buyer's attention was drawn to the disclaimer.

The correspondence preceding the agreement is not a part of the agreement, but is considered in order to determine whether the disclaimer was unbargained for and unanticipated by South Carolina Electric (P). Herr, the disclaimer is clear and unambiguous. The language of the disclaimer came as no surprise to South Carolina Electric (P). There was no factual showing to the contrary. In addition, South Carolina Electric (P) is commercially sophisticated and has bargaining power relatively equal to that of Combustion (D). The size of the transaction and the length of the negotiations show as much. It is not credible that a business like South Carolina Electric (P) would not be aware of the language disclaiming implied warranties. The disclaimer here was effective, notwithstanding its failure to comply with the formal requirements. Affirmed.

### Analysis:

This case is an appeal from a grant of summary judgment, so all the court is saying is that South Carolina Electric (P) did not raise an issue of material fact regarding the disclaimer. In other words, the court is not saying that, as a matter of law, the type of disclaimer used by Combustion (D) will always be sufficient, or even that a large business such as South Carolina Electric (P) will not be able to avoid a disclaimer that is legally insufficient. The court is merely holding that South Carolina Electric (P) did not rebut evidence showing that it had actual notice of the disclaimer. The result of this case could well have been different if there had been no proof that the warranty disclaimer language was discussed before the sales agreement was signed.

# Henningsen v. Bloomfield Motors, Inc.

(Car Buyer) v. (Car Dealer)

32 N.J. 358, 161 A.2d 69, 75 A.L.R.2d 1 (1960)

---

DISCLAIMERS OR OTHER STATEMENTS LIMITING A PARTY'S LIABILITY UNDER A PRIVATE CONTRACT ARE BINDING ONLY IF SUCH LIMITATION IS UNDERSTANDINGLY ACCEPTED BY THE PARTIES

---

■ **INSTANT FACTS** Henningsen sued Bloomfield for breach of warranty after the steering in his new car failed, and Bloomfield countered with a disclaimer written in fine print.

■ **BLACK LETTER RULE** Disclaimers and attempted limitations of warranties or liability, whether in a public, quasi-public, or private contract, are not enforceable unless the limitation is fairly and honestly made and understandingly entered into.

---

■ **PROCEDURAL BASIS**

Appeal from judgment in action for breach of implied warranty of merchantability.

■ **FACTS**

Claus Henningsen (P) bought a new car from Bloomfield Motors, Inc. (Bloomfield) (D). Claus' (P) wife, Helen (P), drove the car ten days later and was injured when the steering mechanism failed. The Henningsens (P) sued Bloomfield (D) and the car's manufacturer, Chrysler Corporation (Chrysler) (D), for breach of an implied warranty of merchantability established by the Uniform Sales Act. Both Bloomfield and Chrysler (D) argue that the warranty had been properly disclaimed under the Act. They (D) pointed to a provision of the purchase contract which provided for a limit on the liability for breach of warranty. Under this provision, liability was limited to replacement of defective parts for up to 90 days after delivery or 4,000 miles of driving, whichever came first. This warranty is a standard one used by car dealers. The provision was contained in an eight-and-a-half point section of fine print on the back of the contract. While most of the contract was printed in twelve-point type, this provision was referred to on the front of the contract by statements printed in six-point type just above the space for signatures. In particular, the contract incorporated the following reference: "I have read the matter printed on the back hereof and agree to it as part of this order the same as if it were printed above my signature." The trial court ruled for the Henningsens (P), and Bloomfield and Chrysler (D) appealed.

■ **ISSUE**

Is a standardized contract with a disclaimer or limitation of warranty automatically enforceable once both parties sign it?

■ **DECISION AND RATIONALE**

(Francis) No. The traditional contract is the product of free bargaining between parties that meet on roughly the same economic level. In present-day commercial life, however, the standardized mass contract has emerged, used primarily by enterprises with strong bargaining power and position. Weaker parties that need goods or services without the ability to "shop around for better terms, either because the one using the form contract has a monopoly or because all competitors use the same kind of contracts. Here, the warranty at issue is imposed on the car-buying customer, who must accept its terms in order to make the purchase. This warranty is used by all the major car manufacturers. Thus, customers like the Henningsens (P) cannot find any better protection than this. Indeed, with the car manufacturers not competing with each other in terms of customer protection, there is no incentive for them to provide better warranties to the customers. Several cases have shown that disclaimers and their resulting limitations of liability will not be given effect if unfairly procured or if not made clear and explicit to the buyer. Disclaimers and attempted limitations of warranties or liability, whether in a public, quasi-public, or private contract, are not enforceable unless the limitation is fairly and honestly made and understandingly entered into. While this rule has usually been applied to cases involving services of a public or semi-public nature, more and more recent cases have applied the rule to private contract disputes. Here, the specific warranty imposed by Bloomfield (D) provided that it (D) would replace defective parts during the first 90 days or 4,000 miles of operation. This apparently served as a remedy for physical deficiencies in the car. Only by abandoning all sense of justice would a court hold that this warranty would indicate that a person accepting it would relinquish any personal injury claim that would result from a defect of the automobile. The court must protect consumers like the Henningsens (P) from such unilateral acts by larger entitles like this disclaimer of liability by Bloomfield and Chrysler (Ds). Judgment affirmed.

**Analysis:**

Remember that the court in *O'Callaghan* stated that the "use of a form contract does not of itself establish disparity of bargaining power," and that the subject of addressing the dangers of exculpatory clauses "is appropriate for legislative rather than judicial action." Here, the court expressly assumes the role of protecting the "ordinary layman . . . [because] . . . there can be no arms length negotiating" between the customer and the manufacturer. It should be noted that since 1960, when *Henningsen* was decided, automobile manufacturers began to extend and advertise their warranties in order to gain a competitive advantage.

## ■ CASE VOCABULARY

INIMICAL: Unfriendly, hostile, or opposed to.

SIGNATURE ELEMENTS: Designated area on contract where parties place their signatures.

# CHAPTER SIX

## Limits on the Bargain and its Performance

### McKinnon v. Benedict

**Instant Facts:** McKinnon loaned the Benedicts $5,000 to purchase their campground, and in return, restricted the Benedicts from making improvements near his property for 25 years.

**Black Letter Rule:** A contract which is harsh, oppressive, and unconscionable may still be enforceable at law, but it is within a court's discretion to not enforce equitable remedies against a party who suffers from such harshness and oppression under the contract.

### Tuckwiller v. Tuckwiller

**Instant Facts:** Ruby Tuckwiller contract to take care of her husband's aunt in exchange for the aunt's farm, but the aunt died shortly after signing the contract.

**Black Letter Rule:** The court should look at a transaction prospectively, from the viewpoint of the parties at the time at the time of the agreement, to determine the fairness of the transaction and the sufficiency of its consideration; once the essential fairness of a contract for real property and the adequacy of its consideration are found, a court of equity can decree specific performance of it.

### Black Industries, Inc. v. Bush

**Instant Facts:** Black claimed that Bush failed to deliver parts according to their contract, while Bush claims that Black would receive excessive profits on its government contracts.

**Black Letter Rule:** It is not the function of the court to interfere in the contractual relationship of two ordinary businessmen dealing at arm's length by trying to determine the validity of the contract on the basis of the adequacy of the consideration.

### O'Callaghan v. Waller & Beckwith Realty Co.

**Instant Facts:** O'Callaghan sued her landlord for negligence after falling in the building courtyard, and her landlord claimed an exculpatory clause in the lease barred the action.

**Black Letter Rule:** Contracts by which one tries to relieve himself or herself from liability for negligence are generally enforced unless it would be against the settled public policy of the State to do so, or there is something in the social relationship of the parties militating against upholding the agreement.

### Graham v. Scissor-Tail, Inc.

**Instant Facts:** After a music promoter signed a mandatory form contract requiring arbitration before a biased panel and then loses his case, he sues to void the contract as unconscionable.

**Black Letter Rule:** Adhesion contracts are enforceable, except for provisions which contradict adherents' reasonable expectations, or are unconscionable.

### Carnival Cruise Lines, Inc. v. Shute

**Instant Facts:** After Shute was injured during a cruise, the cruise line claimed Shute could only file suit in Florida because of terms printed on her ticket.

**Black Letter Rule:** A forum-selection clause should be enforced unless the party claiming unfairness or inconvenience can bear a heavy burden of proof.

### Doe v. Great Expectations

**Instant Facts:** Doe (P) signed up with Great Expectations (D) for dating and introduction services, but she met no one through the service.

**Black Letter Rule:** A consumer injured by a contract that violates statutory requirements may collect actual damages, to be set at the face amount of the contract.

### Williams v. Walker-Thomas Furniture Co.

**Instant Facts:** Williams bought furniture and a stereo on credit from Walker-Thomas while on welfare, and Walker-Thomas repossessed the items when Williams defaulted.

**Black Letter Rule:** A contract is unenforceable if its terms, when considered in light of the circumstances existing when the contract was made, are so extreme as to appear unconscionable according to prevailing mores and business practices.

### Jones v. Star Credit Corp.

**Instant Facts:** While on welfare, the Joneses agreed to buy a $300 freezer on credit, with additional credit and fees running the purchase price up to $1,234.80.

**Black Letter Rule:** A court may find that an entire contract, and not just a particular clause of it, is unconscionable as a matter of law and thereby unenforceable.

### Armendariz v. Foundation Health Psychcare Services

**Instant Facts:** A fired employee challenges her employment agreement, which requires her to arbitrate claims against her employer.

**Black Letter Rule:** Employment contracts' arbitration clauses are enforceable, unless the arbitration procedure is unfair, the arbitration is unilateral, or the clause is unfair procedurally or substantively.

### Scott v. Cingular Wireless

**Instant Facts:** Scott (P) filed a class action suit against Cingular (D) to challenge the legality of certain charges, and Cingular (D) moved to enforce the arbitration clause in its standard contract.

**Black Letter Rule:** An arbitration clause that prohibits consumer class actions is substantively unconscionable in that such a clause undermines enforcement of consumer protection laws, and because such a clause severely limits the remedies of only one side.

### Dalton v. Educational Testing Service

**Instant Facts:** The SAT's administrator reserves the right to cancel disputed scores, but allows test-takers to present evidence proving validity. When the administrator decided a test-taker had an impostor write his test, it ignored the test-taker's proffered evidence.

**Black Letter Rule:** When a contract allows parties to present evidence disputing the other's discretionary determinations, the determiner must review proffered evidence in good faith, and otherwise perform its obligations fairly and faithfully.

### Eastern Air Lines, Inc. v. Gulf Oil Corporation

**Instant Facts:** An airline and its fuel supplier dispute the price terms of their jet fuel contract.

**Black Letter Rule:** UCC § 2–306 asks the parties to output and requirements contracts to conduct their business in good faith and according to commercial standards of fair dealing so that their output or requirements will be reasonably foreseeable.

### Market Street Associates v. Frey [General Electric Pension Trust]

**Instant Facts:** A leaseholder tries to exercise an option which enables him to buy the leased property from its owner.

**Black Letter Rule:** The duty of good faith precludes a party from taking deliberate advantage of an oversight by the other party concerning its rights under the contract.

### Bloor v. Falstaff Brewing Corp.

**Instant Facts:** A brewery fails to use best effort to continue the sales of an acquired label.

**Black Letter Rule:** A contract clause requiring best efforts to ensure profits does not require the promisor to spend itself into bankruptcy in the course of performance.

### Lockewill, Inc. v. United States Shoe Corp.

**Instant Facts:** The new owners of a shoe company breach an exclusivity agreement which was arranged by the prior owner.

**Black Letter Rule:** An agreement which does not state its duration or contain provisions for its termination remains in force until the parties have recouped their investments in the venture.

### Bovard v. American Horse Enterprises, Inc.

**Instant Facts:** A businessman sued to recover payment for selling a business which made drug paraphernalia.

**Black Letter Rule:** Courts cannot hear disputes about contracts which violate public policy by being illegal, or tending to promote illegality.

### X.L.O. Concrete Corp. v. Rivergate Corp.

**Instant Facts:** Rivergate refused to pay XLO an outstanding balance for work XLO had done, claiming that the contract was part of an organized crime racket.

**Black Letter Rule:** A contract will be considered unenforceable if it is so integrally related to the agreement, arrangement or combination in restraint of competition that its enforcement would result in compelling performance of the precise conduct made unlawful by antitrust laws.

### Hopper v. All Pet Animal Clinic

**Instant Facts:** Hopper opened her own veterinary clinic near All Pet after All Pet fired her, and All Pet claimed she violated an agreement not to compete.

**Black Letter Rule:** A covenant not to compete is valid and enforceable only if it is shown that the covenant is (1) in writing; (2) part of a contract of employment; (3) based on reasonable consideration; (4) reasonable in duration and geographical limitation; and (5) not against public policy.

### Sheets v. Teddy's Frosted Foods

**Instant Facts:** An employee is fired for warning his company that they are violating a food labeling statute.

**Black Letter Rule:** An employee who is fired for reasons in contravention of public policy can sue in tort for wrongful termination.

### Balla v. Gambro, Inc.

**Instant Facts** When a dialysis machine marketer fired its general counsel for threatening to report its illegal sale of tampered machines, the counselor sued for wrongful discharge.

**Black Letter Rule** If an attorney is fired for reporting clients' misconduct which the attorney is ethically obligated to report, the attorney has no claim for retaliatory discharge.

### Simeone v. Simeone

**Instant Facts:** An ex-wife sued to void her prenuptial agreement, contending her husband presented it right before the wedding and forced her to sign without opportunity to consult a lawyer.

**Black Letter Rule:** Prenuptial agreements are enforceable as written if they were made after fair financial disclosure.

### In the Matter of Baby M

**Instant Facts:** Stern (P) paid Whitehead (D) $10,000 to bear a child conceived by artificial insemination, and Whitehead (D) refused to relinquish the child to Stern (P) and his wife after Whitehead (D) gave birth.

**Black Letter Rule:** Surrogacy contracts that involve the payment of money to a woman who irrevocably agrees to bear a child and turn it over to another party are illegal and invalid.

# McKinnon v. Benedict

(Homeowner) v. (Campground Owners)
38 Wis.2d 607, 157 N.W.2d 665 (1968)

A COURT CAN DECIDE WHETHER TO ENFORCE A CONTRACT THAT APPEARS TO BE HARSH AND OPPRESSIVE AGAINST ONE OF THE PARTIES TO IT

■ **INSTANT FACTS** McKinnon loaned the Benedicts $5,000 to purchase their campground, and in return, restricted the Benedicts from making improvements near his property for 25 years.

■ **BLACK LETTER RULE** A contract which is harsh, oppressive, and unconscionable may still be enforceable at law, but it is within a court's discretion to not enforce equitable remedies against a party who suffers from such harshness and oppression under the contract.

■ **FACTS**

Roderick McKinnon (P) owned a tract of land consisting of over one thousand acres near a forest lake. In 1960, McKinnon (P) helped Mr. and Mrs. Roy Benedict (D) buy a nearby resort known as Bent's Camp. This camp consisted of about eighty acres, with a lodge and several cabins on the property. This camp was enclosed by the lake and by McKinnon's (P) property. While McKinnon (P) promised to help the Benedicts (D) obtain business, his help came mainly in the form of a $5,000 loan. Only one group occupied the resort as a result of McKinnon's (P) efforts, and that group stayed for less than a week. The Benedicts (D) used this loan as part of its down payment for purchasing the camp from its previous owners. In return for this loan, the Benedicts (D) promised to cut no trees between McKinnon's (P) property and the camp, and to make no improvements "closer to [McKinnon's] property than the present buildings." These restrictions were to remain in effect for 25 years. McKinnon (P) spent his winters out of the state. The Benedicts (D) were able to repay the loan in about seven months, but the resort was not successful. In 1964, they (D) made plans to add a trailer park and tent camp. From the fall of 1964 to the spring of 1965, they invested roughly $9,000 in bulldozing the property and installing utilities. That summer, McKinnon (P) returned, and he (P) later filed suit against the Benedicts (D). The trial court enjoined the Benedicts (D) from continuing work on the additions to the resort. The Benedicts (D) appealed.

■ **ISSUE**

Can a court choose not to enforce a contract when it appears that the contract is unfairly harsh or oppressive for one party?

■ **DECISION AND RATIONALE**

(Heffeman) Yes. A contract which is harsh, oppressive, and unconscionable may still be enforceable at law, but it is within a court's discretion to not enforce equitable remedies against a party who suffers from such harshness and oppression under the contract. Generally, contracts that are oppressive will not be enforced in equity. Also, restrictions on land use are not traditionally favored in the law, and so disputes over such restrictions should normally be resolved in favor of the free use of the property. The great hardship that McKinnon (P) would impose on the Benedicts (D) is clear. The only monetary consideration McKinnon (D) ever provided was a $5,000 loan, interest free, for a period of seven months. Also, McKinnon (P) stated that he would help generate business for the Benedicts (D), but, in the end, his (P) efforts have resulted in only one group's attendance at the resort. For all this, the Benedicts (D) have sacrificed their (D) right to make lawful and reasonable use of their (D) property. Granted, the Benedicts (D) could not have obtained the property without the $5,000 loan. This fact nonetheless demonstrates how the Benedicts (D) were unable to deal at arm's length with McKinnon (P). The Benedicts (D) need for the loan was apparently so great that they (D) were willing to enter a contract that resulted in gross inequities. The benefits that McKinnon (P) would enjoy from this agreement are more than outweighed by the burdens imposed on the Benedicts (D). McKinnon (P) cannot see the proposed trailer camp from his (P) home, and neither can the campsite be seen from that location during the summer, when the leaves are on the trees. Thus, the damage to McKinnon (P) would be minimal. Moreover, McKinnon (P) was a well-established businessman, as well as a former government official, at the time he (P) entered the contract. Mr. Benedict (D), by contrast, was a retail jeweler with limited financial ability. These factors further demonstrate the unfairness of the transaction. Judgment reversed

## Analysis:

A court is generally given discretion to deny specific performance. In withholding this remedy, the courts find justification in the fact that such a decision does not leave a claimant without any remedy at all if the claimant can still make a claim for damages. With a case like *McKinnon*, however, that remedy could be essentially meaningless. Here, the damages suffered by McKinnon (P) would be almost impossible to quantify.

## ■ CASE VOCABULARY

*SINE QUA NON*: Latin for "without which not"; used to describe a necessary precondition.

# Tuckwiller v. Tuckwiller

(Niece) v. (Aunt's Executor)
413 S.W.2d 274 (Mo. 1967)

A COURT SHOULD LOOK AT A TRANSACTION PROSPECTIVELY, NOT RETROACTIVELY, TO DETERMINE ITS FAIRNESS AND THE ADEQUACY OF ITS CONSIDERATION

■ **INSTANT FACTS** Ruby Tuckwiller contract to take care of her husband's aunt in exchange for the aunt's farm, but the aunt died shortly after signing the contract.

■ **BLACK LETTER RULE** The court should look at a transaction prospectively, from the viewpoint of the parties at the time at the time of the agreement, to determine the fairness of the transaction and the sufficiency of its consideration; once the essential fairness of a contract for real property and the adequacy of its consideration are found, a court of equity can decree specific performance of it.

■ **PROCEDURAL BASIS**

Appeal from judgment in action for injunctive relief.

■ **FACTS**

John and Ruby Tuckwiller (P) lived on the Hudson family farm. John's aunt, Metta Hudson Morrison, lived in New York and owned 160 acres of the farm property. When she was about 70 years old, Morrison contracted Parkinson's disease. Morrison had been educated at several schools, including Columbia, and had been a teacher for many years. After learning of her condition, Morrison returned to the Hudson farm in early 1963. Around this time, Morrison first asked Ruby (P) to quit her (P) job and care for her the rest of her life. In April 1963, Morrison had to be hospitalized for about a week. She was thought to have had a stroke, but on May 1st, her doctor found her mental state to be as "clear as a bell." The doctor also said that Morrison was aware that Parkinson's disease is a progressive condition which leaves its victims completely dependent on outside care. After Morrison was released from the hospital, she and Ruby (P) again discussed the possibility of Ruby Tuckwiller (P) providing care for her. On May 3, Morrison signed a paper written by Ruby (P) in which Ruby (P) offered to provide food and nursing care to Morrison during her lifetime. In exchange, Morrison would pass the family farm to her by will when she died. On May 6, Ruby (P) resigned from her job, and Morrison made an appointment with her lawyer to change her will. Later that day, however, Morrison had to be taken to the hospital. Before leaving for the hospital, Morrison had the aforementioned paper dated and signed by the two ambulance attendants as witnesses. Ruby (P) spent much time with Morrison at the hospital, even though Morrison was attended by special nurses. Except for four days, Morrison stayed at the hospital until she died on June 14. Morrison's will, prepared in 1961, was never changed. It provided for the sale of the farm, with the proceeds going into a student loan fund at Davidson College (Davidson) (D). Ruby (P) sued Davidson (D) and Marion Tuckwiller (D), Morrison's executor, for specific performance of her contract with Morrison. The trial court ruled for Ruby (P), and Davidson and Marion (D) appealed.

■ **ISSUE**

Can a court decree specific performance of a contract if it is unfair or has inadequate consideration?

the adequacy of the consideration. To declare a contract void against public policy, the contract must be invalid on the basis of recognized legal principles. The contract here does not fit that description. It is not a contract to pay one of the parties for inducing a public official to act in a certain way; it is not a contract to commit an illegal act; nor is it a contract which refers to collusive bidding on a government contract. The contract's only effect on the government was that Bush's (D) goods were to be used in products that the government would ultimately buy. Thus, the contract cannot be declared void as against public policy as Bush (D) contends. Granted, Black (P) would very likely have received a very high profit on the sale of the parts. Nonetheless, relative values of the consideration in a contract between businessmen, without any evidence of fraud, will not affect the validity of the contract. The mere fact that the government is the ultimate purchaser of the parts involved does not change this standard. To find that this contract would violate public policy solely because of the profit Black (P) could make would needlessly burden the courts with an extremely heavy regulatory function. Bush's (D) motion for summary judgment denied.

### Analysis:

Courts are reluctant to police contracts on the basis of their substance. In his 1958 work, *An Apology for Consideration*, Edwin Patterson suggested three reasons for such reluctance. One is that preventing the courts from setting fair prices makes the efficient administration of the law of contracts possible. A second reason is that ambiguous terms like "fair" and "reasonable" make it difficult to establish a bright-line test for enforceability. The third reason rests on the idea that mature and competent persons should have the freedom to make both wise and unwise contracts.

### ■ CASE VOCABULARY

COLLUSIVE: Performing toward a secret agreement, usually for an illegal or dishonorable purpose.

# O'Callaghan v. Waller & Beckwith Realty Co.

(Tenant) v. (Landlord)

15 Ill.2d 436, 155 N.E.2d 545 (1958)

---

AN EXCULPATORY CONTRACT WILL NOT BE ENFORCED IF SUCH ENFORCEMENT WOULD VIO-LATE THE PUBLIC POLICY OF THE STATE OR IF THE NATURE OF THE RELATIONSHIP OF THE PARTIES JUSTIFIES NO ENFORCEMENT

---

■ **INSTANT FACTS** O'Callaghan sued her landlord for negligence after falling in the building courtyard, and her landlord claimed an exculpatory clause in the lease barred the action.

■ **BLACK LETTER RULE** Contracts by which one tries to relieve himself or herself from liability for negligence are generally enforced unless it would be against the settled public policy of the State to do so, or there is something in the social relationship of the parties militating against upholding the agreement.

---

■ **PROCEDURAL BASIS**

Appeal from judgment in negligence action for damages.

■ **FACTS**

Ella O'Callaghan (P) was a tenant in a large apartment building maintained and operated by Waller & Beckwith Realty Co. (Waller & Beckwith) (D). O'Callaghan (P) was injured when she (P) fell while crossing the paved courtyard between the garage and her apartment. O'Callaghan (P) sued Waller & Beckwith (D) for negligence, claiming that her (P's) injuries were caused by defective pavement in the courtyard. Before the case was tried, O'Callaghan (P) died. Her (P) administrator was substituted as plaintiff in this action. The jury returned a verdict for $14,000 for O'Callaghan (P) and judgment was entered on the verdict. Waller & Beckwith (D) appealed. The Appellate Court held that the action was barred by an exculpatory clause in O'Callaghan's (P) lease, and that a verdict should have been directed for Waller & Beckwith (D). The trial court judgment was then reversed and the cause was remanded with directions to enter a judgment accordingly. Leave to appeal was granted.

■ **ISSUE**

Can a contract which contains a clause allowing one party to relieve itself of liability for negligence be valid and enforceable?

■ **DECISION AND RATIONALE**

(Schaefer) Yes. Contracts by which one tries to relieve himself or herself from liability for negligence are generally enforced unless it would be against the settled public policy of the State to do so, or there is something in the social relationship of the parties militating against upholding the agreement. O'Callaghan (P) argues that the exculpatory clause at issue here is contrary to public policy when included in a lease of residential property and invalid. Freedom of contract is basic to our law. If that freedom, however, is used to absolve one party from the consequences of his or her own negligence, then the standards of conduct which have developed for the protection of others may be diluted. The courts have refused to enforce exculpatory contracts between common carriers and freight companies

---

or passengers, and between telegraph companies and those sending. There is an obvious public interest involved in those transactions. Here, however, an essentially private transaction involving a lessor and lessee is involved. Clauses that exculpate the landlord from the consequences of his or her negligence have been sustained in residential as well as commercial leases. Contracts with such clauses can benefit both landlords and tenants. The risk of potential financial burden becomes widely dispersed among many tenants, and the impact of sanctions against a landlord to induce adherence to certain standards of care is lessened. O'Callaghan (P) claims that the shortage of housing has led to a disparity of bargaining power between lessors and lessees, with landlords receiving an unconscionable advantage over tenants. In pointing to a housing shortage through the existence of rent controls and numerous statutes, O'Callaghan (P) asks that the court augment a presumably inadequate response to this problem by the legislature. The relationship of landlord and tenant, however, does not have the same monopolistic characteristics as other relationships where exculpatory clauses have been considered invalid. There are thousands of landlords in competition with one another. The use of a form contract does not automatically establish disparity of bargaining power between landlord and tenant. Housing shortages are temporary, transitory events. The legislature, not the court, should be responsible for making policy decisions regarding such matters. Judgment of Appellate Court affirmed.

---

**Analysis:**

Most states have laws that provide that statements or clauses in residential leases that allow a landlord to escape liability to the tenant for negligence are ineffective. In other states, common law rules produce a similar result. Still other states have adopted variant statutory rules. For example, a tenant in Maine may enter into a written agreement by which the tenant will accept specific conditions that violate the warranty of fitness for human habitation. In return, the tenant can receive fair consideration, such as a written reduction in rent. Also, a tenant in Texas may waive certain responsibilities owed to him or her by the landlord, provided the waiver meets certain statutory form requirements for knowledge, voluntariness, and consideration. Moreover, several states, including illinois, have enacted statutory limitations on exculpatory provisions in commercial leases.

---

### ■ CASE VOCABULARY

ADMINISTRATOR: A person legally responsible for overseeing an estate after its owner's death.

EXCULPATORY: That which tends to clear someone from liability or guilt.

INDEMNIFY: To compensate for injury or loss.

# Graham v. Scissor-Tail, Inc.

(Music Promoter) v. (Musician's Corporation)

28 Cal.3d 807, 171 Cal.Rptr. 604, 623 P.2d 165 (1990)

## ADHESION CONTRACTS ARE ENFORCEABLE UNLESS UNCONSCIONABLE

■ **INSTANT FACTS** After a music promoter signed a mandatory form contract requiring arbitration before a biased panel and then loses his case, he sues to void the contract as unconscionable.

■ **BLACK LETTER RULE** Adhesion contracts are enforceable, except for provisions which contradict adherents' reasonable expectations, or are unconscionable.

■ **PROCEDURAL BASIS**

In contract arbitration seeking damages, appeal from appellate affirmation of award for defendant.

■ **FACTS**

Graham (P), an experienced music promoter and producer, contracted with singer Leon Russell's corporation Scissor-Tail, Inc. (D) to promote Russell's multi-city concert tour. The contract was an industry-standard form promulgated by the American Federation of Musicians ("A.F. of M.") and provided any disputes would be arbitrated by the A.F. of M's executive board. A.F. of M. required its producer-members to use only its form contract, and membership was virtually required to work in the industry. Some of Russell's concerts proved unprofitable, and disputes arose about whether losses could be applied to offset lucrative concerts' profits. Graham (P) sued for contract breach, but Scissor-Tail, Inc. (D) moved to compel arbitration, and won. At arbitration, the board found for Scissor-Tail (D). Graham (P) appealed, contending the agreement was unenforceable as an adhesion contract, and the arbitration clause was unconscionable. The appellate court affirmed the arbitrators' award. Graham (P) appeals again.

■ **ISSUE**

Is a standard form contract requiring disputes to be arbitrated before a industry panel void?

■ **DECISION AND RATIONALE**

Yes. Adhesion contracts are enforceable, except for provisions which contradict adherents' reasonable expectations, or are unconscionable. Adhesion contracts are a familiar part of the modern legal landscape, and an inevitable fact of life for businessmen and consumers alike. Here, Graham's (P) contract was adhesive; despite Graham's (P) prominence, he was required to be an A.F. of M. member, and thus obligated to use its form contracts, which reduced him to a humble adherent. However, adhesion contracts are generally enforceable, except for provisions which contradict adherents' reasonable expectations, or are unconscionable in context. Here, the arbitration clause was not contrary to Graham's (P) reasonable expectations, since he previously used such contracts. [However, the clause requiring arbitration before the A.F. of M. was unconscionable, since the A.F. of M. is presumably biased by reason of its status and identity.] Reversed.

**Analysis:**
Form contracts offer some efficiency gains by reducing the need to hire lawyers to draft individualized contracts. Adhesion contracts are unenforceable, however, when they undermine adherents' "reasonable expectations," which often happens when a contract that ostensibly confers some boon whittles away most of the expected benefit. Further, clauses that are "unconscionable" are unenforceable. Courts evaluating unconscionability use a process akin to measuring the sufficiency of consideration, deciding whether the contract mostly benefits one side. However, the standard of review is much higher. Unequal contracts are not unconscionable unless the inequality "shocks the conscience," or the terms are so oppressive that no reasonable person would knowingly and willingly assent.

### ■ CASE VOCABULARY

ADHESION CONTRACT: Standard form contract usually promulgated by parties with superior bargaining power. The counterparty must accept the contract as is, without the opportunity to negotiate terms.

UNCONSCIONABLE: Contracts are "unconscionable" when they are too favorable to one side to enforce against the other. A common test mandates that contracts should be voided as unconscionable, in whole or part, if they are so oppressive that no free and reasonable person would have consented to them freely.

# Carnival Cruise Lines, Inc. v. Shute

(Cruise Line) v. (Passenger)

499 U.S. 585, 111 S.Ct. 1522, 113 L.Ed.2d 622 (1991)

A FORUM-SELECTION CLAUSE SHOULD GENERALLY BE ENFORCED UNLESS A PARTY CLAIMING UNFAIRNESS CAN BEAR A HEAVY BURDEN OF PROOF

■ **INSTANT FACTS** After Shute was injured during a cruise, the cruise line claimed Shute could only file suit in Florida because of terms printed on her ticket.

■ **BLACK LETTER RULE** A forum-selection clause should be enforced unless the party claiming unfairness or inconvenience can bear a heavy burden of proof.

■ **PROCEDURAL BASIS**

Appeal from summary judgment in action for damages.

■ **FACTS**

The Shutes (P) bought passage for a cruise on the *Tropicale*, a ship owned and operated by Carnival Cruise Lines, Inc. (Carnival) (D). They (P) paid their (P) fare to a travel agent in Arlington, Washington, who then forwarded their (P) payment to Carnival's (D) headquarters in Miami, Florida. Carnival (D) prepared the tickets and sent them to the Shutes (P) at their (P) home in Washington. Each ticket contained a warning at its lower left-hand comer which read "SUBJECT TO CONDITIONS OF CONTRACT ON LAST PAGES IMPORTANTI PLEASE READ CONTRACT—ON PAGES 1, 2, 3." Page one of the contract provided, in part, that "... all disputes and matters whatsoever arising under, in connection with or incident to this Contract shall be litigated, if at all, in and before a Court located in the State of Florida, U.S.A., to the exclusion of the Courts of any other state or country." This was the forum-selection clause of the contract. The Shutes (Ps) boarded the *Tropicale* in Los Angeles, California. The ship sailed to Mexico and then returned to Los Angeles. While the ship was in international waters off the Mexican coast, Mrs. Shute (P) took a guided tour of the ship's galley. During this tour, Mrs. Shute (P) slipped on a deck mat and was injured. The Shutes (P) filed suit against Carnival (D), claiming that Mrs. Shute (P) was injured as a result of the negligence of Carnival (D) and its (D) employees. This suit was raised in the United States District Court for the Western District of Washington. Carnival (D) moved for summary judgment, arguing that the forum-selection clause on the tickets required the Shutes (P) to bring their suit in a court in Florida. Alternatively, Carnival (D) claimed that its contacts were insufficient for the District Court to have personal jurisdiction. The District Court granted the motion, finding that Carnival's (D) contacts with Washington were constitutionally insufficient to support the exercise of personal jurisdiction. The Court of Appeals reversed, reasoning that the Shutes (P) would not have even taken the cruise if Carnival (D) did not have such extensive contacts with the State of Washington through its advertisements and solicitations of business. Thus, the Court of Appeals concluded that the exercise of personal jurisdiction was justified.

■ **ISSUE**

Is a forum-selection clause found in a pre-printed form contract or ticket generally enforceable?

# Doe v. Great Expectations

(Customer) v. (Dating Service)

10 Misc.3d 618, 809 N.Y.S.2d 819 (N.Y.City Civ. Ct. 2005)

DATING CONTRACTS MUST COMPLY WITH THE LAW

I paid Great Expectations, but they didn't introduce me to anyone.

That's terrible, Doe.

stus.com

■ **INSTANT FACTS** Doe (P) signed up with Great Expectations (D) for dating and introduction services, but she met no one through the service.

■ **BLACK LETTER RULE** A consumer injured by a contract that violates statutory requirements may collect actual damages, to be set at the face amount of the contract.

■ **PROCEDURAL BASIS**

Decision after a small claims court hearing.

■ **FACTS**

Doe (P) and Roe (P) signed form contracts for services to be rendered by Great Expectations (D). Doe (P) paid $1,000 for a six-month contract, and Roe (P) paid $3,790 for a thirty-six month contract that was eventually extended to a total duration of fifty-four months. The contracts stated that Great Expectations (D) would provide photo shoots and dating advice, but would provide no social referrals. The contracts also stated that Doe (P) and Roe (P) did not wish to receive referrals from Great Expectations (D). Roe's (P) contract included a handwritten notation indicating that she was informed orally that she would be introduced to twelve people through Great Expectations (D). Doe (P) met no one through Great Expectations (D), but at some point stopped checking with the service. Roe (P) received no introductions, but met one person who approached her after seeing her information.

■ **ISSUE**

Are Doe (P) and Roe (P) entitled to collect damages from Great Expectations (D)?

■ **DECISION AND RATIONALE**

(Lebedeff, J.) Yes. A consumer injured by a contract that violates statutory requirements may collect actual damages, to be set at the face amount of the contract. The contract here is subject to the New York Dating Services Law, N.Y. Gen. Bus. Law § 394–c, which applies to all services "providing matching of members of the opposite sex ... for the purpose of dating and general social contact." The law has been held to apply to services that match members by creating a location and mechanism for members to assess one another.

There are two principal departures from the requirements of the law in this case. First, the charges are excessive. When no assurances are provided that a service will furnish a client with a specified number of referrals per month, the maximum charge is twenty-five dollars. Roe (P) was told that she would get twelve introductions over the course of thirty-six months, but that is not an assurance of a specified number each month. The second departure is that the form contract violates every provision of the Dating Services Law, with the exception of the mandatory three-day cooling-off period. The provisions omitted include stating a "specified number of social referrals per month," disclosure of the option to cancel and obtain a refund, a statement that personal information will not be revealed without consent, the client's right to place a membership on hold for a year, the return of personal information at the end of the contract, the maximum distance for a face-to-face meeting, and the policy to be applied if the customer moves out of the service area. Great Expectations (D) also failed to provide written notice of the mandatory "Dating Service Consumer Bill of Rights."

The Dating Service Law provides that a person injured by a violation of the law may bring an action to recover his or her actual damages or fifty dollars, whichever is greater. In this case, the actual damages include the difference between each contract price and the maximum twenty-five dollar fee permitted. Doe (P) and Roe (P) seek restitution of the full balance paid, including the twenty-five dollars. The court finds that they would not have signed contracts violating the applicable laws if they had known of their rights, so they are also entitled to a refund including the twenty-five dollar balance. The statutory language regarding actual damages was added along with a provision authorizing the Attorney General to bring enforcement actions and seek civil penalties. Consumers were offered a single remedy of restitution, available through a private lawsuit or through an enforcement action by the Attorney General. The addition of "actual damages" to the law does not erode the commitment to protect consumers from price-gouging by dating services.

The contracts of Doe (P) and Roe (P) are terminated, Doe's (P) by expiration and Roe's (P) by reason of this action. Great Expectations (D) may wish to return personal material to them, or face adverse consequences outside the scope of this litigation. The court has the discretion to report unlawful conduct to the appropriate authorities. This matter impacts the public interest in that it violates the rules of a regulated industry, and a similar course of conduct by Great Expectations (D) has previously been litigated. In addition, the court's truth-determining function will not be impacted by a report. Accordingly, the court will report this matter to the appropriate officials. Judgment ordered in favor of Doe (P) and Roe (P).

## Analysis:

Did the court award Doe (P) and Roe (P) damages, or did it impose a penalty on their behalf? If the case is looked at strictly as a breach of contract matter, without reference to the Dating Services Law, there is no proof that Great Expectations (D) breached the contract. From a strictly contractual point of view, there are no damages. The court, however, presumes damage from the statutory violations. Doe (P) and Roe (P) would not, in the court's reasoning, have signed the contract in the first place if they knew the contract was illegal, and the full contract price is, therefore, the amount by which they were damaged.

# Williams v. Walker-Thomas Furniture Co.

(Welfare Customer) v. (Furniture Store)

350 F.2d 445, 18 A.L.R.3d 1297 (D.C. Cir. 1965)

---

**CONTRACTS WITH APPARENTLY UNCONSCIONABLE TERMS ARE UNENFORCEABLE**

---

■ **INSTANT FACTS** Williams bought furniture and a stereo on credit from Walker-Thomas while on welfare, and Walker-Thomas repossessed the items when Williams defaulted.

■ **BLACK LETTER RULE** A contract is unenforceable if its terms, when considered in light of the circumstances existing when the contract was made, are so extreme as to appear unconscionable according to prevailing mores and business practices.

■ **PROCEDURAL BASIS**

Appeal from judgment in action for replevin.

■ **FACTS**

Walker-Thomas Furniture Company (Walker-Thomas) (D) runs a retail furniture store. From 1957 to 1962, Williams (P) and others (P) bought several household items from Walker-Thomas (D). Payments for these items were to be made through installment plans. The terms of each purchase were contained in a printed form contract which stated the value of the purchased item and the amount of monthly rent payment to be made by the customer. The contract also provided that Walker-Thomas (D) would remain the owner of the purchased item until all monthly payments were made. At that point, the customer could take title to the goods. In the event of a default in the payment of any monthly installment, Walker-Thomas (D) could repossess the item. Moreover, under the contract, any payments made would be credited pro rata on all outstanding balances. In other words, if a customer had bought more than one item on installments, his or her payments would be credited to all the debts for all the different items. This overall balance would then exist until all balances due were paid in full. On April 17, 1962, Williams (P) bought a stereo set for $514.95. By that point, Williams had an outstanding balance of about $164 for previously purchased goods. Her (P) new balance thus increased to $679. Williams (P) was receiving a $218 stipend from the government every month. Walker-Thomas (D) was aware of Williams' (P) financial status when selling the stereo to her (P), and Williams' (P) social worker's name was even written on the back of the contract. Williams (P) eventually defaulted on her (P) payments shortly thereafter, and Walker-Thomas (D) sought to replevy all the items she (P) purchased after December 1957. The Court of General Sessions granted judgment for Walker-Thomas (D). The District of Columbia Court of Appeals affirmed, and leave to appeal was granted.

■ **ISSUE**

Can a contract which appears unconscionable at the time it is made be enforceable?

■ **DECISION AND RATIONALE**

(Wright) No. A contract is unenforceable if its terms, when considered in light of the circumstances existing when the contract was made, are so extreme as to appear unconscionable according to prevailing mores and business practices. Congress should consider enacting corrective legislation to protect the public from such exploitative contracts as were used by Walker-Thomas (D) in this case. In fact, Congress has recently enacted the Uniform Commercial Code, which specifically provides that the court may refuse to enforce a contract which it finds to be unconscionable at the time it was made. This court now holds in accordance with this position. Unconscionability has generally been considered as including the absence of meaningful choice for one party combined with contract terms which are unreasonably favorable to the other party. Whether a party has a meaningful choice may depend on several factors, including the manner in which the contract was entered, or the disparity of bargaining power. Granted, a party that signs a contract without full knowledge of its terms may often be assumed to have entered a one-sided bargain. It is unlikely, though, that a party with little bargaining power or choice when entering such a contract could give his or her consent to all the terms of the contract. In determining the reasonableness or fairness of a contract, the primary concern must be with the terms, considered in light of the circumstances existing when the contract was made. This test cannot be mechanically applied. Case remanded to trial court for further proceedings.

## ■ DISSENT

(Danaher) There must be thousands upon thousands of this kind of transaction occurring everyday. Because the law has long allowed parties such latitude in making contracts, any approach to this problem should be a cautious one. Here, Williams (P) apparently knew precisely where she (P) stood in this contract. The District of Columbia Court of Appeals was correct in its disposition of the issues.

## Analysis:

As it turned out, Williams (P) had bought about sixteen items from Walker-Thomas (D) between 1957 and 1962. She owed only twenty-five cents on the first item, three cents on the second item, and similarly trivial amounts on the other items, except for the stereo. Thus, if Walker-Thomas (D) had applied Williams's (P) payments in relation to the original debt for each item, she would have paid in full for about a dozen of the sixteen items she bought. The manner of apportioning payments has been widely prescribed by various statutes. A broad consumer-protection rule of the Federal Trade Commission applied in this case, would have limited Walker-Thomas (D) to reserving an interest in any items it sold so that only the unpaid price of the item or items subject to that transaction would be secured. In other words, the stereo could only serve as collateral for the outstanding balance on the stereo alone. This kind of regulation would offer far more protection to Williams (P) than the original plan.

## ■ CASE VOCABULARY

LOAN SHARK: One who lends money to others at extremely high rates of interest, often threatening violence against the borrower if he or she defaults.

PRO RATA: At a proportional rate.

REPLEVIN: An action to recover taken property, and not the value of the property.

# Jones v. Star Credit Corp.

(Welfare Customer) v. (Credit Company)

59 Misc.2d 189, 298 N.Y.S.2d 264 (Sup.Ct. 1969)

---

AN ENTIRE CONTRACT, NOT JUST A CLAUSE OF A CONTRACT, CAN BE CONSIDERED UNCON-SCIONABLE AND THEREBY UNENFORCEABLE BY THE COURT

---

**INSTANT FACTS** While on welfare, the Joneses agreed to buy a $300 freezer on credit, with additional credit and fees running the purchase price up to $1,234.80.

■ **BLACK LETTER RULE** A court may find that an entire contract, and not just a particular clause of it, is unconscionable as a matter of law and thereby unenforceable.

■ **PROCEDURAL BASIS**

Breach of contract action for damages.

■ **FACTS**

The Joneses (P) are welfare recipients. On August 30, 1965, the Joneses (P) agreed to buy a home freezer unit for $900 as the result of a visit from a salesman from Your Shop at Home Service, Inc. The purchase price, including credit charges, credit life insurance, credit property insurance, and sales tax, totaled $1,234.80. By the time this action commenced, the Joneses (P) had paid $619.88 toward their (P) purchase. Star Credit Corp. (D) argues that, with additional charges for an extension of the plan, the Joneses (P) still owe a balance of $819.81. The uncontroverted proof at the trial established that the freezer unit had a maximum retail value of about $300 at the time of purchase.

■ **ISSUE**

Can a contract be declared unenforceable if only one term of it, such as its price, can be considered unconscionable?

■ **DECISION AND RATIONALE**

(Wachtler) Yes. A court may find that an entire contract, and not just a particular clause of it, is unconscionable as a matter of law and thereby unenforceable. The poorer members of the community, often uneducated and illiterate, should be protected from overreaching by those with greater bargaining power. Common law and statutory law have recognized the importance of free enterprise and yet have provided legal armor to protect customers from unconscionable contracts. Section 2–302 of the Uniform Commercial Code allows a court to manipulate fluid rules of contract law and determinations based upon a presumed public policy. There is no reason to doubt that this section was also intended to cover the price term of an agreement. The statutory language itself makes clear that not only a clause of the contract, but the contract in its entirety, may be found unconscionable as a matter of law. No other provision of an agreement affects the question of unconscionability more that those affecting price. There is no fraud in this case, but fraud is not necessary. The sale of a $300 freezer for over $1,400 is unconscionable as a matter of law. This does not mean that § 2–302 should be reduced to a solely mathematical formula. Limited financial resources of the customer, as was the case with Jones (P), should also be considered. Indeed, a gross inequality of bargaining power can negate any meaningfulness of choice. Granted, Installment payment plans and extensions of credit are often desirable, even necessary, for people to obtain the most basic conveniences. A merchant may also charge additional costs above the retail value of an item to protect against those who may default on such arrangements. Neither of these premises, however, can validate this arrangement. Star Credit (D) has already been amply compensated for the freezer. The payment provision should be limited to amounts already paid by the Joneses (P) and the contract should be reformed and amended to only call for the amount already paid by the Joneses (P).

### Analysis:

The courts have generally been more hesitant to determine the fairness of the price term of a contract than the fairness of other clauses. The price term is special, because a party can rarely claim surprise regarding price. Indeed, the price is often a negotiable term. Further, evaluating the fairness of the price term is not easy for the courts. Most courts have been satisfied with relatively crude, simple calculations in price unconscionability cases. There are questions regarding how much weight should be given to certain factors, including a seller's markup, any difference between the seller's price and that of other sellers and the potential profit for a seller. For these and other reasons, most courts have avoided ruling that an unfair price, without other evidence of unfairness, is unconscionable.

### ■ CASE VOCABULARY

CAVEAT: A warning against performing a certain act.

INTRINSIC: Having to do with the essential nature of something.

OVERREACHING: Taking unfair advantage of another through abuse of one's superior bargaining power or through fraud.

# Armendariz v. Foundation Health Psychcare Services

(Employee) v. (Employer)

24 Cal.4th 83, 99 Cal.Rptr.2d 745, 6 P.3d 669 (2000)

## EMPLOYMENT AGREEMENTS' ARBITRATION CLAUSES ARE GENERALLY ENFORCEABLE

■ **INSTANT FACTS** A fired employee challenges her employment agreement, which requires her to arbitrate claims against her employer.

■ **BLACK LETTER RULE** Employment contracts' arbitration clauses are enforceable, unless the arbitration procedure is unfair, the arbitration is unilateral, or the clause is unfair procedurally or substantively.

■ **PROCEDURAL BASIS**

In wrongful termination suit, appeal from appellate affirmation of judgement for plaintiff.

■ **FACTS**

Ms. Armendariz (P) was employed by Foundation Health Psychcare Services, Inc. ("Employer") (D). Armendariz's (P) employment agreement included a clause requiring arbitration of employees' wrongful termination claims. Later, Armendariz (P) was fired, ostensibly because her position was eliminated. Armendariz (P) sued for wrongful termination and employment law violations, alleging she was fired for refusing coworkers' sexual advances. Armendariz (P) claimed she could not be compelled to arbitrate because her employment agreement's arbitration clause was unconscionable, and made the entire agreement void. At trial, the court found the arbitration clause unconscionable and invalidated the whole agreement. On appeal, the Court of Appeal reversed, finding the clause unenforceable but the remaining agreement valid. Employer (D) appeals.

■ **ISSUE**

Is an adhesive employment contract's unilateral arbitration clause void?

■ **DECISION AND RATIONALE**

(Mosk) Yes. Employment contracts' arbitration clauses are enforceable, unless the arbitration procedure is unfair, the arbitration is unilateral, or the clause is unfair procedurally or substantively. [We hold that employment agreements may properly require employees to arbitrate *statutory* [employment discrimination] claims, as long as the arbitration procedure is fair, and includes (i) a neutral arbiter, (ii) adequate discovery, (iii) written decisions allowing some judicial review, and (iv) reasonable arbitral fees. We now turn to whether employment agreements requiring arbitration for *general* claims are unconscionable.] *Scissor-Tail* held that, if a contract is adhesive, then courts must determine whether other factors are present to render it void, e.g., undermining adherents' "reasonable expectations" or setting oppressive or "unconscionable" terms. California's *Civil Code* allows courts to void unconscionable contractual provisions, including arbitration clauses. Evaluating "unconscionability" has a "procedural" element (for oppression/surprise due to unequal bargaining power) and a "substantive" one (for overly-harsh or one-sided results); both facets must be present to find unconscionability. Here, we find Armendariz' (P) employment agreement adhesive, since it was imposed as a condition of employment, without opportunity to negotiate. Further, employment contracts allow employers to exert economic pressure on most employees. While arbitration may be cost-efficient, studies show it awards employees less damages. Since arbitration's justification is its voluntariness, we must be sensitive of forced arbitration. Here, Armendariz (P) contends the agreement is unconscionabile because it requires employees to arbitrate against Employer (D), but allows Employer (D) to litigate claims against employees, relying on *Stirlen v. Supercuts, Inc.* [high-level employee may void one-sided arbitration clause]. However, *Stirlen* required only a "modicum of bilaterality" in adhesion contracts; complete mutuality is not required. However, *Stirlen* does not mean that arbitration clauses are illusory or suspect, as long as the arrangement has some reasonable justification other than maximizing employers' advantage. An adhesive arbitration agreement which requires only 1 party to arbitrate claims arising from the same transaction(s) is non-mutual and unfair. Here, we find Armendariz's (P) arbitration agreement was unconscionable, since it required employees to arbitrate wrongful termination claims, but implicitly allowed Employer (D) the option of litigating against employees. The fact that employers are unlikely to sue employees is no justification for unilateral arbitration agreements. Reversed.

---

**Analysis:**

*Armendariz* considers a type of adhesion contract that is prevalent in fact, but that is not usually thought of in the same context as a standard adhesion contract. Of course, prospective employees are even more vulnerable to oppression than consumers. Large employers enjoy vastly more bargaining power than almost any employee, since just about any worker could be replaced. *Armendariz* caused a flurry of litigation and efforts to redraft arbitration clauses to be enforceable, but in the end, it offers little clear guidance on exactly when an employment agreement or arbitration clause will be considered valid.

---

# Scott v. Cingular Wireless

(Telephone Customer) v. (Telephone Service Provider)

160 Wash.2d 843, 161 P.3d 1000 (2007)

---

## CLASS ACTIONS VINDICATE CONSUMER RIGHTS

---

■ **INSTANT FACTS** Scott (P) filed a class action suit against Cingular (D) to challenge the legality of certain charges, and Cingular (D) moved to enforce the arbitration clause in its standard contract.

■ **BLACK LETTER RULE** An arbitration clause that prohibits consumer class actions is substantively unconscionable in that such a clause undermines enforcement of consumer protection laws, and because such a clause severely limits the remedies of only one side.

---

■ **PROCEDURAL BASIS**

Appeal from an order granting a motion to compel arbitration.

■ **FACTS**

Scott (P) and other plaintiffs purchased cellular telephones and calling plans from Cingular (D). The contracts were all standard preprinted agreements that contained a clause requiring mandatory arbitration. The arbitration clause prohibited consolidation of cases, class action suits, and class arbitration. Cingular (D) also reserved the right to unilaterally revise the agreement.

The agreement was modified in July 2003 by a monthly "bill stuffer." The revised agreement continued to prohibit class actions, and it also provided that arbitration would be conducted according to the rules of the American Arbitration Association. The agreement further provided that Cingular (D) would pay the fees associated with the arbitration unless the customer's claim was frivolous, that Cingular (D) also would pay the customer's attorney's fees and expenses if the customer received at least the demanded amount, and that arbitration would take place in the county of the customer's billing address. Limitations on punitive damages were removed.

Scott (P) brought suit against Cingular (D), claiming that customers were overcharged for long distance and out-of-network roaming calls. Customers were overcharged up to approximately $45 per month, according to the suit. Scott (P) admitted that the loss to each individual customer was small, but in the aggregate, Cingular (D) overcharged the public by a significant amount. Cingular (D) moved to compel individual arbitration. Scott (P) argued that the class action waiver was substantively and procedurally unconscionable. The trial court granted Cingular's (D) motion to compel, finding that although the contract was a contract of adhesion, it was not sufficiently complex, illegal, or misleading to be procedurally unconscionable.

■ **ISSUE**

Was the class action waiver clause unconscionable?

■ **DECISION AND RATIONALE**

(Chambers, J.) Yes. An arbitration clause that prohibits consumer class actions is substantively unconscionable in that such a clause it undermines enforcement of consumer protection laws, and

---

because such a clause severely limits the remedies of only one side. An agreement is against public policy if it is against the public good or is injurious to the public. Washington law authorizes class actions and shows a state policy of favoring the aggregation of small claims for efficiency, deterrence, and the access to justice. When consumer claims are small but numerous, a class-based remedy is the only effective way to vindicate the public's rights. Individual actions by defrauded consumers are often impracticable because the amount of an individual's recovery may be too small to justify bringing a separate suit. Class remedies not only resolve the claims of the individual class members, but can also deter future similar conduct. Consumers who bring actions under the Consumer Protection Act do not merely vindicate their own rights, they represent the public interest. Courts have held that class actions are a critical part of the enforcement of the consumer protection laws. Without class actions, many meritorious claims would never be brought, and there would be far less opportunity to vindicate the Consumer Protection Act. The class action waiver in the instant case is a substantively unconscionable violation of the state's policy, because it drastically forestalls attempts to vindicate consumer rights. It is unnecessary to address the claims of procedural unconscionability.

The class action waiver is also unconscionable for effectively exculpating Cingular (D) for a large class of wrongful conduct. Contract provisions that exculpate the drafter for wrongdoing undermine the public good, especially when the drafter is exculpated for intentional wrongdoing. Exculpation for unfair or deceptive acts or practices in commerce clearly violates public policy. On its face, the class action waiver does not exculpate Cingular (D) from anything. The waiver merely channels disputes into individual arbitration or small claims court. But in effect, the waiver does exculpate Cingular (D) whenever the cost of pursuing a claim outweighs the potential of recovery. The realistic alternative to a class action, as Judge Posner points out, is not millions of individual suits, but zero individual suits "as only a lunatic or a fanatic sues for $30." In cases involving smaller claims, the ability to proceed as a class transforms a merely theoretical remedy into a real one. Without a class action, many consumers may not even realize that they have a claim, but class actions have a mechanism to alert potential claimants.

Shifting the arbitration cost to Cingular (D) does not seem likely to make it worth the time, expense, and effort to pursue individual small claims. Scott (P) presented evidence that the cost does prevent claims. It appears that no claims from Washington customers have been brought to arbitration against Cingular (D) in the past six years. Cingular (D) claims that its promise to pay the costs associated with arbitration removes any concerns about access to a remedy. This promise, however laudable, does not ensure that a remedy is practically available. Attorney's fees are awarded only if the consumer recovers at least the full amount of his or her demand. A consumer could recover ninety-nine percent of a claim and still be denied attorney's fees. In addition, the arbitrator still may consider the amount in controversy when awarding fees. Although customers are not barred from hiring an attorney, it is made impracticable for them to do so. The class action waiver thus prohibits one party to the contract, the consumer, from pursuing small claims. It is therefore substantively unconscionable for denying any meaningful remedy.

The class action waiver states that if it is found to be unenforceable, the entire arbitration clause is null and void. There is thus no basis on which to compel arbitration. Reversed and remanded.

■ **DISSENT**

(Madsen, J.) If there is a public policy forbidding class action waivers, it should come from the legislature, not the court. The new policy of the majority disfavors arbitration, contradicting the strong public policy favoring arbitration embodied in the Federal Arbitration Act. Under the Act, every arbitration agreement is presumed valid. This policy is of particular force where, as here, the arbitration agreement includes significant financial protections for consumers. If this arbitration clause violates "public policy," then it is difficult to imagine any in the consumer context that would not.

The majority also departs from the usual case-by-case analysis for determining contract unconscionability in favor of a sweeping rule. This rule will invalidate thousands of arbitration contracts without regard to the specific terms of those contracts.

**Analysis:**

In a footnote, the majority says that, contrary to the claims of the dissent, it is not holding that the Consumer Protection Act invalidates all class action waivers, but only those that effectively prohibit enforcement of the Consumer Protection Act. It is not clear when the waivers would be permitted, as the majority's language seems absolute. The case cited as an example in the footnote, *Hangman Ridge Training Stables, Inc. v. Safeco Tit. Ins. Co.,* 105 Wash. 2d 778, 719 P. 2d 531 (1986), does not mention arbitration or class actions. Interestingly, the court's opinion in the instant case also specifically states that "class-wide" arbitration would not be prohibited under its ruling.

### ■ CASE VOCABULARY

CLASS ACTION: A lawsuit in which a single person or small group of people represents the interests of a larger group. Federal procedure has several requirements for maintaining a class action: (1) the class must be so large that individual suits would be impracticable, (2) there must be legal or factual questions common to the class, (3) the claims or defenses of the representative parties must be typical of those of the class, and (4) the representative parties must adequately protect the interests of the class. Fed. R. Civ. P. 23.

PROCEDURAL UNCONSCIONABILITY: Unconscionability resulting from improprieties in contract formation (such as oral misrepresentations or disparities in bargaining position) rather than from the terms of the contract itself.

SUBSTANTIVE UNCONSCIONABILITY: Unconscionability resulting from actual contract terms that are unduly harsh, commercially unreasonable, and grossly unfair given the existing circumstances.

UNCONSCIONABILITY: 1. Extreme unfairness. Unconscionability is normally assessed by an objective standard: (1) one party's lack of meaningful choice, and (2) contractual terms that unreasonably favor the other party. 2. The principle that a court may refuse to enforce a contract that is unfair or oppressive because of procedural abuses during contract formation or because of overreaching contractual terms, especially terms that are unreasonably favorable to one party while precluding meaningful choice for the other party. Because unconscionability depends on circumstances at the time the contract is formed, a later rise in market price is irrelevant.

UNCONSCIONABLE: Showing no regard for conscience; affronting the sense of justice, decency, or reasonableness.

# Dalton v. Educational Testing Service

(SAT Test-Taker) v. (SAT Test Administrator)

87 N.Y.2d 384, 639 N.Y.S.2d 977, 663 N.E.2d 289 (Ct. App. 1995)

---

**ALL CONTRACTS IMPLY A DUTY TO PERFORM OBLIGATIONS FAIRLY AND IN GOOD FAITH**

---

■ **INSTANT FACTS** The SAT's administrator reserves the right to cancel disputed scores, but allows test-takers to present evidence proving validity. When the administrator decided a test-taker had an impostor write his test, it ignored the test-taker's proffered evidence.

■ **BLACK LETTER RULE** When a contract allows parties to present evidence disputing the other's discretionary determinations, the determiner must review proffered evidence in good faith, and otherwise perform its obligations fairly and faithfully.

---

■ **PROCEDURAL BASIS**

In contract action seeking specific performance, appeal from appellate affirmation of judgement for plaintiff.

■ **FACTS**

Student Dalton (P) registered to take the Scholastic Aptitude Test (SAT), administered by Educational Testing Service ("ETS") (D). In registering, Dalton (P) signed ETS' (D) standard agreement, allowing ETS (D) "the right to cancel any test score ... if ETS believes ... there is reason to question the score's validity." The agreement also provided that, if "the validity of a test score is questioned because it may have been obtained unfairly, ETS [will notify] the test taker or the reasons for questioning the score" and giving the test taker the option of either providing an explanation, taking a free retest, canceling the score and obtaining a refund, appealing to the college receiving the score, or arbitrating. Since Dalton's (P) score on his second attempt rose substantially over his first, ETS (D) flagged his exam. ETS' (D) officials and handwriting experts analyzed Dalton's (P) test, opining someone else had written Dalton's (P) second test for him. ETS (D) decided preliminarily to cancel his second score unless he provided explanation. Dalton (P) offered evidence that he was sick with mononucleosis (a lingering, fatigue-inducing infection) the first time, and witness testimony confirming he was present at the testing center the second time. However, ETS (D) merely submitted Dalton's (P) 2 exams to another handwriting analyst, who again opined they were discrepant. [Meaning ETS (D) ignored Dalton's (P) explanations.] Dalton (P) sued ETS (D) for breach of contract, demanding ETS (D) release his score and contending ETS' (D) dispute-resolution procedures implied an obligation to review evidence in good faith. ETS (D) defended, contending Dalton's (P) proof of illness and presence were irrelevant to the disparate handwriting. [Huh? And ETS (D) is testing *our* abstract reasoning ability?] At trial, the judge held for Dalton (P), finding ETS (D) breached by failing to investigate Dalton's (P) furnished information, and ordered ETS (D) to release his score. On appeal, the Appellate Division affirmed. ETS (D) appeals.

■ **ISSUE**

When a contract allows parties to present evidence disputing the other's discretionary determinations, must the determiner review proffered evidence?

---

requirements are reasonably foreseeable. Eastern (P) and Gulf (D) have supply contracts which extend back over thirty years. During this time, Eastern's (P) fuel requirements have continually changed with the vagaries of the airline industry. As a result, Eastern (P) has occasionally requested large amounts of fuel at particular Gulf (D) stations. The parties have always been aware of this problem and, indeed, it has played a part in their contract negotiations. We can conclude from these facts that fuel freighting is simply a part of the airline business. In addition, it has long been a part of the dealings between the parties. There is no evidence that Eastern (P) is abusing the privilege to raise and lower its requirements as needed. It is still constrained by its established routes to buy fuel when and where they need it. This case would be different if Eastern (P) was asking for unreasonable amounts of fuel, or requesting no fuel at all. This is not the case, however. Gulf (D) is complaining of a practice that is common in the industry and between the parties. With this in mind, it cannot be said that Eastern (P) acted in bad faith. [For this reason and others, the court granted Eastern's (P) request for a permanent injunction, requiring Gulf (D) to continue supplying fuel at the posted rates.]

## Analysis:

The requirement of good faith in commercial dealings may seem a bit malleable. That is as it should be. The Uniform Commercial Code attempts, through gap-filling and other provisions, to preserve an already dynamic and specialized system of commercial transactions. The drafters recognized that many long term transactions develop lives of their own, based on the parties' knowledge of each other and their industry. The implied duty of good faith is designed to respect the relationship of the parties without defining the actual requirements of good faith in every case. As a result, the question of good faith is necessarily a factual one that can only be answered on a case-by-case basis. However, as with all rules, its refinement through case law can provide some guidance for the parties to future transactions. In this way, the rule provides general guidance for every commercial transaction and specific guidance under previously recognized circumstances.

## ■ CASE VOCABULARY

FREIGHTING: The practice of buying extra fuel at an airport where the price is low to avoid needing fuel at a stop where the price is higher.

GOOD FAITH: Good faith is a phrase which can have a variety of meanings depending upon the legal context in which it used. Many areas of the law rely on a definition of good faith which is unique to that practice area. The UCC's definition governs commercial transactions. The UCC, however, defines good faith differently from one article to the next. Article 1 posits a subjective definition of good faith as "honesty in fact in the conduct or transaction concerned." Article 2 requires honesty in fact as well as the objective observance of "reasonable commercial standards of fair dealing in the trade."

# Market Street Associates v. Frey [General Electric Pension Trust]

(Lessee) v. (Property Owner)

941 F.2d 588 (7th Cir. 1991)

## COURT OF APPEALS DESCRIBES THE BOUNDARIES OF AN IMPLIED DUTY OF GOOD FAITH

■ **INSTANT FACTS** A leaseholder tries to exercise an option which enables him to buy the leased property from its owner.

■ **BLACK LETTER RULE** The duty of good faith precludes a party from taking deliberate advantage of an oversight by the other party concerning its rights under the contract.

## ■ PROCEDURAL BASIS

Appeal from a trial court judgement for the defendant in an action for specific performance on a lease option.

## ■ FACTS

J.C. Penney entered into a fairly complicated financial arrangement with General Electric Pension Trust (GE) (D). Under the resulting agreement, J.C. Penney sold its property to GE (D) and then leased it back from them. This transaction was supposed to provide J.C. Penney with capital for growth enhancement. Paragraph 34 of the agreement required GE (D) to give reasonable consideration to any requests from J.C. Penney for the financing of improvements. In addition, paragraph 34 gave J.C. Penney the right to buy back its property if negotiations for improvements broke down, and if J.C. Penney's property had an average annual appreciation over 6%. A successor of J.C. Penney's under one of its leases, Market Street Associates (Market Street) (P), was interested in buying the property back from GE (D). GE's (D) representative, Erb, did not respond to inquiries. Market Street (P) subsequently sent two letters to Erb, requesting financing for improvements. They never mentioned paragraph 34 in these letters. Erb denied Market Street's (P) request because they asked for an amount less than the minimum loan of $7 million. Market Street (P) then tried to exercise the buyback option under paragraph 34. GE (D) refused this request as well, forcing Market Street (P) to sue for specific performance. The district court granted summary judgement to GE (D), finding that Market Street (P) violated its duty of good faith under the agreement. Market Street's (P) representative, Orenstein, admitted that he did not think Erb knew about paragraph 34 when it made its request for financing. The district court decided that Market Street (P) had deliberately manufactured the circumstances which triggered the buyback option. Market Street (P) appeals this determination.

## ■ ISSUE

Does the duty of good faith require a party to protect against another party's ignorance of a contract term?

## ■ DECISION AND RATIONALE

(Posner) Yes. The district court felt that Market Street (P) had an obligation to remind GE (D) of paragraph 34, even though GE (D) was likely to discover the paragraph when it processed Market Street's (P) request for financing. It was correct, but this approach has its limits. The duty of good faith does not require parties to look out for each other's financial well being. In fact, a party to a contract is fully entitled to take advantage of its superior knowledge or financial position when dealing with another party. A party cannot, however, take advantage of an oversight by the other party which affects its rights under the contract. In this case, it is not clear whether Orenstein took advantage of Erb's lack of knowledge regarding paragraph 34, or if he simply assumed that GE (D) would discover the paragraph on its own. This question cannot be answered on summary judgement. Instead, it requires an inquiry into Orenstein's state of mind at the time. As a result, the district court's grant of summary judgement is reversed and the case is remanded for trial.

## Analysis:

Judge Posner's opinion in this case is interesting because it demonstrates that law and economics are not ruthless, but simply appreciate efficiency. In other words, there are limits to the sort of behavior that can be tolerated and still maintain a healthy market for contracts. Judge Posner and Judge Easterbrook, his fellow judge on the Seventh Circuit, are respected for their cohesiveness and their clarity, if not yet fully embraced by the entire legal establishment. On a separate note, the district court ultimately found for GE (D) on remand. As it turns out. Orenstein knew that GE (D) was unaware of paragraph 34, but continued to write letters that failed to clarify the parties' respective rights. This was a violation of the duty of good faith, as described by Judge Posner, and led the district court to deny its request for specific performance.

# Bloor v. Falstaff Brewing Corp.

(Reorganization Trustee) v. (Brewery)
601 F.2d 609 (2nd Cir. 1979)

COURT OF APPEALS PERMITS A FACT-SPECIFIC INQUIRY TO DETERMINE A PARTY'S OBLIGATIONS UNDER A BEST EFFORTS CLAUSE

■ **INSTANT FACTS** A brewery fails to use best effort to continue the sales of an acquired label.

■ **BLACK LETTER RULE** A contract clause requiring best efforts to ensure profits does not require the promisor to spend itself into bankruptcy in the course of performance.

## ■ PROCEDURAL BASIS

Appeal by both parties from a district court judgement for the plaintiff in a breach of contract action.

## ■ FACTS

Falstaff Brewing Corporation (Falstaff) (D) bought the rights to produce and market beer which formerly produced by P. Ballantine & Sons (Ballantine). The contract required Falstaff (D) to use best efforts to promote Ballantine's labels and to maintain a high volume of sales. In addition, Falstaff (D) was supposed to pay Ballantine $.50 per barrel in royalties for six years. If Falstaff (D) ever substantially discontinued the sale of Ballantine beer, it would trigger an onerous liquidated damages clause. The Ballantine label had been in trouble for years before Falstaff (D) stepped in. Ballantine had already been taken over once and had failed to turn a profit. Falstaff (D) continued the effort, but Ballantine performed more poorly than any of Falstaff's (D) other beers. In fact, Falstaff (D) was approaching the point where it would be unable to meet their payroll or other credit obligations. A change in Falstaff's (D) corporate control, however, resulted in a healthy infusion of cash and a subsequent reduction in its effort to market Ballantine beer. It reduced the advertising budget for Ballantine from $1,000,000 to $115,000 and closed or restructured the distribution centers which handled Ballantine beer. This caused a drop in Ballantine sales which was, again, far worse than that suffered by Falstaff's (D) other brands. Ballantine's reorganization trustee, Bloor (P), ultimately sued Falstaff (D) for breach of contract, making two claims. First, Bloor (P) claimed that Falstaff (D) failed to use best efforts to maintain Ballantine's sales. As a result, Bloor (P) claimed that Falstaff (D) also triggered the liquidated damages clause by substantially discontinuing the distribution of Ballantine beer. The district court found for Bloor (P) on the first claim and for Falstaff (D) on the second claim. Both parties appeal this result. Falstaff's (D) arguments are the focus of the decision.

## ■ ISSUE

Does a best efforts clause require the promisor to satisfy its contractual obligations at any expense?

## ■ DECISION AND RATIONALE

(Friendly) No. Falstaff (D) argues that the district court held it to a "best efforts" standard which required it to continue marketing Ballantine beer regardless of the consequences. This is not true. The district court did cite to a case which required performance even to the point of financial difficulty or economic hardship. Falstaff (D) cites an alternative case, *Feld v. Henry S. Levy & Sons, Inc.* [performance is not required to result in bankruptcy] which held that a party would be excused from performance if its losses were more than trivial. The dispute over precedent is unnecessary, however, because the district court did not apply the rule it cited. Instead, the court examined the evidence to determine whether Falstaff (D) used its best efforts to "promote and maintain a high volume of sales" for Ballantine. This evidence did not favor Falstaff (D). In fact, it was not until *after* Falstaff (D) returned from the brink of insolvency that its controlling shareholder, Kalmanovitz, announced a policy which abandoned any efforts to resuscitate Ballantine. Falstaff (D) closed key Ballantine distributorships and, at times, placed Ballantine's distribution in the hands of its competitors. It also rejected other offers to distribute Ballantine, focused attention on their own beers—which were free of the $.50 per barrel royalty—and adopted a general policy favoring profit over volume. In essence, it violated its duty of good faith by preferring its own interests to Ballantine's, well beyond the point necessary to preserve its survival. The only excusable act which Falstaff (D) committed was spending more to advertise its beers than Ballantine's in regions which were traditionally Falstaff (D) territory. Otherwise, it demonstrated a lack of attention to Ballantine which was not consistent with its duty to maintain a high volume of sales. This duty was linked to the royalty payments, which were such an inextricable part of the purchase price for Ballantine that they were protected by a liquidated damages clause. As a result, the district court correctly found for Bloor (P) and calculated Ballantine's damages against the sales of comparable northeast beers. The judgement of the district court is affirmed [including the rejection of Bloor's (P) liquidated damages claim—presumably to avoid giving Bloor (P) double damages for the same breach].

**Analysis:**

Judge Friendly's opinion follows a familiar theme in contract law that requires a case-by-case analysis under certain circumstances. However, he never really announces a rule of law that governs this case. Instead, he relies on the findings of the district court, implicitly endorsing a factual inquiry rather than a bright line rule. Judge Friendly may have followed this approach because, as he notes, the specific language in the contract called for a *high* volume of sales. In other words, the contract itself set a standard for Falstaff's (D) best efforts. The contract also contained a notable synergy between the purchase price for Ballantine and the best efforts clause. In essence, Falstaff (D) ignored an implied obligation to supply Ballantine with royalties that were an intended part of Ballantine's consideration for the right to promote its beers. It not only breached its duty, but circumvented the intent of the agreement and gained a windfall in the process. On a separate note, the opinion places the burden of proof on Falstaff (D) to show that there was nothing it could have done to avert Ballantine's difficulties. Judge Friendly does not say so, but the disposition of the case presumes that Falstaff (D) failed to meet this burden.

**■ CASE VOCABULARY**

REORGANIZATION TRUSTEE: A reorganization trustee holds title to and is responsible for protecting the fiduciary interests of a corporation which is undergoing bankruptcy, merger, or a variety of other possible organizational or financial changes.

# Lockewill, Inc. v. United States Shoe Corp.

(Distributor) v. (Shoe Manufacturer)

547 F.2d 1024 (8th Cir. 1976), cert. denied, 431 U.S. 956 (1977)

COURT OF APPEALS IMPLIES A RIGHT TO RECOUP ONE'S INVESTMENT IN AN AGREEMENT WITH NO TERMINATION PROVISION

■ **INSTANT FACTS** The new owners of a shoe company breach an exclusivity agreement which was arranged by the prior owner.

■ **BLACK LETTER RULE** An agreement which does not state its duration or contain provisions for its termination remains in force until the parties have recouped their investments in the venture.

■ **PROCEDURAL BASIS**

Appeal from a district court judgement for the plaintiff in a breach of contract action.

■ **FACTS**

Grant Williams [presumably the owner of Lockewill, Inc.] (Williams) (P) entered into an oral agreement with a representative from Pappagallo, Inc. for the exclusive right to market Pappagallo shoes in St. Louis. The contract did not state the duration of their agreement, nor did it make any provision for its termination. Nonetheless, Pappagallo's representative, Maurice Bandler, assured Williams (P) that a verbal contract was sufficient to protect their respective interests. Williams (P) subsequently made all of the necessary logistic and financial arrangements to sell Pappagallo shoes at a shop in St. Louis which operated for years afterwards. Pappagallo, Inc. was ultimately taken over by another company, United States Shoe Corp. (USSC) (D), which bought out Bandler's interest. USSC (D) promptly made arrangements for Pappagallo shoes to be sold in a St. Louis department store, in competition with Williams (P). Williams (P) wrote to USSC (D) to complain but to no avail. The deal went ahead and the department store began selling Pappagallo shoes six months later. Williams (P) then sued USSC (D) for breach of contract, claiming that they violated the exclusivity provision of his distributorship agreement. The trial court found for Williams (P). USSC (D) appeals.

■ **ISSUE**

Can a party terminate an agreement at will if the agreement does not state its duration or make provisions for its termination?

■ **DECISION AND RATIONALE**

(Henley) Yes. According to Missouri law, an exclusivity or distributorship agreement which does not state its duration and is silent on the provisions for its termination is terminable at will by either party. That said, a party cannot be unjustly deprived of its good faith investment in the expected relationship. At the very least, the parties are entitled to a reasonable opportunity to recoup their expenses through the operation of the agreement. If this opportunity is denied, they can recover in quantum meruit for their time, labor and expenses. In this case, Pappagallo and USSC (D) had a binding contract with Williams (P) for the exclusive distribution of Pappagallo shoes. He had a right to an unimpeded opportunity to recover his investment and expenses for a reasonable period after he opened his shop in St. Louis. In fact, Williams (P) had over 8 years to accomplish this. We consider this a reasonable period. As of 1973, Pappagallo and USSC (D) were entitled to cancel their agreement or limit its exclusivity at will. This is especially true since Williams (P) had known for some time that USSC (D) was considering a change in distribution. As a result, the district court erred in finding that USSC (D) breached the contract. USSC (D) had a right to terminate the contract at will, considering that its duration was indefinite and that Williams (P) had ample time to recoup his investment. The judgement of the district court is reversed.

### Analysis:

There are certain considerations that will guide a court's decision to imply a particular obligation. First, the court may consider the extent of the defendant's losses if the relevant obligation is enforced. The court may also consider the extent of the plaintiff's losses if the court does not create a protected right in its favor. Judge Henley relies on the second of these two approaches in his opinion. He is clearly concerned with the financial impact that an at-will termination of the exclusivity agreement would have. Once he demonstrates that Williams (P) will not suffer in the event of a cancellation, Judge Henley resolves the issue in USSC's (D) favor. In the process, he puts future parties on notice that similar agreements may give rise to obligations that the parties might prefer to avoid. He also demonstrates the danger in leaving important terms to chance and relying on an ad hoc verbal agreement to secure the parties' rights.

### ■ CASE VOCABULARY

AT WILL: A common designation for employment contracts; "at will" generally describes both parties' right to cancel an agreement whenever they like, without legal consequences.

# Bovard v. American Horse Enterprises, Inc.

(Business Seller) v. (Business Buyer)

201 Cal.App.3d 832, 247 Cal.Rptr. 340 (1988)

COURTS MUST REFUSE TO HEAR DISPUTES ABOUT CONTRACTS WHICH ARE ILLEGAL OR IMMORAL, ON POLICY GROUNDS

■ **INSTANT FACTS** A businessman sued to recover payment for selling a business which made drug paraphernalia.

■ **BLACK LETTER RULE** Courts cannot hear disputes about contracts which violate public policy by being illegal, or tending to promote illegality.

■ **PROCEDURAL BASIS**

In contract action seeking damages, appeal from dismissal.

■ **FACTS**

American Horse Enterprises, Inc.'s (D) owner Bovard (P) sold the corporation to Ralph (D), in exchange for Ralph's (D) promissory notes. When Ralph (D) defaulted, Bovard (P) sued Ralph (D) and American Horse (D) for breach of contract. At trial, testimony revealed American Horse (D) manufactured jewelry, and also drug paraphernalia (bongs and roach clips) used to smoke marijuana. At the time of the contract, manufacturing drug paraphernalia was legal, though later it was criminalized. The trial court held the contract was illegal and void for public policy (because it aided drug abuse), and denied restitution. Bovard (P) appeals, contending the corporation's business was perfectly legal.

■ **ISSUE**

May a court mediate a contractual dispute involving the sale of a corporation which manufactures drug paraphernalia?

■ **DECISION AND RATIONALE**

(Puglia) No. Courts cannot hear disputes about contracts which violate public policy by being illegal, or tending to promote illegality. Whether a contract contravenes public policy is a question of law for the court. Whenever a court becomes aware a contract is illegal, it has a duty to refrain from enforcing it. Furthermore, the court will not permit the parties to maintain, settle, or compromise claims based on an illegal contract. Courts should not refuse enforcement unless it is entirely plain the contract violates public policy. The burden is on defendants to prove that enforcement would violate the state's settled policy or injure the people's morals. Bovard (P) cites *Moran v. Harris*, wherein we held 2 lawyers' fee-splitting agreement was enforceable, even though the bar association later prohibited such arrangements. Unlike in *Moran*, here there was a positive law effective on the transaction date, which prohibited using marijuana. Applying the standards of *Restatement 2d § 178*, we conclude the interest in enforcing this contract is tenuous. Neither party was reasonably justified in expecting the government would not effectively geld American Horse (D), a business harnessed to the production of paraphernalia used to facilitate use of illegal drugs. Though voiding this contract imposes a forfeiture on Bovard (P), it is mitigated because he may still recover the only asset usable for lawful purposes, i.e., the machinery used to manufacture jewelry. Finally, there is no special public interest in enforcing this contract, only the general interest in preventing contractual parties from avoiding debts. On the other hand, the public policy factors against enforcing this contract are strong. The statutory prohibition of marijuana use and possession implies a policy against manufacturing paraphernalia which facilitates its use. It is immaterial that American Horse's (D) business was not expressly banned when Bovard (P) and Ralph (D) contracted, since both knew the corporation's product would be used for illegal purposes. Affirmed.

## Analysis:

*Bovard* illustrates the question of a contract that was not illegal in itself, but nevertheless was sufficiently related to proscribed crimes to be deemed corrupting. Criteria for evaluating whether contracts should be enforced are found in Restatement (Second) of Contracts § 178, which urges courts to weigh (i) parties' reasonable expectations that the contract's subject would remain legal, (ii) whether non-enforcement would impose an unfair forfeiture on one party, (iii) whether enforcing the contract furthered some special public interest, and (iv) statutes and legislative policy statements indicating the desire to restrict such related activities. While courts are understandably unenthusiastic about enforcing illegal contracts, the refusal to do so may have arguably unfair distributive effects between two equally dishonest parties. Here, presumably both Bovard (P) and Ralph (D) knew equally well that American Horse (D) was semi-legal, but Ralph (D) is allowed to keep his ill-gotten gains, and Bovard (P) bears all of the loss.

## ■ CASE VOCABULARY

GELD: To castrate, as done to horses and cattle.

# X.L.O. Concrete Corp. v. Rivergate Corp.

(Subcontractor) v. (General Contractor)

83 N.Y.2d 513, 611 N.Y.S.2d 786, 634 N.E.2d 158 (1994)

---

A CONTRACT WILL BE UNENFORCEABLE IF IT IS SO RELATED TO AN AGREEMENT THAT RESTRAINS COMPETITION THAT ITS ENFORCEMENT WOULD COMPEL CONDUCT THAT VIOLATES ANTITRUST LAWS

---

■ **INSTANT FACTS** Rivergate refused to pay XLO an outstanding balance for work XLO had done, claiming that the contract was part of an organized crime racket.

■ **BLACK LETTER RULE** A contract will be considered unenforceable if it is so integrally related to the agreement, arrangement or combination in restraint of competition that its enforcement would result in compelling performance of the precise conduct made unlawful by antitrust laws.

■ **PROCEDURAL BASIS**

Appeal from dismissal of complaint in action for breach of contract and unjust enrichment.

■ **FACTS**

In New York City, there was [is???] a criminal operation in effect known as the "Club." This "Club" was an arrangement between a ruling body consisting of four of the city's five major organized crime family bosses known as the "Commission," seven concrete construction companies operating in the city, and the District Council of Cement and Concrete Workers, Laborers International Union of North America. The Commission decided which concrete companies would take on construction jobs in the city that were worth over two million dollars. The Commission also fixed the bidding to ensure that their chosen company for a given job would submit the lowest bid. Any contractors who took on such jobs had to pay the Commission two percent of the contract price to guarantee "labor peace." This system was enforced through threatened or actual labor unrest or violence. In May 1981, X.L.O. Concrete Corp. (XLO) (P) became the last concrete contractor in New York City to join the Club. In May 1983, XLO (P) later entered into a written contract with Rivergate Corporation (Rivergate) (D) for construction work on a project in Manhattan. XLO (P) was to be the subcontractor, and Rivergate (D) was to be the general contractor. The Commission gave this project to XLO (P) on the assumption that it would not exceed $15 million. XLO (P) and Rivergate (D) agreed on a figure of $16,300,000. This price exceeded the amount approved by the Commission, prompting the Commission to request that XLO (P) abandon the project. XLO (P) refused, claiming that the Commission had not designated XLO (P) for any work for over 18 months. The Commission decided to allow XLO (P) to work on the project, which led XLO (P) to give a $50,000 gift to a Commission representative for speaking on XLO's (P) behalf. Rivergate (D) negotiated the contract with full knowledge of the Club and its rules. XLO (P) completed its performance of the contract, but Rivergate (D) refused to pay the full balance, claiming that the contract was an integral feature of the Club's bribery and extortion operations, and thus violated antitrust laws. XLO (P) sued for breach of contract and unjust enrichment. The Supreme Court dismissed the complaint and certain counterclaims. The Appellate Division modified the judgment.

## ■ ISSUE

Should a contract be considered unenforceable if it is integrally related to another agreement which if complied with, would violate antitrust laws?

## ■ DECISION AND RATIONALE

(Ciparick) Yes. A contract will be considered unenforceable if it is so integrally related to the agreement, arrangement or combination in restraint of competition that its enforcement would result in compelling performance of the precise conduct made unlawful by antitrust laws. Generally, the use of antitrust defenses in contract actions is not encouraged, out of fear that one who successfully uses such a defense will reap the benefits of a contract while escaping the corresponding burdens of it. Still, antitrust defenses will be upheld in cases where judicial enforcement of a contract would result in enforcement of the exact kind of conduct an antitrust act forbids. Likewise, a contract which is legal on its face and does not call for unlawful conduct in its performance is not voidable simply because it resulted from an antitrust conspiracy. The key issue is whether the given contract is so integrally related to the agreement in restraint of competition that its enforcement would result in compelling performance of the precise conduct made unlawful by the antitrust laws. Here, that question cannot be answered without further development at trial. The extent to which the contract price is excessive and fails to reflect fair market value at the time the contract was made should be determined. In addition, the potentially unlawful use of market power to inflate the contract price and eliminate competition should also be developed. The equities, relative culpability, bargaining power, and knowledge of the parties should all be considered, as well, along with the public policy interest in discouraging such unlawful schemes as the Club. In light of this analysis, Rivergate's (D) remaining contention that the contract is per se illegal is rejected. Order affirmed, with costs.

## Analysis:

In this case, the parties were "in part delicto" (of equal fault), since Rivergate (D) was fully aware of X.L.O.'s (P) illegal involvement with the Club's extortion and bid-rigging racket. In cases of equal fault, courts often automatically hold for defendants, under the maxim "in pari delicto potior est condition defendantis" (in [case of] equal fault, the stronger position is that of the defendant). Of course, this motto is arbitrary, and if literally enforced would often have the dubious effect of unjustly enriching one crook at the expense of another who is no more reprehensible. The rule seems to be a reflection of courts' unwillingness to lend official auspices to mediating disputes between crooks, and their preference for leaving the parties as they found them (with the defendant presumably in possession of the money). The courts' "hands-off" policy in shady contracts is debatable, since the upshot is that Mafiosos and semi-legitimate businesses are left to "self-help," often through violence or further wrongdoing.

## ■ CASE VOCABULARY

DEPRECATE: To disapprove of.

QUANTUM MERUIT: An action for recovery of the reasonable value of services rendered on the basis of an implied contract or promise.

# Hopper v. All Pet Animal Clinic

(Veterinarian) v. (Former Employer)

861 P.2d 531 (Wyo. 1993)

---

A COVENANT NOT TO COMPETE WILL BE VALID AND ENFORCEABLE IF IT IS REASONABLE GIVEN THE CIRCUMSTANCES OF THE PARTICULAR CASE

---

■ **INSTANT FACTS** Hopper opened her own veterinary clinic near All Pet after All Pet fired her, and All Pet claimed she violated an agreement not to compete.

■ **BLACK LETTER RULE** A covenant not to compete is valid and enforceable only if it is shown that the covenant is (1) in writing; (2) part of a contract of employment; (3) based on reasonable consideration; (4) reasonable in duration and geographical limitation; and (5) not against public policy.

---

■ **PROCEDURAL BASIS**

Appeal from action for damages and injunctive relief.

■ **FACTS**

After completing her (D) education, Dr. Glenna Hopper (D) started working part-time at the All Pet Animal Clinic, Inc. (All Pet) (P) in Laramie, Wyoming. She (D) eventually began full-time work at All Pet (P). Hopper (D) and All Pet (P) executed an agreement, effective March 1989, which provided, in part, that "[u]pon termination, Dr. Hopper [(D)] agrees that she will not practice small animal medicine for a period of three years from the date of termination within 5 miles of the corporate limits of the City of Laramie, Wyoming." In addition, the provision also expressed Hopper's (D's) agreement that "the duration and geographic scope of that limitation is reasonable." After this agreement was executed, All Pet's (P) president, Dr. R.B. Johnson, heard a rumor that Hopper (D) was considering buying a competing practice. When Johnson suggested to Hopper (D) that she (D) buy her way out of the agreement, she (D) replied that she (D) could do whatever she (D) wanted. Hopper (D) was then discharged. In July 1991, having bought the other practice, she (D) began operating the Gem City Veterinary Clinic. In November, All Pet (P) sued Hopper (D) for an injunction and also for damages. Alpine Animal Clinic, Inc. (Alpine) (P), another practice in which Johnson and Hopper (D) had also been associated, joined All Pet (P) in this action. The case came to trial almost two years after Hopper (D) was actually discharged. All Pet and Alpine (P) did not seek a temporary injunction. The evidence showed that a little more than half of Hopper's (D) practice came from small animal medicine, and that there was a substantial overlap of about 187 clients between Hopper's (D) current and former practices. The trial court granted the injunction, but concluded that damages were too speculative to be awarded. Hopper (D), All Pet (P), and Alpine (P) all appealed.

■ **ISSUE**

Can an agreement not to compete with a previous employer for a given period of time and within a certain distance of the employer be considered enforceable?

---

## ■ DECISION AND RATIONALE

(Taylor) Yes. The common law policy against contracts made in restraint of trade is very old and very firmly established. The initial burden is on the employer to prove the agreement is fair and reasonable, and that is necessary for the protection of his or her business interests. While an employer can make such an agreement to protect from unfair and improper competition, no such protection can be sought for normal competition. A covenant in restraint of trade will only be enforced if there is a proper balance between the interests of the employer and those of the employee. Thus, a covenant not to compete is valid and enforceable only if it is shown that the covenant is (1) in writing; (2) part of a contract of employment; (3) based on reasonable consideration; (4) reasonable in duration and geographical limitation; and (5) not against public policy. The reasonableness of the covenant must be determined in relation to all the facts and circumstances of the particular case. Here, Hopper (D) moved to Laramie right after completing her education and had no professional contacts. In working for All Pet (P), she (D) gained valuable exposure to All Pet's and Alpine's (D) clients and client records, as well as knowledge of their (D) pricing policies and practice development techniques. The knowledge that she (D) acquired through working at these two clinics (P) clearly had monetary value. All Pet and Alpine (D) are entitled to reasonable protection from irreparable harm that could result from Hopper's (D) use of this information. The established loss of 187 clients to Hopper's (D's) practice sufficiently demonstrated the actual loss suffered as a result of this unfair competition. Enforcement of the practice restrictions in Hopper's (D) agreement with All Pet (P) not to compete does not result in an unreasonable restraint of trade. Hopper (D), working in Wyoming, could have earned a living practicing large animal medicine without relocating. The public would not have suffered injury from enforcement of this agreement. The five mile limit was also reasonable, considering the distribution of clients throughout the county, and not just within the boundaries of Laramie. A one-year limit, however, would be sufficient to protect All Pet and Alpine (P) from unfair competition. Case remanded for modification of judgment.

## ■ DISSENT

(Cardine) Hopper (D) has essentially beaten the system with this ruling. The majority has decided that as a matter of law that a one-year non competition restriction is reasonable, and that a longer period is unreasonable. Hopper (D) should be enjoined from that part of the practice of veterinary medicine specified in the covenant starting from the date the trial court, on remand, enters its modified judgment, and for at least the one-year period set by this court.

---

### Analysis:

Generally, post-employment restraints are sustained only if, like Hopper (P) did here, an employee acquires confidential information, or a "trade secret," regarding some process or method involved in the operation of the business, or if the employee acquires information that could be used to lure away existing clients. Such information could consist of customer name lists, mailing lists, client histories and financial records, and other forms of data. Typically, these kinds of restraints are justified by the public interest in a smooth, efficient employer-employee relationship. This interest in a workable relationship is balanced by the public interest in individual economic autonomy, free dissemination of ideas and information, and the shifting of labor to areas with the greatest productivity. These restraints invariably involve a larger, employer-entity that can subject employees to unanticipated hardship. Because of this, the agreements are more closely scrutinized than those creating other restraints of trade, like those for the sale of a business.

---

## ■ CASE VOCABULARY

DE NOVO: Latin for "new," or a "second time"; in a hearing of this kind, the reviewing court acts as though it were the court where the case originated, and the findings of the lower courts are used only if they are helpful to the reviewing court.

# Sheets v. Teddy's Frosted Foods

(Employee) v. (Employer)

179 Conn. 471, 427 A.2d 385 (1980)

## CONNECTICUT SUPREME COURT RECOGNIZES TORT REMEDY FOR VIOLATION OF EMPLOYMENT CONTRACT RIGHTS

■ **INSTANT FACTS** An employee is fired for warning his company that they are violating a food labeling statute.

■ **BLACK LETTER RULE** An employee who is fired for reasons in contravention of public policy can sue in tort for wrongful termination.

■ **PROCEDURAL BASIS**

Appeal from a trial court judgement for the defendant in a wrongful termination tort action [yes, you're still in the right casebook].

■ **FACTS**

The following facts are based on the allegations in Sheets' (P) complaint. Sheets (P) worked for Teddy's Frosted Foods (TFF) (D) for four years. He began as its quality control inspector and later, took on the job of operations manager as well. Sheets (P) received several raises and bonuses during his employment. However, trouble began when he noticed that the labels on some of TFF's (D) foods did not correspond to the quality and weight of the ingredients. This was a violation of the Connecticut Uniform Food, Drug and Cosmetic Act. Sheets (P) warned TFF (D) of the problems and suggested changes which might have corrected the situation. TFF (D) ignored his warnings. In fact, it fired Sheets (P) six months later, claiming that his performance was unsatisfactory. However, he was actually fired in retaliation for trying to bring TFF (D) into compliance with Connecticut's food labeling laws. Sheets (P) subsequently sued TFF (D) for wrongful termination. He claimed that TFF (D) breached an implied contract for employment, violated public policy, and was guilty of malicious discharge. TFF (D) made a motion to strike Sheets' (P) pleadings and he declined to amend them. The trial court then found for TFF (D). Sheets (P) appeals. In his appeal, Sheets (P) concedes that indefinite employment contracts are terminable at will. He similarly concedes that TFF (D) was not required to fire him for just cause. Connecticut has not placed such a requirement on employment contracts, in any event. Instead, he relies almost exclusively on the claim that TFF (D) terminated his employment in violation of public policy. If this were so, he would be entitled to tort damages for wrongful termination. It is this argument which the court addresses on appeal.

■ **ISSUE**

Can the firing of an at-will employee give rise to a tort action for wrongful termination?

■ **DECISION AND RATIONALE**

(Peters) Yes. An employee who is fired for reasons in contravention of public policy can sue in tort for wrongful termination. This is not unusual. Certain contract rights give rise to tort remedies, while certain tort principles have found their way into contract claims. Wrongful termination is a tort claim which stems from the improper violation of an employee's contract rights. This claim has generally been recognized when the termination of an employee violates public policy. For instance, courts have found termination to be wrongful when employees were fired for refusing to commit perjury, for filing a workman's comp claim, for engaging in union activity, or for serving on a jury. More importantly, courts have recognized claims for retaliatory discharge when an employee's responsibilities were linked to the public interest and they were fired under circumstances which were similar to this case. Sheets (P) worked in an area which was regulated by statute. That statute, prohibiting the mislabeling of food, is intended to protect the public health and welfare. In fact, TFF's (D) violations could have subjected Sheets (P) to criminal liability. In essence, Sheets (P) was forced to choose between possible criminal prosecution or the loss of his job. This is a situation for which the law has increasingly recognized a remedy, a tort action for wrongful termination. Considering the burgeoning acceptance of this remedy and the facts of the case, the trial court inappropriately ruled for TFF (P). The court's decision is reversed and the case is remanded for further proceedings.

■ **DISSENT**

(Cotter) I dissent from the court's opinion for the following reasons. First, the facts of the case are not sufficient to support an action for wrongful discharge. The alleged public policy concerns are limited to frozen food entrees which may not measure up to their purported quality. This is not the same as depriving an employee of his right to file a workman's compensation claim o?? his right to engage in union activity. In those cases, the employer actually violated a statute in the termination itself. In this case, the statutory violation is only tangential to the firing. In addition, Sheets (P) need not have lost his job over the statutory violation. He could have informed the commissioner of consumer affairs anonymously and never faced the prospect of termination. The second problem with the court's opinion is the danger it creates by relying on such meager facts to satisfy a claim for wrongful termination. Other jurisdictions have been far more careful in recognizing this claim. The court's lack of caution will lead to a flood of cases whose nuisance value alone will negatively impact employers. In addition, ill-intentioned employees can now file suit despite the absence of a direct statutory violation. They will bring suit for any statutory violation which can be linked, no matter how distantly, to their termination in the hopes that the alleged infraction will satisfy a particular court's definition of public policy. Because of the factual insufficiency of this case and the expansion it permits of a previously limited doctrine, I would deny Sheets' (P) claim and affirm the decision of the trial court.

---

**Analysis:**

Justice Peters alludes to a longstanding synergy between contract doctrine and tort doctrine. For instance, a tort action for misrepresentation may be available even if an action for breach of an implied warranty is not. In this case, Sheets (P) did not have a strong argument for breach of an employment contract because he was an at-will employee. However, he did have at least a colorable claim for wrongful termination since he was fired not long after he warned TFF (D) of its statutory violations. The most generally accepted claim for wrongful discharge results from termination for an employee's refusal to engage in illegal activity. In strict at-will jurisdictions, however, an employee can be fired for virtually any reason, including his or her refusal to break the law. A plaintiff can, and should, pursue every relevant theory of recovery for a particular harm, including remedies in tort *and* contract if the case warrants that approach. However, the plaintiff can only recover damages under one type of claims.

---

■ **CASE VOCABULARY**

JUST CAUSE: Another limitation on at-will employment doctrine. A state may create a statutory exception which requires employers to terminate workers for just cause. In other words, the employer must advance a proper, good-faith reason for the firing.

WRONGFUL TERMINATION: A tort cause of action which is generally brought for the termination of an employee for refusing to break the law. In essence, a state that recognizes wrongful termination claims creates a public policy exception to at-will employment doctrine.

# Balla v. Gambro, Inc.

(In-House Counsel) v. (Employer)

145 Ill.2d 492, 164 Ill.Dec. 892, 584 N.E.2d 104 (1991)

LAWYERS FIRED FOR WHISTLE-BLOWING CANNOT SUE FOR WRONGFUL DISCHARGE

■ **INSTANT FACTS** When a dialysis machine marketer fired its general counsel for threatening to report its illegal sale of tampered machines, the counselor sued for wrongful discharge.

■ **BLACK LETTER RULE** If an attorney is fired for reporting clients' misconduct which the attorney is ethically obligated to report, the attorney has no claim for retaliatory discharge.

■ **PROCEDURAL BASIS**

In wrongful discharge suit seeking damages, appeal from appellate reversal of summary judgement for defendant.

■ **FACTS**

Attorney Balla (P) was in-house counsel and "manager of regulatory affairs" at Gambro, Inc. ("Gambro") (D), a distributor of kidney dialysis equipment. When Gambro (D) agreed to import German equipment which failed to comply with FDA regulations, Balla (P) protested its resale plan was illegal, in vain. When Balla (P) insisted the purchase be stopped, Gambro (D) fired him. Balla (P) complained to the FDA, which seized the shipment and found it adulterated. Balla (P) then sued Gambro (D) for retaliatory discharge. Gambro (D) moved for summary judgement, contending it had an absolute right to fire Balla (P). At trial, the judge granted Gambro's (D) motion. On appeal, the Court of Appeals reversed and remanded, holding Balla (P) may sue for retaliatory discharge. Gambro (D) appeals.

■ **ISSUE**

If a firm fires its attorney for threatening to report its dangerous illegal misconduct, may the attorney sue for retaliatory discharge?

■ **DECISION AND RATIONALE**

(Clark) No. If an attorney is fired for reporting clients' misconduct which the attorney is ethically obligated to report, the attorney has no claim for retaliatory discharge. Generally, in-house counsel do not have tort claims for retaliatory discharge, which is a narrow exception to the general rule of at-will employment. Here, the public policy—protecting citizens' lives—is adequately safeguarded without extending the tort of retaliatory discharge. Balla (P) was subject to the Code of Professional Responsibility, which states "A lawyer *shall* reveal information about a client to the extent it appears necessary to prevent the client from committing an act that would result in death or serious bodily injury." Thus, Balla (P) was obligated professionally to report Gambro's (D) intent to sell misbranded or adulterated dialyzers, which could cause serous injury. Balla (P) contends that not permitting suits for retaliatory discharge would present attorneys with a "Hobson's choice" of either violating the law and risking professional and criminal sanctions, or losing their jobs, but we find no such dilemma, since lawyers are ethically obligated to report such conduct. [Misses the point, doesn't it?] Additionally, we believe that restricting employers' rights to fire counselors at will encourages employers to be less than candid in revealing their questionable conduct to their counselors. Also, we believe it inappropriate for employer-clients to bear the cost of their in-house counsel's adherence to their ethical obligations, since the employer would be forced to mitigate the attorney's harm suffered for having to adhere to professional conduct codes. We believe all attorneys should know that, in their professional careers, they sometimes must forego economic gains to protect the legal profession's integrity. [Remember, a judge is only some lawyer who knew a Senator.] Balla (P) argues that, since he learned of Gambro's (D) violation in his capacity as manager of regulatory affairs, he should be allowed to sue as a mere "employee" (rather an as its "attorney"), but we find Balla (P) learned this information from working as its lawyer. Reversed.

## Analysis:

Apparently, the law in illinois was that ordinary "employees" could sue for wrongful discharge, but whistle-blowing "lawyers" could not. Thus, Balla (P) attempted to portray himself as Gambro's (D) compliance officer employee rather than its lawyer, but the court rejected this concocted duality. For no apparent reason, Justice Clark decides that, when clients violate the law, their lawyers should lose their jobs without compensation for doing the right thing; he forgets that it is Gambro (D), not Balla (P), who committed the violation. Needless to say, this discourages attorneys from reporting misconduct by effectively allowing criminals to punish whistle blowers. Fortunately, *Balla's* reasoning was rejected three years later.

# Simeone v. Simeone

(Ex-Wife) v. (Ex-Husband)

525 Pa. 392, 581 A.2d 162 (1990)

## PRENUPTIAL AGREEMENTS ARE ENFORCEABLE IF SIGNED AFTER FAIR FINANCIAL DISCLOSURE

■ **INSTANT FACTS** An ex-wife sued to void her prenuptial agreement, contending her husband presented it right before the wedding and forced her to sign without opportunity to consult a lawyer.

■ **BLACK LETTER RULE** Prenuptial agreements are enforceable as written if they were made after fair financial disclosure.

## ■ FACTS

Catherine Walsh ("Catherine") (P) was engaged to Dr. Frederick Simeone ("Frederick") (D). On the eve of their wedding, Frederick (D) presented Catherine (P) with a prenuptial agreement limiting her alimony to $25K. Catherine (P) signed, without consulting an attorney or seeking explanation from Frederick's (D) lawyer. They married the next day, but separated 7 years later. Catherine (P) sued for divorce and alimony *pendente lite*. Frederick (D) defended, contending he had already paid support payments of $25K after they separated. At trial, the master upheld the prenuptial agreement. On appeal, the appellate court affirmed. Catherine (P) appeals again, contending the payment cap was unreasonable, and that she was not properly informed of her rights before signing.

## ■ ISSUE

Is a prenuptial agreement void if the signatory did not understand its terms or have opportunity to consult an attorney?

## ■ DECISION AND RATIONALE

(Flaherty) No. Prenuptial agreements are enforceable as written if they were made after fair financial disclosure. Catherine (P) relies on *Estate of Geyer*, which held a prenuptial agreement is valid if either it made reasonable provisions, or was entered after full and fair disclosure of the parties' general finance positions and the statutory rights being relinquished. However, we reject *Geyer*, which was founded on outdated assumptions that women are of inferior status and unable to understand contractual terms. Since then, society has advanced to the point where women are no longer uneducated and "weaker" partners in marriage; they may well be sophisticated breadwinners. Thus, paternalistic presumptions and protections are no longer necessary to shelter women from supposed inferiorities. Furthermore, *Geyer* inappropriately allowed courts to consider parties' knowledge and the sufficiency of consideration in deciding whether to enforce contracts. Prenuptial agreements are just contracts, and should be evaluated similarly. Normally, contracting parties are bound by their agreements, regardless of whether they read or understood them, or whether the bargain was good or reasonable. To impose a requirement that parties entering a prenuptial agreement consult independent counsel would interfere with freedom of contract. Furthermore, permitting courts to investigate prenuptial agreements' reasonableness would undermine such contracts' reliability. But we do not retreat from the principle that parties must make full and fair disclosure of their financial positions, and that material misrepresentations may void the agreement, because at that moment the parties are in a relationship calling for mutual trust and disclosure. Catherine (P) claims duress, contending Frederick (D) presented the agreement on the eve of her wedding, when she could not consult counsel, but the master found Catherine (P) had previously discussed prenuptial agreements and expressed no reluctance. Affirmed.

■ **CONCURRENCE**

(Papadakos) I believe the majority prematurely presumes that gender inequality has been erased. I view prenuptial agreements as adhesion contracts, where one party is subservient. The law should protect the subservient party, regardless of sex, to ensure equal protection.

■ **DISSENT**

(McDermott) Prenuptial agreements should be void if they are inadequate, especially since the state has a paramount interest in preventing underpaid divorcees from becoming wards of the state.

---

**Analysis:**

*Simeone* is a case decided on policy grounds, where the correct policy is not at all clear. There is no law criminalizing prenuptial agreements, and no indication the legislature either approves or disapproves of them. Thus, judges wishing to decide whether to enforce them are forced to make their own policy choice, often selecting between several competing policies. Here, majority judge Flaherty believes the most important policy is to protect freedom of contract, preserve parties' contractual expectations, and affirm gender equality, Concurrer Papadakos predicates his opinion on the assumption that rich men force such contracts on poor women; in his view, the prevalent policy should be to protect weaker parties from overreaching. For dissenter McDermott, the important policy is to ensure divorcees are paid enough to support them, in order to protect the state from having to support them.

---

■ **CASE VOCABULARY**

MASTER: In litigation, a court-appointed fact-finder, usually an expert on calculating damages.

*PENDENTE LITE*: "While the action is pending." A claim for an immediate award of damages, contingent on winning the suit.

# In the Matter of Baby M

(Child Conceived by Surrogacy)

109 N.J. 396, 537 A.2d 1227 (1988)

CONTRACTS THAT PAY FOR CHILDBEARING ARE ILLEGAL

In this case, I'm gonna split the baby.

?!?

stus.com

■ **INSTANT FACTS** Stern (P) paid Whitehead (D) $10,000 to bear a child conceived by artificial insemination, and Whitehead (D) refused to relinquish the child to Stern (P) and his wife after Whitehead (D) gave birth.

■ **BLACK LETTER RULE** Surrogacy contracts that involve the payment of money to a woman who irrevocably agrees to bear a child and turn it over to another party are illegal and invalid.

■ **PROCEDURAL BASIS**

Appeal from an order upholding the validity of a surrogacy contract and terminating the parental rights of Whitehead (D)

■ **FACTS**

Stern (P) and Whitehead (D) entered into a written surrogacy contract. The contract provided that, in return for payment of $10,000, Whitehead (D) would be inseminated with Stern's (P) sperm. Any child conceived as a result of the insemination would be turned over permanently to Stern (P), and Whitehead (D) would voluntarily relinquish her parental rights.

Whitehead (D) delivered a baby girl, Baby M, but she refused to turn the child over to Stern (P). Stern (P) brought an action for specific enforcement of the contract. The trial court upheld the validity of the contract, and awarded custody of Baby M to Stern (P). The trial court also terminated Whitehead's (D) parental rights.

■ **ISSUE**

Was the surrogate parenting agreement enforceable?

■ **DECISION AND RATIONALE**

(Wilentz, C.J.) No. Surrogacy contracts that involve payment of money to a woman who irrevocably agrees to bear a child and turn it over to another party are illegal and invalid. The conclusion that these contracts are invalid is based on their direct conflict with existing statutes, and on a conflict with the public policy of the state, as expressed in statutory and case law. The monetary inducement is unlawful in and of itself. Moreover, the irrevocable agreement made before birth or conception to surrender the child would be unenforceable in a normal private placement adoption. The agreement not to contest termination of parental rights and the contractual concession that the child's best interests would be served by adoption by the natural father and his wife are equally invalid.

The contract conflicts with statutory provisions prohibiting the use of money in connection with adoptions, requiring proof of parental unfitness or abandonment before termination of parental rights or adoption is granted, and making the surrender of custody and consent to adoption revocable in private placement adoptions. Although private placement adoptions are allowed in New Jersey, they are disfavored. Paying or accepting money in connection with a private placement adoption is a high misdemeanor. The evils inherent in baby-bartering are loathsome for many reasons. The child is sold without regard to whether the purchasers will be suitable parents, the birth mother does not receive the benefit of counseling and guidance to assist her in making the decision, and the monetary incentive may make her decision less voluntary. Although the surrogacy contract in the instant case was carefully structured to avoid the statutory prohibition, it seems clear that money was paid and accepted in connection with the adoption. The provision in the contract, agreed to before conception, requiring Whitehead (D) to surrender custody without any right of revocation is a further indication that the essential nature of this transaction is to create a contractual system of termination and adoption that circumvents the statutes.

The surrogacy contract is also invalid as against the public policy of New Jersey. The premise of the contract, that the natural parents can decide in advance of a child's birth which one of them is to have custody, bears no relationship to the settled law that custody is determined by the best interests of the child. Under the contract, Whitehead (D) is irrevocably committed to surrender Baby M before she knows the strength of her bond with the child. She does not make a totally voluntary, informed decision, because any decision before birth is uninformed and any decision after that is compelled by a pre-existing contractual commitment, the threat of a lawsuit, and payment of $10,000, all of which make the decision less than totally voluntary.

Worst of all is the contract's total disregard of the best interests of the child. There is no suggestion that any inquiry will be made to determine the fitness of Stern (P) or his wife to be parents, their superiority to Whitehead (D), or the effect on Baby M of not living with her biological mother. This is the sale of a child, or at least the sale of a mother's right to her child. The only mitigating factor is that one of the purchasers is the father.

Almost every evil that prompted the prohibition on the payment of money in connection with adoptions exists here. First, and perhaps most important, all of the parties concede that it is unlikely that surrogacy will survive without money. If there are no payments, there will be few, if any, surrogates. In an adoption, the adoption itself relieves the mother of the financial burden of supporting an infant and is in some sense the equivalent of payment. Second, the use of money in adoptions does not produce the problem. Conception and, usually, birth occur before the illicit funds are paid. With surrogacy, the problem—the purchase of a woman's procreative capacity, at the risk of her life—is caused by, and originates with, the offer of money. Third, the prohibition of using money in connection with adoptions means that the financial pressure of an unwanted pregnancy and the resulting support obligation will not lead the mother to the highest-paying, yet ill-suited, adoptive parents. She is just as well-off surrendering her child to an approved agency. In surrogacy for money, the highest bidders become the adoptive parents, regardless of their suitability. Fourth, in an adoption, a mother's consent to surrender her child is revocable. If the surrender is to an approved agency, there are protections against an ill-advised surrender. In surrogacy, the consent is irrevocable, and it occurs so early that no amount of advice would be sufficient.

In the surrogacy transaction, the predominant motive is profit. A middleman promoted the sale, and he was propelled by profit. There is a shortage of infants available for adoption, and that makes the situation ripe for middlemen who will bring some equilibrium into the market by increasing the supply through the use of money. It is irrelevant that Whitehead (D) agreed to the transaction, supposedly with a full understanding of the consequences. In a civilized society, there are some things that money cannot buy. A surrogacy contract guarantees the separation of a child from its mother, it looks to adoption regardless of suitability, it completely ignores the child, it takes the child from his or her mother without regard to her wishes and her maternal fitness, and all of this is accomplished through the use of money. The court cannot say whether this principle recommends a prohibition of surrogacy. It is merely noted that Whitehead's (D) consent here is irrelevant.

Beyond the other policy considerations is the potential degradation of women that may result from these arrangements. The fact that some women may see surrogacy as an opportunity does not diminish its potential for devastation of other women. The unregulated use of surrogacy can bring suffering to all involved, including the surrogate mother and her family, the biological father and his wife, and, most importantly, the child. Although the present law prohibits surrogacy for pay, there is nothing that prohibits voluntary surrogacy when there is no payment and the mother is given the right to change her mind and to assert her parental rights. Moreover, the legislature is free to deal with this issue as it sees fit, subject only to constitutional constraints. Reversed and remanded to determine Whitehead's (D) visitation rights with Baby M.

---

**Analysis:**

When this case was pending, Whitehead (D) received public support from all parts of the political spectrum. Some prominent feminists, as well as some conservative commenters, criticized the trial court's apparent rejection of the mother-child bond. Liberal supporters often noted the class distinctions—Whitehead (D) was a high-school dropout married to a sanitation worker, and Stern (P) was a physician married to a biochemist. In 2004, Baby M turned eighteen. She filed court proceedings to terminate Whitehead's (D) parental rights and formalize her adoption by Stern's (P) wife.

---

■ **CASE VOCABULARY**

PRIVATE ADOPTION: An adoption that occurs independently between the biological mother (and sometimes the biological father) and the adoptive parents without the involvement of an agency. Also called *private-placement adoption.*

# CHAPTER SEVEN

## Remedies for Breach

### Campbell Soup Co. v. Wentz

**Instant Facts:** Wentz (D) refused to sell carrots to Campbell Soup Co. (P) as agreed, and Campbell's (P) brought suit to compel specific performance of the contract.

**Black Letter Rule:** The test for whether goods are "unique" is not always determined by objective standards, but may be based on the value of the item to the party requesting relief.

### Klein v. PepsiCo

**Instant Facts:** PepsiCo (D) agreed to sell a Gulfstream corporate jet to Universal Jet Sales ("UJS") (P) for resale to Klein (P), but before the airplane could be delivered to UJS (P), PepsiCo (D) reneged and Klein (P) and UJS (P) sued for specific performance.

**Black Letter Rule:** Specific performance cannot be granted where damages are recoverable and adequate.

### Morris v. Sparrow

**Instant Facts:** Sparrow (P) sought specific enforcement of an agreement by Morris (D) to give him a horse as part of the consideration for working on Morris's (D) ranch.

**Black Letter Rule:** Equity will grant specific performance of a contract for the sale of chattels if there are special and peculiar reasons that make it impossible for money damages to provide relief to the injured party.

### Laclede Gas Co. v. Amoco Oil Co.

**Instant Facts:** Laclede (P) sought injunctive relief when Amoco (D) unilaterally terminated an agreement with Laclede (P) to supply propane gas distribution systems to various residential developments.

**Black Letter Rule:** Specific performance will not be ordered when the party claiming the breach of contract has an adequate remedy at law.

### Northern Delaware Industrial Development Corp. v. E. W. Bliss Co.

**Instant Facts:** The court denied Northern (P) an order of specific performance of a contract to compel E.W. Bliss (D) to add workers, for the period that one of Phoenix Steel's (P) mills had to be shut down, because of a delay of the work.

**Black Letter Rule:** With regard to a construction contract, a court should not order specific performance which would be impractical to enforce and supervise.

### Walgreen Co. v. Sara Creek Property Co.

**Instant Facts:** Walgreen (P) sought to enjoin Sara Creek (D) to enforce the exclusivity clause in their lease in which Sara Creek (D) promised not to lease space in a mall to another store that has a pharmacy.

**Black Letter Rule:** In making a decision about injunctive relief, a judge should balance the cost and benefits between the injunctive relief and damages.

### Vitex Manufacturing Corp. v. Caribtex Corp.

**Instant Facts:** Caribtex breached a contract to supply Vitex with woolen material, and Vitex sued to recover for its lost profits.

**Black Letter Rule:** When overhead expenses are not affected by the performance of a particular contract, such expenses should not constitute a performance cost to be deducted when computing lost profits.

### Laredo Hides Co., Inc. v. H & H Meat Products Co., Inc.

**Instant Facts:** Laredo Hides had to buy hides on the open market to fulfill another contract with a tannery when H & H breached its contract with Laredo Hides.

**Black Letter Rule:** Under UCC § 2–712, when a seller refuses to acknowledge a contract or refuses to deliver the goods under contract, a buyer may "cover by making in good faith and without unreasonable delay any reasonable purchase of or contract to purchase goods in substitution for those due from the seller," and recover damages in the form of "the difference between the cost of cover and the contract price together with any incidental or consequential damages."

### R.E. Davis Chemical Corp. v. Diasonics, Inc.

**Instant Facts:** Davis (P) had to breach a purchase contract with Diasonics (D), and when Diasonics (D) resold the equipment, Davis (P) sued to get its full deposit back.

**Black Letter Rule:** A seller who wishes to resell goods after a buyer breaches a given contract can seek damages equal to the difference between the contract price and market price at the time and place for tender under UCC § 2–708; but to receive lost profits, the seller must establish both that he or she would have been able to produce the breached goods and the resold goods and that it would have been profitable to produce and sell both sets of goods.

### United States v. Algernon Blair, Inc.

**Instant Facts:** When Blair refused to pay crane rental costs, Coastal Steel terminated its performance and sued to recover for labor and equipment it had already furnished.

**Black Letter Rule:** The measure of recovery for quantum meruit is the reasonable value of the performance, and recovery is undiminished by any loss which would have been incurred by complete performance.

### Rockingham County v. Luten Bridge Co.

**Instant Facts:** Luten Bridge Co. continued building a bridge even after Rockingham County notified the company not to proceed with the work.

**Black Letter Rule:** A plaintiff must, so far as he or she can without loss to himself or herself, mitigate the damages caused by a defendant's wrongful act; a plaintiff cannot hold a defendant liable for damages which need not have been incurred.

### Tongish v. Thomas

**Instant Facts:** Tongish contracted to sell his sunflower seed crop to the Coop Association, but repudiated that contract when the market price for seeds went up.

**Black Letter Rule:** If a seller breaches a contractual obligation to deliver goods, and the buyer fails to go into the market and "cover," the buyer's damages will be measured by the difference between the market price and the contract price according to UCC § 2–713.

### Parker v. Twentieth Century-Fox Film Corp.

**Instant Facts:** Parker contracted to act in a musical in California, but Fox abandoned the musical and offered her a role in a western in Australia.

**Black Letter Rule:** A wrongfully discharged employee's rejection of or failure to seek other available employment of a different or inferior kind cannot be used by the employer as a means of mitigating damages.

### Jacob & Youngs v. Kent

**Instant Facts:** Jacob & Youngs (P) constructed a house using two types of pipe, and Kent (D) refused to make full payment because the contract called for the exclusive use of pipe manufactured by Reading.

**Black Letter Rule:** Insubstantial departures from express contract language may be remedied by damages based on the diminution in market value rather than the cost of replacement.

### Groves v. John Wunder Co.

**Instant Facts:** John Wunder Co. agreed to remove sand and gravel from the Groves land and keep the land level when finished, but later breached this agreement.

**Black Letter Rule:** When a party willfully fails to perform under a contract, the other party will be entitled to damages equal to the reasonable cost of having performance carried out, and not the difference in value resulting from non-performance.

### Peevyhouse v. Garland Coal and Mining Co.

**Instant Facts:** The Peevyhouses (P) leased their farm to Garland (D) for strip mining, but Garland (D) failed to do specific remedial work at the end of the lease.

**Black Letter Rule:** The measure of damages in an action by a lessor against a lessee for breach of contract is ordinarily the reasonable cost of performance of the work; however, if the breached provision is merely incidental to the main purpose of the contract, and the economic benefit to be gained by the lessor from full performance is grossly disproportionate to the cost of performance, then the damages which may be recovered are limited to the diminution of value to the property caused by non-performance.

### Hadley v. Baxendale

**Instant Facts:** Baxendale failed to deliver a broken mill shaft for Hadley on time, and the delay prevented Hadley from reopening the mill on time.

**Black Letter Rule:** A party injured by another party's breach of contract can only recover those damages that may fairly and reasonably be considered either as arising naturally, or as may reasonably be supposed to have been in the contemplation of both parties, at the time the contract was made, as the probable result of such a breach of the contract.

### Delchi Carrier SpA v. Rotorex Corp.

**Instant Facts:** A parts supplier refused to ship conforming goods to a buyer.

**Black Letter Rule:** Under international commercial law, a buyer may recover lost profits and other incidental damages caused by the seller's breach of contract if those lost profits were foreseeable.

### Kenford Co. v. County of Erie

**Instant Facts:** A company bought land, anticipating it would substantially appreciate due to a stadium being built nearby, and sued when the stadium was not built.

**Black Letter Rule:** An injured party is not entitled to recover damages that the parties did not contemplate the breaching party would assume.

### Fera v. Village Plaza, Inc.

**Instant Facts:** After the Plaza refused to give Fera the store space they had agreed upon, Fera sued and tried to claim lost profits as damages.

**Black Letter Rule:** Future lost profits are allowed as an element of damage in any case where, by reason of the nature of the situation, the profits may be established with reasonable certainty.

### Wasserman's Inc. v. Township of Middletown

**Instant Facts:** The Township canceled a lease with Wasserman's but refused to pay the damages outlined in the cancellation clause of the lease.

**Black Letter Rule:** Provisions for liquidated damages are enforceable only if the amount fixed for damages is a reasonable forecast of just compensation for the harm that is caused by the breach and that harm is incapable or very difficult of accurate estimate.

### Dave Gustafson & Co. v. State

**Instant Facts:** The State withheld part of the payment owed to Gustafson & Co. as liquidated damages under the contract after a job was delayed 67 days.

**Black Letter Rule:** A provision for payment of a stipulated sum as a liquidation of damages will be sustained if it appears that 1) at the time the contract was made the damages in the event of breach were incapable or very difficult of accurate estimation, 2) there was a reasonable endeavor by the parties to fix fair compensation, and 3) the amount stipulated bears a reasonable relation to probable damages and is not disproportionate to any damages reasonably to be anticipated.

### Raffles v. Wichelhaus

**Instant Facts:** Two parties to a cotton transaction disagree as to the exact identity of a ship named in their contract.

**Black Letter Rule:** A contract can be voided if it contains an ambiguous term which was, in fact, interpreted differently by the parties.

### Oswald v. Allen

**Instant Facts:** Two coin collectors each have a different interpretation of a contract for the sale of Swiss coins.

**Black Letter Rule:** A contract should be voided if the parties each held different understandings of an ambiguous term and neither party should have been aware of the other's understanding.

# Campbell Soup Co. v. Wentz

(Buyer of Carrots) v. (Grower)

172 F.2d 80 (3d Cir. 1948)

UNIQUENESS OF GOODS DEPENDS ON VALUE TO PURCHASER

I need uniform-looking carrots for my children.

You want to fight in court just to stop your kids from fighting with each other?

stus.com

■ **INSTANT FACTS** Wentz (D) refused to sell carrots to Campbell Soup Co. (P) as agreed, and Campbell's (P) brought suit to compel specific performance of the contract.

■ **BLACK LETTER RULE** The test for whether goods are "unique" is not always determined by objective standards, but may be based on the value of the item to the party requesting relief.

## ■ PROCEDURAL BASIS

Appeal from judgments for Wentz (D) and Lojeski (D).

## ■ FACTS

Campbell Soup (P) contracted to buy all of the Chantenay red cored carrots to be grown on fifteen acres of the farm owned by Wentz (D) during the 1947 season. Campbell's (P) used large quantities of the Chantenay carrots because of the uniformity of their appearance, and because their blunt shape made them easier to handle and process. The price for the carrots was $30 per ton for deliveries made in January 1948, and Campbell's (P) furnished the seeds to the growers.

In early January 1948, Wentz (D) informed Campbell's (P) that the carrots would not be delivered at the contract price. The market price at the time was at least $90 per ton, and Chantenay carrots were virtually unobtainable. Wentz (D) sold approximately sixty-two tons of carrots to Lojeski (D). Lojeski (D) resold approximately fifty-eight tons of the carrots, half to Campbell's (P) and half to other buyers. Campbell's (P) suspected that Lojeski (D) was selling its "contract carrots," and refused to buy any more. Campbell's (P) brought actions against Wentz (D) and Lojeski (D), seeking specific performance.

The trial court denied relief, noting that Campbell's (P) had not proved what proportion of its carrots was used to make stock, and what proportion was used as identifiable ingredients in soups. The court concluded that Campbell failed to establish that the carrots, "judged by objective standards," were unique goods.

## ■ ISSUE

Did Campbell's (P) establish that it was entitled to equitable relief?

## ■ DECISION AND RATIONALE

(Goodrich, J.) Yes. The test for whether goods are "unique" is not always determined by objective standards, but may be based on the value of the item to the party requesting relief. The goods contracted for here were unavailable on the open market. Campbell's (P) had contracted to purchase them well in advance of its needs. The uniformity of the appearance of carrots in soups marketed and sold under the Campbell's (P) name is a matter of considerable commercial significance, and one that should be taken into account when determining whether a substitute ingredient will be just as good. Campbell's (P) has built up a general reputation for its products, and the uniformity of the appearance of those products is important.

There is no reason why a court should be reluctant to grant specific relief when it can be given without supervision of the court or other time-consuming processes. There is considerable authority showing liberality in the granting of an equitable remedy. Affirmed.

**Analysis:**

Although the court agreed with Campbell's (P) contention that equitable relief was appropriate, enforcement of the contracts was denied as unconscionable. The unconscionable provision was one that prevented Wentz (D) from selling the carrots to anyone else if, due to circumstances beyond the control of either party, Campbell's (P) could not take possession of them. The court did not analyze this provision in detail, but said it was "carrying a good joke too far." Although Wentz's (D) conduct was a breach of the contract, equity would not enforce an unconscionable bargain. 172 F. 2d at 83.

### ■ CASE VOCABULARY

EQUITABLE REMEDY: A remedy, usually a nonmonetary one such as an injunction or specific performance, obtained when available legal remedies, usually monetary damages, cannot adequately redress the injury.

SPECIFIC PERFORMANCE: The rendering, as nearly as practicable, of a promised performance through a judgment or decree; specifically, a court-ordered remedy that requires precise fulfillment of a legal or contractual obligation when monetary damages are inappropriate or inadequate, as when the sale of real estate or a rare article is involved. Specific performance is an equitable remedy that lies within the court's discretion to award whenever the common-law remedy is insufficient, either because damages would be inadequate or because the damages could not possibly be established.

# Klein v. PepsiCo

(Buyer) v. (Seller of Plane)

845 F.2d 76 (4th Cir. 1988)

---

IF GOODS THAT ARE FOR SALE ARE UNIQUE, IT IS OKAY TO GRANT SPECIFIC PERFORMANCE

---

■ **INSTANT FACTS** PepsiCo (D) agreed to sell a Gulfstream corporate jet to Universal Jet Sales ("UJS") (P) for resale to Klein (P), but before the airplane could be delivered to UJS (P), PepsiCo (D) reneged and Klein (P) and UJS (P) sued for specific performance.

■ **BLACK LETTER RULE** Specific performance cannot be granted where damages are recoverable and adequate.

---

■ **PROCEDURAL BASIS**

Appeal from ruling of specific performance for breach of contract.

■ **FACTS**

PepsiCo (D) agreed to sell a Gulfstream corporate jet (G-II's) to UJS (P) for resale to Klein (P) for $4.6 million. The plane was flown to Savannah, Georgia for an inspection and was to be flown to New York for specific repairs promised by PepsiCo (D) representatives. However, the plane was sent to pick up a stranded PepsiCo (D) Chairman of the Board from Dulles airport, who decided that PepsiCo (D) should not sell the plane. The Chairman told PepsiCo (D) representatives to withdraw the plane from the market. Klein (P) and UJS (P) sued and the district court granted specific performance.

■ **ISSUE**

Can specific performance be granted where damages are recoverable and adequate?

■ **DECISION AND RATIONALE**

(Ervin) No. Specific performance cannot be granted where damages are recoverable and adequate. The State of Virginia has adopted the Uniform Commercial Code which permits a jilted buyer of goods to seek specific performance of the contract if the goods sought are unique, or in other proper circumstances. In this case, there was testimony that twenty-one G-II's were on the market, three of which were roughly comparable. It is noted that subsequent to the PepsiCo (D) deal falling through, UJS (P) purchased two other G-II's and Klein (P) made bids on them. Because of price, Klein (P) decided to purchase a G-III aircraft instead. Price Increases alone are no reason to order specific performance and, given these facts, it is very difficult to support a ruling that the aircraft was so unique as to merit such an order. Reversed and remanded as to the specific performance.

---

**Analysis:**

In order to get equitable relief, damages must be an inadequate remedy. Under the UCC, the sale of goods generally must be unique (i.e., rare or of sentimental value) in order to be subject to specific performance. The UCC provides that even if not unique, other proper circumstances may arise in which specific performance can be granted. The Fourth Circuit did not see such circumstances in this case. Klein (P) could have bought another G-II from UJS (P) for more money, and in fact had that opportunity. Money damages were therefore adequate.

## ■ CASE VOCABULARY

ABROGATE: To annul, cancel, repeal or destroy.

EXTRINSIC EVIDENCE: External evidence, or that which is not contained in the body of an agreement, contract, and the like; may also refer to evidence not legitimately before the tribunal in which the determination is made.

MAXIM: An established principle or proposition; a principle of law universally admitted as being a correct statement of the law, or as agreeable to reason. Maxims are but attempted general statements of rules of law and are law only to the extent of application in adjudicated cases.

# Morris v. Sparrow

(Rancher) v. (Cowboy)

225 Ark. 1019, 287 S.W.2d 583 (1956)

● A TRAINED HORSE HAS UNIQUE VALUE TO THE TRAINER

I turned your "worthless" pony into prize. What d'ya think of that?

I think I want to change our deal.

stus.com

■ **INSTANT FACTS** Sparrow (P) sought specific enforcement of an agreement by Morris (D) to give him a horse as part of the consideration for working on Morris's (D) ranch.

■ **BLACK LETTER RULE** Equity will grant specific performance of a contract for the sale of chattels if there are special and peculiar reasons that make it impossible for money damages to provide relief to the injured party.

■ **PROCEDURAL BASIS**

Appeal from a decree of the chancery court.

● ■ **FACTS**

Morris (D), a rancher who participated in rodeos, met Sparrow (P) at a rodeo in Florida. The two agreed that Sparrow (P), a cowboy who was experienced in training horses, would stay at Morris's (D) ranch in Arkansas and do the necessary work while Morris (D) travelled to Canada. Sparrow (P) was to work sixteen weeks and receive $400. Sparrow (P) also alleged that he was to receive a brown horse named Keno. When Sparrow (P) arrived at Morris's (D) ranch, Keno was practically unbroken. During his spare time, Sparrow (P) trained the horse so that, with a little additional training, Keno would be a first class roping horse.

Morris (D) paid Sparrow (P) the agreed-upon money. He refused to turn Keno over to him, claiming that Sparrow (P) was to get the horse only if his work was satisfactory, and that Sparrow (P) did not do a good job.

■ **ISSUE**

Was Sparrow (D) entitled to specific enforcement of the agreement?

■ **DECISION AND RATIONALE**

(Robinson, J.) Yes. Equity will grant specific performance of a contract for the sale of chattels if there are special and peculiar reasons that make it impossible for money damages to provide relief to the injured party. Sparrow (P) made a roping horse out of a green, unbroken pony. Such a horse would have a peculiar and unique value. If Sparrow (P) is to prevail, he has a right to the horse instead of its market value in money.

● Morris (D) contends that Sparrow's (P) right to receive Keno was conditioned upon doing a satisfactory job at Morris's (D) ranch. Both parties were in the chancery court, and the chancellor had a better opportunity to evaluate the testimony regarding the quality of Sparrow's (P) work. Affirmed.

**Analysis:**

Sparrow (P) cannot adequately be compensated by money damages, not because Keno has some intrinsic value, or because he is a trained and broken horse. Keno's unique quality is that he was trained and broken by Sparrow (P) over the course of sixteen weeks. The implication is that the quality that makes Keno special makes him special only to Sparrow (P). If Morris (D) had promised the horse to someone else, that other party might not be able to make the same claim for specific performance that Sparrow (P) does.

### ■ CASE VOCABULARY

CHANCERY: A court of equity, or, collectively, the courts of equity; the system of jurisprudence administered in courts of equity.

# Laclede Gas Co. v. Amoco Oil Co.

(Distributing Utility) v. (The Supplier)
522 F.2d 33 (8th Cir. 1975)

■ **INSTANT FACTS** Laclede (P) sought injunctive relief when Amoco (D) unilaterally terminated an agreement with Laclede (P) to supply propane gas distribution systems to various residential developments.

■ **BLACK LETTER RULE** Specific performance will not be ordered when the party claiming the breach of contract has an adequate remedy at law.

■ **PROCEDURAL BASIS**

Appeal from denial of breach of contract and injunctive relief.

■ **FACTS**

Laclede (P) and Amoco (D) entered into a long term agreement whereby Amoco would supply propane gas distribution systems to various residential developments until such time as natural gas mains were extended into those areas. The contract gave Laclede (P) broad cancellation rights. However, Amoco (D) could not cancel the contract unless the subdivisions subsequently converted to natural gas. After performing under the contract for some time, Amoco (D) notified Laclede (P) that the price of propane had increased by three cents per gallon and subsequently terminated the agreement, telling Laclede (P) that the agreement lacked mutuality. The district court ruled in favor of Amoco (D), agreeing that the contract was invalid because of a lack of mutuality. The district court denied injunctive relief. On appeal, the Circuit Court ruled that there was a contract and that the contract had been breached by Amoco (D).

■ **ISSUE**

Will specific performance be ordered when the party claiming the breach of contract has an adequate remedy at law?

■ **DECISION AND RATIONALE**

(Ross) No. Specific performance generally will not be ordered when the party claiming breach of contract has an adequate remedy at law. The remedy at law must be certain, prompt, complete and efficient to attain the ends of justice as in a decree of specific performance. The contract between Laclede (P) and Amoco (D) is for a long-term supply of propane to the subdivisions of the development and there was uncontradicted expert testimony that Laclede (P) probably could not find another supplier of propane willing to enter into such a long-term contract. Even if Laclede (P) could obtain supplies of propane for the affected developments, there is no guarantee that Laclede (P) would be able to find propane in the future years, in which case the damages could not be estimated in advance. Specific performance is the proper remedy in this situation and it should be granted by the district court. Reversed and remanded.

**Analysis:**

Generally, the determination of whether to order specific performance of a contract lies within the sound discretion of the trial court. The Eighth Circuit in this case held that the remedy at law was not adequate in part because it believed money could not purchase a substitute performance (i.e., future propane gas) for the subdivisions of the development. The court noted that there was a public interest directly involved in supplying customers with the propane. It should also be noted that the court dismissed Amoco's (D) contention that the remedy of specific performance would be difficult for the court to administer without constant and long-continued supervision. The court stated that this is merely a discretionary rule that is frequently ignored when the public interest is involved, and noted that the public interest in providing propane to retail customers is manifest, while any supervision required will be far from onerous.

---

### ■ CASE VOCABULARY

ARBITRARY: Not done according to reason or judgement; depending on will alone; failure to exercise honest judgement.

MUTUALITY OF REMEDY: The right to performance must be mutual to grant specific performance.

ONEROUS: Unreasonably burdensome or one-sided.

REPUDIATE: To put away, reject, disclaim, or renounce a right, duty, obligation or privilege.

# Northern Delaware Industrial Development Corp. v. E. W. Bliss Co.

(Development Corporation) v. (General Contractor)

245 A.2d 431 (Del.Ch.1968)

## A COURT GENERALLY WILL NOT GRANT EQUITABLE RELIEF IN CONSTRUCTION CONTRACTS WHERE ENFORCEMENT AND SUPERVISION BY THE COURT IS IMPRACTICAL

■ **INSTANT FACTS** The court denied Northern (P) an order of specific performance of a contract to compel E.W. Bliss (D) to add workers, for the period that one of Phoenix Steel's (P) mills had to be shut down, because of a delay of the work.

■ **BLACK LETTER RULE** With regard to a construction contract, a court should not order specific performance which would be impractical to enforce and supervise.

■ **PROCEDURAL BASIS**

Appeal from denial of specific performance for breach of contract.

■ **FACTS**

E.W. Bliss (D) contracted to modernize Phoenix Steel's (P) plant, which was spread over a 60-acre site, for $27,500,000. Work did not progress as rapidly as expected in the contract and Phoenix (P) sought a court order of specific performance to compel E.W. Bliss (D) to add 300 more workmen, to make up a full second shift during the period that one of the mills had to be shut down, because of a delay of the work. The court denied specific performance.

■ **ISSUE**

Should a court grant specific performance of any building contract in a situation in which it would be impractical to carry out such an order?

■ **DECISION AND RATIONALE**

(Marvel) No. The court of equity should not order specific performance of any building contract in a situation in which it would be impractical to carry out such an order unless there are special circumstances or public interest is directly involved. To grant specific performance in this case would be inappropriate in view of the imprecision of the contract provision relied upon and the impracticability if not impossibility of effective enforcement by the Court of a mandatory order designed to keep a specific number of men on the job at the site of a steel mill which is undergoing extensive modernization and expansion. If Northern (P) has suffered loss as a result of actionable building delays, they may, at an appropriate time, resort to law for fixing of their claimed damages. Affirmed.

---

**Analysis:**

Here, the court did not find special circumstances or an important public interest. For the *Northern* court, the problems of supervising the performance of the complex work involved in construction contracts and assessing the adherence to an order were deemed greater than the benefits to be gained by specific performance. Although equitable relief is now considered more often than in the past with regard to construction contracts, the difficulties in enforcement and supervision generally outweigh the benefits of specific performance.

■ **CASE VOCABULARY**

COURT OF EQUITY: Court which administers justice according to the system of equity, using well-settled and well-understood rules, principles and precedents.

MINISTERIAL ACT: Act performed in obedience to mandate of legal authority, without regard to one's own judgment upon the propriety of the act being done.

# Walgreen Co. v. Sara Creek Property Co.

(Tenant) v. (Landlord)

966 F.2d 273 (7th Cir.1992)

## INJUNCTIVE RELIEF IS APPROPRIATE WHEN THE CALCULATION OF DAMAGES IS UNCERTAIN

■ **INSTANT FACTS** Walgreen (P) sought to enjoin Sara Creek (D) to enforce the exclusivity clause in their lease in which Sara Creek (D) promised not to lease space in a mall to another store that has a pharmacy.

■ **BLACK LETTER RULE** In making a decision about injunctive relief, a judge should balance the cost and benefits between the injunctive relief and damages.

## ■ PROCEDURAL BASIS

Appeal from award of permanent injunction for breach of contract.

## ■ FACTS

Walgreen (P) is a discount chain store that has a pharmacy. As part of its lease with Sara Creek (D), Sara Creek (D) agreed not to lease a space in the mall to another store operating a pharmacy. In 1990, fearful that its largest tenant was about to close its store, Sara Creek (D) informed Walgreen (P) that it intended to buy out that tenant and install in its place a "deep discount" store that would contain a pharmacy. Walgreen (P) sought an injunction against Sara Creek (D) until its contract expired in ten years. The Court entered a permanent injunction against Sara Creek (D).

## ■ ISSUE

In making a decision about injunctive relief, should the judge balance the cost and benefits between the injunctive relief and damages?

## ■ DECISION AND RATIONALE

(Posner) Yes. In deciding whether to grant injunctive relief, a judge should weigh the cost and benefits of granting damages versus an injunction. The district judge did not exceed the bounds of reasonable judgement in concluding that the costs of the damages remedy would exceed the cost of injunctive relief. The determination of Walgreen's (P) damages would have been costly in forensic resources and inescapably inaccurate. The lease had ten years to run. Walgreen (P) would have had to project costs over the next ten years, and then project the impact on those figures of its new competitor, and then discount that impact to present value. All but the last step would have been fraught with uncertainty. Affirmed.

---

**Analysis:**

The court here went into a lot of detail regarding weighing the cost and benefits of damages versus an injunction. The appellate court was comfortable that the district court at least had this analysis in mind when granting the injunction and did not question it further. However, the Seventh Circuit found that the calculations of damages were at best "fraught with uncertainty." The result may have been different if the contract was for a shorter term, or involved a different industry. Nevertheless, judges do

deducted when computing lost profits. In other words, because overhead is fixed and nonperformance of the contract would produce no overhead cost savings, no deduction from profits should result. Here, Vitex (P) had closed its plant when business activity had temporarily slowed down. If Vitex (P) had entered no other contracts for the rest of the year, Vitex's (P's) profits would have been determined by deducting its production costs and overhead from gross profits resulting from previous transactions. When Vitex (P) contracted to process Caribtex's (D's) wool, the only new costs that Vitex (P) would incur would be those of reopening its (P's) plant and the direct costs of processing, such as labor, chemicals, and the like. Overhead costs would have been constant, regardless of whether Vitex (P) contracted with Caribtex (D) or Vitex (P) actually processed Caribtex's (D's) wool. Because overhead remained constant and was totally unaffected by the Caribtex (D) contract, it would be improper to consider it as a cost of Vitex's (P's) performance and deduct it from the gross proceeds of the Caribtex (D) contract. Carlbtex (D) may argue that this position is incorrect, as overhead is as much a cost of production as other expenses. Granted, successful businessmen do set prices at a level high enough to recoup all expenses, including overhead, and reap profits. Still, this does not automatically mean that fixed overhead costs, even when allocated in part to each transaction, should be considered a cost factor when computing lost profits on individual transactions. While overhead is paid for by the proceeds of the business, such costs generally do not bear a direct relationship to individual transactions to be considered a cost in determining lost profits. Moreover, with fewer transactions, overhead is spread out to a far lesser degree; these overhead costs would then lead to a loss of profitability for each existing transaction. This loss should thus be considered a compensable item of damage. The UCC provides that, if the difference between the contract price and market price is insufficient to put a seller in as good a position as if the contract had been fully performed, a different measure of damages should be used. The measure of damages should then be the profit, *including reasonable overhead* which the seller would have received from the buyer. Judgment of district court affirmed.

### Analysis:

UCC § 2–708(2) states that the measure of damages is "the *profit (including overhead)* which the seller would have made from full performance by the buyer." In the case of *Universal Power Sys. v. Godfather's Pizza,* 818 F.2d 667 (8th Cir. 1987), the Eighth Circuit gave a ruling similar to that of the Third Circuit in *Vitex,* holding that the measure of damages under § 2–708(2) should be read as not subtracting fixed costs when calculating profit. Instead, only variable overhead costs, such as those for electrical power or heat that can be turned off once a breach occurs, were to be considered in such calculations. Thus, when overhead costs are variable, they should be included in the general formula for measuring damages, which finds damages equal to the loss in value plus any other loss, minus any *cost avoided* and loss avoided as a result of the breach. When the overhead is a fixed cost, as was the case here, it makes no sense to include the overhead in the formula. Costs like insurance premiums, property taxes, and the like cannot be avoided simply by having one party breach the contract.

### ■ CASE VOCABULARY

DUTY-FREE: Term to describe goods which are free from customs payments when imported into a county.

TARIFFS: A list of articles which outlines the rates of duties, or taxes, that are to be imposed upon goods imported into a country.

# Laredo Hides Co., Inc. v. H & H Meat Products Co., Inc.

(Cattle Hide Buyer) v. (Cattle Hide Seller)

513 S.W.2d 210 (Tex. Civ. App. 1974)

---

UCC § 2–712 PROVIDES THAT IF A SELLER BREACHES A CONTRACT, A BUYER MAY "COVER" AND BE ENTITLED TO DAMAGES BY MAKING A REASONABLE PURCHASE OF SUBSTITUTE GOODS

---

■ **INSTANT FACTS** Laredo Hides had to buy hides on the open market to fulfill another contract with a tannery when H & H breached its contract with Laredo Hides.

■ **BLACK LETTER RULE** Under UCC § 2–712, when a seller refuses to acknowledge a contract or refuses to deliver the goods under contract, a buyer may "cover by making in good faith and without unreasonable delay any reasonable purchase of or contract to purchase goods in substitution for those due from the seller," and recover damages in the form of "the difference between the cost of cover and the contract price together with any incidental or consequential damages."

■ **PROCEDURAL BASIS**

Appeal from take nothing judgment in action for breach of contract.

■ **FACTS**

H & H Meat Products Company, Inc. (H & H) (D) is a Texas meat processing and packing corporation. H & H (D) also sells cattle hides as a side business. Laredo Hides Company, Inc. (Laredo) (P) is a Texas corporation which purchases cattle hides from various meat packers in the United States and ships them to tanneries in Mexico. On February 29, 1972, the two companies (P and D) executed a contract by which Laredo (P) agreed to buy all of H & H's (D's) cattle hide production from March through December, 1972. On March 3, 1972, Laredo (P) contracted to sell all the hides it would purchase from H & H (D) to a Mexican tannery. A disagreement over payment for the second shipment resulted in H & H (D) stating it (D) would deliver no more hides. [The appellate court held that H & H's (D's) refusal to deliver more hides was unjustified as it amounted to a breach by repudiation of the contract. Thus, Laredo (P) was not obligated to fulfill the remaining months of the contract.] To fulfill its (P's) contract with the tannery, Laredo (P) was forced to purchase hides on the open market in substitution for the H & H (D) hides. Unfortunately for Laredo (P), the market price for cattle hides had steadily increased after Laredo (P) contracted with H & H (D). Laredo's (P's) total additional cost of purchasing substitute hides from other suppliers was $142,254.48. Further, the transportation and handling costs which resulted from having to deal with additional suppliers was $3,448.95. The Texas Business and Commerce Code, mirroring the UCC, provides guidelines for fixing a buyer's remedies when a seller breaches a contract for the sale of goods. When a seller repudiates the contract or refuses to deliver the contracted goods, a buyer may cover under § 2–711. The seller could be entitled to damages under § 2–712 "by making in good faith and without unreasonable delay any reasonable purchase of or contract to purchase goods in substitution for those due from the seller." The seller could thus recover damages under this section in the amount of the difference between the cost of cover and the contract price, plus incidental damages. Laredo (P) began this action in May 1972, requesting specific performance, or in the alternative, damages equaling at least $100,000. This figure constituted the rough amount of damages caused by H & H's (D's) breach. A take nothing judgment was rendered in favor of H & H (D). Laredo (P) appealed.

■ **ISSUE**

Is a buyer entitled to damages if he or she "covers" himself or herself by purchasing substitute goods when a seller breaches a contract for a sale of goods?

■ **DECISION AND RATIONALE**

(Bissett) Yes. Under UCC § 2–712, when a seller refuses to acknowledge a contract or refuses to deliver the goods under contract, a buyer will be entitled to damages if he or she covers "by making in good faith and without unreasonable delay any reasonable purchase of or contract to purchase goods in substitution for those due from the seller." The buyer can then recover damages in the form of "the difference between the cost of cover and the contract price together with any incidental or consequential damages." Here, Laredo (P) offered evidence of H & H's (D's) hide production from April to December, 1972. Laredo (P) also demonstrated the price for the hides it had to buy elsewhere and the fact that it (P) had to buy them often, as the hides would decompose if allowed to age. A certified public accountant also demonstrated the costs of buying the substitute hides based on purchase invoices. It is clear that Laredo (P) opted to pursue the remedy provided by § 2–712. Its (P's) pleadings and evidence also brings Laredo (P) under the "cover" provisions of that section of the Code. Also, if the buyer complies with the requirements of § 2–712, any purchase by the buyer is presumed to be proper. The seller bears the burden of proof to show that "cover" was not properly obtained. Here, H & H (D) offered no evidence to counter this presumption. The difference between the contract price and the cover price for the steer hides has thus been shown to be $134,252.82; the difference for the bull hides has been shown to be $8,001.66. The total contract/cover difference, then, is $142,254.48. Further, Laredo (P) offered evidence of $1,435,77 in increased transportation costs, and $2,013.18 in increased handling charges. These costs are certainly recoverable as incidental damages where a buyer elects to "cover." There is no evidence that Laredo (P) tried to increase its damages after H & H (D) refused to deliver the contracted hides. By purchasing the other hides, Laredo (P) acted promptly and in a reasonable manner. The record does not support the trial court's decisions of fact and of law. Laredo (P) is entitled to $152,960.04 in damages plus interest. Judgment reversed and rendered.

**Analysis:**

Generally speaking, a buyer's damages when a seller fails to deliver goods is equal to the amount of the replacement price (the "cover" price) minus the contract price, plus the cost of any other loss incurred because of the breach. According to the Code commentary, though, the replacement transaction must be an appropriate one, according to the aforementioned requirements of good faith and reasonableness, for this formula to apply. Still, the Code suggests that it is immaterial whether later information proves the resale transaction was "not the cheapest or most effective." Also, cover does not have to be identical to the breached goods, but can be goods that are "commercially usable as reasonable substitutes under the circumstances." Quality is also not a major factor. If the goods for cover are in any way superior or inferior, this discrepancy can be compensated for in a separate monetary award between the parties. It is important to note, though, that cover *is not mandatory*. If a replacement transaction is not conducted, or is insufficient for cover under the Code, the buyer's damages will simply be calculated without regard to such a transaction.

■ **CASE VOCABULARY**

TAKE NOTHING JUDGMENT: Judgment which provides that one party is not entitled to certain damages.

TANNERY: A place where animal hides are converted into leather.

# R.E. Davis Chemical Corp. v. Diasonics, Inc.

(Equipment Buyer) v. (Equipment Manufacturer)

826 F.2d 678 (7th Cir. 1987)

**A SELLER WHO WISHES TO RESELL GOODS AFTER A BUYER BREACHES A CONTRACT CAN BE ENTITLED TO DAMAGES AS CALCULATED UNDER UCC § 2–708**

■ **INSTANT FACTS** Davis (P) had to breach a purchase contract with Diasonics (D), and when Diasonics (D) resold the equipment, Davis (P) sued to get its full deposit back.

■ **BLACK LETTER RULE** A seller who wishes to resell goods after a buyer breaches a given contract can seek damages equal to the difference between the contract price and market price at the time and place for tender under UCC § 2–708; but to receive lost profits, the seller must establish both that he or she would have been able to produce the breached goods and the resold goods and that it would have been profitable to produce and sell both sets of goods.

■ **PROCEDURAL BASIS**

Appeal from order denying motion for summary judgment in action for restitution.

■ **FACTS**

On or about February 23, 1984, R.E. Davis Chemical Corporation (Davis) (P) contracted to purchase a piece of medical diagnostic equipment from Diasonics, Inc. (Diasonics) (D), a manufacturer and seller of such equipment. In accordance with this agreement, Davis (P) paid Diasonics (D) a $300,000 deposit on February 29, 1984. Before making this agreement with Diasonics (D), Davis (P) had contracted with Dobbin and Valvassori to establish a medical facility where the Diasonics (D) equipment was to be used. Sometime after the Diasonics (D) contract was made, however, Dobbin and Valvassori breached their contract with Davis (P). Davis (P) then breached its contract with Diasonics (D) by refusing to take delivery of the equipment and withholding payment of the rest of the balance due under the agreement. Diasonics (D) eventually resold the equipment to a third party for the same price at which it was to be sold to Davis (P). Davis (P) sued Diasonics (D), asking for restitution of its $300,000 down payment under UCC § 2–718(2). Diasonics (D) counterclaimed, arguing that it (D) was entitled to an offset under § 2–718(3). Diasonics (D) claimed it was a "lost volume seller," and thus lost one sale's worth of profit when Davis (P) breached. To be put in as good a position as it would if Davis (P) had performed, Diasonics (D) claimed, it (D) should be entitled to recover its lost profits under UCC § 2–708(2). The district court held that lost volume sellers were limited to recovering only the difference between a resale price and a contract price, plus incidental damages, under UCC § 2–706(1). Davis (P) was awarded $322,656, which represented Davis' (P's) down payment plus pre-judgment interest, minus Diasonics' (D's) incidental damages. Diasonics (D) appealed.

■ **ISSUE**

Can a lost volume seller wishing to resell goods after a buyer breaches a contract of sale seek lost profits under UCC § 2–708?

■ **DECISION AND RATIONALE**

(Cudahy) Yes. A seller who wishes to resell goods after a buyer breaches a given contract can seek damages under UCC § 2–708, but to receive lost profits, the seller must establish, not only that he or she would have been able to produce the breached goods and the resold goods, but also that it would have been profitable to produce and sell both sets of goods. Two measures of damages are provided by § 2–708. The first, in § 2–708(1), calculates damages by subtracting the market price at the time and place of tender from the contract price. Diasonics (D) is requesting the second, in § 2–708(2), which is a profit measure of damages. This should only be applied when the former measure of damages is inadequate to put the seller in as good a position as performance of the contract would have done. Diasonics (D) claims that § 2–708(1) provides only inadequate damages for lost volume sellers. The breach would have effectively cost the seller a "profit," and thus the seller can only be made whole again by receiving damages equal to its "lost profit." Diasonics (D) is correct that the measure provided by 2–708(1) will not put a reselling seller in as good a position as it would have been in had the buyer performed; this is because the breach resulted in the loss of sales volume for the seller. Whether a person is a lost volume seller, however, should depend on two questions. The first is whether the seller could have produced the breached units in addition to its actual volume; the second is whether it would have been profitable for the seller to produce both units. This position reflects the economic law of diminishing returns: as a seller's volume increases, at some point the cost of selling each additional item will be so high that it is unprofitable to make another sale. Thus, it is possible that granting a lost volume seller its presumed lost profit would overcompensate the seller. The measure of damages of 2–708(2) would not take effect because the damage formula in 2–708(1) would place the seller in as good a position as if the buyer had not breached. On remand, then, Diasonics (D) must prove not only that it (D) had the capacity to produce the breached unit in addition to the unit resold, but also that it would be profitable to have produced and sold both. Dlasonics (D) carries this burden because it generally falls on the party claiming injury to establish the amount of damages, and this issue is raised by Diasonics' (D's) counterclaim. If Diasonics (D) successfully establishes these facts, then the district court will calculate damages under 2–708(2). Summary judgment reversed and remanded with instructions.

## Analysis:

On remand, the district judge ruled that Diasonics (D) had demonstrated lost profit damages equaling $453,050. Judgment was then entered for that sum, minus the $300,000 deposit that Diasonics (D) kept for the equipment. Davis (P), unsurprisingly, appealed this judgment as well. The court of appeals upheld this judgment, noting the evidence was undisputed that Diasonics (D) could produce one more piece of the diagnostic equipment. Also, Diasonics (D) had shown it was "beating the bushes for all possible sales." In reality, a decision on lost volume in a given case will likely turn on who has the burden of proof on that issue. Most jurisdictions place that burden on the seller, as was done here. The Ninth Circuit, however, in *Islamic Republic of Iran v. Boeing Co.*, 771 F.2d 1279 (9th Cir. 1985), rejected the idea of imposing a "rigid and complex" burden of proof on a seller under UCC § 2–708(2), instead, the Court held that a seller only needs to show that it could have supplied both the breaching buyer and the resale buyer, and not that it could have made a profit from both sales.

# United States v. Algernon Blair, Inc.

(Owner of Naval Hospital) v. (Construction Company)

479 F.2d 638 (4th Cir. 1973)

THE MEASURE OF RESTITUTION IN THE FORM OF QUANTUM MERUIT RECOVERY IS THE REASONABLE VALUE OF THE PERFORMANCE RENDERED, AND CANNOT BE DIMINISHED BY ANY LOSS THAT WOULD HAVE RESULTED FROM COMPLETE PERFORMANCE

■ **INSTANT FACTS** When Blair refused to pay crane rental costs, Coastal Steel terminated its performance and sued to recover for labor and equipment it had already furnished.

■ **BLACK LETTER RULE** The measure of recovery for quantum meruit is the reasonable value of the performance, and recovery is undiminished by any loss which would have been incurred by complete performance.

■ **PROCEDURAL BASIS**

Appeal from award of damages in action for breach of contract.

■ **FACTS**

Algernon Blair, Inc. (Blair) (D) entered a contract with the United States (U.S.) (P) for the construction of a naval hospital. Blair (D) then contracted with Coastal Steel Erectors, Inc. (Coastal) (P) to conduct steel erection operations and supply equipment as part of Blalr's (D's) contract with the U.S. (P). Coastal (P) began performing its obligations and supplied its own cranes for handling and placing the required steel. Blair (D) claimed that the cost of crane rental was not its (D's) responsibility under its (D's) subcontract with Coastal (P), and refused to pay those costs. Because of this refusal to pay, Coastal (P) terminated its performance. This occurred after Coastal (P) had completed roughly 28 percent of its subcontract. Blair (D) went ahead and completed its contract with the U.S. (P) with a new subcontractor. Coastal (P) sued in the name of the United States (P) under the Miller Act to recover damages for labor and equipment already furnished. The district court found that Blair (D) was required under the subcontract to pay for crane use. Also, the refusal to pay was a material breach and justified Coastal's (P's) termination of performance. This finding is not questioned on appeal, but the court also found that Coastal (P), less what it (P) was already paid, was owed roughly $37,000. Moreover, the court found that Coastal (P) would have actually lost $37,000 (as compared to making $37,000) if performance was completed. The court thus denied recovery to Coastal (P), finding that any amount due would have to be reduced by any loss that would have resulted from complete performance of the contract.

■ **ISSUE**

Should a subcontractor who justifiably ceases work after the main contractor breaches the contract be entitled to restitution based on the value of the services already rendered?

■ **DECISION AND RATIONALE**

(Craven) Yes. The measure of recovery for quantum meruit is the reasonable value of the performance, and recovery is undiminished by any loss which would have been incurred by complete performance. In *United States for Use of Susi Contracting Co. v. Zara Contracting Co.*, 146 F.2d 606 (2d.Cir.1944), the

Second Circuit faced a similar situation involving a prime contractor who had unjustifiably breached a subcontract after partial performance by a subcontractor. There, the court stated that the subcontractor could choose not to file suit based on the contract, and instead could make a claim for the reasonable value of his or her performance. Here, Coastal (P) paid for the costs of labor and equipment that Blair (D) has used. Blair (D) then breached the subcontract and retained the benefits of this labor and equipment without having fully paid for them. Based on these facts, it is clear that Coastal (P) is entitled to restitution in quantum meruit. As Fuller & Perdue wrote in their piece on The Reliance Interest in Contract Damages, 46 Yale L.J. 52, 56 (1936), "if A not only causes B to lose one unit but appropriates that unit to himself, the resulting discrepancy between A and B is not one unit but two." Quantum meruit allows a promisee to recover the value of services he or she gave to the promisor. This recovery is possible regardless of whether the promisee would have lost money on the contract and been unable to recover in a suit on the contract. The standard measuring the reasonable value of the services rendered is the amount for which such services could have been purchased from one in the plaintiff's position at the time and place the services were rendered. The district court must determine the reasonable value of the labor and equipment that Coastal (P) provided for Blair (D). This amount should then be awarded to Coastal (P), minus any payment Blair (D) may have already made under the contract. Decision reversed and remanded with instructions.

---

**Analysis:**

Many courts have made similar rulings on questions of this nature. In addition to the Fourth Circuit here, the Second Circuit in *Scaduto v. Orlando*, 381 F.2d 587 (2d Cir. 1967), and in the afore mentioned *Zara Contracting* case, ruled that the subcontractor should recover the "actual value of labor and materials" from the contractor in the event of the contractor's breach. Generally, the courts that follow this reasoning must face the minor problem of measuring the benefit received by the breaching party. This difficulty is greatly eased by relying on the reasonable value of the services rendered, as trying to measure the benefit based on the other party's expectation interest will be far more difficult. Indeed, the use of the reasonable value standard is favorable, for even if the party in breach abandons the contractual enterprise entirely, any performance taken by the nonbreaching party will be, presumably, for the benefit of the party in breach. This was certainly the case here, as the steel erection and crane usage provided by Coastal (P) certainly helped Blair's (D's) construction work.

---

### ■ CASE VOCABULARY

SURETY: A person or entity who is held liable for the payment of a debt or performance of an obligation by another person or entity.

# Rockingham County v. Luten Bridge Co.

(County) v. (Bridge Building Company)

35 F.2d 301, 66 A.L.R. 735 (4th Cir. 1929)

A PLAINTIFF CANNOT HOLD A DEFENDANT LIABLE FOR DAMAGES WHICH NEED NOT HAVE BEEN INCURRED

■ **INSTANT FACTS** Luten Bridge Co. continued building a bridge even after Rockingham County notified the company not to proceed with the work.

■ **BLACK LETTER RULE** A plaintiff must, so far as he or she can without loss to himself or herself, mitigate the damages caused by a defendant's wrongful act; a plaintiff cannot hold a defendant liable for damages which need not have been incurred.

■ **PROCEDURAL BASIS**

Appeal from action at law for damages.

■ **FACTS**

The Board of County Commissioners of Rockingham County, North Carolina (D) entered a contract with Luten Bridge Company (Luten) (P) on January 7, 1924 to build a bridge within the county limits. A significant amount of the public opposed the building of the bridge. On February 21, 1924, the Board (D) notified Luten (P) that the County (D) was refusing to recognize the contract as valid and that Luten (P) should not proceed with further work. [The appellate court eventually held that this refusal to recognize the contract was unjustifiable.] By this point, Luten (P) had already spent about $1900 for labor and materials for the bridge. After receiving notice from the Board (D), Luten (P) continued to build the bridge according to the terms of the contract. Luten (P) filed suit to recover $18,301.07, which Luten (P) claimed it (P) was owed for work done before November 3, 1924. The trial court directed a verdict for Luten (P) for this amount. The County (D) appealed.

■ **ISSUE**

If one party unjustifiably rescinds a contract, is the other party entitled to recover damages if he or she continues performance under the contract?

■ **DECISION AND RATIONALE**

(Parker) No. A plaintiff must, so far as he or she can without loss to himself or herself, mitigate the damages caused by a defendant's wrongful act; a plaintiff cannot hold a defendant liable for damages which need not have been incurred. Granted, the County (D) had no right to rescind the contract, and its notice to Luten (P) constituted a breach of the contract by the County (D). Once Luten (P) received this notice of the breach, however, it was Luten's (P's) duty to do nothing to pile up damages flowing from this breach. Luten (P) should have treated the contract as broken at that point and simply sued for any damages resulting from that breach, as well as any profits that would have resulted from performance, and any losses that were incurred. The bridge involved here was to have been built in the forest as part of a future roadway. The County (D) later decided not to build the road, and thus the bridge would have been of no value to the County (D). Luten (P) had no right to pile up damages by continuing to build a useless bridge. Judgment reversed.

**Analysis:**

The ruling here does not mean that a party who has notice of another party's breach of their contract is automatically barred from continuing performance. For example, it may still be reasonable for an injured party to perform if the breach comes with assurances that the breaching party will still perform. In addition, UCC § 2–704(2) provides that a seller who was also supposed to manufacture the contracted goods may finish manufacturing them when the buyer repudiates the contract. This provision is meant to save the seller/manufacturer the cost of stopping production and salvaging the goods and materials, on the belief the seller/manufacturer will exercise "reasonable commercial judgment" to avoid such loss.

# Tongish v. Thomas

(Sunflower Seed Farmer) v. (Second Seed Buyer)

251 Kan. 728, 840 P.2d 471 (1992)

MARKET DAMAGES SHOULD BE AWARDED IN THE EVENT OF A SUPPLIER'S BREACH OF ITS CONTRACTUAL OBLIGATION TO DELIVER GOODS

■ **INSTANT FACTS** Tongish contracted to sell his sunflower seed crop to the Coop Association, but repudiated that contract when the market price for seeds went up.

■ **BLACK LETTER RULE** If a seller breaches a contractual obligation to deliver goods, and the buyer fails to go into the market and "cover," the buyer's damages will be measured by the difference between the market price and the contract price according to UCC § 2–713.

## ■ FACTS

Tongish (D) was a farmer who grew sunflower seeds. Tongish (D) contracted with the Coop Association (Coop) (P) to grow 116.8 acres of sunflower seeds and sell the seeds to Coop (P) at $13 per hundredweight for large seeds and $8 per hundredweight for small seeds. The seeds were to be delivered in thirds by December 31, 1988, March 31, 1989, and May 31, 1989. Coop (P) also contracted to deliver these seeds to Bambino Bean & Seed for the same price it (P) paid to Tongish (D), minus a 55 cent per hundredweight handling fee as profit. In January 1989, the market price of sunflower seeds had risen to double the price named in the Tongish (D) contract. This was the result of a small seed crop, bad weather, and other factors. Tongish (D) notified Coop (P) that he (D) would end deliveries and sold his (D's) remaining seed crop to Danny Thomas for about $20 per hundredweight. Thomas' total purchase price amounted to $14,714, which was $5,153 more than the Coop (P) contract price. Coop (P) sued Tongish (D) and was awarded $455 in damages for its (P's) loss of handling charges. Coop (P) appealed, and the Court of Appeals reversed so that damages could be measured according to the market price under UCC § 2–713. Tongish appealed, claiming that the trial court ruling was correct under UCC § 1–106, which was intended to place an injured party "in as good a position as if the other party had fully performed."

## ■ ISSUE

If a seller fails to deliver goods under a contract, can the buyer recover the difference between the market price and the contract price of goods under UCC § 2–713, even if such an award will be greater than the buyer's loss under the terms of the contract?

## ■ DECISION AND RATIONALE

(McFarland) Yes. In *Allied Canners & Packers, Inc. v. Victor Packing Co.*, 162 Cal.App.3d 905, 209 Cal.Rptr. 60 (1984), the court faced a somewhat similar situation of a farmer being unable to deliver a crop to a buyer. There, the court noted that where a seller knows a buyer has a resale contract for goods, and the seller has not breached the contract in bad faith, then the buyer is limited to actual loss of damages under § 1–106. The farmer in the earlier case, however, could not deliver the crop because it had been destroyed by heavy rains. Here, Tongish (D) did have a crop to deliver, but instead took advantage of the sunflower seed market and sold it to Thomas. The trial court found there was no valid reason for this kind of breach. Thus, the breach in *Allied* is much different than the breach found here. Granted, the market damages remedy conflicts with the idea that contract damages should only make the injured party whole, and not penalize a breaching party. Still, the *Allied* decision has been sharply criticized for its rejection of market damages. The rule of market damages under UCC § 2–713 is the more reasonable standard, for while it may not reflect the buyer's actual loss, it encourages efficiency in the market and guards against the breach of contracts. While this solution may seem unfair, allowing damages under § 1–106 would allow Tongish (D) to consider the contract price with Coop (P) as a mere "floor" price for the seeds, ignore his (D's) obligation to Coop (P) and take the seeds out on the market to sell to the highest bidder. In other words, this would encourage Tongish (D) to breach the contract. Using market damages would encourage market stability and the honoring of contracts. Judgment of Court of Appeals affirmed.

## Analysis:

The courts have been split for over sixty years on the measure of damages when a supplier breaches delivery obligations. The majority of courts award damages in the amount of the difference between the market price and the contract price, even when it would be in excess of a plaintiff's actual loss under the contract. A strong minority would limit market damages to actual loss, however, even if the defendant would have a relative windfall because of it. Most experts still favor the market damages rule, because it effectively penalizes parties for violating their own agreements for the sake of their own profits from the market. At least one scholar, Schneider, in a 1986 article mentioned in the opinion, criticized the *Allied* decision as ignoring the intent behind § 2–713 to "award expectation damages in accordance with the allocation of risk as measured by the difference between contract price and market price on the date set for performance." Another scholar, Scott, argued in the University of Chicago Law Review that the lost profits rule of *Allied* encourages parties to break agreements if the market changes to their advantage, thereby creating instability in the market and in the agreements themselves.

## ■ CASE VOCABULARY

HUNDREDWEIGHT: A unit of weight equaling one hundred (100) pounds.

# Parker v. Twentieth Century-Fox Film Corp.

(Actress) v. (Film Studio)
3 Cal.3d 176, 89 Cal.Rptr. 737, 474 P.2d 689 (1970)

AN ACTRESS' REFUSAL TO TAKE A DIFFERENT KIND OF ROLE IN A DIFFERENT PRODUCTION CANNOT BE USED AS A REASON FOR MITIGATING DAMAGES IN A BREACH OF CONTRACT DISPUTE

■ **INSTANT FACTS** Parker contracted to act in a musical in California, but Fox abandoned the musical and offered her a role in a western in Australia.

■ **BLACK LETTER RULE** A wrongfully discharged employee's rejection of or failure to seek other available employment of a different or inferior kind cannot be used by the employer as a means of mitigating damages.

■ **PROCEDURAL BASIS**

Appeal from summary judgment in breach of contract action for damages.

■ **FACTS**

Mrs. Parker (P), known professionally as Shirley MacLaine, was [and still is, "Mrs. Winterbourne" notwithstanding] a prominent film actress. Under a contract with Twentieth Century-Fox Film Corporation (Fox) (D), dated August 6, 1965, Parker (P) was to play the female lead in Fox's (D's) proposed production of a film entitled "Bloomer Girl." Fox (D) agreed to pay Parker (P) a total of $750,000 over a period of 14 weeks, beginning May 23, 1966. This contract also provided Parker (P) with certain rights of approval regarding the choice of director and content of the screenplay. Before May 1966, however, Fox (D) decided not to produce the film. In a letter dated April 4, 1966, Fox (D) notified Parker (P) of this decision, and with the express purpose "to avoid any damage to you," offered Parker (P) the leading female role in another film, tentatively entitled "Big Country, Big Man." ("Big Country") The monetary compensation for this new role was to be identical to the amount offered previously. "Big Country," however, was a dramatic "western" movie, while "Bloomer Girl" was to have been a musical production. Also, "Big Country" was to be filmed in Australia, while "Bloomer Girl" had been set for production in California. Moreover, Parker (P) was not given director and screenplay approval by the "Big Country" contract. Parker (P) was given a week to accept this second contract. She (P) did not accept Fox's (D's) offer, and then filed suit seeking recovery of the agreed guaranteed compensation. She (P) set forth a cause of action under the contract itself, and another for damages from the breach of the contract. Fox (D) admitted the existence and validity of the contract, and that it (D) had breached and repudiated the contract. Fox (D) denied, however, that Parker (P) was entitled to any money under the contract or as a result of the breach. Fox (D) claimed, as an affirmative defense, that Parker (P) deliberately failed to mitigate her (P's) damages by unreasonably refusing to accept the role in "Big Country." Parker (P) moved for and was granted summary judgment, with an award of $750,000 plus interest. Fox (D) appealed.

■ **ISSUE**

Should a wrongfully discharged employee's rejection of an offer of different and inferior employment by his or her employer be considered when measuring damages for the employer's breach?

## ■ DECISION AND RATIONALE

(Burke) No. A wrongfully discharged employee's rejection of or failure to seek other available employment of a different or inferior kind cannot be used by the employer as a means of mitigating damages. Generally, a wrongfully discharged employee is entitled to recover the amount of salary he or she was promised. This amount is to be reduced by the amount that the employer affirmatively proves the employee has earned or could have earned with reasonable effort since being discharged. The employer must show, however, that any job opportunities that the employee rejected were comparable, or substantially similar, to the original job that the employee had agreed to perform. Here, Fox (D) has raised no issue as to the reasonableness of Parker's (P's) efforts to gain other employment. The only issue is whether her (P's) refusal of the "Big Country" role may be used to mitigate her (P's) damages. It is clear that Parker's (P's) refusal to accept the latter role offered by Fox (D) should not be applied in mitigation of damages. This is because the "Big Country" lead was different from and inferior to the role offered for "Bloomer Girl." The female lead as a dramatic actress in a western style motion picture cannot be considered substantially similar to a female lead in a song-and-dance production. In addition, no expertise is required to see that the "Big Country" offer, which proposed to eliminate or impair Parker's (P's) director and screenplay approval rights under the "Bloomer Girl" contract, was an offer of inferior employment. Parker's (P's) rejection of the role in "Big Country" should not be a means of mitigating damages. Judgment affirmed.

## ■ DISSENT

(Sullivan) Only in California is there a rule that an employee is only required to accept employment that is "substantially similar." There is no historical or theoretical justification for adopting a standard regarding employment of a "different or inferior kind." It has never been the law that the mere existence of differences between two jobs in the same field is sufficient to excuse an employee from accepting an alternative offer of employment in order to mitigate his or her own damages. All the majority has done is attempt to prove their proposition that the two roles offered by Fox (D) were different by repeating the idea that they were different. The relevant question is not whether one offer of employment is different from the other, but whether there are enough differences in the kind of employment, or whether one offer is truly inferior to the other. These questions are part of the ultimate issue, which is whether or not the employee in question has acted reasonably. Summary judgment should be withheld.

Analysis:

The question of what is an appropriate substitute offer of employment will depend greatly on the facts and circumstances of each case. Factors may include the work the injured party is to perform, the time and place at which the performance is to be rendered, and the compensation to be given for the work. The cases where latter offers of employment have not been found to be appropriate have tended to involve very vivid situations. The Eighth Circuit in *Jackson v. Wheatley School Dist.*, 464 F.2d 411 (8th Cir. 1972), for example, held that a job that would require a teacher to live apart from her husband was not an appropriate substitute for a job in the same school where the husband also worked as a teacher. In addition, the court in *State ex rel. Freeman v. Sierra County Bd. of Educ.*, 49 N.M. 54, 157 P.2d 234 (1945), found that a principal and teacher in a school could not be required to accept a job as fourth-grade teacher in the same school.

# Jacob & Youngs v. Kent

(Contractor) v. (Homeowner)

230 N.Y. 239, 129 N.E. 889, 23 A.L.R. 1429 (1921)

FREEDOM OF CONTRACT BATTLES EQUITY IN DETERMINING THE APPROPRIATE MEASURE OF DAMAGES

■ **INSTANT FACTS** Jacob & Youngs (P) constructed a house using two types of pipe, and Kent (D) refused to make full payment because the contract called for the exclusive use of pipe manufactured by Reading.

■ **BLACK LETTER RULE** Insubstantial departures from express contract language may be remedied by damages based on the diminution in market value rather than the cost of replacement.

## ■ PROCEDURAL BASIS

Appeal from reversal of directed verdict that denied damages for failure to pay on a contact.

## ■ FACTS

Jacob & Youngs ("Jacob") (P) contracted to build a country residence for Kent (D). The express terms of the contract required Jacob (P) to use only pipes manufactured by Reading. However, Jacob (P) used Reading pipes for less than half of the plumbing. Upon discovering this defect, Kent (D) withheld the final payment of over $3000, and Jacob (P) sued for payment. At trial, Jacob (P) attempted to enter into evidence the fact that the non-Reading pipes were identical in quality and price to the Reading pipes. The trial court excluded the evidence and directed a verdict for Kent (D). The appellate division reversed and granted a new trial. In order for Jacob (P) to remedy the defect, he would have been required to tear down most of the house, as almost all of the pipes were encased within the walls. Thus, the cost of replacing the non-Reading pipes would have been tremendous, especially in comparison to the negligible decrease in value caused by using non-Reading pipes. Kent (D) appealed the appellate division's decision.

## ■ ISSUE

Where the cost of replacement is grossly disproportionate to the good to be attained, may diminution in value constitute the appropriate measure of damages?

## ■ DECISION AND RATIONALE

(Cardozo, J.) Yes. Where the cost of replacement is grossly disproportionate to the good to be attained, diminution in value may constitute the appropriate measure of damages. Thus, the trial court erred in not admitting evidence of the relative quality of the non-Reading pipes. The evidence, if admitted, would have supplied some basis for the inference that the defect was insignificant in relation to the project. A trivial and innocent omission will sometimes be atoned for by allowance of the resulting damage, and will not always constitute a breach of contract. Indeed, in some situations, substitution of equivalents will have great significance. Departure from the strict terms of the contract will not be tolerated if it is so dominant and pervasive so as to frustrate the purpose of the contract. However, in the instant situation, the triers of fact should have been allowed to determine the significance of Jacob's (P) use of non-Reading pipe. Where the performance has been substantial, an equitable remedy exists where the defects are trivial. We think that the measure of damages must be shaped to the same end. Although cost of replacement is typically the appropriate measure of damages, we think the correct measure in this case should have been the difference in value. The cost of replacement was grossly and unfairly out of proportion to the good to be attained, i.e. the construction of adequate plumbing in the residence. Affirmed.

### ■ DISSENT

(McLaughlin, J.) Jacob (P) contracted to construct the residence out of Reading pipe, and Jacob (P) failed to comply with this express contractual mandate. Thus, Jacob (P) failed to perform its contract. Kent (D) had the right to contract for what he wanted, and Kent (D) clearly bargained for the exclusive use of Reading pipes in the building. His reason for requiring this kind of pipe is of no importance. Thus, the rule of substantial performance, with damages for unsubstantial omissions, has no application.

### Analysis:

This case involves the determination of appropriate measure of damages. As a note following the case recommends, it may be easier to assume that Kent (D) had paid Jacob (P) full price and that Kent (D) was suing for damages. In this scenario, it is easy to see that Kent (D) would be arguing for the "cost of replacement" measure of damages, whereas Jacob (P) would be pushing for the lower "diminution in value" measure. If diminution in value was the appropriate measure, then Jacob (P) should have been allowed to enter evidence of the relative quality of the non-Reading pipes. The majority opinion attempts to achieve a just result. It makes sense that Jacob (P) should not be forced to tear down the building and reconstruct it using only Reading pipes, if the non-Reading pipes were just as good. On the other hand, Kent (D) did expressly contract for the exclusive use of Reading pipes. As the dissent contends, a party has the right to expect the performance that he bargained for at the contract-formation stages. All in all, the case presents an interesting example of competing forces in the law of contracts: the principle of freedom of contract versus the ability of a court to achieve a more equitable result that contradicts express contractual language.

### ■ CASE VOCABULARY

MINUTIAE: Litte, insignificant details.

MULTIFARIOUS: Having great variety and diversity.

# Groves v. John Wunder Co.

(Land Owner) v. (Land User)

205 Minn. 163, 286 N.W. 235 (1939)

A DELIBERATE BREACH OF A CONTRACT BY A PARTY WILL LEAD TO DAMAGES EQUAL TO THE COST OF REMEDYING THE FAILURE IN PERFORMANCE

■ **INSTANT FACTS** John Wunder Co. agreed to remove sand and gravel from the Groves land and keep the land level when finished, but later breached this agreement.

■ **BLACK LETTER RULE** When a party willfully fails to perform under a contract, the other party will be entitled to damages equal to the reasonable cost of having performance carried out, and not the difference in value resulting from non-performance.

■ **PROCEDURAL BASIS**

Appeal from judgment in action for breach of contract.

■ **FACTS**

S.J. Groves & Sons Company (Groves) (P) owned a 24-acre tract of land which contained a significant deposit of sand and gravel. Groves (P) operated a plant on this land for excavating and screening the gravel. John Wunder Co. (Wunder) (D) owned and operated a similar plant nearby. In August 1927, Groves (P) and Wunder (D) entered a contract by which Groves (P) would lease its (P) land to Wunder (D) for seven years. Wunder (D) agreed to remove the sand and gravel, and also to leave the property "at a uniform grade, substantially the same as the grade now existing at the roadway ... on said premises..." The lease also provided that Wunder (D), in clearing away any of the materials covering the sand and gravel, would use such materials "for the purpose of maintaining and establishing said grade." Further, Wunder (D) would acquire the Groves (P) screening plant on the property and eliminate Groves (P) as a competitor. Groves (P) was paid $105,000 under the lease. Wunder (D) breached this contract deliberately, removing only "the richest and best of the gravel" from the land and leaving the property "broken, rugged, and uneven." Groves (P) sued Wunder (D) for breach of contract. The lower court found that, to leave the property at the required uniform grade, 288,495 cubic *yards* of material would have to be excavated and deposited elsewhere. The cost of doing this would be over $60,000. If Wunder (D) did leave the land at a uniform grade, however, the reasonable value of the property would have been only $12,160. The lower court awarded damages to Groves (P) for approximately $15,000, measuring them by the difference between the market value of the land in the condition it was in when the contract was made and the condition the land would have been in had Wunder (D) performed. Groves (P) appealed the amount of damages.

■ **ISSUE**

Should a party injured by another party's willful failure to perform under a contract be entitled to damages based on the cost of performance?

■ **DECISION AND RATIONALE**

(Stone) Yes. When a party willfully falls to perform under a contract, the other party will be entitled to damages equal to the reasonable cost of having performance carried out, and not the difference in value resulting from non-performance. Wunder's (D) breach of contract was certainly willful in this case, with nothing of good faith about it. The lower court's decision to award damages for only $15,000 effectively rewards bad faith and the deliberate breach of a contract. That outcome is unacceptable. A contractor who willfully and fraudulently varies from a contract cannot sue based on the contract and expect to have the benefit of the doctrine of substantial performance. Here, there is not even substantial performance on the part of Wunder (D). As Justice Cardozo wrote in *Jacob & Youngs v. Kent*, change will not be tolerated "If it is so dominant or pervasive as in any real or substantial measure to frustrate the purpose of the contract." Clearly, Wunder (D) acted against Groves' (P) explicit wish to improve the land after the lease was concluded. Further, it would be wrong to measure damages according to the difference in value of the land if the contract were fulfilled and the value of the land without performance. Value of the land is no proper part of any measure of damages for willful breach of a building contract. Previous cases have never suggested that the lack of value in land furnished to a contractor who had promised to improve it allows the contractor to breach such a contract without harsh consequences. Here, the contractor, Wunder (D) was paid in advance and refused to improve the land as it (D) promised. Groves' (P) desire to see its (P) land improved should not be impaired by the small value of the land itself. Instead, Groves (P) is entitled to compensation for the work it (P) has been promised by Wunder (D), yet been deprived of by Wunder (D) after payment has already been made. Groves (P) would not be unjustly or unconscionable enriched by forcing Wunder (D) to give what it (D) had already promised and received payment for. Judgment reversed and new trial ordered.

## ■ DISSENT

(Olson) The diminished value rule should be applied here because of the lack of evidence to show that the completed performance would satisfy the personal taste of Groves (P). The willfulness of Wunder's (D) breach should have no effect on the measure of damages.

## Analysis:

The court's focus on the willfulness of the breach in justifying a higher award of damages should be noted. Remember that the cost of performance, namely the cost of leaving the land at the required grade, would be roughly $60,000. Also, the potential increase in the market value of the land would be only $12,160, barely one-fifth of the cost. From these facts alone, it seems that Wunder's (D) decision not to leave the property at a uniform grade was the only economically sensible decision that that company (D) could make. Had Groves (P) attempted to show there was some special value to the land that was not necessarily reflected in its market value, then perhaps the award would not seem too excessive. For instance, if Groves (P) owned adjacent land that could only be used productively if the land in question were restored, then the award would possibly make better sense. Without such an indication of special value, however, one may find difficulty justifying a large award of damages, like the one here, solely because the breach was *willful.* After all, there was no evidence that the breach was necessarily *malicious,* accompanied by the intent to cause harm to Groves (P). As it stands, defining "willfulness" in this context may be difficult, as it is unclear whether purposeful intent to commit the act, or purposeful intent to commit the act in a harmful way, would satisfy the definition.

## ■ CASE VOCABULARY

GRADE: The degree of slope or inclination for a road or other segment of land.

OVERBURDEN: Dirt and other unimportant materials that cover a deposit of more useful geological materials or bedrock.

# Peevyhouse v. Garland Coal and Mining Co.

(Farm Owners) v. (Coal Miners)

382 P.2d 109 (Okla.1962), cert. denied, 375 U.S. 906 (1963)

THE AMOUNT OF DAMAGES AWARDED WHEN A CONTRACT PROVISION IS BREACHED WILL DEPEND ON THE IMPORTANCE OF THE PROVISION TO THE CONTRACT'S OVERALL PURPOSE AND THE RELATION OF THE COST OF PERFORMANCE TO THE BENEFIT OF PERFORMANCE

■ **INSTANT FACTS** The Peevyhouses (P) leased their farm to Garland (D) for strip mining, but Garland (D) failed to do specific remedial work at the end of the lease.

■ **BLACK LETTER RULE** The measure of damages in an action by a lessor against a lessee for breach of contract is ordinarily the reasonable cost of performance of the work; however, if the breached provision is merely incidental to the main purpose of the contract, and the economic benefit to be gained by the lessor from full performance is grossly disproportionate to the cost of performance, then the damages which may be recovered are limited to the diminution of value to the property caused by non-performance.

■ **PROCEDURAL BASIS**

Appeal from judgment in action for damages for breach of contract.

■ **FACTS**

In 1954, Willie and Lucille Peevyhouse (P) leased their farm to Garland Coal & Mining Co. (Garland) (D). The lease was for a five-year term, and would allow Garland (D) to strip mine for coal. As part of this lease, Garland (D) agreed to perform specific kinds of restorative and remedial work on the land at the end of the lease. Garland (D) failed to do this work, which would have involved moving many thousands of cubic yards of dirt. This operation would have cost Garland (D) roughly $29,000, but would have only increased the market price of the farm by about $300. The Peevyhouses (P) sued for $25,000 in damages, The trial court awarded $5,000 in damages. Both the Peevyhouses (P) and Garland (D) appealed.

■ **ISSUE**

Should a party injured by another party's failure to perform automatically be allowed to recover damages equal to the cost of performance when the cost of performance is disproportionate to the end to be attained by performance?

■ **DECISION AND RATIONALE**

(Jackson) No. The measure of damages in an action by a lessor against a lessee for damages for breach of contract is ordinarily the reasonable cost of performance of the work. If, however, the breached provision is merely incidental to the main purpose of the contract, and the economic benefit to be gained by the lessor from full performance is grossly disproportionate to the cost of performance, then the damages which may be recovered are limited to the diminution of value to the property caused by non-performance. The Peevyhouses (P) point to the decision in *Groves v. John Wunder Co.* [when a party willfully fails to perform under a contract, the other party will be entitled to damages equal to the reasonable cost of having performance carried out, and not the difference in value resulting from non-performance] to justify their (P) claim. It should be noted that that particular case is the only one in which the cost of performance rule was followed where the cost of performance greatly exceeded the decrease in value caused by the breach of contract. Moreover, that case was decided by a mere plurality of the court. Here, unlike previous cases, a "building and construction" or "grading and excavation" contract is not at issue. The contract was meant to accomplish the economical recovery and marketing of coal from the property for the benefit of all the parties. The provisions of the lease contract relating to the remedial work were incidental to this main purpose. In McCormick, Damages, Section 168, it is said with regard to building and construction cases that ". . . in cases where the defect is one that can be repaired or cured without undue expense," then damages should be measured by the cost of performance. If, however, ". . . the defect in material or construction is one that cannot be remedied without an expenditure for reconstruction disproportionate to the end to be attained," then the value rule should be allowed. This idea was also conveyed in *Jacob & Youngs, Inc. v. Kent* [substantial performance on a contract will outweigh trivial variations in performance which might ordinarily cause the failure of a condition]. Thus, because of the disproportion between the potential $300 increase in the value of the land and the enormous, $29,000 cost of remedial work, damages should be limited to the difference in value. Judgment reduced to $300 and affirmed.

## ■ DISSENT

(Irwin) The Peevyhouses (P) had insisted that the provisions for the remedial work be included in the contract, and they (P) would not agree to the lease unless those provisions were included. The Peevyhouses (P) were entitled to specific performance of the contract, and because Garland (D) failed to perform, damages should be awarded according to the cost of performance. Any other measure of damages would ignore the express provisions of the contract and nullify Garland's (D) obligations. Thus, a new contract would be made, for the benefit of Garland (D) and to the detriment of the Peevyhouses (P).

## Analysis:

The Restatement (Second) does not take willfulness into consideration in its damages formulation. Following the *Groves* rule here would lead to a damages award of nearly one *hundred* times the potential effect on the Peevyhouses' (P) land. Such an award would be quite unfair to some and economically ridiculous to others. Looking back at an earlier case, a $29,000 award here would lead to the same kind of economic waste that would have resulted had Jacob & Youngs been forced to demolish the walls in Kent's home in order to replace the pipes. Admittedly, this is a case that pits a farm couple (P) against a larger coal mining company (D), and strip mining is particularly damaging to surface land, with large expanses of earth being excavated a layer at a time. Still, the cost of restoring the land could have been mitigated, perhaps if Garland (D) agreed, as a term of its (D) lease, to allot a small percentage of profits over the five years to the Peevyhouses (P) for the purpose of funding the remedial work at the end of the lease.

# Hadley v. Baxendale

(Mill Operators) v. (Delivery Service)

9 Ex. 341, 156 Eng.Rep. 145 (1854)

A PARTY INJURED BY A BREACH OF CONTRACT CAN ONLY RECOVER THOSE DAMAGES THAT MAY REASONABLY BE CONSIDERED AS ARISING NATURALLY FROM THE BREACH, OR AS HAVING BEEN CONTEMPLATED BY THE PARTIES IN ADVANCE AS A LIKELY RESULT OF THE BREACH

■ **INSTANT FACTS** Baxendale failed to deliver a broken mill shaft for Hadley on time, and the delay prevented Hadley from reopening the mill on time.

■ **BLACK LETTER RULE** A party injured by another party's breach of contract can only recover those damages that may fairly and reasonably be considered either as arising naturally, or as may reasonably be supposed to have been in the contemplation of both parties, at the time the contract was made, as the probable result of such a breach of the contract.

■ **PROCEDURAL BASIS**

Rule nisi for new trial in action for damages for breach of contract of carriage.

■ **FACTS**

The Hadleys (P) operated a mill in Gloucester. This mill had to be shut down on May 11, 1854, when the crankshaft of the steam engine which ran the mill became broken. The Hadleys (P) arranged to have the manufacturers of their (P) engine make a replacement one based on the pattern of the broken shaft. To accomplish this, a representative of the Hadleys (P) went to Baxendale (D) at Pickford & Co., a well-known carrier [delivery and transport] business, on May 13. This representative told the Baxendale's (D) clerk that the Hadleys' (P) mill was stopped, and that the shaft must be sent immediately to the manufacturers at Greenwich. The clerk assured the Hadleys' (P) servant that it could be delivered in a day. The next morning, Baxendale (D) took the shaft and was paid to deliver it to Greenwich. This delivery was delayed by Baxendale's (D) neglect. As a result, the completion of repairs and the reopening of the mill were delayed by five days. In that time, the Hadleys (P) were compelled to pay wages. The Hadleys (P) claimed they (P) also lost wages totaling 300£ [pounds] and sought judgment for that amount. Baxendale (D) claimed these damages were too remote, and that liability should not be found. The jury awarded 25£ in damages to the Hadleys (P). Baxendale (D) appealed.

■ **ISSUE**

Should the measure of damages awarded to a party who is injured by a breach of contract be limited to only those damages that are not considered remote by the parties?

■ **DECISION AND RATIONALE**

(Alderson) Yes. A party injured by another party's breach of contract can only recover those damages that may fairly and reasonably be considered either as arising naturally, or as may reasonably be supposed to have been in the contemplation of both parties, at the time the contract was made, as the probable result of such a breach of the contract. In other words, if the special circumstances under which a contract is made are described by one party to another, it follows that both sides are aware of these special circumstances. Thus, any damages caused by a breach would have been reasonably contemplated by the parties. The measure of those damages would be the amount of injury which would ordinarily follow from such a breach under these circumstances. If, however, a party that breaches the contract did not know of these special circumstances, then he or she could only be presumed to have knowledge of the kind of injury that would result generally from a breach. This is because parties with knowledge of special circumstances regarding a contract could very well provide for them. It would be unfair for this advantage to be taken away from such parties by presuming otherwise. Here, the Hadleys' (P) servant only told Baxendale's (D) clerk at the time the contract was made that the mill shaft was broken, and that the Hadleys (P) operated that mill. It is unclear how these circumstances could reasonably show that the mill's profits would be stopped if the delivery of the shaft to the manufacturer were unreasonably delayed. Baxendale (D) had no idea of whether the Hadleys (P) had an extra shaft at the mill, or whether the steam engine was otherwise defective, etc. Ordinarily, a miller sending an engine shaft to a third person by a common carrier would not result in a loss of profits and a stopped mill. The special circumstances here that would lead to such a situation were never communicated to Baxendale (D). Therefore, the loss of profits in this case cannot reasonably be considered such a consequence of the breach of the contract as could have been fairly and reasonably contemplated by both parties when they made this contract. The jury should not have taken the loss of profits into consideration when measuring damages. A new trial is necessary in this case. Rule absolute.

---

**Analysis:**

Consequential damages are affected by the circumstances under which the contract was made, such as the amount of information provided by one party to another. The court here said the loss of profits for the mill could not have been in Baxendale's (D) "contemplation" because he (D) did not know if Hadley (P) had an extra mill shaft, if the mill engine was otherwise faulty, etc. This "contemplation" requirement imposed on the recovery of breach of contract damages was more severe than the test for substantial or proximate cause used in actions for tort or breach of warranty. Shortly after the *Hadley* decision, it appeared that both English and American courts would transform this contemplation test into an even stricter one. Some courts supported the idea that a party could not be held liable for consequential damages unless that party had made a "tacit agreement" to assume that particular risk when making the contract. Fortunately, this restrictive test has not survived to this day, and is explicitly rejected in the comments to the UCC. The modern trend has been to define the test as one of "foreseeability." A party must only have been given notice of facts that made a loss foreseeable to be held liable. Both the Restatement (Second) and the UCC have adopted this standard.

---

### ■ CASE VOCABULARY

COMMON CARRIER: A business that offers its services to the public for transportation of people, goods, or messages.

CRANK SHAFT/CRANKSHAFT: Shaft which drives the main moving parts of an engine.

NISI: Latin for "unless"; denotes a ruling that will be declared final unless the party adversely affected by it can show cause as to why the ruling should not take effect.

NOLLE PROSEQUI: A formal declaration that a prosecutor or plaintiff will "no longer prosecute" a particular case.

RULE ABSOLUTE: A rule which commands that an order be forthwith enforced.

# Delchi Carrier SpA v. Rotorex Corp.

(Manufacturer) v. (Parts Supplier)

71 F.3d 1024 (2nd Cir. 1995)

DAMAGED PARTY MAY RECOVER FORESEEABLE DAMAGES, EVEN UNDER INTERNATIONAL LAW

■ **INSTANT FACTS** A parts supplier refused to ship conforming goods to a buyer.

■ **BLACK LETTER RULE** Under international commercial law, a buyer may recover lost profits and other incidental damages caused by the seller's breach of contract if those lost profits were foreseeable.

■ **PROCEDURAL BASIS**

Appeal of district court judgment on breach of contract action for incidental and consequential damages.

■ **FACTS**

Rotorex Corp. (Rotorex) (D) agreed to supply three shipments of compressors to Delchi Carrier SpA, (Delchi) (P), an Italian air conditioner manufacturer. When the second shipment was en route, Delchi (P) discovered that the compressors in the first shipment were not the kind the contract required. Delchi (P) asked Rotorex (D) to supply conforming compressors, but Rotorex (D) refused. Delchi (P) canceled the contract and sought another source. As a result, Delchi's (P) plant was shut down for four days. Delchi (P) also incurred expenses shipping the nonconforming goods back to Rotorex (D). Delchi (P) sued Rotorex (D) for incidental and consequential damages. The judgment was for Delchi (P) for $1,248,332. The damages included lost profits for unfilled orders from Delchi (P) affiliates in Europe and from sales agents in Italy. The damages did not include consequential and incidental damages for shipping, customs, and related matters for the two returned shipments. Both parties appealed.

■ **ISSUE**

Under international commercial law, may a buyer recover lost profits and other incidental damages caused by the seller's breach of contract?

■ **DECISION AND RATIONALE**

(Winter, J.) Yes, if the damages are foreseeable. This case is governed by the Convention for the International Sale of Goods (CISG), an international treaty between the United States and other countries, including Italy. The CISG has virtually no case law interpreting it, but it directs that its interpretation should be informed by the need to promote uniformity and good faith. Case law interpreting the UCC may inform the court where the language of the CISG tracks the UCC. Article 74 of the CISG provides that damages for breach of contract may not exceed the loss that was foreseeable at the time of the conclusion of the contract, in light of the facts and matter of which the breaching party knew or ought to have known as a possible consequence of the breach. Rotorex (D) argues that the district court improperly awarded Delchi (P) lost profits. We disagree. The CISG requires that damages be limited by foreseeability as established in *Hadley v. Baxendale* [landmark English case holding that party injured by breach of contract may recover damages that were reasonably foreseeable at the time the contract was made]. Here, it was reasonably foreseeable that Delchi (P) would take orders for sales based on the number of compressors it had. On Delchi's (P) appeal of the district court's denial of damages for shipping, customs, and storage charges for the two returned shipments, we hold that these expenses were reasonably foreseeable. They are legitimate consequential damages that do not duplicate lost profits damages. Delchi's (P) labor expenses incurred as a result of the shutdown of its production line are also a reasonably foreseeable result of Rotorex's (D) shipment of nonconforming goods. We remand to the district court to determine whether Delchi's (P) labor costs during this four-day period were variable or fixed. Affirmed in part, and reversed and remanded in part.

## Analysis:

Where a seller delivers goods to a manufacturer knowing they are to be used in the manufacturing process, the seller has reason to know that nonconforming goods may disrupt production and result in lost profits. Therefore, the foresee ability rule allowed Delchi (P) to recover its lost profits from lost sales due to Rotorex's (D) breach and the costs Delchi (D) Incurred to return the shipments to Rotorex (D). This case demonstrates the universal acceptance of *Hadley v. Baxendale.* It remains the leading case on contract damages, even when international law is at issue. Note that *Delchi* holds that where the language of the CISG tracks the UCC, case law interpreting the UCC may be relevant However, Article 74 of the CISG provides that a party injured by a breach of contract may recover foreseeable *possible* consequences of the breach. UCC § 2–715(2) provides that consequential damages Include any loss resulting from general or particular requirements and need of which the seller at the time of contracting had reason to know and that could not reasonably be prevented by cover or otherwise. Thus, the language of the CISG would allow for broader damages than the UCC. Note that both § 351 of the Restatement and *Hadley v. Baxendale* refer to the *probable* results of the breach.

## ■ CASE VOCABULARY

SELF-EXECUTING AGREEMENT: An international treaty that does not require enabling legislation from Congress to be implemented.

# Kenford Co. v. County of Erie

(Land Owner) v. (County)

73 N.Y.2d 312, 540 N.Y.S.2d 1, 537 N.E.2d 176 (1989)

NEW YORK HIGH COURT LIMITS CONTRACT DAMAGES TO THOSE WHICH THE BREACHING PARTY ASSUMED

■ **INSTANT FACTS** A company bought land, anticipating it would substantially appreciate due to a stadium being built nearby, and sued when the stadium was not built.

■ **BLACK LETTER RULE** An injured party is not entitled to recover damages that the parties did not contemplate the breaching party would assume.

■ **PROCEDURAL BASIS**

Appeal of breach of contract action for specific performance, or in the alternative, damages.

■ **FACTS**

In 1968, the County of Erie (the County) (D) passed a law authorizing it to finance and construct a domed sports stadium near Buffalo. The County (D) authorized a $50 million bond issue to finance the stadium construction. Kenford Co. (Kenford) (P) offered to donate to the County (D) the land upon which to build the stadium if the County (D) would allow Dome Stadium, Inc. (DSI) (P) to lease or manage the stadium. The County (D) accepted Kenford's (P) offer and the parties engaged in contract negotiations. During this time, Edward Cottrell, Kenford's (P) president and sole shareholder, purchased land in Lancaster. In 1969, the County (D), Kenford (P), and DSI (P) entered into an agreement whereby Kenford (P) would donate land in Lancaster to the County (D) for the stadium, the County (D) would begin construction within 12 months, and the County (D) would agree to negotiate a 40-year lease with DSI (P) through which the County (D) would receive lease revenues of at least $63.75 million. The revenues included increased real property taxes resulting from the increased value of peripheral lands. "Peripheral lands" was defined in the contract as land owned by Cottrell or Kenford (P) located in Lancaster. If DSI (P) and the County (D) could not agree on the lease terms, DSI (P) and the County (D) were to enter into a 20-year management agreement. When the County (D) learned that the stadium would cost about $72 million to build [shouldn't it have gotten an estimate before issuing the bonds? ], it terminated the contract. Kenford (P) and DSI (P) sued. The jury awarded Kenford (P) $18 million for its lost appreciation in its property located near the proposed stadium site, and $6 million for out-of-pocket expenses. DSI (P) was awarded $25.6 million in lost profits under the 20-year management contract. On appeal, the Appellate Division reversed the award to DSI (P) for lost profits and a portion of the award to Kenford (P) for out-of-pocket expenses. The Appellate Division also held that Kenford (P) could recover for lost appreciation of its property, but remanded the case to obtain proper appraisal evidence. DSI (P) appealed the reversal of its damages to the Court of Appeals [New York's highest court]. The Court of Appeals affirmed the Appellate Division's ruling on the basis that the County's (D) liability for DSI's (P) lost profits was not in the contemplation of the parties when the contract was executed and the damages were too speculative. On retrial of Kenford's (P) damages for loss of anticipated land appreciation, the jury awarded Kenford (P) $6.5 million, and the Appellate Division affirmed. The County (D) appealed.

# ■ ISSUE

May an injured party recover damages that the parties did not contemplate the breaching party would assume?

# ■ DECISION AND RATIONALE

(Mollen, J.)   No.   A nonbreaching party may recover general damages that are the natural and probable consequences of the breach.   Unusual damages are recoverable only if they were within the contemplation of the parties as the probable result of a breach at the time of the contract.   Here, at the time of contracting, the parties expected that the stadium would result in increased land values and increased property taxes.   However, this expectation does not necessarily lead to the conclusion that the parties contemplated that the County (D) would assume liability for Kenford's (P) loss of anticipated appreciation if the stadium were not built.   The contract did not provide this remedy and there is no evidence that the parties contemplated it.   This is supported by the fact that Kenford (P) had no contractual obligation with the County (D) to acquire land near the stadium.   Kenford (P) bought the land with the hope that it would benefit from the stadium.   Kenford (P) voluntarily and knowingly assumed the risk that if the stadium were not built, it would not realize a financial gain.   To hold otherwise would lead to the irrational conclusion that the County (D) provided a guarantee that if the stadium were not built, Kenford (P) would still receive a financial benefit from the peripheral lands.   Kenford (P) argues that it should realize all of its anticipated gains with or without the stadium.   Clearly this is illogical.   Law dating back to *Hadley v. Baxendale* [landmark English case holding that party injured by breach of contract may recover only those damages that were reasonably foreseeable at the time the contract was made] provides that damages are limited to those that were reasonably foreseen or contemplated at the time the parties executed the contract.   This limits liability for unassumed risks, and diminishes the risks of entering into a business enterprise.   Reversed.

## Analysis:

The court here went beyond *Hadley v. Baxendale* and limited breach of contract damages even more. It relied on *Globe Refining Co. v. Landa Cotton Oil Co.,* in which Justice Oliver Holmes proposed the "tacit agreement" test, holding that contract damages are limited to "the liability the defendant fairly may be supposed to have assumed consciously, or to have warranted the plaintiff reasonably to suppose that it assumed, when the contract was made."   Thus, the court looked not at what damages were objectively foreseeable, but at what the defendant subjectively contemplated.   This test is not widely used and, in fact, was expressly rejected by the UCC.   It is interesting to wonder whether Kenford (P) could have recovered under the objective test of foreseeability in *Hadley v. Baxendale*.   All the parties expected and anticipated that Kenford's (P) land would appreciate in value after the stadium was built.   There was no way that Kenford (P) could "cover" its loss, i.e., find some other way to cause its land to appreciate in value, and this inability to cover was reasonably foreseeable to the County (D).

# Fera v. Village Plaza, Inc.

(Store Operator) v. (Plaza Operator)

396 Mich. 639, 242 N.W.2d 372 (1976)

EVEN A NEW BUSINESS CAN RECOVER DAMAGES FOR FUTURE LOST PROFITS PROVIDED IT CAN ESTABLISH THOSE PROFITS WITH REASONABLE CERTAINTY

■ **INSTANT FACTS** After the Plaza refused to give Fera the store space they had agreed upon, Fera sued and tried to claim lost profits as damages.

■ **BLACK LETTER RULE** Future lost profits are allowed as an element of damage in any case where, by reason of the nature of the situation, the profits may be established with reasonable certainty.

## ■ FACTS

On August 20, 1965, Fera (P) and Village Plaza, Inc. (VPI) (D) entered into a ten-year lease for a new "book and bottle" shop to be located in VPI's (D) proposed shopping center. This shop was not part of a continuing business. Fera (P) paid a $1,000 deposit according to the lease. In addition, the lease provided for a minimum $1,000 monthly rent plus 5% of annual receipts in excess of $240,000 to be paid to VPI (D). After the lease was executed, Fera (P) agreed to give up 600 square feet of its leased space to another tenant. In exchange, VPI (D) agreed to exclude Fera's (P) liquor sales from the 5% rent provision of the lease. Numerous work stoppages occurred afterwards, and VPI (D) ended up transferring the deed to Bank of the Commonwealth in lieu of foreclosure after defaulting. When the space was finally ready for occupancy, Fera (P) was told that the lease had been misplaced and that the space had been rented to other tenants. Fera (P) refused an offer of alternative space, saying the alternative space was unsuitable for the intended business. Fera (P) filed suit in Wayne Circuit Court, alleging, among other things, a claim for anticipated lost profits. The jury returned a verdict for Fera (P) against VPI (D) and those managing the property for the Bank (D) for $200,000. The Court of Appeals reversed and remanded for new trial on the issue of damages, holding that the trial court was wrong to allow lost profits to be used as the measure of damages for breach of the lease.

## ■ ISSUE

Can future lost profits be considered as an element of damages?

## ■ DECISION AND RATIONALE

(Kavanagh) Yes. Future lost profits are allowed as an element of damage in any case where, by reason of the nature of the situation, the profits may be established with reasonable certainty. Some cases have held that prospective profits are so uncertain that they cannot be included when measuring damages. This rule is simply an application of the general doctrine that a plaintiff must be able to provide a sufficient basis for a reasonable estimate of the degree of harm he or she has suffered in order to be entitled to a verdict or judgment for damages for breach of contract. Future profits should not be excluded from the measure of damages simply because they are profits. If the profits can be established with reasonable certainty, they should be allowed in setting damages. When an already established business is interrupted, a reasonable prediction can often be made as to its future profits based on its past profits. Granted, a new business will not have the kind of financial history to prove its future profits with reasonable accuracy through the use of facts. Still, such future profits would not necessarily be too uncertain to allow recovery in the case of new businesses. In this case, the trial judge stated that the issue of the speculative nature of future profits was probably the most completely tried issue in the entire dispute. Days of direct and cross-examination were devoted to the topic, with proofs of damage ranging from zero to $270,000. In the end, the jury set damages for Fera (P) at $200,000, a figure well within the range provided by the evidence. The jury apparently chose to believe Fera (P), and it was well within its rights to make such a choice. Also, there was no evidence of abuse of discretion by the trial judge in denying VPI's (D) motion for a new trial. Court of Appeals reversed and trial court judgment reinstated.

## Analysis:

The element of certainty as a limit on damages was introduced by American Judges at around the same time that English judges introduced foreseeability. As outlined in a leading New York case, *Griffin v. Colver,* the doctrine of certainty originally required that damages "be shown, by clear and satisfactory evidence, to have actually been sustained" and "be shown with certainty, and not left to speculation or conjecture." This is the "general doctrine" mentioned by the court here. It resulted in a widespread reluctance on the part of the judges to recognize interests that were too difficult to measure in monetary terms. This certainty requirement has been greatly relaxed in recent years, however. The Restatement (Second) for example, bars recovery "for loss beyond an amount that the evidence permits to be established with reasonable certainty." The comments to the Uniform Commercial Code also note that damages are "at best approximate," and do not have to be completely mathematically accurate. Instead, the UCC allows damages to be set with "whatever definiteness and accuracy the facts permit." In addition, the courts are less demanding with this certainty requirement when a party willfully breaches a contract. Moreover, the courts ease this standard in cases where precise proof of damages is inherently impossible, as in claims for loss of "good will."

## ■ CASE VOCABULARY

INTER ALIA: Latin for "among other things."

# Wasserman's Inc. v. Township of Middletown

(Store Operators) v. (Township)
137 N.J. 238, 645 A.2d 100 (1994)

A LIQUIDATED DAMAGES PROVISION WILL ONLY BE ENFORCED IF ITS LEVEL OF DAMAGES IS A REASONABLE FORECAST OF JUST COMPENSATION FOR A POTENTIAL BREACH AND THE POTENTIAL HARM IS TOO DIFFICULT TO ESTIMATE

■ **INSTANT FACTS** The Township canceled a lease with Wasserman's but refused to pay the damages outlined in the cancellation clause of the lease.

■ **BLACK LETTER RULE** Provisions for liquidated damages are enforceable only if the amount fixed for damages is a reasonable forecast of just compensation for the harm that is caused by the breach and that harm is incapable or very difficult of accurate estimate.

■ **PROCEDURAL BASIS**

Appeal from summary judgment in action for breach of contract for damages.

■ **FACTS**

The Township of Middletown (Township) (D) owned a section of land in one of its commercial areas. From 1948 to 1968, Wasserman's, Inc. (Wasserman's) (P) leased the property from the Township for a 3,200-square-foot store. In 1969 and 1970, the Township (D) accepted bids to lease the property, which the Township (D) had evaluated at $47,500. Wasserman's (P) submitted the only bid each time. Eventually, a new lease was approved on September 22, 1970 and signed on May 21, 1971. The thirty-year lease set a constant monthly rental rate. A cancellation clause also stated that if the Township (D) canceled the lease, it (D) would pay Wasserman's (P) a pro-rata reimbursement of Improvement costs. This reimbursement would be based on the total value of the improvements, and the proportion of time remaining in the lease. In addition, the Township (D) would have to pay damages equal to twenty-five percent of Wasserman's (P) average gross receipts for one year. Wasserman's (P) eventually spent $142,336.01 in renovating and expanding the store. In August 1973, Wasserman's (P) apparently sold its (P) corporate assets and sublet the premises to Jo-Ro, Inc. (Jo-Ro) (P). The sublease provided that Jo-Ro (P) would pay Wasserman's (P) a monthly rent, and that any payments made by the Township (D) if the lease were canceled would be split between the two (P). By a December 7, 1987 letter, the Township (D) canceled the lease effective December 31, 1988. In June 1989, the Township (D) sold the property at auction for $610,000, but refused to pay damages for canceling the lease. Wasserman's and Jo-Ro (Ps) filed for summary judgment, as did the Township (D). The Law Division held that the lease and cancellation clause were enforceable, requiring the Township (D) to pay $346,058.44 plus interest in damages. The Appellate Division affirmed.

■ **ISSUE**

Is a liquidated damages clause in a contract automatically enforceable once the parties to a contract agree to adopt it?

■ **DECISION AND RATIONALE**

(Pollock) No. Provisions for liquidated damages are enforceable only if the amount fixed for damages is a reasonable forecast of just compensation for the harm that is caused by the breach and that harm is incapable or very difficult of accurate estimate. Historically, courts have been reluctant to enforce penalty clauses of contracts. This stems from the use of early penalty clauses as a means of oppression or extortion, as debtors would be bound for twice the amount of their actual debts. Over the years, courts have distinguished nonenforceable penalty clauses from enforceable provisions for "liquidated damages." Liquidated damages are the result of a good faith effort to estimate in advance the actual damages that would probably result from a breach. A penalty, by contrast, is intended to serve as a punishment for a breaching party, and thus deter a future breach. It is settled in this State that a contract which fixes penalties for breach is unlawful. As the law has evolved, the reasonableness standard has been used to determine the validity of stipulated damages clauses. Accordingly, the New Jersey courts have viewed enforceability of such clauses as depending on whether the fixed amount is a reasonable forecast of just compensation for the harm caused by the breach and whether that harm is too difficult or impossible to be estimated accurately. Likewise, the greater the difficulty of estimating or proving damages, the more likely the stipulated amount will be considered reasonable. In addition, the New Jersey courts have long relied on the circumstances of each case, and not the words of the parties, to determine enforceability. Both the Uniform Commercial Code and the Restatement (Second) of Contracts allow for the liquidation of damages within a contract at an amount that is reasonable in light of the actual or anticipated harm from a breach, as well. Following this trend, most courts today have held that liquidated damages clause: are presumptively reasonable, and anyone challenging such a clause bears the burden of proving otherwise. It should be noted that such a clause is unreasonable if it does more than compensate injured parties for the actual damages from a breach. Also, damages based on gross receipts run the risk of being found unreasonable, due to the uncertainty involved and the possibility of a windfall. Here, the 25% of Jo-Ro's (P) average gross receipts that the Township (D) would presumably have to pay would be nearly $300,000. This figure, however, would not represent the actual losses of Jo-Ro and Wasserman's (P) through operating expenses or relocation costs and the like. The Township (D) is liable to Wasserman's and Jo-Ro (P) for terminating the lease, and they (P) should be awarded $55,748.27 for renovation costs. The Law Division, however, should determine whether the gross receipts clause of the contract is a reasonable one, and as such a valid liquidated damages clause. Judgment of Appellate Division affirmed in part, reversed in part, and matter remanded to Law Division.

### Analysis:

There are policy considerations on both sides of the question of stipulated damages clauses. Proponents of stipulated damages claim the clauses allow parties to control their exposure to risk by setting payments for a potential breach well in advance. In addition, the judicial process is avoided in setting damages, saving the parties a great deal of time and expense. Moreover, stipulated damages clauses allow the parties to set a damage formula that can include elements not otherwise considered by most courts in their rules of damages. Such clauses are not universally praised, however. Stipulated damages go against the ordinary practice of allowing public law, not private law, to define contract remedies. Courts must thus be involved in order to prevent private parties from exceeding the principle of allowing compensatory damages. A minority of courts treat these provisions as unconscionable if the amount of liquidated damages is clearly disproportionate to actual damages. The Uniform Commercial Code follows the reasonableness standard mentioned above.

### ■ CASE VOCABULARY

PRO RATA: According to a certain rate or percentage.

# Dave Gustafson & Co. v. State

(Road Construction Company) v. (State)

83 S.D. 160, 156 N.W.2d 185 (1968)

THE PARTIES TO A CONTRACT WITH A LIQUIDATED DAMAGES PROVISION MAY ALSO BE REQUIRED TO SHOW A REASONABLE ATTEMPT TO FIX FAIR COMPENSATION FOR THAT PROVISION TO BE SUSTAINED

■ **INSTANT FACTS** The State withheld part of the payment owed to Gustafson & Co. as liquidated damages under the contract after a job was delayed 67 days.

■ **BLACK LETTER RULE** A provision for payment of a stipulated sum as a liquidation of damages will be sustained if it appears that 1) at the time the contract was made the damages in the event of breach were incapable or very difficult of accurate estimation, 2) there was a reasonable endeavor by the parties to fix fair compensation, and 3) the amount stipulated bears a reasonable relation to probable damages and is not disproportionate to any damages reasonably to be anticipated.

■ **PROCEDURAL BASIS**

Appeal from judgment in action for damages.

■ **FACTS**

Dave Gustafson & Co. (Gustafson) (P) contracted with the State (D) to surface a new state highway which ran parallel to an older road. Gustafson (P) was to receive $530,724.14 for the work. The State (D), however, withheld $14,070 as liquidated damages after completion was delayed by 67 days. The contract included a graduated scale of liquidated damages per day. Under this scale, a contract in an amount from $500,001 to $1,000,000 would be accompanied by damages of $210 per day. This rate over 67 days amounted to $14,070. When Gustafson (P) sued for this remaining amount, the trial court upheld the State's (D) claim. Gustafson (P) appealed.

■ **ISSUE**

Can a contract provision for liquidated damages be sustained if it employs a graduated scale of liquidated damages per day?

■ **DECISION AND RATIONALE**

(Hanson) Yes. A provision for payment of a stipulated sum as a liquidation of damages will be sustained if it appears that: 1) at the time the contract was made the damages in the event of breach were incapable or very difficult of accurate estimation, 2) there was a reasonable endeavor by the parties to fix fair compensation, and 3) the amount stipulated bears a reasonable relation to probable damages and is not disproportionate to any damages reasonably to be anticipated. The recent trend has been to enforce liquidated provisions in contracts when they amount to fair and reasonable attempts to fix just compensation for anticipated loss resulting from a breach of contract. Such provisions are especially useful when damages are uncertain or immeasurable. Here, the provision at issue is not a penalty, but rather a valid damages clause. The exact damages for delays in constructing a new highway are immeasurable. Further, the amount stated in the clause demonstrates an attempt to set a fair level of compensation for the loss, inconvenience, extra costs, and deprivation of use of the road that are all caused by such a delay. Indeed, the daily amount of damage is dependent on the overall size of the work to be performed; smaller projects presumably incur smaller damage costs, while larger projects incur larger damage costs. Therefore, the amount stipulated in the contract bears a reasonable relation to probable damages. Moreover, the amount is not disproportionate to the damage reasonably to be anticipated from this unexcused delay in performance. Judgment affirmed.

## Analysis:

The liquidated damages for government contracts described here have widespread practical effects. As at least one scholar has noted, high levels of liquidated damages can make contractors and others who perform construction work for the government rather "jittery." For instance, the potential threat of significant penalties for delays in performance can leave companies open to pressure from labor groups. Unions and other workers' organizations can employ considerable leverage in persuading employers to comply with their demands, whether such demands are reasonable or not. Such negotiations for benefits or other working conditions between labor and individual government contractors can, in turn, affect other contractors. Businesses outside these isolated transactions may feel pressured to give the same benefits to their employees or face the same type of labor pressure, and thus may not have the security to take on lucrative public projects.

# CHAPTER EIGHT

## Performance and Breach

### Luttinger v. Rosen

**Instant Facts:** The prospective buyers of a piece of real estate try to get their deposit back after failing to get a mortgage.

**Black Letter Rule:** The failure of a condition precedent renders a contract unenforceable.

### Internatio-Rotterdam, Inc. v. River Brand Rice Mills, Inc.

**Instant Facts:** A rice processor refuses to complete the delivery of a shipment of rice to an exporter when a contract condition fails.

**Black Letter Rule:** A condition whose satisfaction is "of the essence" must be performed by the date specified in the contract in order to bind the parties.

### Peacock Construction Co. v. Modern Air Conditioning, Inc. [and Overly Manufacturing]

**Instant Facts:** A general contractor did not make final payments to two of his subcontractors after he failed to receive payment from the owner of the project.

**Black Letter Rule:** A contract condition may be interpreted as a question of law when the circumstances are so common that the parties' intent can be gleaned from their relationship.

### Gibson v. Cranage

**Instant Facts:** A parent refuses to pay for a satisfaction-guaranteed photograph of his daughter.

**Black Letter Rule:** A contract condition which guarantees the satisfaction of a party grants that party complete discretion with regard to their approval over performance.

### McKenna v. Vernon

**Instant Facts:** A movie theater owner refuses to make final payment to the theater's builder.

**Black Letter Rule:** Waiver of a contract condition may be inferred from the conduct of the parties.

### Hicks v. Bush

**Instant Facts:** The parties to a failed merger agreement dispute the existence of a parol condition on that agreement.

**Black Letter Rule:** Evidence of an oral condition to a written contract will be admissible so long as it does not contradict the express terms of the agreement.

### Kingston v. Preston

**Instant Facts:** A silk mercer refuses to turn over his business, as promised, to his apprentice.

**Black Letter Rule:** A contract for the exchange of promised performances may give rise to an implied condition on that exchange, making each party's performance dependent on the other's.

### Stewart v. Newbury

**Instant Facts:** A builder walks off of a construction job after the client refuses to pay his first installment bill.

**Black Letter Rule:** In the absence of agreement to the contrary, a court cannot imply a condition to make payments at reasonable intervals rather than upon completion of the contract.

### Jacob & Youngs v. Kent

**Instant Facts:** A general contractor installed the wrong kind of pipe in a newly constructed house and refused to tear out the walls in order to remove it.

**Black Letter Rule:** Substantial performance on a contract will out-weigh trivial variations in performance which might ordinarily cause the failure of a condition.

### Plante v. Jacobs

**Instant Facts:** Homeowners refuse to make their final payment to the contractor who built their house.

**Black Letter Rule:** Substantial performance on construction contracts may be less than perfect, but recovery will be reduced by the diminished value of the project or the cost of completion of the unfinished work.

### Gill v. Johnstown Lumber Co.

**Instant Facts:** A lumber driver requests full payment for his work, despite losing a percentage of his client's logs.

**Black Letter Rule:** If a contract is severable, as opposed to entire, then payment may be requested for the measure of performance which was completed.

### Britton v. Turner

**Instant Facts:** An employee breaks a one-year contract with his employer after ten months, suing to recover wages for that period.

**Black Letter Rule:** A party may recover in quantum meruit [restitution] despite being in breach of their contract.

### Kirkland v. Archbold

**Instant Facts:** A homeowner refuses to pay the contractor who has been working on her house for two months.

**Black Letter Rule:** A court may grant recovery in quantum meruit to a party, despite their being in breach of contract and without interpreting the contract as severable.

### Walker & Co. v. Harrison

**Instant Facts:** A dry cleaner stops making rental payments on his neon sign when the sign company refuses to clean it according to routine maintenance.

**Black Letter Rule:** A party may discontinue performance on a contract which has been materially breached by the other party.

### K & G Construction Co. v. Harris

**Instant Facts:** A general contractor stops paying his subcontractor after the subcontractor refuses to pay for damage that an employee did at the job site.

**Black Letter Rule:** A party who materially breaches a contract may not respond to non-breacher's cessation of performance by repudiating the contract.

### Iron Trade Products Co. v. Wilkoff Co.

**Instant Facts:** A rail supplier cannot find enough rails to satisfy a contract because his buyer has purchased a significant portion of the available rails.

**Black Letter Rule:** Performance on a contract may be excused if one party intentionally makes the other party's performance impossible.

### New England Structures, Inc. v. Loranger

**Instant Facts:** A general contractor fires his roofing subcontractor on narrower grounds than he alleges in court.

**Black Letter Rule:** A party who terminates an agreement is not restricted at trial to the claims made at the time of termination unless the other party has relied on the earlier claims to his detriment.

### Hochster v. De La Tour

**Instant Facts:** A prospective employer cancels a contract to hire a courier before their contract was due to be performed.

**Black Letter Rule:** A party who announces its intention to breach a contract releases the other party from any obligations under the contract.

### Kanavos v. Hancock Bank & Trust Co.

**Instant Facts:** A stockholder violated a right of first refusal granted to a prospective buyer by selling their stock to a third party.

**Black Letter Rule:** A contract party cannot recover damages for repudiation if they were unable to perform their own obligations under the contract.

### McCloskey & Co. v. Minweld Steel Co.

**Instant Facts:** A subcontractor is accused of repudiating a contract despite their difficulty in getting supplies due to market and governmental forces beyond their control.

**Black Letter Rule:** Anticipatory repudiation can only be demonstrated by an absolute and unequivocal refusal to perform or a distinct and positive statement of an inability to do so.

### C.L. Maddox, Inc. v. Coalfield Services, Inc.

**Instant Facts:** A mining subcontractor began excavating while awaiting a final contract. When the general contract repeatedly delayed signing, the subcontractor stopped work and sued.

**Black Letter Rule:** Contractual parties are justified in suspending performance when the counterparty shows an intent to not perform the contract as agreed, e.g., by refusing to sign a contract or clarify vague terms, failing to make progress payments *upon demand,* or demanding contract modifications.

### Cosden Oil & Chemical Company v. Karl O. Helm Aktiengesellschaft

**Instant Facts:** A polystyrene supplier is taken to court when they fail to meet their obligations to their buyer.

**Black Letter Rule:** A buyer's damages for anticipatory repudiation are measured by the difference between the contract price and the market price at a commercially reasonable time after the repudiation.

### United States v. Seacoast Gas Co.

**Instant Facts:** A utility company repudiates its agreement with the government and then tries to retract its repudiation.

**Black Letter Rule:** A party cannot freely retract its repudiation of a contract once the other party has filed suit or given it a limited time to retract.

### Pittsburgh-Des Moines Steel Co. v. Brookhaven Manor Water Co.

**Instant Facts:** A steel company requests assurances of performance from its client when it finds out that the client has failed to qualify for a bank loan.

**Black Letter Rule:** Under the UCC, a party may not seek assurances of performance from another party unless it has reasonable grounds for insecurity regarding that party's ability to perform.

### Norcon Power Partners v. Niagara Mohawk Power Corp.

**Instant Facts:** When an electricity distributor calculated its supplier would owe it $610 million, it demanded reasonable assurances of future payment.

**Black Letter Rule:** In New York, corporate parties to long-term complex commercial contracts may, upon having reasonable grounds to doubt the other party will fulfill its contractual obligations, demand adequate assurances.

# Luttinger v. Rosen

(Prospective Purchasers) v. (Landowner)
164 Conn. 45, 316 A.2d 757 (1972)

CONNECTICUT SUPREME COURT EXPLAINS THE CONSEQUENCES OF A FAILED CONTRACT CONDITION

■ **INSTANT FACTS** The prospective buyers of a piece of real estate try to get their deposit back after failing to get a mortgage.

■ **BLACK LETTER RULE** The failure of a condition precedent renders a contract unenforceable.

■ **PROCEDURAL BASIS**

Appeal from a trial court judgement for the plaintiffs in a breach of contract action.

■ **FACTS**

The Luttingers (P) contracted to purchase an $85,000 property owned by Rosen (D). They also paid him an $8500 deposit on the property. In addition, the purchase contract was subject to a condition that the Luttingers (P) obtain a mortgage from a bank or lending institution for $45,000. The mortgage would have to be for a term of at least twenty years and financed at no more than 8½ percent. The Luttingers (P), in turn, agreed to use due diligence to acquire the mortgage. The parties also agreed that the Luttingers' deposit would be refunded if they could not satisfy the mortgage condition. Unfortunately, the Luttingers (P) were unable to get a mortgage for less than 8¾ percent. Their lawyer knew the rates being offered by the various local banks and applied to the one bank that he knew might make the loan. Rosen (D) offered to finance the extra ¼ percent in order to meet the contract condition, but he refused to return the Luttingers' (P) deposit. The Luttingers (P) declined his offer and sued him for breach of contract. Rosen (D) claimed that the Luttingers (P) failed to use due diligence in obtaining a mortgage because they did not apply to other lenders. The trial court ruled for the Luttingers (P). Rosen (D) appeals.

■ **ISSUE**

Is it necessary for a party to follow every possible course of action in order to satisfy a contract condition requiring due diligence?

■ **DECISION AND RATIONALE**

(Loiselle) No. Rosen (D) claims that the Luttingers did not try hard enough to get a qualifying mortgage. However, it is not necessary to perform futile acts in order to satisfy a condition requiring due diligence. In this case, the Luttingers' (P) lawyer knew that no other lending institution would make the loan that they needed. It would have been pointless to apply to those banks under the circumstances. Rosen (D) also claims that the mortgage condition was satisfied, obviating the need to return the Luttingers' (P) deposit, because he offered to make the additional loan necessary to bring the mortgage down to 8½ percent. However, the condition states that the loan must come from a bank or another lending institution. The Luttingers (P) were under no obligation to accept Rosen's (D) offer. As a result, the condition failed and the Luttingers were entitled to the return of their deposit. Affirmed.

**Analysis:**

The mortgage condition in the Luttingers' (P) contract is referred to as a "condition precedent." The court defines a condition precedent as a fact or event that must exist or take place before there is a right to performance. In other words, the parties agree to a set of circumstances that must exist before they will be bound by their contract. This case deals with an agreement requiring the Luttingers' (P) due diligence in trying to satisfy the contract conditions. The agreement only binds the Luttingers (P) to their precontractual behavior. However, as this case demonstrates, if the Luttingers failed to exercise due diligence, they might have forfeited their deposit. As a result, the failure of a condition can have a significant impact on the parties to an agreement.

## ■ CASE VOCABULARY

CONDITION PRECEDENT: A condition precedent is a circumstance which must exist before the parties to a contract will be bound. Similarly, a condition *subsequent* voids an already binding contract depending upon circumstances not existing at the time of contracting.

# Internatio-Rotterdam, Inc. v. River Brand Rice Mills, Inc.

(Exporter) v. (Rice Processor)

259 F.2d 137 (2nd Cir. 1958), cert. denied, 358 U.S. 946 (1959)

COURT OF APPEALS VOIDS A CONTRACT AFTER A CONDITION FAILS WHICH WAS "OF THE ESSENCE"

■ **INSTANT FACTS** A rice processor refuses to complete the delivery of a shipment of rice to an exporter when a contract condition fails.

■ **BLACK LETTER RULE** A condition whose satisfaction is "of the essence" must be performed by the date specified in the contract in order to bind the parties.

■ **PROCEDURAL BASIS**

Appeal from the district court's dismissal of the plaintiff's complaint.

■ **FACTS**

River Brand Rice Mills, Inc. (River Brand) (D) agreed to supply Internatio-Rotterdam, Inc. (Internatio) (P), an exporter, with a large quantity of rice. Their agreement stated the amount of rice for delivery, the price, the delivery instructions, and the payment arrangements. Among other terms, 95,600 pockets of rice were to be delivered during the month of December and within two weeks of Internatio's (P) request. The rice was to be delivered to either of two ports: Lake Charles or Houston. In addition, payment for the shipment was to be secured by a letter of credit on Internatio's behalf (P). When December arrived, Internatio (P) was still trying to get an export license approved for the rice. To make matters worse, December is a peak shipping month for rice and the ports were getting crowded. River Brand (D) finally received their shipping instructions on December 10th and began delivery of 50,000 pockets of rice at Lake Charles. The remainder was to be delivered to Houston. However, if the Houston delivery did not start by the 17th, River Brand (D) would not be able to complete delivery within the two-week window provided by the purchase agreement. Unfortunately, Internatio (P) was not able to secure a dock in Houston by this date. On the morning of the 18th, River Brand (D) rescinded the contract for the Houston shipment. They continued making the Lake Charles deliveries and completed them on December 31st. It is quite likely that River Brand's (D) quick recision of the Houston contract was due to a sharp rise in the market price of rice from $8.25 per pocket to $9.75 per pocket. River Brand (D) had agreed to sell the rice to Internatio (P) for $8.25 a pocket and stood to make a large profit from other buyers if they voided that agreement. Internatio (P) subsequently sued River Brand (D) for breach of contract. The trial court dismissed their complaint, however, and Internatio (P) appeals.

■ **ISSUE**

Can a condition to an agreement extend beyond the date specified for its performance?

■ **DECISION AND RATIONALE**

(Hincks) Potentially. Internatio (P) concedes that they were obligated to supply River Brand (D) with complete shipping instructions for both ports by December 17th. Otherwise, River Brand (D) would not be able to complete delivery within the two weeks allotted and still deliver in December. Nonetheless,

# Peacock Construction Co. v. Modern Air Conditioning, Inc. [and Overly Manufacturing]

(General Contractor) v. (Subcontractors)

353 So.2d 840 (Fla. 1977)

## SUPREME COURT OF FLORIDA INTERPRETS CONTRACT CONDITIONS AS A QUESTION OF LAW

■ **INSTANT FACTS** A general contractor did not make final payments to two of his subcontractors after he failed to receive payment from the owner of the project.

■ **BLACK LETTER RULE** A contract condition may be interpreted as a question of law when the circumstances are so common that the parties' intent can be gleaned from their relationship.

■ **PROCEDURAL BASIS**

Two cases, both joined on appeal by the state supreme court after successful motions for summary judgement by the plaintiffs in breach of contract actions which were affirmed by the court of appeals.

■ **FACTS**

Modern Air Conditioning, Inc. (Modern Air) (P) and Overly Manufacturing (Overly) (P) were hired by Peacock Construction Co. (Peacock) (D) as subcontractors on a condominium construction project for which Peacock (D) was the general contractor. Modern Air (P) was hired to install the heating and air conditioning. Overly (P) was hired to install a rooftop swimming pool. Both of their contracts indicated that-final-payment would arrive within thirty days of the completion of their work. The payment clause concluded with the phrase, "written acceptance by the Architect and full payment therefor by the Owner." This clause provides the central controversy for the actions for breach of contract which both subcontractors brought after the Peacock (D) failed to pay them. Peacock (D) claimed that he never received full payment from the Owner. He argues that the payment clause is a condition precedent to his obligation to pay the subcontractors—a condition which failed. In each case, the trial court granted the subcontractors' motions for summary judgement. Peacock (D) appealed both judgements. The judgements were affirmed by the court of appeal. Peacock (D) now appeals to this court.

■ **ISSUE**

Is it appropriate for a court to grant summary judgement, ruling as a matter of law on an ambiguous condition to a contract?

■ **DECISION AND RATIONALE**

(Boyd) Yes. The trial court's grant of summary judgement implies that the payment clause was not a condition on Peacock's (P) obligation to pay his subcontractors. Similarly, the court of appeals follows the majority rule which interprets provisions like the one at issue here as "absolute promises to pay." Consequently, the owner's payment to the general contractor merely sets a reasonable time limit on the general contractor's payment to the subcontractors. Both of these opinions conflict with Florida precedent which calls for an interpretation consistent with the intent of the parties to the contract. This is potentially a factual determination which would be inappropriate for a grant of summary judgement. Peacock (P) argues that, at best, the trial court must hear evidence before granting a directed verdict on the issue. However, this outcome is not required. The general rule is that the interpretation of a document is a question of law rather than a question of fact. It is quite possible for the court to determine the parties' intent from the language of the contract. This is particularly so when the relationship between the parties, like the one between general contractors and subcontractors, is so common that their intent rarely varies from transaction to transaction. In most cases, the subcontractor would not willingly assume the risk of the owner's nonpayment. This is a burden that the general contractor must bear unless the risk is unambiguously shifted in the agreement with the subcontractor. As a result, the trial court and the court of appeals ruled correctly in this matter. To the extent that Florida precedent is at odds with this outcome it is overruled.

## Analysis:

Justice Boyd's approach to this case should seem familiar. The canon of contract interpretation is brought to bear on one more element of contracts: the condition. As in the cases dealing with the construction bidding process, the courts have found ways of dealing with certain familiar business transactions. Judges can apply a single rule that is based on the most common dealings between parties. As Justice Boyd notes, the parties can always contract around the application of this rule, but they must do so unambiguously. This protects subcontractors, who are the most likely parties to suffer from a misapplication of the rule. In the bidding cases, it seemed as if the subcontractors were being short changed because the general contractors were not obligated to hire them even if they used their bids. Here, Justice Boyd recognizes that it may seem as if general contractors are unfairly bearing all of the risk of non-payment. However, in both cases the court understood that an equitable allocation of risk between the parties demanded the particular outcome.

## ■ CASE VOCABULARY

QUESTION OF FACT: Questions of fact are classically the province of the jury. They involve the interpretation of evidence against everyday experience. This is particularly well-suited to the role of the jury as members the general community.

QUESTION OF LAW: Questions of law are the province of the judge. The judge rules on the interpretation and application of legal rules and may, if necessary, determine the outcome of a case as a matter of law.

# Gibson v. Cranage

(Photographer) v. (Parent)
39 Mich. 49 (1878)

## MICHIGAN SUPREME COURT GRANTS COMPLETE DISCRETION TO A PARTY WITH APPROVAL UNDER A SATISFACTION CLAUSE

■ **INSTANT FACTS** A parent refuses to pay for a satisfaction-guaranteed photograph of his daughter.

■ **BLACK LETTER RULE** A contract condition which guarantees the satisfaction of a party grants that party complete discretion with regard to their approval over performance.

■ **PROCEDURAL BASIS**

Appeal from a trial court judgement for the defendant in an action in assumpsit.

■ **FACTS**

Gibson (P) offered to have an enlarged photograph made of Cranage's (D) deceased daughter. He told Cranage (D) that he would not have to pay for the enlargement if it was not "perfectly satisfactory to [him] in every particular." As it turns out, Cranage (D) was not happy with the finished photograph and refused to accept it. Gibson (P) sent it back for refinishing and presented it to Cranage (D) a second time after it returned. Cranage (D) refused to look at the photograph and, again, refused to accept it. Gibson (P) subsequently brought an action in assumpsit for payment on the contract. The trial court ruled for Cranage (D). Gibson (P) appeals.

■ **ISSUE**

Is an express condition enforceable which relies solely on the satisfaction of one party to an agreement?

■ **DECISION AND RATIONALE**

(Marston) Yes. An agreement to perform a service at the complete discretion and satisfaction of one party is perfectly enforceable. This may be difficult for an artist or a photographer to accept since they have a more sophisticated view of their own work which may be at odds with the person who ordered it. However, the contract was agreed to by both parties and, as such, it will be enforced. Judgement affirmed.

**Analysis:**

This is a rare contract case in which the reasonable man standard does not apply because of the personal nature of the contract. There is nothing by which to judge Cranage's (D) satisfaction with a deeply personal item like a portrait of his deceased daughter. On the other hand, a satisfaction-guaranteed contract that takes place in a commercial setting might be subject to an implied range of reasonableness, since there will be objective standards by which to measure the quality of the goods. Ordinarily, this type of guarantee is referred to as a satisfaction clause. This kind of agreement can have an enormous impact on the allocation of risk between the parties by requiring one of them to run the risk of forfeiture.

## ■ CASE VOCABULARY

ASSUMPSIT:  An action for recovery of money owed on a contract.  Frequently an equitable action but also available at law.

FORFEITURE:  Forfeiture occurs when one party has performed but their performance does not meet the satisfaction of the other party.  There is no remedy for this if the refusing party's decision falls within the scope of the satisfaction clause.

SATISFACTION CLAUSE:  A contract condition which gives one party the right to judge the acceptability of the other's performance.  This clause may explicitly limit the discretion of that party.  If it does not, it may be interpreted to grant complete discretion, or require an honest or reasonable refusal of performance depending upon the circumstances.

# McKenna v. Vernon

(Builder) v. (Theater Owner)

258 Pa. 18, 101 A. 919 (1917)

PENNSYLVANIA SUPREME COURT IMPLIES WAIVER OF A CONDITION FROM THE CONDUCT OF THE PARTIES

■ **INSTANT FACTS** A movie theater owner refuses to make final payment to the theater's builder.

■ **BLACK LETTER RULE** Waiver of a contract condition may be inferred from the conduct of the parties.

■ **PROCEDURAL BASIS**

Appeal from a trial court judgment for the plaintiff in a breach of contract action.

■ **FACTS**

McKenna (P) contracted to build a movie theater for Vernon (D). The contract called for several installment payments during the course of the work and final payment within 30 days of completion. In addition, the work was to be supervised by an architect whose certificate was a required condition on all of the payments. However, upon completion, Vernon (D) had not paid more than $6000 on an $8750 job. He had made almost all of the installment payments without requiring McKenna (P) to produce the architect's certificate. McKenna (P) subsequently sued for breach of contract. Vernon (D) claimed that the work was defective and, therefore, payment was not required. The architect, however, had no complaints about McKenna's (P) work. The trial court held for McKenna (P). Vernon (D) appeals.

■ **ISSUE**

Can a party waive a contract condition by ignoring it?

■ **DECISION AND RATIONALE**

(Stewart) Yes. Vernon (D) claims that he was not required to pay McKenna (P) because McKenna (P) never secured a certificate from the architect. However, Vernon (D) did not require the builder to produce the certificate for six out of seven installment payments. As a result, they waived the right to request the certificate for final payment. In addition, they are estopped from claiming that failure of the certificate condition relieved them of their contractual obligations.

**Analysis:**

A party who, by its behavior, waives the obligation that a condition places on the other party, cannot later complain that the contract is void for failure of that condition. This concept is referred to as estoppel. Estoppel precludes a party from making a particular claim due to its own conduct. For instance, once a condition has been waived, it can only be reinstated if the other party has not relied to its detriment on the waiver. In this case, the builder presumably continued on with his work under the assumption that the architect's certificate was no longer required for payment. It would be unfair to let

Vernon (D) out of the contract, since he induced McKenna's (P) reliance by ignoring the conditions for payment.

## ■ CASE VOCABULARY

ESTOPPEL: Once a party has waived a contract condition, they may not reinstate that condition once the other party has relied to an extent that it would be unfair to release the waiving party from their obligations.

WAIVER: A party may waive the enforcement of a condition. As above, conduct alone may be sufficient to constitute waiver. When in doubt, courts will lean towards enforcing the overall contract at the expense of a condition whose waiver may be implied.

# Hicks v. Bush

(Merging Company) v. (Non-Merging Company)

10 N.Y.2d 488, 225 N.Y.S.2d 34, 180 N.E.2d 425 (1962)

NEW YORK COURT OF APPEALS APPLIES THE PAROL EVIDENCE RULE TO A CONDITION PRECE-
DENT

■ **INSTANT FACTS** The parties to a failed merger agreement dispute the existence of a parol
condition on that agreement.

■ **BLACK LETTER RULE** Evidence of an oral
condition to a written contract will be admissible
so long as it does not contradict the express
terms of the agreement.

■ **PROCEDURAL BASIS**

Appeal from a trial court judgement for the defendant in a breach of contract action.

■ **FACTS**

Hicks (P) agreed to a merger with the Clinton G. Bush Company (Bush) (D) [don't ask]. Each party
was supposed to transfer their current shares to a third holding company. Hicks (P) transferred his
shares but the other parties did not. As a result, the merger never happened. When Hicks (P) sued
Bush (D) for specific performance, Bush (D) claimed that the parties had agreed to a parol condition
which made the contract ineffective until they had raised a certain amount of money to fund the merger.
Hicks (P) denies that this condition ever existed. Despite this, the trial court found for Bush (D). Hicks
appeals.

■ **ISSUE**

Can a condition which is agreed to orally be admitted as evidence to question the existence of a written
contract?

■ **DECISION AND RATIONALE**

(Fuld) Yes. Parol testimony is admissible to prove a condition precedent to the existence of a contract
if the condition does not contradict the express terms of the contract. The question in this case is
whether the condition contradicts the contract. It does not. In fact, there is no mention in the contract
of the need to raise funds to support the merger. Hicks (P) claims that the condition contradicts a term
which would annul the merger if the new corporation does not accept any of their stock within 25 days.
However, these conditions can coexist without negating each other. They are simply complementary
conditions which bear on the viability of the merger. The oral condition, in particular, is not the sort of
condition which would be included in a written agreement to which the public has access. Consequently, the trial court did not err in admitting evidence of the extra condition. Bush (D) was perfectly
justified in not transferring their stock until it was satisfied. Judgement affirmed.

**Analysis:**

The normal rules of contract interpretation apply to conditions. Although conditions are not binding
promises, they are interpreted as ordinary promises due to their potential to vitiate a contract, leaving

the parties with heavy losses. This is especially true with regard to the parol evidence rule. It would be easy for a party who wanted to get out of a contract to claim that a condition that was agreed to, orally, failed, leaving them without obligations, which is why Justice Fuld notes that the funding condition on the merger contract is not the sort that would be put in writing. In a sense, he was testing the condition against common sense: is this the sort of condition that parties would deliberately leave *out* of a written agreement? In this case, it might be. The merging companies would not want a public document, intended to attract investors, to reflect the potential instability of their merger. Since the condition had some semblance of rationality, and since it did not contradict the written agreement, it supplemented that agreement, voiding it when it failed.

## ■ CASE VOCABULARY

HOLDING COMPANY: As it sounds, a holding company can be used to hold the stock of other companies. In this case, the holding company was probably a form of security for the two merging companies—a neutral entity to hold their stock during the merger process.

MERGER: As opposed to a takeover, a merger is generally a friendly, negotiated agreement between two companies to combine their assets. Only one of the merging companies survives as a legal entity. In addition, mergers require approval by the board of directors as well as the shareholders.

PAROL EVIDENCE RULE: A longstanding rule of evidence which is found in the Uniform Commercial Code as well in the Restatement (Second) of Contracts. The basic rule is that an oral agreement which contradicts the terms of a current written agreement is not admissible into evidence. If it does not contradict the written agreement, the oral agreement may be used to supplement the terms of the written agreement.

# Kingston v. Preston

(Apprentice) v. (Silk Mercer)

Lofft 194, 2 Doug. 689, 99 Eng.Rep. 437 (King's Bench 1773)

KING'S BENCH IMPLIES A CONDITION PRECEDENT ON A CONTRACT TO PROTECT A PARTY FROM THE OTHER'S NONPERFORMANCE

■ **INSTANT FACTS** A silk mercer refuses to turn over his business, as promised, to his apprentice.

■ **BLACK LETTER RULE** A contract for the exchange of promised performances may give rise to an implied condition on that exchange, making each party's performance dependent on the other's.

■ **PROCEDURAL BASIS**

Arguments before the King's Bench, the trial court in this case.

■ **FACTS**

Kingston (P) apprenticed himself to Preston (D) a silk mercer (a textile merchant). They agreed that after a year and three months, Kingston (P) would take over the business with a partner appointed by Preston (D). Kingston (P) was supposed to pay for his share of the business in 250£ installments after the business changed hands. He was required to provide Preston (D) with security for the debt at that time. However, after a year and three months, Preston (D) refused to turn over the business. Kingston (P) sued Preston (D) for breach of contract. Preston (D) defended his actions, claiming that Kingston (P) had not provided him with sufficient security. A trial ensued.

■ **ISSUE**

Can a party to a contract be required to perform despite nonperformance by the other party?

■ **DECISION AND RATIONALE**

(Mansfield) Potentially. There are three kinds of covenants: 1) mutual and independent, 2) conditional and dependent, and 3) mutual conditions. In the first instance, if a party breaches an independent covenant, the plaintiff can recover damages regardless of whether he has performed his end of the contract. In the second instance, if a party causes a condition to fall, the other party is excused from performance altogether. Finally, if parties agree to mutual conditions, they must both be prepared to perform at the same time. If one party is prepared to perform and the other party is not, the prepared party can sue for the other's breach. In order to determine which of the above covenants applies to a particular case, the court must look at the language of the agreement. By looking at the agreement, the court can determine what the order and status of performance should be in order to best fulfill its language. In this case, the agreement between the parties was subject to a dependent condition, as in example two above, which required the apprentice to produce sufficient security before Preston (D) was required to turn over his business. Since the security was insufficient, Preston (D) was under no further obligation. Judgement for the Preston (D).

## Analysis:

Consider Lord Mansfield's three categories of covenants with regard to the cases from the first section of this chapter. All of these cases fit under the rubric of dependent conditions. In fact Lord Mansfield refers to the security agreement in this case as a condition precedent—a form of dependent condition. The first types of conditions, mutual and independent conditions, are now discussed with regard to material or immaterial breaches. If a party's breach of a promise to perform is material, the other party is excused from performance. If the breach is immaterial, then the other party's performance is not excused. The second type of condition, a condition dependent, has already been discussed as the implied condition in this case. The third type of condition, mutual condition, is also referred to as concurrent condition and is discussed more fully in your casebook. It should also be noted that Lord Mansfield implied a condition that did not exist in the contract between Kingston (P) and Preston (D). This is called a constructive condition. In some cases, courts will subject an agreement to a constructive condition in order to excuse a party's performance when the other party fails to perform.

## ■ CASE VOCABULARY

CONCURRENT CONDITIONS: Concurrent conditions govern an agreement between parties which requires that they each be prepared to perform obligations which are mutually dependent. Performance does not actually need to be concurrent, but there must at least be the ability to satisfy the obligation when required.

CONSTRUCTIVE CONDITIONS: Also referred to as constructive conditions of exchange. If a party fails to perform on a bilateral contract—an exchange of promised obligations, the court may imply a condition on their exchange in order to protect the non-breaching party from having to perform.

KING'S BENCH: Until 1875, England's trial court was called the King's (or Queen's) Bench. This court also handled certain appeals. From the court's discussion in this case, it appears that this was a first adjudication of the parties dispute.

# Stewart v. Newbury

(Builder) v. (Client)

220 N.Y. 379, 115 N.E. 984 (1917)

NEW YORK COURT OF APPEALS REJECTS AN IMPLIED CONDITION OF REASONABLE PROGRESS PAYMENTS FOR LARGE CONSTRUCTION JOBS

■ **INSTANT FACTS** A builder walks off of a construction job after the client refuses to pay his first installment bill.

■ **BLACK LETTER RULE** In the absence of agreement to the contrary, a court cannot imply a condition to make payments at reasonable intervals rather than upon completion of the contract.

■ **PROCEDURAL BASIS**

Appeal to the state supreme court from an intermediate appellate affirmance of the trial court's judgment for the plaintiff in a breach of contract action.

■ **FACTS**

Stewart (P), a builder, agreed to do the excavation work for Newbury's (D) building. Stewart (P) contends that Newbury (D) agreed, in a subsequent telephone conversation, to make periodic payments for the work in progress, reserving a percentage for security. He claims that this is standard construction industry practice. Newbury (D) denies these payment terms. Instead, he claims that he was not required to pay for the work until it was completed. Stewart (P) submitted his first installment bill which Newbury (D) refused to pay. As a result, Stewart (P) stopped work on the project. A subsequent exchange of phone calls and letters failed to clear up the parties' difference of opinion on the payment terms. In fact, the parties also differed on who was responsible for Stewart's (P) leaving the job. Stewart (P) claimed that he was terminated in a letter from Newbury (D) and sued for breach of contract. Newbury (D) defended on the ground that Stewart (P) abandoned the project of his own free will. A jury trial resulted in a judgement for Stewart (P) for the unpaid bill, but not for damages for breach of contract. The judge had instructed the jury that Newbury (D) would be responsible for making payments at reasonable intervals if the jury found that the parties had not otherwise agreed to payment terms. The intermediate court of appeals affirmed. Newbury appeals to this court.

■ **ISSUE**

In the absence of any agreement to the contrary, can a contract condition be implied which requires payments at reasonable intervals?

■ **DECISION AND RATIONALE**

(Crane) No. The default rule states that a contract must be substantially performed before payment can be requested. The parties to a contract can circumvent this rule by agreeing to whatever payment terms they choose. As a result, the trial court wrongly instructed the jury on this issue. However, this was not the only question in this case. The jury was also required to determine whether Newbury (D) breached his contract by refusing to allow Stewart (P) to continue working on the job. Newbury (D) alleges that the builder's work was not up to specifications and there is evidence to support this claim. However, the jury's findings on this issue are not clear. They obviously thought Stewart (P) was entitled to damages for the unpaid bill. On the other hand, they did not grant him damages for breach of contract. It appears that the jury found that Stewart (P) left the job justifiably after he was not paid. If this is the case, then the jury reached this conclusion in reliance on the judge's erroneous instructions. Alternatively, they may have believed that the parties *did* have an agreement which was made during the disputed telephone call. It also appears that the jury found, since Stewart was already off the job, that Newbury (D) did not breach their contract by then firing him. While these are reasonable explanations for the jury's findings, they are not as apparent as they should be. Given the confusion surrounding the improper jury instructions and the uncertainty of their findings, this case must be reversed and remanded for further proceedings.

### Analysis:

Consider in each case whether a party has substantially or materially breached its contractual obligations. If not, the party walking away may turn out to be the breacher. In this case, it is not clear whether the jury found that Stewart (P) and Newbury (D) had agreed to payment terms. They might have found that there were no agreed terms and then applied the default terms. While Stewart (P) did not make out badly on these terms, the new default terms will not be as attractive on remand. As a result, he should have been more careful when dealing with Newbury (D). For instance, he could have stayed on the job until the dispute was resolved in order to protect himself. It should be noted that most contractors now explicitly agree to terms that include progress payments for large jobs. These agreements should help circumvent the effects of the rule announced in this case.

# Jacob & Youngs v. Kent

(General Contractor) v. (Homeowner)

230 N.Y. 239, 129 N.E. 889, 23 A.L.R. 1429 (1921)

NEW YORK COURT OF APPEALS UPHOLDS COMPENSATION DESPITE PERFORMANCE WHICH DIFFERS FROM THE CONDITIONS OF THE CONTRACT

■ **INSTANT FACTS** A general contractor installed the wrong kind of pipe in a newly constructed house and refused to tear out the walls in order to remove it.

■ **BLACK LETTER RULE** Substantial performance on a contract will out-weigh trivial variations in performance which might ordinarily cause the failure of a condition.

■ **PROCEDURAL BASIS**

Appeal from an intermediate appeals court reversal and grant of a new trial after a trial court judgment for the defendant in a breach of contract action.

■ **FACTS**

Jacob & Youngs (J&Y) (P) was the general contractor on a home construction job for Kent (D), the homeowner. The parties had an agreement which stated, among other things, that Kent (D) would make monthly progress payments provided that J&Y (P) produced an architect's certificate each month. In addition, any brand name material listed in the agreement could not be substituted without the architect's consent, final decisions regarding construction were to be made by the architect, and any non-conforming work would have to be torn out and replaced. Kent (D) also had the right to accept non-conforming work but to be paid the difference in value by J&Y (P). During the course of construction, Kent (D) discovered that J&Y (P) had installed pipes in the house that did not conform to the brand specified in the construction agreement. It was an oversight which escaped even the attention of the architect. Kent (D) asked J&Y (P) to replace the pipes. In order to remove them, however, J&Y (P) would have to destroy a great deal of completed work. They refused. Ultimately, J&Y (P) were denied an architect's certificate for final payment and sued Kent (D) to recover. The trial court found for Kent (D), refusing to allow J&Y (P) to introduce evidence that the installed pipes were virtually the same in every significant respect as the ones specified in the agreement. The intermediate court of appeals reversed and granted a new trial. Kent (D) now appeals.

■ **ISSUE**

Can a potentially trivial discrepancy in performance give rise to a forfeiture of the performer's right to compensation?

■ **DECISION AND RATIONALE**

(Cardozo) Yes. However, the court must determine just how trivial the failure of performance was. If the failure was trivial, then it will not be allowed to void a condition upon which compensation for substantial performance rests. The difference between a trivial and a non-trivial failure of performance is similar to the difference between independent and dependent promises. Independent promises are not conditions of each other. In other words, the performance of one promise does not depend on the performance of a return promise. Dependent promises, however, can never exist without each other.

They are, thus, conditions on each other. Finally, some promises are dependent on each other, but would not be substantially compromised if performance on one of the promises varied to an insignificant degree. Only a court can determine the degree to which performance has varied in order to decide whether to grant recovery. The court is guided by principles of fairness which are not subject to exact measurement. By the same token, the court will not interpret a deviation in performance so as to frustrate the purpose of the contract. In fact, the parties to a contract are entitled to circumvent this process by drafting an agreement which makes every aspect of performance vital to compensation. These parties did not do so, and as a result, the court must step in. In this case, J&Y (P) was precluded from presenting evidence which would have shown that the difference in performance was insubstantial. As a result, the measure of damages should reflect the triviality of this difference. Kent (D) is entitled to the difference in value between the house with the specified pipe, and the house as it stands with the unspecified pipe. This difference is admittedly small, but it reflects the degree of the contractor's error. This error was not significant enough to cause the conditions of performance to fail and thus, J&Y (P) is entitled to compensation for the work done. Judgement affirmed and directed for J&Y (P).

## ■ DISSENT

(McLaughlin) This court applies a rule which has no application to this case: the rule of substantial performance. To put it simply, J&Y (P) did not perform their end of the contract. For whatever reason, they installed the wrong pipe in the house. In fact, two-fifths of the pipe was non-conforming. This amounts to 1000 to 1500 feet of pipe which was of a brand not specified in the contract. This is not a minor omission, and if this omission is to be excused by the doctrine of substantial performance, it can only be done so by showing good faith on the part of the contractor. Unfortunately, good faith is lacking here. It is not important why Kent (D) selected the pipe that he did. It is enough to know that wrong pipes were installed. Recovery for J&Y (P) should be denied and a verdict should be directed for Kent (D).

## Analysis:

Justice Cardozo is clearly worried about forfeiture—the result of a failed condition that denies payment to a party even though it has tendered substantial performance. In this case, denying the contractor recovery for work done because of a mix-up in the use of virtually identical pipes seems arbitrary and unfair. Justice McLaughlin is far more worried about the letter of the contract than about overarching fairness. He measures J&Y's (P) mistake in pipe feet and brand names. Compare this case to the satisfaction clause cases. In those cases, there were times when satisfaction was measured according to a reasonable person standard. In the same way, Kent's (D) desire for a specific brand of pipe is measured against a standard that has reasonableness written all over it. The difference between Justice Cardozo and Justice McLaughlin, thus, comes down to a fundamental conflict over the interpretation of contracts, Justice Cardozo is willing to bring fairness concerns to bear on the contract while trying to maintain its integrity.

## ■ CASE VOCABULARY

SUBSTANTIAL PERFORMANCE: A doctrine which permits recovery for performance which, while not perfect, is substantial. The inquiry into substantiality is heavily dependent on the facts of the case and subject to the discretion of the court and the dictates of fairness.

# Plante v. Jacobs

(General Contractor) v. (Homeowners)

10 Wis.2d 567, 103 N.W.2d 296 (1960)

WISCONSIN SUPREME COURT APPLIES DIMINISHED-VALUE RULE TO SUBSTANTIALLY PERFORMED CONSTRUCTION CONTRACT

■ **INSTANT FACTS** Homeowners refuse to make their final payment to the contractor who built their house.

■ **BLACK LETTER RULE** Substantial performance on construction contracts may be less than perfect, but recovery will be reduced by the diminished value of the project or the cost of completion of the unfinished work.

■ **PROCEDURAL BASIS**

Appeal from a trial court judgement for the plaintiff in a suit to establish a lien on the defendant's property.

■ **FACTS**

Plante (P) a contractor, agreed to build a house for the Jacobs (D) for $26,765. After $20,000 worth of work was paid for, the parties had a falling out which resulted in Plante (P) walking off of the job. He had not completed the house. In fact, there was at least $1601.95 worth of work to be completed. Despite this, he sued to establish a lien on the Jacobs' (D) property in order to recover the remainder of the construction price. He admits that he is not entitled to compensation for the uncompleted work. The Jacobs' (D) complain that, among other defects, Plante (P) misplaced the wall between their living room and kitchen by a foot. As a result, they claim that he is not entitled to compensation because he has not substantially performed the contract. It would cost roughly $4000 to tear down and rebuild the wall. However, the placement of the wall has no effect on the market value of the house. The trial court found for Plante (P). The Jacobs (D) appeal.

■ **ISSUE**

Can performance be considered substantial despite mistakes which will be costly to correct?

■ **DECISION AND RATIONALE**

(Hallows) Yes. The first question is whether substantial performance has been tendered. This cannot be answered according to precise formulae, especially with regard to construction contracts. In other cases, substantial performance was denied because performance was useless to the other party or a total failure with regard to the object of the contract. In construction cases, the rule is that something less than perfection will count as substantial performance unless the parties indicate otherwise in the contract. In this case, Plante (P) was not given any blueprints for the house. He built it based on standard floor plans, resolving problems by practical experience. Given the circumstances surrounding construction, and notwithstanding the Jacobs' (D) unhappiness with the job, the trial court did not err in finding substantial performance. However, this is not the end of our inquiry. The house was still left uncompleted. The next question which must be answered is how to measure the damages owed to Plante (P). Normally, he would receive the full contract price, minus the damages caused by incomplete performance. The damages caused by incomplete performance should be determined by comparing the diminution in value of the house, against the cost of completing the work. When the cost of completion is prohibitive, the diminution in value should be applied. The trial court parsed out the defects, applying the diminished-value rule to some defects, and the cost of completion rule to others. While the trial court applied cost of completion to some defects which this court may not have, we cannot say that their judgement was so erroneous as to require reversal. In particular, the trial court measured the misplaced wall by the diminished-value rule. This was appropriate. The Jacobs (P) never made it clear that the wall was being built in the wrong place. In addition, replacing the wall would require substantial demolition of the existing structure. This would be economically wasteful and unreasonable. Since the trial court did not err in its measure of damages, the judgement will be affirmed.

### Analysis:

Justice Hallows's approach in this case is not wholly different from Justice Cardozo's approach in *Jacob & Youngs*. Both justices realize that a mathematical formula is unsuited ... determining substantial performance in construction cases. The work is simply too complicated and unpredictable to give rise to exact measurements regarding performance. On the other hand, Justice Hallows has broader concerns in the apportionment of damages than are evident in *Jacob & Youngs*. While both courts desired an equitable result, Justice Hallows is more explicitly concerned with efficiency than fairness. In fact, the diminished-value rule is a rule of efficiency. It is wasteful, albeit also unfair, to force parties to pay for defects that would be costly to repair, but have little impact on the value of the house.

### ■ CASE VOCABULARY

COST OF COMPLETION: A measure of damages, frequently present in construction cases, which compensates the injured party for the cost of repairing or completing defective or unfinished work. This measure of damages will be granted unless it is grossly disproportionate to the value which is produced by the work. If it is grossly disproportionate, damages will be measured by the diminution in value.

DIMINUTION IN VALUE: As it sounds, the diminution in market value of a construction project is one possible measure of damages resulting from defective or incomplete performance by the builder. The court determines the market value of the project as completed per the contract and subtracts the value of the structure as it stands.

# Gill v. Johnstown Lumber Co.

(Lumber Driver) v. (Lumber Mill)

151 Pa. 534, 25 A. 120 (1892)

PENNSYLVANIA SUPREME COURT PERMITS RECOVERY ON A SEVERABLE DELIVERY CONTRACT

■ **INSTANT FACTS** A lumber driver requests full payment for his work, despite losing a percentage of his client's logs.

■ **BLACK LETTER RULE** If a contract is severable, as opposed to entire, then payment may be requested for the measure of performance which was completed.

■ **PROCEDURAL BASIS**

Appeal from a trial court directed verdict for the defendant in a breach of contract action.

■ **FACTS**

Gill (P), a lumber driver, had an agreement with Johnstown Lumber Co. (Johnstown) (D) to deliver a load of logs and cross-ties to a variety of locations, Including Johnstown's (D) mill. The delivery was to be made by river from certain specified points of departure to specified locations. In addition, Johnstown (D) promised to pay Gill (P) rates which varied according to the types of logs and the delivery destinations. Unfortunately, a flood hit while Gill (P) was delivering the logs and he permitted a large percentage of them to float past Johnstown's (D) mill. Undaunted, he sued Johnstown (D) in assumpsit for the money he was owed under the contract. The trial court directed a verdict for Johnstown (D), holding that the contract was entire—in other words, not subject to a disaggregation of obligations and payment that would permit partial recovery. Gill (P) appeals.

■ **ISSUE**

Can a contract which is "entire" give rise to a recovery for a party tendering incomplete performance?

■ **DECISION AND RATIONALE**

(Heydrick) No. However, the contract in this case is not entire. A contract is entire if only one payment is made for the completion of performance. It does not matter whether a single act is promised, or If several distinct acts make up the completed performance. On the other hand, a contract is severable if it divides payment up among several distinct acts which constitute performance. The contract is also severable if it does not specify how payment is to be made for these distinct acts. In this case, Gill (P) had a variety of responsibilities. He had to deliver logs made of different woods to different locations. He also had to deliver cross-ties to varying locations. The contract specifically apportioned payment among the types of wood, cross-ties, and shipping locations. As a result, the agreement is severable, not entire. Accordingly, Gill (P) is entitled to payment for the work completed. He is not, however, entitled to payment for the logs which were lost. Johnstown (D) promised to pay for all of the lumber which was delivered. They should not have to pay for lumber which was not delivered. However, since Gill (P) is otherwise entitled to compensation, the judgement of the trial court is reversed and a *venire facias de novo* is ordered.

**Analysis:**

A court's interpretation of a contract as divisible is much like the determination of substantial performance in that there is no set rule determining the outcome. According to the Restatement, courts should determine whether the elements of performance can be paired up with a promise of payment. For instance, in the above case, Johnstown (D) promised to pay one dollar per thousand feet of oak logs delivered. Gill (P) promised to deliver the logs for that amount. It is easy to see each pair of promises functioning as an individual mini-agreement within the contract. In addition, the court must determine whether it is appropriate to treat the pair of promises as "agreed equivalents." This means that the promises that were exchanged are worth the same to the parties regardless of the rest of the contract. If Johnstown's (D) oak logs, for instance, were worthless to them if the pine logs were not delivered, then it seems unfair to make them pay for the delivery of the oak logs. This item is not severable because Johnstown's (D) promise to pay for the delivery is now worth more to Gill (P) than his promise to deliver the remaining logs—they are no longer agreed equivalents.

## ■ CASE VOCABULARY

ASSUMPSIT: An action for the recovery of damages due to a breach of contract.

ENTIRE: A contract is "entire" when a single payment is promised for the performance of all of its terms.

SEVERABLE: A contract is "severable" when payment is divided among the terms of the contract. In that event, a party can recover payment for part performance. This rule is subject to the limitations which are discussed above.

VENIRE FACIAS DE NOVO: An order for a new jury. This order may be given after some irregularity or impropriety in the original jury's conduct or verdict. A court ordering a new jury is, in essence, ordering a new trial.

# Britton v. Turner

(Employee) v. (Employer)

6 N.H. 481 (1834)

NEW HAMPSHIRE SUPREME COURT GRANTS RESTITUTION TO A PARTY IN BREACH

■ **INSTANT FACTS** An employee breaks a one-year contract with his employer after ten months, suing to recover wages for that period.

■ **BLACK LETTER RULE** A party may recover in quantum meruit [restitution] despite being in breach of their contract.

■ **PROCEDURAL BASIS**

Appeal from a trial court jury verdict for the plaintiff in an action for assumpsit and quantum meruit.

■ **FACTS**

Britton (P) had an employment contract with Turner (D) for a period of one year. Turner (D) promised to pay Britton (P) $120 for the year. However, Britton (P) quit, without reason, after ten months. He then sued Turner (D) in assumpsit, adding a count of quantum meruit for $100. The $100 was intended to compensate him for the time that he worked. The trial court instructed the jury that if they accepted all of the facts as alleged, Britton (P) was entitled to reasonable compensation for his ten months work. The jury subsequently awarded Britton (P) $95 [minimum wage must have been a fantasy back then]. Turner (D) appeals.

■ **ISSUE**

Can a party recover in quantum meruit for part performance despite being in breach of contract?

■ **DECISION AND RATIONALE**

(Parker) Yes. It goes without saying that a party who breaks a contract cannot recover on the contract itself. Similarly, courts have held that a party who breaches a contract for labor promised at a specific rate cannot recover for part performance of that labor. The effects of this rule can be harsh. For instance, a party may be liable for damages to their employer for breaching a contract before performance begins. By the same token, a party who performs nearly all of their contract, but falls short of complete performance, may be subject to the same damages in addition to the loss of their contribution to complete performance. This puts the performing breacher in a worse position than the non-performing breacher. In this case, Britton (P) worked for nearly ten months on a one-year contract. The jury valued this work at $95. If the rule of recovery is applied as above, he would forfeit that compensation, and the value of his performance, to Tumer (D). In addition, he might still be liable to Turner (D) for damages for breach of contract. However, this case should be considered in light of rules which are applied in other contexts. Specifically, when a party contracts for the construction of a home, he need not accept the home if it does not conform to his requested specifications. If he does accept the home, he must pay for the construction, minus an offset for any defects. Similarly, when a buyer receives and makes use of defective goods, he may be able to return the unused goods to the seller. Nonetheless, the seller is entitled to recover the value of the goods which the buyer used. The principle of these cases is that a party cannot accept the benefit of performance on a contract without compensation. This principle can be applied to the current dispute. An employer receives a benefit every moment of his employee's labor. The employer knows this, regardless of whether the contract calls for periodic compensation, or for compensation at the end of the employee's term. The employer also knows that the employee may fail to complete this term. Despite this, he accepts the benefit of performance on a daily basis and should have to compensate the employee for this benefit. This result would relieve the unfair effect of forfeiture, plus the danger of breach of contract damages, which faces an employee who cannot complete his contract. Consequently, we announce a rule which covers two types of cases. First, no compensation will be required for part performance on a special contract [see vocabulary below] which explicitly states that payment is not due until performance is complete. However, if a party receives a benefit from performance on an ordinary contract, the court may imply a provision which grants compensation for that performance. In a sense, part performance counts as consideration for a new, implied subsidiary agreement for which compensation may be ordered. This rule does not affect those occasions when the non-breaching party can refuse the object of performance, like a defectively built house, and thereby derive no benefit from it. Nor does this rule affect contracts which are entire, and therefore not subject to an apportionment of performance and compensation. Employment contracts, on the other hand, are inherently divisible unless they specifically state that the employee forfeits any right to compensation if he fails to complete his term. Otherwise, in the event of a breach, the employer should be entitled to the damages resulting from the breach, minus the value of the benefit he received from part performance. This rule can be applied without hesitation in this case. Britton (P) worked for a period of time under a contract which did not include a forfeiture provision as above. As a result, the trial court correctly instructed the jury that he was entitled to a share of the total contract price. While Turner (D) raised a defense of breach of contract, he did not allege any damages. As a result, the judgement of the trial court is affirmed, notwithstanding Turner's (D) right to bring a separate suit for breach of contract.

## Analysis:

Remember that restitution is a separate cause of action, not a form of recovery on the contract. A party who is in breach is not entitled to sue on the contract. However, that does not mean that they surrender all of their rights to compensation. Restitution, divisibility, and substantial performance provide the primary means by which the harsh effects of forfeiture can be avoided in the event of a breach of contract. Justice Parker does an excellent job of surveying the entire landscape of remedies and bringing them to bear on the dispute between Britton (P) and Turner (D). He traces a line of cases from substantial performance, through a common law modification on the perfect tender rule, and ends by distinguishing entire from divisible employment contracts. In doing so, he wrote a landmark opinion that set the stage for a reversal of the traditional doctrine, which denied compensation to parties in breach.

## ■ CASE VOCABULARY

QUANTUM MERUIT: Literally, "as much as deserved." Quantum meruit is the precursor to the modern cause of action for restitution. It was generally a specific count which was added to a cause of action in assumpsit [an action for contract damages]. See RESTITUTION below.

RESTITUTION: Technically, restitution is a separate cause of action in equity based on the concept of unjust enrichment. The complainant must show that they conferred a benefit on the other party and that it would be unjust to permit that party to retain the benefit. If this test can be met, the complainant is entitled to the reasonable value of the benefit conferred.

SPECIAL CONTRACT: [A special contract is...uh...well...special.] It is a contract which contains specific terms detailing the obligations of the parties. In addition, the contract may have an unusual objective which is not easily subject to judicially implied terms.

# Kirkland v. Archbold

(Contractor) v. (Homeowner)

113 N.E.2d 496 (Ohio App. 1953)

OHIO COURT OF APPEALS GRANTS RECOVERY TO A BUILDER DESPITE HIS BREACH OF CONTRACT

■ **INSTANT FACTS** A homeowner refuses to pay the contractor who has been working on her house for two months.

■ **BLACK LETTER RULE** A court may grant recovery in quantum meruit to a party, despite their being in breach of contract and without interpreting the contract as severable.

■ **PROCEDURAL BASIS**

Appeal from the plaintiff after a trial court judgment which limited the requested damages in a breach of contract action.

■ **FACTS**

Kirkland (P), a contractor, agreed to make some repairs on a home owned by Archbold (D). Their contract stated, among other things, that Archbold (D) would pay Kirkland (P) $1000 after ten days of satisfactory work, $1000 after twenty days of work, $1000 after thirty days of work, $1000 upon completion of the job, and $2000 within thirty days of completion. Kirkland (P) worked for two months before Archbold (D) asked him to stop. During this time, Kirkland (P) had only been paid $800. His expenses, up to this point, were $2985. He sued Archbold (D) for the difference in a breach of contract action. The trial court found that Kirkland (P) himself was in breach of contract by ignoring certain contract specifications for work that he completed. As a result, the court found that Archbold (D) fired him justifiably. However, since Archbold (D) had already paid Kirkland (P) $800, she was deemed to have accepted his first ten days work as satisfactory. The trial court granted Kirkland (P) the $200 difference. Kirkland (P) now appeals.

■ **ISSUE**

Can a party who is in breach of contract bring an action to recover for part performance?

■ **DECISION AND RATIONALE**

(Skeel) Yes. Traditionally, a plaintiff could not sue on a contract that he had breached unless he had substantially performed. However, this rule has changed over time. Beginning with *Britton v. Turner* [permitting a party to recover in quantum meruit despite being in breach of their contract], courts began allowing contractors to recover in quantum meruit for work which bestowed a benefit on the other party. Recovery was based on the concept of unjust enrichment, and represented a quasi-contract in which one party promised to pay for a benefit received from the other. Generally, the plaintiff's recovery was reduced by the amount of damages which resulted from the breach of contract. This doctrine is not the same as substantial performance even though courts use substantial performance to protect builders against the same result—the forfeiture of work without compensation after a breach. However, even if a builder has not substantially performed, there is no justice in forcing him to forfeit compensation for work which benefited his client. In this case, Kirkland (P) never claimed that he had substantially performed. He only sought compensation for the work that he completed. Unfortunately, the trial court interpreted the contract as severable [divisible], denying Kirkland (P) compensation for work which was done after the first ten day period. A court should deny compensation only when the owner received no benefit from the work, or the work was entirely nonconforming to the contract, or the builder left the work unfinished. Finally, recovery should not be granted to a contractor who willfully, as opposed to negligently, abandons his contract. In this case, Kirkland's (P) claim does not violate any of these caveats. He was fully entitled to compensation for the work that he completed, minus any damages which resulted from his breach of contract. As a result, the judgement of the trial court should be reversed and the cause remanded for further proceedings.

## Analysis:

Quantum meruit was generally added as a count to a claim in assumpsit essentially a breach of contract action. Currently, however, restitution is a more common off-the-contract remedy for these sorts of cases. A party who willfully breaches his contract is frequently not entitled to recover in restitution, but a party who *intentionally* breaches a contract does not necessarily do so "willfully." In the context of breaches, the word "willful" connotes a more malevolent, craven reason for breaching the contract. For Instance, a party who breached a contract because it was financially advantageous for it to do so might be seen as having done so willfully. Considering that this language is fairly slippery, it is understandable that the Restatement (Second) of Contracts abandoned the concept of willfulness as an absolute bar to recovery.

## ■ CASE VOCABULARY

QUASI-CONTRACT: A quasi-contract is no different from an implied contract. In the context above, a court may find an implied or quasi-contract to pay for services which benefited one of the parties to an existing agreement.

# Walker & Co. v. Harrison

(Sign Company) v. (Dry Cleaner)

347 Mich. 630, 81 N.W.2d 352 (1957)

MICHIGAN SUPREME COURT HOLDS REPUDIATING PARTY LIABLE FOR CONTRACT WHICH WAS NOT MATERIALLY BREACHED BY THE OTHER PARTY

■ **INSTANT FACTS** A dry cleaner stops making rental payments on his neon sign when the sign company refuses to clean it according to routine maintenance.

■ **BLACK LETTER RULE** A party may discontinue performance on a contract which has been materially breached by the other party.

■ **PROCEDURAL BASIS**

Appeal from a trial court judgement for the plaintiff in an action for assumpsit.

■ **FACTS**

Walker & Co. (Walker) (P) agreed to provide Harrison (D) with a neon sign for his dry cleaning business. Walker (P) rented the sign to Harrison (D) subject to a number of terms contained in the lease. These included a rental price of $148.50 per month, a term of 36 months, and a maintenance clause which required Walker (P) to clean and repaint the sign whenever necessary to keep it in "first class advertising condition." The sign was installed in July. Soon after, it began to fall into disrepair. Someone had thrown a tomato at it, and it was also covered with graffiti, cobwebs, and rust. Harrison (D) complained again and again but Walker (P) never serviced the sign. Consequently, Harrison (D) only made one rental payment. Finally, in October, Harrison (D) sent Walker (P) a telegram, renouncing their contract and any further obligations to pay rent for the sign. Walker (P) responded with a letter, drawing Harrison's (D) attention to a Breach of Agreement clause in the contract. This clause stated that, in the event of the lessee's failure to pay rent, Walker (P) could remove the sign and demand the remainder of the rental payments. Harrison (D) never responded, so Walker (P) sued in assumpsit for the entire balance due under the contract, $5197.5. Harrison (D) claimed that Walker (P) had already materially breached their agreement by the time he stopped paying rent. He claims that his repudiation was justifiable under the circumstances. Nonetheless, the trial court found for Walker (P). Harrison (D) appeals.

■ **ISSUE**

Can a party cease performance on a contract once the other party has materially breached the agreement?

■ **DECISION AND RATIONALE**

(Smith) Yes. A material breach by one party entitles the other party to discontinue performance on the contract. However, a party who responds to a material breach in this manner does so at his own peril. It is difficult to determine the point at which a breach becomes material. The Restatement [First] of Contracts provides some criteria which are helpful to this end. A court engaged in this analysis should examine the extent to which the non-breaching party will obtain the substantial benefit from the contract which they reasonably anticipated, the extent to which damages can adequately compensate the non-breacher, the extent to which the breacher has performed or prepared to perform, the hardship on the breacher of terminating the contract; the willful, negligent, or innocent behavior of the breacher; and the likelihood that the breacher will complete performance. Taking these elements together, it is clear that Walker (P) did not materially breach their obligations under the lease. First, Harrison (D) is unclear on the number of times he actually complained to Walker (P). In addition, it appears that some of the problems with the sign, notably the cobwebs and rust, were easily within Harrison's (D) reach. He could have taken care of those problems himself. The rust, itself, could not have been very severe since the sign had only recently been installed. Finally, Walker (P) repaired the sign within a week of Harrison's (D) telegram. Given Harrison's (D) complaint, which can be reduced to a stain from a thrown tomato, it cannot fairly be said that Walker (P) was guilty of a material breach in not repairing the sign sooner. The trial court did not err in its analysis. As a result, their judgment will be affirmed.

---

**Analysis:**

Many people think that any deviation from the terms of an agreement gives them the right to stop paying the landlord, the plumber, or any other party with whom they have a disagreement. Since this is not the case, it is one of the most dangerous misconceptions. While this case makes it clear that a material breach is difficult to quantify, it is always necessary to analyze a breach according to the criteria that the court outlines. At the very least, this analysis will provide some indication of the breach's magnitude and suggest an outcome in one party's favor.

---

**■ CASE VOCABULARY**

MATERIAL BREACH: If one party to a contract materially (or substantially, or totally) breaches the contract, the other party may be excused from performance. In this event, the non-breaching party may still sue on the contract to recover damages due to lack of performance. In order to determine whether a breach is material, a court is likely to consider the elements outlined by Justice Smith, above.

# K & G Construction Co. v. Harris

(General Contractor) v. (Subcontractor)

223 Md. 305, 164 A.2d 451 (1960)

MARYLAND COURT OF APPEALS SORTS OUT COMPLICATED BREACH AND REPUDIATION CONSTRUCTION DISPUTE

■ **INSTANT FACTS** A general contractor stops paying his subcontractor after the subcontractor refuses to pay for damage that an employee did at the job site.

■ **BLACK LETTER RULE** A party who materially breaches a contract may not respond to non-breacher's cessation of performance by repudiating the contract.

■ **PROCEDURAL BASIS**

Appeal from a trial court judgement on a counterclaim, in favor of the defendant in a breach of contract action.

■ **FACTS**

K & G Construction (K&G) (P) hired Harris and Brooks (Harris) (D) as the excavation and earth-moving subcontractors on a construction job. The agreement required K&G (P) to make monthly progress payments to Harris (D) on the submission of requisitions which were due by the 25th of each month. In addition, Harris (D) promised to perform his work in a "workmanlike manner, and in accordance with the best practices." Finally, Harris (D) was required to carry liability insurance for any property damage which occurred on the job. On August 9th, one of Harris's (D) bulldozer drivers inadvertently demolished a wall and some other portions of a house under construction. Despite the insurance provisions, Harris (D) refused to pay for the damage. He submitted a requisition the following day for work that was done in July. K&G (P) refused to pay the bill since Harris (D) refused to pay for the bulldozer damage. Harris (D) continued on the job until September 12th. At this point, he stopped work because of the unpaid requisition. Up until this time, K&G (P) was satisfied with Harris's (D) work with the exception of the bulldozer accident. Nevertheless, after Harris (D) quit, K&G (P) hired another subcontractor to complete the excavation work for an extra $450. They subsequently sued Harris (D) for breach of contract and for negligence in the bulldozer accident. Harris (D) counterclaimed for the payment due on their excavation, and for lost profits associated with not being permitted to finish the job. A jury found in K&G's (P) favor on the negligence claim. The judge found in Harris's (D) favor on the breach of contract claim. K&G (P) appeals this ruling.

■ **ISSUE**

Can a party to a contract suspend performance if the other party materially breaches the contract?

■ **DECISION AND RATIONALE**

(Prescott) Yes. Ordinarily, contracts give rise to two types of promises: Independent and mutually dependent. Independent promises are exchanged for nothing more than a return promise. They are not exchanged for immediate performance. Mutually dependent promises, on the other hand, are exchanged only on the condition of performance by the other party. These promises may be precedent, subsequent, or concurrent. In other words, either a party must perform before the other party will be bound, after the other party becomes bound, or the parties must perform simultaneously. Courts used to presume that contract promises were independent. However, this trend was reversed when Lord Mansfield developed the concept of constructive conditions in *Kingston v. Preston* [a contract for the exchange of promised performances may give rise to an implied condition on that exchange, making each party's performance dependent on the other's]. Now, contract promises are presumed to be mutually dependent. This does not leave courts free to ignore the intentions of the parties or the good sense of the case, however. In this case, for instance, mutually dependent conditions could work to K&G's (P) disadvantage as they try to cope with the poor workmanship of their subcontractor. K&G (P) would be required to pay for the subcontractor's work, in order not to breach the contract, before suing for the damage done. Instead, we find that Harris's (D) failure to correct the damage done by the bulldozer to be a material breach of the construction contract. Harris (D) agreed to perform his work in a workmanlike manner, in accordance with the best practices. Yet, his negligence led to property damage which was double the value of their final requisition. This clearly amounted to a material breach. The law is settled that if a subcontractor fails to tender substantial performance [another way of describing material breach], the general contractor is entitled to withhold their progress payments. If the general contractor is justified in withholding payment, then a subcontractor's subsequent refusal to work constitutes a wrongful repudiation of the contract. On the other hand, the general contractor may keep the subcontractor on the job and treat the failure of performance as a partial breach. This is what K&G (P) did by keeping Harris (D) on the job despite withholding their payment. However, Harris (D) breached their contract a second time by walking off the job. This breach led to $450 in damages for which K&G (P) is entitled to repayment. Consequently, the judgement of the trial court is reversed and entered in favor of K&G (P).

## Analysis:

Judge Prescott appears to see the doctrines of mutually dependent promises and material breach at odds with each other. This need not be the case. Using the doctrine of mutually dependent promises could have led Judge Prescott to the same conclusion—i.e., that Harris's (D) lack of workmanship relieved K&G's (P) obligation to pay him. The lack of workmanship could either be phrased as the failure of a constructive condition on payment or a material breach of the contract. Either way, these doctrines need not be seen as competing, but rather complementary solutions to a difficult problem of mutual performance.

# Iron Trade Products Co. v. Wilkoff Co.

(Rail Buyer) v. (Rail Supplier)

272 Pa. 172, 116 A. 150 (1922)

PENNSYLVANIA SUPREME COURT REJECTS A BREACHER'S CLAIM THAT THE NON-BREACHER INTERFERED WITH HIS PERFORMANCE

■ **INSTANT FACTS** A rail supplier cannot find enough rails to satisfy a contract because his buyer has purchased a significant portion of the available rails.

■ **BLACK LETTER RULE** Performance on a contract may be excused if one party intentionally makes the other party's performance impossible.

■ **PROCEDURAL BASIS**

Appeal from a trial court judgement for the plaintiff in a breach of contract action.

■ **FACTS**

Wilkoff Co. (Wilkoff) (D) contracted to supply Iron Trade Products Co. (Iron Trade) (P) with 2600 tons of relaying rails at $41 per ton. While Wilkoff was trying to amass the necessary rails, however, Iron Trade (P) was also buying rails on the open market. In fact, Iron Trade's (P) rail purchases were so large—and from the same supplier with which Wilkoff (D) was dealing—that the price rose to a point where Wilkoff (D) could no longer afford them. Iron Trade (P) did not know that rail supplies were limited, nor did they intend to interfere with Wilkoff's (D) ability to buy rails. In any event, Wilkoff (D) was unable to deliver any rails to Iron Trade (P) in the time allotted. Iron Trade (P) was then forced to buy the rails from other suppliers at the current market price of roughly $50 per ton. They sued Wilkoff (D) for breach of contract, requesting damages for the difference in price which they were forced to pay. The trial court ruled in favor of Iron Trade (P). Wilkoff (D) appeals.

■ **ISSUE**

Is a party excused from performance on a contract if the other party interferes with its performance?

■ **DECISION AND RATIONALE**

(Walling) Yes. However, a party cannot be excused from a contract simply because the other party's interference made performance more difficult. Performance must actually be made impossible before its failure can be excused. The true facts of this case reveal that Wilkoff (D) was capable of buying the necessary rails at all times. If nothing else, Iron Trade's (P) ability to buy up large amounts of rails, including the rails that Wilkoff (D) failed to provide, indicates that rails were readily available. In addition, Iron Trade (P) did not know that they were interfering with Wilkoff's (D) ability to buy rails. More importantly, they never intended to make it difficult for him to do so. As a matter of fact, the negotiator with whom both parties were dealing offered Wilkoff (D) a better price than he gave Iron Trade (P). Wilkoff (D) cannot claim, under these circumstances, that it was truly impossible for him to buy enough rails to meet his obligations. However, Wilkoff (D) also claims that he should not be held liable because Iron Trade (P) made a deal to sell Wilkoff's (D) rails even before the parties made their contract. Even if this were true, it represents a transaction which is distinct from the contract between Wilkoff (D) and Iron Trade (P). As a result, it will not be considered in this proceeding. Since there is no excuse for Wilkoff's (D) failure to provide Iron Trade (P) with the necessary rails, the judgement of the trial court is affirmed.

**Analysis:**

It can be difficult to determine whether one party has sufficiently interfered with the other party's ability to perform such that performance should be excused. The inquiry is heavily dependent on the facts of the case, and subject to the court's interpretation of those facts. One way of looking at a party's interference is to consider whether the other party would have agreed to that sort of behavior in the contract. For instance, would Wilkoff (D) have agreed to allow Iron Trade (P) to continue looking for rails while Wilkoff (D) was trying to satisfy its order? Again, the answer to this question depends upon the facts of the case, the circumstances surrounding the transaction, and the relationship of the parties. It is important to this case that Iron Trade (P) did not intend to interfere with Wilkoff's (D) ability to fulfill his obligations. If Wilkoff (D) could have demonstrated malice on Iron Trade's (P) part, he might have been more successful in being excused from performance.

■ **CASE VOCABULARY**

MALICE: You may recall, if you have had Criminal Law, that malice does not mean ill will. The term "malice" usually represents a party's intent to cause a predicted result.

# New England Structures, Inc. v. Loranger

(Subcontractor) v. (General Contractor)

354 Mass. 62, 234 N.E.2d 888 (1968)

MASSACHUSETTS SUPREME COURT PERMITS A PARTY TO MAKE ARGUMENTS AT TRIAL WHICH DIFFER FROM THOSE ADVANCED DURING THE ORIGINAL DISPUTE

■ **INSTANT FACTS** A general contractor fires his roofing subcontractor on narrower grounds than he alleges in court.

■ **BLACK LETTER RULE** A party who terminates an agreement is not restricted at trial to the claims made at the time of termination unless the other party has relied on the earlier claims to his detriment.

## ■ PROCEDURAL BASIS

Appeal from a trial court jury verdict in favor of New England as plaintiff and defendant in two different actions joined for trial.

## ■ FACTS

Loranger (P), a general contractor, hired New England Structures (New England) (R) as the roofing subcontractor on a construction job. Their agreement stated that New England (R) was required, among other things, to provide enough skilled workmen to complete the job according to the pace set by Loranger (P). Loranger (P) was entitled to fire New England (R) with five days written notice if they failed to live up the agreement. In fact, Loranger (P) sent New England (R) a notice of termination after they had been on the job for barely a month. Loranger (P) stated in the notice that New England (R) consistently refused or failed to provide enough skilled workman to maintain satisfactory progress. New England (R) sent back a telegram, claiming that Loranger (P) had been slow in providing approved drawings from which New England (R) could do their work. Despite this, Loranger (P) hired another subcontractor to complete the job. They then sued New England (R) for breach of contract, claiming damages for the payments made to the new subcontractor. New England (R) in turn, sued Loranger (P) for breach of contract resulting from their termination. [??This case arose from two distinct actions. In one action, Loranger sued New England. In another, New England sued Loranger. Since each party is a plaintiff *and* a defendant, they will be referred to as (P)etitioner and (R)espondent for the purposes of this brief.] The two actions were joined for consideration by the trial court. A jury found for New England (R) in both of the predicate actions. Loranger (P) does not challenge the result in New England's (R) claim for breach of contract. The jury found that Loranger (P) violated the provisions of the termination clause by preventing New England's (R) welders from working for five days after they received the notice of termination. However, Loranger (P) does challenge the judge's instructions regarding his claim against New England for breach of contract. At trial, the parties disputed several defects in New England's (R) performance apart from the failure to provide sufficient workman. Nevertheless, the judge told the jury that Loranger (P) could not argue that he fired New England (R) for reasons other than those stated in the notice of termination. The jury was permitted to consider only the evidence which was relevant to these reasons. Loranger (P) argues that this instruction was improper. He appeals the jury's verdict on this issue.

## ■ ISSUE

Can a party who terminates a contract justify the termination at trial on grounds other than those given to the employee at the time of termination?

above, to his right to recover damages. Kanavos (P) relies on case law which states that a real estate purchaser may recover damages for breach of contract, under circumstances similar to this case, regardless of their ability to carry out their end of the contract. However, this approach is no longer taken by the courts, the Restatement (Second) of Contracts, the UCC or the relevant treatises. This does not end our inquiry, however. The question remains as to which party bears the burden of proof on Kanavos' (P) ability to complete the stock purchase. The law is not settled in cases of this type. However, it is our conclusion that Kanavos (P) should bear the burden of proof on this issue because he is better informed regarding his financial state than Hancock (D). This may seem unfair considering that Hancock (D) was responsible for repudiating the contract between the parties. However, this is not a sufficient reason to require that they disprove a fact which is part of Kanavos' (P) case. That said, Kanavos (P) presented evidence from which the jury could have determined his ability to complete the transaction. While he was experiencing some difficulty at the time of the sale, he may have been able to raise the necessary financing through other parties. In addition, he argues that he could have made the necessary arrangements if Hancock (D) had given him notice of the transaction. With that in mind, the trial court erred in overruling Hancock's (D) objection. The only issue for retrial is whether Kanavos (P) would have been financially able to exercise his option if he had received sufficient notice of the pending sale from Hancock (D). Case is remanded for a determination on this issue.

**Analysis:**

In a sense, the court here implied a condition to the option contract that required Kanavos (P) to demonstrate his financial ability to perform. Otherwise, Hancock (D) is released from their obligation to pay damages. This seems reasonable, especially if you were to change the facts of the case slightly. Suppose Hancock (D) warned Kanavos (P) of the impending sale. In order to exercise his option he would have to fulfill his promise to meet the bank's asking price. If he could not do so, his option would lapse and Hancock (D) would be released from any further obligations. Kanavos (P) could not claim damages on a contract for which the condition would have failed regardless of Hancock's (D) behavior. The second part of the court's opinion deals with the burden of proof on the issue presented. The party who has the best information on a particular fact frequently bears the burden of proof associated with that fact. This is particularly relevant in this case, where the determination of that fact is a prerequisite to Kanavos' (P) ability to recover damages for Hancock's (D) repudiation.

■ **CASE VOCABULARY**

RIGHT OF FIRST REFUSAL: As it sounds, a right of first refusal grants the holder an option which is superior to any other buyer. Once an offer is made to sell the relevant property, the holder can purchase the property ahead of any other prospective buyer, as long as he can meet the asking price of the seller.

# McCloskey & Co. v. Minweld Steel Co.

(General Contractor) v. (Subcontractor)

220 F.2d 101 (3rd Cir. 1955)

COURT OF APPEALS DISTINGUISHES BETWEEN ANTICIPATORY REPUDIATION AND STATEMENTS EXPRESSING DOUBT ABOUT PERFORMANCE

■ **INSTANT FACTS** A subcontractor is accused of repudiating a contract despite their difficulty in getting supplies due to market and governmental forces beyond their control.

■ **BLACK LETTER RULE** Anticipatory repudiation can only be demonstrated by an absolute and unequivocal refusal to perform or a distinct and positive statement of an inability to do so.

■ **PROCEDURAL BASIS**

Appeal from a district court judgement for the defendant in a breach of contract action.

■ **FACTS**

McCloskey & Co. (McCloskey) (P), a contractor, hired Minweld Steel Co. (Minweld) (D) as the steel subcontractor on a construction job. Minweld (D) agreed to supply and erect all of the structural steel for two buildings on which McCloskey (P) was working. The parties' contract stated that Minweld (D) could be terminated if they failed to supply enough materials for the job. Minweld (D) agreed to provide samples, drawings, and work schedules when they received the contract drawings or at McCloskey's (P) request. They further acknowledged that the delivery and installation of the steel was of the essence. The trouble began when McCloskey (P) sent the contract drawings to Minweld (D) In May of 1950. McCloskey (P) wanted to know how long it would take them to supply and erect the steel. Minweld (D) sent him a letter stating that the work would take until November 15th. As early as July, however, McCloskey (P) threatened to fire Minweld (D) if they did not assure him that they would have the necessary materials within thirty days. Minweld (D), unfortunately, was having problems buying steel. None of the major steel companies could fill their orders. In addition, the President of the United States further constricted the domestic steel market due to the outbreak of the Korean War in June. Minweld (D) informed McCloskey (P) of these problems and requested their help in lobbying the General State Authority for the necessary steel. McCloskey (P) took this as a repudiation of Minweld's (D) ability to perform their obligations and sued them for breach of contract. The district court found for Minweld (D). McCloskey (P) appeals.

■ **ISSUE**

Can a party be guilty of anticipatory repudiation for announcing difficulties which might preclude them from performing on the contract?

■ **DECISION AND RATIONALE**

(McLaughlin) No. This case is in federal court by way of diversity jurisdiction. Pennsylvania state law applies since the contract was executed there. In that regard, in order for a repudiation to rise to the level of breach of contract, there must be an "absolute and unequivocal refusal to perform or a distinct and positive statement of an inability to do so." Even if a party does nothing in preparation for performance which is due at a later date, it is not tantamount to a repudiation of the contract. In this case, Minweld (D) simply explained the difficulties that they were having. At no time did they refuse to perform the contract or suggest that performance would be impossible for them. They justifiably looked to McCloskey for help and were denied. In fact, McCloskey (P) was able to procure the necessary steel from two different manufacturers in order to have the work completed. One of their suppliers, Bethlehem Steel, was actually in competition with Minweld (D) for the original contract and refused to supply Minweld (D) with steel when they requested it. Nonetheless, McCloskey (P) argues that Minweld (D) specifically repudiated the deadline that McCloskey (P) announced in his July letter. Suffice it to say that Minweld (D) no more repudiated that deadline than they did the entire contract. In any event, there is nothing in the contract which entitles McCloskey (P) to set a deadline for Minweld's (D) assurance of completion. As a result, Minweld's (D) letter does not constitute an anticipatory repudiation of their contract with McCloskey (P). The judgement of the district court will be upheld.

## Analysis:

Pennsylvania's law regarding anticipatory repudiation is typical of most states. Generally, repudiation cannot be assumed from comments that merely place the party's performance in doubt. In fact, the repudiation must be so far-reaching as to offer the injured party a remedy for a total breach of contract. McCloskey (P) took the first sign of trouble as an excuse to discontinue his own performance. This approach does not advance the goal of securing transactions in a competitive marketplace. On the contrary, it would unleash the worst behavior of the parties, each seeking to cut and run whenever a contract became the least bit burdensome or unprofitable. Restatement (Second) of Contracts § 251, however, permits a party to demand assurances of performance from the other party. If the other party does not respond within a reasonable time, the failure may constitute a repudiation of the contract.

## ■ CASE VOCABULARY

TOTAL BREACH: This is a phrase which is used interchangeably with the terms "substantial breach" or "material breach" and which carries the same connotation of a breach serious enough to result in legal liability and to release the other party from their obligations.

# C.L. Maddox, Inc. v. Coalfield Services, Inc.

(General Contractor) v. (Subcontractor)

51 F.3d 76 (7th Cir. 1995)

## CONTRACTORS MAY REPUDIATE WHEN COUNTERPARTY INSISTS ON MODIFYING ORIGINAL AGREEMENT

■ **INSTANT FACTS** A mining subcontractor began excavating while awaiting a final contract. When the general contract repeatedly delayed signing, the subcontractor stopped work and sued.

■ **BLACK LETTER RULE** Contractual parties are justified in suspending performance when the counterparty shows an intent to not perform the contract as agreed, e.g., by refusing to sign a contract or clarify vague terms, failing to make progress payments *upon demand,* or demanding contract modifications.

■ **PROCEDURAL BASIS**

In contract action seeking damages, appeal from judgement for defendant.

■ **FACTS**

Old Ben Coal Company contracted with general contractor C.L. Maddox, Inc. ("Maddox") (P) to demolish and replace its mine loading facility. Maddox (P) decided to rebuild the facility itself, but subcontract the demolition to Coalfield Services, Inc. ("Coalfield") (D). The demolition would have to be completed within 3 weeks for Maddox (P) to finish its work by Old Ben's deadline. Maddox's (P) and Coalfield's (D) representatives met and discussed Coalfield (D) doing the work in 3 weeks for $230K, with biweekly progress payments. Coalfield (D) began work, and faxed Maddox (P) a proposed contract for signature. Maddox (P) stalled on signing the contract, while Coalfield (D) kept working. After 3 weeks of work, Coalfield (D) was only 45% done, and stopped to demand Maddox (P) sign the contract and pay 45% of the price. Maddox (P) apparently agreed, but only if Coalfield (D) agreed to liquidated damages of $1,000 per day beyond the 4-week deadline. Coalfield (D) refused, estimating that completion might take up to 35 days beyond the deadline. Coalfield (D) counter-offered, stating that if Maddox (P) accepted the original proposal with a 1-week extension, Coalfield (D) could resume work within 8 days. [Coalfield (D), in stopping work, had brought its workers and machinery to the mine's surface, and apparently needed 8 days to return them underground.] Maddox (P) sued Coalfield (D) for the cost of hiring a replacement subcontractor to finish work by the deadline. Coalfield (D) countersued for 45% of the contract price. At trial before a magistrate, the magistrate held for Coalfield (D), finding its work stoppage was a legitimate response to Maddox's (P) breach in withholding progress payments. Maddox (P) appeals.

■ **ISSUE**

Is a contractor justified in stopping performance when the counterparty refuses to sign a contract or clarify vague terms, fails to make progress payments, and demands a liquidated damages clause be added?

■ **DECISION AND RATIONALE**

(Posner) Yes. Contractual parties are justified in suspending performance when the counterparty shows an intent to not perform the contract as agreed, e.g., by refusing to sign a contract or clarify vague terms, failing to make progress payments *upon demand,* or demanding contract modifications. [We find there was a valid oral contract.] The magistrate's finding that Coalfield's (D) suspension was in response to Maddox's (P) nonpayment was incorrect, since Coalfield (D) billed Maddox (P) only after it stopped working, and Maddox (P) could not pay before Coalfield (D) specified the percentage of work it had completed. Where a contractual party knows the counterparty is in a hurry, a substantial interruption of work constitutes breach, unless it is excused by the counterparty's own breach or anticipatory repudiation. Here, Coalfield's (D) work stoppage was a substantial interruption, since resuming work would take 8 days, which would impede Maddox's (P) known deadline. But we find Coalfield's (D) stoppage was excused. Maddox's (P) refusal to answer Coalfield's (D) proposal for 3 weeks constituted anticipatory repudiation, since it gave Coalfield (D) substantial grounds for interrupting work in order to avoid incurring additional costs without assurances of payment. Since Maddox (P) had accepted only a basic contract with many omitted terms, it was free to deny acceptance of the additional terms in Coalfield's (D) written proposal. Thus, had Coalfield (D) continued working, it would have incurred costs and put itself at Maddox's (P) mercy. In short, Coalfield's (D) work stoppage was reasonable, especially in light of Maddox's (P) later demand for unusual and unreasonable liquidated damages. Our reaction might be different if liquidated damages clauses were standard in the industry. We do not suggest Maddox's (P) proposal of liquidated damages was itself a breach, since Coalfield (D) was free to refuse. Maddox (P) claims Coalfield (D) initially breached by failing to finish within 3 weeks, then used Maddox's (P) non-signature as a pretext to quit a job which had become unprofitably difficult, but there is no evidence of this. Affirmed and remanded to recompute damages.

---

**Analysis:**

The prolonged failure to sign a contract or clarify a preliminary agreement's vague terms may be a repudiation that justifies stopping performance, because it often signals the non-signatory is planning to deny or modify the contract and is waiting to obtain greater leverage. Generally, failure to make mandatory progress payments also justifies non-performance, since it suggests an unwillingness/inability to make final payments. However, here, the lack of progress payments was not pivotal, since the court effectively found Coalfield (D) had delayed demanding those payments, and thus effectively waived its right. *Insistence* on adding onerous contractual provisions is a breach, since it signals the demander is unwilling to follow the contract as written. But merely *suggesting* unfavorable modifications is not a breach. If the parties are not obligated (or forced) to accept.

---

■ **CASE VOCABULARY**

LIQUIDATED DAMAGES [CLAUSE]: Contractual provision obligating one party to compensate the other a *predetermined amount* for breach or delay. Theoretically, liquidated damages are supposed to provide a reasonable measure of actual damages when proving actual damages in court would prove difficult.

MAGISTRATE JUDGE: Statutory officer who is given a limited grant of power to try some cases. Apparently, in this jurisdiction, parties are given the right to secure an accelerated trial by consenting to having a magistrate try the case, rather than a full judge.

# Cosden Oil & Chemical Company v. Karl O. Helm Aktienge-sellschaft

(Polystyrene Supplier) v. (Buyer)
736 F.2d 1064 (5th Cir. 1984)

COURT OF APPEALS ANNOUNCES THE APPROPRIATE MEASURE OF A BUYER'S DAMAGES RESULTING FROM A SELLER'S ANTICIPATORY REPUDIATION

■ **INSTANT FACTS** A polystyrene supplier is taken to court when they fall to meet their obligations to their buyer.

■ **BLACK LETTER RULE** A buyer's damages for anticipatory repudiation are measured by the difference between the contract price and the market price at a commercially reasonable time after the repudiation.

■ **PROCEDURAL BASIS**

Appeal from a district court valuation of damages resulting from a jury verdict for the plaintiff in a breach of contract action.

■ **FACTS**

Cosden Oil & Chemical Company (Cosden) (P) had a contract to supply Karl O. Helm Aktiengesellschaft [gesundheit] (Helm) (D) with two different grades of polystyrene. Helm (D) ordered a large amount of the product in response to an impending shortage due to political problems in iran, a major petroleum producer. The bulk of Helm's (D) order was high impact polystyrene. They also ordered a small amount of less expensive general purpose polystyrene. In addition, Helm (D) had four options on future purchases, represented by four confirmation numbers from 04 through 07. Numbers 04 and 06 designated the high impact polystyrene. Cosden (P) began delivery on contract 04 in January of 1979. Shortly thereafter, they began experiencing difficulties which forced them to cancel delivery on contracts 05, 06, and 07. One of Cosden's (P) plants had to shut down after the illinois River froze, suspending barge traffic to the plant. Another plant was shut down after a defect was discovered in its production machinery. Cosden (P) made one more delivery on contract 04 and was soon forced to cancel the remainder of that contract as well. To make matters worse, Helm (D) never paid for any of the polystyrene that they received. As a result, Cosden (P) sued them for breach of contract. Helm (D) counterclaimed, alleging that Cosden (P) failed to fulfill their end of the contract. The jury sided with Helm (D), finding that Cosden (P) anticipatorily repudiated orders 05 through 07. In addition, they found that Cosden (P) cancelled order 04 before Helm (D) repudiated by nonpayment. The judge then fixed the damages as the difference between the contract price of the polystyrene and the market price at a commercially reasonable time after repudiation. He then permitted Cosden (P) to deduct the amount they were owed for deliveries under contract 04. Both parties appeal the judge's determination of damages.

■ **ISSUE**

Should the valuation of damages under a repudiated sales contract be made at a commercially reasonable time after repudiation?

## ■ DECISION AND RATIONALE

(Reavley) Yes. Texas adopted the Uniform Commercial Code as Title 1 of their Business and Commerce Code. All further references to "the Code" refer to the Texas code. According to section 2.713, a buyer is entitled to recover damages for a seller's breach as measured by the difference between the contract price and the market price at the time the buyer learned of the breach. The buyer is also entitled to any incidental or consequential damages. This measure is easily applied when the breach takes place at or after the time for performance. However, courts have disagreed over when to measure the damages after anticipatory repudiation. In that event, courts have interpreted "the time the buyer learned of the breach" to mean 1) when the buyer learns of the repudiation, 2) when the buyer learns of the repudiation plus a reasonable commercial time, or 3) when performance is due under the contract. Code section 2.610 on anticipatory repudiation, on the other hand, permits buyers to wait a commercially reasonable time before suing for breach. They cannot recover additional damages incurred after that point. Consequently, this Code section marks the outer boundaries of a buyer's recovery at a commercially reasonable time after learning of the repudiation. Any interpretation of section 2.713 which limited this range of recovery would be at odds with the buyer's rights under 2.610. Both parties rely on these rights to guide their behavior in the event of a breach. It may be more profitable for a seller to breach the contract and pay damages than to continue performance. This cannot be done if the seller is unsure of how the buyer's damages will be measured. Similarly, the buyer needs time to determine whether to cover [see vocabulary below]. If the buyer chooses not to cover, the court will still determine damages by the point at which the buyer *could* have covered. Our conclusions are further supported by the courts of appeals for the 3rd and 10th circuits and the Code's reliance on commercial reasonableness in a variety of contexts. As a result, we uphold the district court's determination of damages at a commercially reasonable time after Helm (D) learned of Cosden's (P) breach. Nevertheless, Cosden (P) challenges the valuation of damages, arguing that Helm (D) attempted to cover after Cosden (P) breached and that the price that Helm (D) paid for polystyrene should mark the ceiling for their damages. However, the jury found that Helm's (D) purchases during this period did not count as cover. As a result, we cannot follow Cosden's (P) suggestion. We affirm the trial court's determination as to when to measure the damages, but remand for a recalculation based on other issues [Cosden (P) was not entitled, as the jury found, to a set-off for impracticability because they failed to meet the demands of the doctrine].

---

## Analysis:

A buyer's remedies for a seller's breach are codified in UCC § 2–712 through § 2–715. The Texas code does not differ markedly from the UCC. You can tell from looking at the Texas code that the rights of the buyer with regard to recovery and cover closely resemble the expectation measure of damages. Under the expectation measure, buyers are entitled to damages that place them in the position they would have occupied if the contract had been performed as promised. Similarly, a buyer is entitled to damages that reflect the expected price of the goods that he sought to purchase. This purchase price fluctuates, however, with the market. In addition, this measure of damages is subject to the buyer's mitigation by way of cover. As is the case with the expectation measure, if the buyer does not cover, he suffers the consequences of his failure to mitigate. According to UCC § 2–713, the court will calculate the damages at the time of the breach if the buyer chooses not to cover. This rule may be a blessing or a curse depending upon how the market functions after the breach.

---

## ■ CASE VOCABULARY

CONSEQUENTIAL DAMAGES: Consequential damages represent costs which are not associated with an attempt to cover, but which still result from the seller's breach. These are typically late fees associated with the buyer's inability to satisfy subsequent commitments to other clients after the seller's breach.

COVER: In the event of a seller's breach, the buyer has a right to cover "with reasonable goods in substitution." Essentially, the buyer is entitled to investigate alternatives to the seller's failed performance. The buyer is under no obligation to cover, however. If the buyer chooses not to cover, the measure of damages will be the market price at the time of the breach minus the contract price. The buyer will also recover for incidental and consequential damages as below.

INCIDENTAL DAMAGES: Incidental damages represent the costs associated with the buyer's attempt to cover. For instance, the buyer might incur extra shipping or warehousing costs as a result of trying to replace the original seller's undelivered goods.

# United States v. Seacoast Gas Co.

(The Government) v. (Utility Company)

204 F.2d 709 (5th Cir. 1953), cert. denied, 346 U.S. 866 (1953)

## COURT OF APPEALS REJECTS A REPUDIATING PARTY'S ATTEMPT TO RESCIND ITS REPUDIATION

■ **INSTANT FACTS** A utility company repudiates its agreement with the government and then tries to retract its repudiation.

■ **BLACK LETTER RULE** A party cannot freely retract its repudiation of a contract once the other party has filed suit or given it a limited time to retract.

## ■ PROCEDURAL BASIS

Appeal from a district court judgement in favor of the defendant in a breach of contract action.

## ■ FACTS

Seacoast Gas Co. (Seacoast) (D) had a year long contract to provide gas to a federal housing project. Seacoast (D) repudiated the contract several months into performance, blaming its anticipated cancellation on the United States' (P) breach of contract. It gave the United States (P) a month's notice before the threatened cancellation. The United States (P), in turn, notified Seacoast (P) that it was going to solicit bids from other gas companies. It ultimately received a low bid from the Trion Company. At this point, it gave Seacoast (D) three days to retract its repudiation. If not, the United States (P) would hold it (and its surety) liable for breach of contract. Seacoast (D) did not respond in time and, as a result, the United State's (P) hired the Trion Company in its place. As it happens, Trion and Seacoast (D) had the same president, Zell. He notified the Public Housing Authority that Seacoast (D) was retracting its repudiation. This was not until three days after Trion was hired and two days before Seacoast (D) planned on cancelling its service as threatened. Despite the fact that the United States (P) and Trion had not yet signed their contract, it refused Seacoast's (D) retraction. The United States (P) also sued Seacoast (D) for breach of contract. Seacoast (D) argued that its repudiation was healed before the United States (P) relied on it to its detriment. The district court agreed and found in its favor. The United States (P) appeals, arguing that Seacoast's (D) retraction was too late.

## ■ ISSUE

Can a party retract an anticipatory repudiation if the other party has not changed position in reliance on the repudiation?

## ■ DECISION AND RATIONALE

(Hutcheson) Yes. A party may withdraw its repudiation if the other party has not yet relied on it. However, the other party has the power to finalize the repudiation at will. It may either bring suit for breach of contract, or may notify the guilty party that its repudiation will be final if a retraction is not received within a specified time. Seacoast (D) argues that the United States (P) did not rely on its repudiation because it was retracted before the new utility contract was signed. This is beside the point. The United States had already warned Seacoast (D) that it was soliciting bids and gave it three days to retract its repudiation. At this point, the *locus poenitentiae* for a retraction was reduced from one month, as originally threatened by Seacoast (D), to three days as announced by the United States

(P). This conclusion seems particularly compelling since Seacoast (D) and Trion's mutual president, Zell, was involved in this dispute at all times. The United States (P) repeatedly asked him for a retraction and he repeatedly refused. Zell did not attempt to rectify the situation until just before Trion and the United States (P) were ready to sign their contract. In fact, the signing was delayed because Trion was late in filing its bond. This behavior, coupled with the United States' (P) limitation on the acceptable time for a retraction, justifies our decision. The judgment of the trial court will be reversed and remanded for a judgment in favor of the United States (P).

**Analysis:**

The court lists at least two ways that Seacoast's (D) repudiation might become final. First, the United States (P) might file suit. Second, it might rely on Seacoast's (D) repudiation but give it a chance to retract. However, it was not required to do so in order to preserve Seacoast's (D) liability. If the United States (P) had materially changed position in reliance on the repudiation, it would have become final regardless of whether it notified Seacoast (D). A third option, not mentioned in the case, would be for the United States to ignore the repudiation and hope that Seacoast (D) performed when the time arrived. This is obviously the least desirable option since the United States (P) would be leaving itself open to an eventual breach. In any event, the circumstances of the parties' dispute will help determine the appropriate response to an anticipatory breach of contract. In this case, for instance, the United States (P) was certainly hoping to avoid the uncertainty of a new bidding process and the unpredictability of a new utility provider by giving Seacoast (D) a chance to retract.

**■ CASE VOCABULARY**

LOCUS POENITENTIAE: Literally, a place for repentance. The phrase signifies an opportunity to change one's mind, such as that granted by the United States (P) to Seacoast (D).

# Pittsburgh-Des Moines Steel Co. v. Brookhaven Manor Water Co.

(Steel Company) v. (Water Company)

532 F.2d 572 (7th Cir. 1976)

---

**COURT OF APPEALS REJECTS A PARTY'S REQUEST FOR ASSURANCES OF PERFORMANCE**

---

■ **INSTANT FACTS** A steel company requests assurances of performance from its client when it finds out that the client has failed to qualify for a bank loan.

■ **BLACK LETTER RULE** Under the UCC, a party may not seek assurances of performance from another party unless it has reasonable grounds for insecurity regarding that party's ability to perform.

---

■ **PROCEDURAL BASIS**

Appeal from a district court judgement notwithstanding the verdict, in favor of the defendant in a breach of contract action.

■ **FACTS**

Brookhaven Manor Water Co. (Brookhaven) (D) hired the Pittsburgh-Des Moines Steel Co. (Pittsburgh) (P) to build an elevated water tank. The original agreement called for Brookhaven (D) to make periodic progress payments. However, it renegotiated the contract to call for full payment within 30 days of the project's completion. Thus, Pittsburgh (P) became nervous when it heard that Brookhaven (D) was in the process of applying for a loan. It wrote to the prospective lender and to Brookhaven (D), requesting that $175,000 be put in escrow for the contract. In the meantime, Brookhaven's (D) loan fell through: At this point, Pittsburgh (P) wrote directly to the president of Brookhaven (D), demanding that he personally guarantee Brookhaven's (D) payment. In addition, it now demanded the establishment of an escrow account. The president responded by simply providing Pittsburgh (P) with a statement of his personal worth. Pittsburgh (P) subsequently stopped work on the tank and never completed it. It then sued Brookhaven (D) for breach of contract, claiming that Brookhaven (D) repudiated the agreement by failing to provide the necessary assurances of performance. Brookhaven (D) counterclaimed, alleging that Pittsburgh (P) was the party in breach. Despite a jury verdict in Pittsburgh's (P) favor, the district court entered a judgment notwithstanding the verdict, for Brookhaven (D). Pittsburgh (P) appeals.

■ **ISSUE**

Can a party to a contract seek assurances from the other party when it has reason to doubt that party's ability to perform?

■ **DECISION AND RATIONALE**

(Pell) Yes. Preliminarily, it should be noted that this contract is governed by the UCC as an agreement for the purchase of goods. That said, UCC § 2–609 grants a party to a contract the right to seek assurances of performance from the other party. This request must be made in writing. In addition, there must be reasonable grounds for insecurity before this right can be exercised. In this case, Pittsburgh (P) made its requests in writing—as long as its demands for an escrow account can be interpreted as requests for assurances of performance. The problem is that Pittsburgh (P) did not have reasonable grounds to fear that Brookhaven (D) would be unable to pay the contract price. There is no evidence that Pittsburgh (P) was concerned about Brookhaven's (D) finances at the time of contracting. In fact, it agreed to a change in the contract to more liberal payment terms. In addition, Pittsburgh's (P) credit department had reviewed Brookhaven's (D) credit and saw no change over the period of time taken up by this dispute. Indeed, all of Brookhaven's (D) actions are consistent with ordinary business sense. There was no reason for Brookhaven (D) to rush the initial loan negotiations. It would not want to pay interest on a loan which it did not need for several months. Similarly, Brookhaven's (D) small cash reserves were not unusual for a company in its line of work. Finally, Brookhaven's (D) president would naturally reject any attempt to hold him personally liable for the company's debts. Each of these considerations could have been the subject of contract negotiations but they were not. Pittsburgh (P) cannot now complain that it is reasonably concerned about Brookhaven's (D) financial condition when it ignored the situation at the time of contracting. This is especially true since Brookhaven's (D) condition has not changed markedly since that time. Under the circumstances, it was Pittsburgh (P) who was at fault, and Brookhaven (D) who is entitled to a recovery for anticipatory repudiation. The judgment of the district court is affirmed.

# ■ CONCURRENCE

(Cummings) The majority's conclusion is correct, but for the wrong reasons. Despite the majority's interpretation of UCC § 2–609, it is inappropriate to confine its language to cases where a party has experienced a fundamental change in financial position. Pittsburgh (P) may have had reasonable grounds for insecurity when Brookhaven's (D) loan fell through. Any prudent businessman might have had similar concerns. However, this is a question for the jury. More importantly, Pittsburgh's (P) letters to Brookhaven (D) asked for more than it may have been entitled to under the § 2–609. It is on this ground that I would support the majority's conclusion and the district court's judgment.

## Analysis:

The parties to a contract should draft their agreement so as to avoid the sort of dispute that arose in this case. Pittsburgh (P) made a number of realizations during the course of performance that made it nervous, but that were no different than concerns it should have had during contract negotiations. There is always a struggle when drafting a contract between accounting for every possible eventuality and leaving certain things to chance. This struggle is, in many respects, an economic one. It is too costly and time consuming to draft a perfectly comprehensive agreement. By the same token, the parties to a contract must consider the likely costs of ending up in court because a term that should have been included was left undefined.

# Norcon Power Partners v. Niagara Mohawk Power Corp.

(Electricity Supplier) v. (Electricity Distributor)

92 N.Y.2d 458, 682 N.Y.S.2d 664, 705 N.E.2d 656 (1998)

## NEW YORK ADOPTS UCC RIGHT TO DEMAND "REASONABLE ASSURANCES"

■ **INSTANT FACTS** When an electricity distributor calculated its supplier would owe it $610 million, it demanded reasonable assurances of future payment.

■ **BLACK LETTER RULE** In New York, corporate parties to long-term complex commercial contracts may, upon having reasonable grounds to doubt the other party will fulfill its contractual obligations, demand adequate assurances.

■ **PROCEDURAL BASIS**

In contract action seeking declaration and Injunction, appeal from appellate affirmation of judgement for defendant, on certified question.

■ **FACTS**

Power supplier Norcon Power Partners ("Norcon") (P) agreed to supply electricity to energy retailer Niagara Mohawk Power Corp. ("Niagara Mohawk") (D). Under the 25-year contract, the fee for power varies; in the relevant period, Niagara Mohawk (D) is to pay an "avoided price equal to the price of obtaining electricity from the next-best supplier. Thus, if prevailing electricity prices fall below a specified "floor," Norcon (P) must make payments to Niagara Mohawk's (D) "adjustment account. When prices fell, Niagara Mohawk (D) calculated Norcon (P) would owe $610M, and demanded Norcon (P) provide adequate assurances it would be able to pay. Norcon (P) sued Niagara Mohawk (D), seeking a declaration that Niagara Mohawk (D) had no right to additional assurances, and an injunction to keep it from terminating anticipatorily. Niagara Mohawk (D) countersued for a declaration that its demand for assurances was proper. At trial, the District Court found for Norcon (P), holding that common law allows demand for assurances only when a party becomes insolvent. On appeal, the Second Circuit affirmed preliminarily, but certified the "issue" below to the New York Court of Appeals (since it involved New York law). The Court of Appeals granted certification.

■ **ISSUE**

"Does a party have the right to demand adequate assurance of future performance where [there are reasonable indications] the other party will commit . . . non-performance of a contract governed by New York law, where the other party is solvent and [the UCC is inapplicable]?"

■ **DECISION AND RATIONALE**

(Bellacosa) Yes. In New York, corporate parties to long-term complex commercial contracts may, upon having reasonable grounds to doubt the other party will fulfill its contractual obligations, may demand adequate assurances. At common law, the doctrine of "anticipatory repudiation" provides that, if a party repudiates by word or voluntary affirmative act, the aggrieved party may stop its performance and sue for full damages. But this right is clear only when the breacher's words or deeds are unequivocal. If the repudiation is equivocal, counterparties face a dilemma with hard choices and serious consequences: if they terminate and sue prematurely, they are in breach, but if they continue performance, they may be denied recovery for failure to mitigate damages after repudiation. To avoid such uncertainty, the law created the right to demand adequate assurances. Under the UCC, if parties to a contract for the sale of goods have "reasonable grounds for insecurity," they may demand assurances of future performance. If adequate assurances are not forthcoming, the party withholding them is deemed to admit repudiation, and the nonbreacher may act accordingly. UCC 2–609. This UCC policy is so effective at encouraging certainty that many states adopted similar policies into their common law. Restatement 2d of Contracts § 251. Commentators have approved, noting the policy is equally applicable to non-goods contracts. Until now, New York's common law has not expanded the right to demand assurances, unless the contract is governed by the UCC, or unless a contractual party becomes insolvent. While we are reluctant to alter our state common law suddenly and sweepingly by applying the UCC approach to all contracts, we now permit requests for reasonable assurances in long-term commercial contracts between corporations, where the contract is so complex it cannot realistically specify all anticipated security features, and where a party has reasonable grounds for insecurity. We need not decide how this answer to the certified question applies here.

### Analysis:

The Court of Appeals is technically correct, it need only answer the certified question of law in the abstract, and need not actually resolve the dispute. *Norcon* indicates that the Restatement urges states to adopt similar policies for non-goods contracts at common law, and most states have done so. With *Norcon,* New York adopted this policy, at least for commercial long-term contracts. Unfortunately, even the "reasonable assurances" policy is not a panacea, since the doctrine is subject to *some* of the same uncertainties that plague the "was that really a repudiation?" decision. The demand for *assurances* is not merely a demand for unsecured promises; usually, parties demand "assurances by requiring additional collateral or contractual obligations, *which imposes additional costs* or *liabilities'* on one contractual party. Thus, demanding such assurances at an unreasonable time, or demanding concessions to an unreasonable extent, may itself constitute a repudiation.

### ■ CASE VOCABULARY

INSOLVENT: Unable to make payments when due. This does not necessarily imply the insolvent party has more liabilities than assets, or has formally declared bankruptcy.

# CHAPTER NINE

## Third Party Beneficiaries

### Stees v. Leonard

**Instant Facts:** Stees (P) contracted with Leonard (D) to complete a building on Sees's (P) lot, but because the ground was composed of quicksand, Leonard (D) refused to complete the contract.

**Black Letter Rule:** If a person binds himself to a contract, mistake is no reason for rescission, and nothing short of "absolute impossibility" will excuse that party from fulfilling his duties.

### Renner v. Kehl

**Instant Facts:** A purchaser of real estate leases sought to rescind the sales contract on the ground that, although the parties were under the belief that the land was suitable for farming, the water wells on the land proved inadequate.

**Black Letter Rule:** A party who rescinds a contract based on mutual mistake is not entitled to recover consequential damages.

### Mineral Park Land Co. v. Howard

**Instant Facts:** Mineral Park (P) contracted with Howard (D) for Howard (D) to buy as much gravel from Mineral Park (P) as Howard (D) would need to build a bridge.

**Black Letter Rule:** Even though there is an existing impracticality, as opposed to a supervening one, at the time of entering the contract, the court can excuse a buyer from his duties if he can't perform them in an ordinary manner and without paying prohibitive cost.

### Taylor v. Caldwell

**Instant Facts:** Taylor (P) entered into a contract with Caldwell (D) to rent Caldwell's (D's) music hall, but the music hall burned down before Taylor (P) could use it.

**Black Letter Rule:** A promisor is excused from contract performance if such performance is made impractical because the subject matter of the contract is destroyed prior to such performance and the promisor wasn't responsible for such destruction.

### Transatlantic Financing Corporation v. United States

**Instant Facts:** Transatlantic (P) contracted with the United States (D) to deliver cargo to Iran, but contrary to usual practice, it sailed around the Cape of Good Hope instead of the Suez Canal.

**Black Letter Rule:** A court won't grant a party additional costs other than that agreed in the contract if the party relies on a theory of quantum meruit (under this equitable doctrine, the court will imply a promise to pay for labor and goods if a party stands to unjustly enrich himself on the labor and gods of another) and the party cannot show that its contract performance was impractical.

### Selland Pontiac-GMC, Inc. v. King

**Instant Facts:** A company which contracted to buy bodies for several school busses brought an action for breach of contract, claiming that the seller was not excused from performance simply because its supplier went into receivership and ceased to continue manufacturing the bodies.

**Black Letter Rule:** A seller's duty to perform under a contract may be excused when unexpected events render the seller unable to obtain supplies from a source expressly identified in the contract.

### Canadian Industrial Alcohol Co. v. Dunbar Molasses Co.

**Instant Facts:** Canadian (P) entered a contract with Dunbar (D) to purchase a supply of Dunbar's (D's) molasses, but Dunbar (D) failed to deliver the agreed amount because the sugar company didn't produce enough sugar to supply Dunbar (D).

**Black Letter Rule:** If a seller fails to take all due precautions to ensure a steady supply of raw materials to complete his goods, then the court will not excuse his performance when such raw materials run out.

### Eastern Air Lines, Inc. v. Gulf Oil Corporation

**Instant Facts:** In the midst of an oil embargo, Gulf Oil attempts to get out of its requirements contract with Eastern Air claiming the increased cost of oil made performance impracticable.

**Black Letter Rule:** The party seeking to establish commercial impracticality bears the burden to show that the events causing impracticality were not foreseeable and that the cost increase complained of was unjust.

### Krell v. Henry

**Instant Facts:** Krell (P) rented a room in his hotel to Henry (D) and both believed that the room would be used to watch the King's coronation.

**Black Letter Rule:** Even though performance isn't Impractical, a court can still excuse performance on the basis of frustration of purpose as long as there is a non-existence of events which both parties considered as the foundation of the contract.

### Swift Canadian Co. v. Banet

**Instant Facts:** Banet (D) contracted with Swift (P) to buy lamb pelts from Swift (P) but a government regulation prevented their importation into America.

**Black Letter Rule:** A buyer cannot claim frustration of purpose—and thus be excused from performance—even if a supervening event prevents him from receiving his goods, as long as a free on board term (F.O.B.) allows the seller to complete his duties simply by delivering the goods to a carrier, and the seller then actually delivers the goods to that carrier.

### Chase Precast Corp. v. John J. Paonessa Co.

**Instant Facts:** Chase (P) contracted with Paonessa (D) to supply concrete dividers but a supervening event obviated the need for Paonessa (D) to buy more dividers from Chase (P).

**Black Letter Rule:** A court can excuse performance on the basis of frustration of purpose only if the contract didn't allocate to one of the parties the risk of a supervening event.

### Northern Indiana Public Service Co. v. Carbon County Coal Co.

**Instant Facts:** Northern Indiana Public Service Company (P) (NIPSCO) entered a contract with Carbon (D) which was a long-term contract that didn't allow NIPSCO (P) to renegotiate its terms.

**Black Letter Rule:** Even though there is a force majeure clause (a clause which lists certain events that are beyond the control of the parties and thus excuses performance), a party has assumed the risks for market fluctuations if that party has agreed to a fixed-priced contract.

### Young v. City of Chicopee

**Instant Facts:** Young (P) contracted with Chicopee (D) to repair Chicopee's bridge, but a fire burned and destroyed the bridge.

**Black Letter Rule:** If a supervening event renders performance impractical for a repair contract, the owner must compensate the repairer only to the extent of actual repair done on the owner's property.

# Stees v. Leonard

(Lot Owner) v. (Construction Company Owner)

20 Minn. 494, 20 Gil. 448 (1874)

PARTIES TO A CONTRACT ARE BOUND TO COMPLY WITH THE TERMS UNLESS IT IS ABSOLUTELY IMPOSSIBLE TO PERFORM

■ **INSTANT FACTS** Stees (P) contracted with Leonard (D) to complete a building on Sees's (P) lot, but because the ground was composed of quicksand, Leonard (D) refused to complete the contract.

■ **BLACK LETTER RULE** If a person binds himself to a contract, mistake is no reason for rescission, and nothing short of "absolute impossibility" will excuse that party from fulfilling his duties.

■ **PROCEDURAL BASIS**

Appeal from judgment in favor of Stees (P) on an action for negligence.

■ **FACTS**

Stees (P) contracted with Leonard (D) to complete a building on Sees' (P's) lot. But Leonard (D) refused to complete the building because he (D) discovered that the ground was composed of quicksand.

■ **ISSUE**

May a party refuse to fulfill his contractual duties because of a mistake of fact?

■ **DECISION AND RATIONALE**

(Young) No. If a person binds himself to a contract, nothing short of "absolute impossibility" will excuse that party from fulfilling his duties. In this case, Leonard (D) discovered a mistake of fact when he discovered after making the contract that the ground was composed of quicksand. However, because Leonard (D) promised Stees (P) that he (D) would fulfill his duties, Leonard must use all necessary means to overcome this problem. Leonard (D), for example, can use stronger footings or even drain the land. Either way, Leonard (D) must fulfill his contractual promise because there isn't any "absolute impossibility" preventing him. Judgment affirmed.

**Analysis:**

Is the court in *Stees* being unfair? Think about policy. On the one hand, the law of contracts, like law in general, encourages predictability. When people sign a contract, they should feel confident that promises will be fulfilled. Is the standard of "absolute impossibility too high? Consider what might be a possible result if Stees (P), and not Leonard (D), had specified all the material provisions, including for the foundation. If Leonard (D) fails to complete his duties, should the court refuse to excuse him? Isn't Stees (P) responsible for having drafted inaccurately? In *United States v. Spearin*, 248 U.S. 132, 136–37 (1918), the Court stated that, although "one who undertakes to erect a structure upon a particular site, assumes ordinarily the risk of subsidence of the soil," nevertheless, "if the contractor is bound to build according to plans and specifications prepared by the owner, the contractor will not be responsible for the consequences and defects in the plans and specifications.''

## ■ CASE VOCABULARY

MISTAKE: According to the Restatement Second § 151, a ''mistake'' in contract law occurs when a party's beliefs contradict the facts.

PAROL AGREEMENT: An oral or verbal agreement outside of the written contract itself.

# Renner v. Kehl

(Jojoba Farmer) v. (Seller of Land)
150 Ariz. 94, 722 P.2d 262 (1986)

A CONTRACT MAY BE RESCINDED IF THE PARTIES WERE BOTH MISTAKEN AS TO A BASIC ASSUMPTION UPON WHICH THE CONTRACT WAS FORMED

■ **INSTANT FACTS** A purchaser of real estate leases sought to rescind the sales contract on the ground that, although the parties were under the belief that the land was suitable for farming, the water wells on the land proved inadequate.

■ **BLACK LETTER RULE** A party who rescinds a contract based on mutual mistake is not entitled to recover consequential damages.

## ■ PROCEDURAL BASIS

Appeal to the Supreme Court of Arizona to review the decision of the appellate court affirming the judgment of the trial court, which rescinded a real estate contract on the ground of mutual mistake.

## ■ FACTS

The Kehls (D) and Moyles (D) sold to Roy Renner (P) certain leases of unimproved land for about $100 per acre for over two thousand acres. Renner (P) had made dear to the Kehls (D) and Moyles (D) that he was interested in the land only for the cultivation of jojoba and that he required adequate supply of water for that purpose. After making a down payment, taking the conveyance and undertaking some test drills, Renner (P) abandoned the project due to an insufficient supply of water. Renner (P) brought an action to rescind the sales contract on the ground of mutual mistake of the parties. After finding that the sale would not have taken place if the parties involved did not believe the land was suitable for commercial cultivation of jojoba, the trial court concluded that Renner (P) was entitled to a rescission of the contract. The trial court ordered the Kehls (D) and Moyles (D) to reimburse Renner (P) the amount of the down payment and the expenses incurred in developing the land and conducting drilling tests. The court of appeals affirmed.

## ■ ISSUE

When seeking to rescind a contract on the basis of mutual mistake is a party entitled to recover consequential damages?

## ■ DECISION AND RATIONALE

(Gordon, V.C.J.) No. A party who rescinds a contract based on mutual mistake is not entitled to recover consequential damages. Since both parties were mistaken as to a basic assumption upon which the contract was based - i.e. that the land contained a suitable quantity of water - the contract was voidable and Renner (P) was entitled to a rescission. However, mutual mistake implies freedom of fault on the part of both parties. Thus, the trial court improperly awarded Renner (P) the full cost of his expenses. When a party rescinds a contract in the absence of fraud or misrepresentation, he is entitled only to restitution for any benefit conferred on the other party by way of part performance or reliance. In this case, Renner (P) was entitled to the down payment and the value of any improvements made to the land. However, the Kehls (D) and Moyles (D) were entitled to the fair rental value of their land during the time it was occupied by Renner (P). Additionally, Renner (P) is not entitled to development expenses because that would shift the entire risk of mistake onto the Kehls (D) and Moyles (D), an allocation of risk which is incompatible with equitable rescission.

### Analysis:

Traditionally, the analysis employed by courts confronted with a case of mutual mistake involved an abstract inquiry into whether the mistake involved the substance of the contract or a only a quality or value thereof. The court here holds that rescission is proper where the parties' mistake concerns "a basic assumption" upon which the contract was formed. The "basic assumption" formulation used in the Second Restatement is the more modern approach. After a court determines that the parties have made a mistake as to a basic assumption of fact, the court should go on to ask which party is in the best position to bear the risk. However, the court here appears to assume that the sellers bore the risk. This assumption may be questioned in light of two facts. First, because Renner (P) was the person proposing the farming, he was in the best position to determine which land was most suitable for his needs. The second, and most important, fact that leads to a conclusion that Renner (P) should have borne the risk was that he conducted the water drilling test after purchasing the land. If Renner (P) wanted to assure himself of the quality of the land, he should have made the purchase contingent on the tests providing satisfactory results.

### ■ CASE VOCABULARY

JOJOBA: An evergreen shrub (pronounced "ho *ho* buh").

MUTUAL MISTAKE: Courts will excuse a party's contractual obligation where the parties entered into a contract on mistaken assumption as to a basic fact.

RESCISSION: A contractual remedy where courts nullify a contract.

# Mineral Park Land Co. v. Howard

(Gravel Owner) v. (Gravel Purchaser)

172 Cal. 289, 156 P. 458 (1916)

## AN IMPRACTICALITY EXISTING AT THE TIME A CONTRACT IS MADE MAY EXCUSE PERFORMANCE

■ **INSTANT FACTS** Mineral Park (P) contracted with Howard (D) for Howard (D) to buy as much gravel from Mineral Park (P) as Howard (D) would need to build a bridge.

■ **BLACK LETTER RULE** Even though there is an existing impracticality, as opposed to a supervening one, at the time of entering the contract, the court can excuse a buyer from his duties if he can't perform them in an ordinary manner and without paying prohibitive cost.

■ **PROCEDURAL BASIS**

Appeal from judgment on an action for breach of contract.

■ **FACTS**

Mineral Park (P) contracted with Howard (D) for Howard (D) to buy as much gravel from Mineral Park (P) as Howard (D) would need to build a bridge. But Howard (D) discovered that only a certain amount of Mineral Park's (P) gravel was above water. Because getting the underwater gravel would be too much trouble. Howard (D) decided to buy the rest of the gravel from someone else. Mineral Park (P) claims that Howard (D) breached the contract.

■ **ISSUE**

Even though there is an existing impracticality, as opposed to a supervening one, at the time of entering the contract, can the court excuse a buyer from his duties if he can't perform them in an ordinary manner and without paying prohibitive cost?

■ **DECISION AND RATIONALE**

(Sloss) Yes. Even though there is an existing impracticality, as opposed to a supervening one, at the time of entering the contract, the court can excuse a buyer from his duties if he can't perform them in an ordinary manner and without paying prohibitive cost. Here, the impracticality existed at the time Mineral Park (P) and Howard (D) entered the contract: Some of the gravel was already underwater. Howard (D) couldn't remove the underwater gravel by resorting to ordinary means and without paying prohibitive costs. The difference in cost between using Mineral Park's (P) underwater gravel and someone else's gravel is so high that forcing Howard (D) to do so would be impractical. Judgment reversed.

**Analysis:**

In *Mineral Park*, the court stressed the differences in costs in deciding to excuse the buyer, Howard (D). In fact, it seems to be the only justification for excusing performance on the basis of impracticality. But for impracticality cases in general, courts very rarely rely on price differentials to excuse performance. Another thing to consider with regard to *Mineral Park* is the difference between supervening impracticality and existing impracticality. Supervening impracticality occurs when an event occurs after two parties enter into contract. But an existing impracticality already exists even before the parties enter the contract. A party arguing existing impracticality may also have a claim of mistake. The two doctrines are similar. For the doctrine of mutual mistake, a court is likely to consider the effect upon both parties in deciding to enforce performance. But for impracticality, the court tends to concentrate only on the burdens of the party that must perform.

### ■ CASE VOCABULARY

PROHIBITIVE COST: An unreasonably high cost.

REQUISITE QUANTITY: The amount of stuff that the buyer agreed to purchase.

# Taylor v. Caldwell

(Renter of Music Hall) v. (Music Hall Owner)

3 B. & S. 826, 122 Eng.Rep. 309 (1863)

A COURT WILL EXCUSE CONTRACT PERFORMANCE IF THE SUBJECT OF SUCH PERFORMANCE IS IMPRACTICAL

■ **INSTANT FACTS** Taylor (P) entered into a contract with Caldwell (D) to rent Caldwell's (D's) music hall, but the music hall burned down before Taylor (P) could use it.

■ **BLACK LETTER RULE** A promisor is excused from contract performance if such performance is made impractical because the subject matter of the contract is destroyed prior to such performance and the promisor wasn't responsible for such destruction.

## ■ PROCEDURAL BASIS

Appeal from judgment in favor of Caldwell (D) on an action for breach of contract.

## ■ FACTS

Taylor (P) entered a contract with Caldwell (D) to rent Caldwell's (D) music hall, but the music hall burned down before Taylor (P) could use it. Neither party was responsible for having burned down the hall. Taylor (P) claimed that he had spent money advertising his music hall concerts and also for preparing for the concerts. Taylor (P) wanted Caldwell (D) to reimburse him for such costs now that the concerts were made impossible. Taylor (P) claimed that Caldwell (D) breached his contract duties in failing to provide a music hall as promised.

## ■ ISSUE

Is a party excused from contract performance if such performance is made impractical because the subject matter of the contract is destroyed prior to such performance and neither party was responsible for such destruction?

## ■ DECISION AND RATIONALE

(Blackburn) Yes. The promisor is excused from contract performance if such performance is made impractical because the subject matter of the contract is destroyed prior to such performance and the promisor wasn't responsible for such destruction. We will imply that such an exception exists even though the contract itself says nothing explicitly about what to do in the event that the subject matter of the contract is destroyed. Here, the subject matter of the contract was the music hall. And because it was burned down, the subject matter was destroyed. Neither party was responsible for burning down the building. Thus, both parties are excused from their contract performances. Judgment affirmed.

---

**Analysis:**

In *Stees,* the court stated that a party won't be excused from performance unless there's "absolute impossibility." However, in *Taylor*, the court stated a party will be excused from performance if such performance is made "impractical." According to the Uniform Commercial Code, impracticability is a defense for performance in the sale of goods (UCC § 2–215). Moreover, today courts tend to adopt the impracticability test for contract cases in general. UCC § 2–613 states: A seller is excused from his duty if "the contract requires for its performance goods identified before the contract is made, and the goods suffer casualty without fault of either party before the risk of loss passes to the buyer." Would *Stees* come out differently under the UCC?

## ■ CASE VOCABULARY

BAILEE: This is the person who accepts the goods in a bailment.

BAILMENT: A type of delivery of property where the acceptee promises to use the property for a particular purpose as explained by the owner. After using the property, the acceptor must deliver the property back to the owner or use it in a manner told to him by the owner.

CHATTEL: Personal property, not real property.

# Transatlantic Financing Corporation v. United States

(Ship Operator) v. (Cargo Owner)

363 F.2d 312 (D.C. Cir. 1966)

UNDER A THEORY OF QUANTUM MERUIT A COURT WILL NOT GRANT ADDITIONAL EXPENSES OVER AND ABOVE WHAT WAS AGREED TO IN A CONTRACT

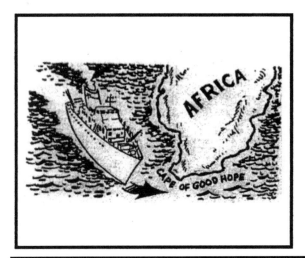

■ **INSTANT FACTS** Transatlantic (P) contracted with the United States (D) to deliver cargo to Iran, but contrary to usual practice, it sailed around the Cape of Good Hope instead of the Suez Canal.

■ **BLACK LETTER RULE** A court won't grant a party additional costs other than that agreed in the contract if the party relies on a theory of quantum meruit (under this equitable doctrine, the court will imply a promise to pay for labor and goods if a party stands to unjustly enrich himself on the labor and gods of another) and the party cannot show that its contract performance was impractical.

■ **PROCEDURAL BASIS**

Appeal from dismissal of a libel (in admiralty law, this used to be the equivalent of a complaint) on an action for quantum meruit resulting from impracticability.

■ **FACTS**

Transatlantic (P) contracted with the United States (D) to deliver cargo to Iran. Both parties intended that Transatlantic (P) would go through the Suez Canal. But because of military unrest, this wasn't an option. So Transatlantic (P) sailed around the much longer route of the Cape of Good Hope. The United States (D) never promised Transatlantic (P) that it (D) would reimburse Transatlantic (P) for the extra costs of going around the Cape. Transatlantic (P) safely delivered the cargo to Iran. The United States (D) paid Transatlantic (P) the contract price. Transatlantic (P) then demanded that the United States (D) reimburse Transatlantic (P) for the extra costs of having to go around the Cape instead of through the Suez.

■ **ISSUE**

Will a court grant a party additional costs other than that agreed in the contract if the party relies on a theory of quantum meruit and the party cannot show that its contract performance was Impractical?

■ **DECISION AND RATIONALE**

(Wright) No. A court won't grant a party additional costs other than that agreed in the contract if the party relies on a theory of quantum meruit and the party cannot show that its contract performance was impractical. Here, Transatlantic (P) relied on a theory of quantum meruit in order to collect the additional cost of going around the Cape. Was Transatlantic (P) able to show that its contract performance was impracticable? To be impracticable, all three of the following conditions must be met: 1) something unexpected must have occurred; 2) the risk of the unexpected occurrence must not have been allocated either by agreement or by custom; and 3) occurrence of the unexpected event must have rendered performance commercially impracticable. Here, the first requirement was met when the Suez was blocked off because of political unrest. The second requirement wasn't met. Transatlantic (P) assumed the risk. Transatlantic (P) like most commercial shippers knew that the Suez could become a dangerous place. It (P) nonetheless entered the contract. The third requirement wasn't met either. Transatlantic's (P) performance wasn't commercially impractical. Transatlantic (P) was financially and physically able to sail around the Cape without problems. This is a generally used alternative course on which ships rely if the Suez is blocked. Granted, Transatlantic (P) incurred extra expenses of $43,972 beyond the contract price. Still, to show impracticability, there must be a greater difference between the contract price and the actual costs incurred to perform the duties. Thus, Transatlantic (P) wasn't faced with impracticability, and accordingly, it (P) can't receive through the theory of quantum meruit any additional costs incurred outside of the contract price.

### Analysis:

*Transatlantic* focuses on the issue of foreseeability. Citing Uniform Commercial Code § 2–615, the court stated that foreseeability alone doesn't necessarily mean that a party has assumed the risks. However, it is one factor that the court will consider in deciding whether there was legal impossibility. Consider the Restatement (Second), Introductory Note to Chapter 11: "The fact that the event was unforeseeable is significant as suggesting that its nonoccurrence was a basic assumption. However, the fact that it was foreseeable, or even foreseen, does not, of itself, argue for a contrary conclusion, since the parties may not have thought it sufficiently important a risk to have made it a subject of their bargaining."

### ■ CASE VOCABULARY

LIBEL: In admiralty law, this used to be the equivalent of a complaint.

QUANTUM MERUIT: Under this equitable doctrine, the court will imply a promise to pay for labor and goods if a party stands to unjustly enrich himself on the labor and goods of another.

# Selland Pontiac-GMC, Inc. v. King

(Buyer) v. (Seller of School Bus Bodies)

384 N.W.2d 490 (Minn. App. 1986)

---

IN DECIDING A CASE OF IMPRACTICABILITY, SOME COURTS WILL FOCUS ON THE LANGUAGE OF THE CONTRACT TO DETERMINE WHETHER THE RISK WAS SOMEHOW ALLOCATED TO EITHER PARTY

---

■ **INSTANT FACTS** A company which contracted to buy bodies for several school busses brought an action for breach of contract, claiming that the seller was not excused from performance simply because its supplier went into receivership and ceased to continue manufacturing the bodies.

■ **BLACK LETTER RULE** A seller's duty to perform under a contract may be excused when unexpected events render the seller unable to obtain supplies from a source expressly identified in the contract.

---

■ **PROCEDURAL BASIS**

Appeal to the Minnesota Court of Appeals to review the decision of the trial court denying the plaintiff's motion of a new trial and/or amended findings of fact and conclusions of law.

■ **FACTS**

In May of 1983, Selland Pontiac-GMC, Inc. (Selland) (P) contracted to buy four school bus bodies from King (D). The contract expressly stated that the bodies were to be manufactured by Superior Manufacturing (Superior). The contract contained no clause which excused King's performance should he no longer have a viable supply. In reliance on the contract with King (D), Selland (P) purchased four chassis upon which the bodies were to be built. In early July, Superior went into receivership. Although the parties disputed their respective reactions to the news of Superior's condition, the trial court found that Selland (P) decided to wait and see if Superior would come out of receivership. Superior never fully recovered. In December, Selland (P) canceled their order and sold the chassis at a loss.

■ **ISSUE**

May a seller's contractual obligation be excused if his source of supply terminates even if the contract does not provide for that contingency?

■ **DECISION AND RATIONALE**

(Randall, J.) Yes. A seller's duty to perform under a contract may be excused when unexpected events render the seller unable to obtain supplies from a source expressly identified in the contract. Section 2-615(a) of the U.C.C. provides, in pertinent part, that a seller is not in breach of his duty to sell if "performance as agreed has been made impracticable by the occurrence of a contingency the non-occurrence of which was a basic assumption on which the contract was made...." The trial court found that the contract between Selland (P) and King (D) expressly identified Superior as King's (D) supplier and that the bodies were to be manufactured by Superior. Accordingly, the supply of bus bodies made by Superior was a basic assumption upon which the contract was made. The supply of

Superior bodies became impracticable when Superior ceased manufacturing. Although § 2-615(c) goes on to require the seller to give notice of non-delivery, Selland (P) canceled the contract before such notice could be given. Thus, Selland (P) cannot avoid its loss by claiming it did not receive notice as required by statute.

## Analysis:

As judicial adherence to the requirement of physical impossibility began to wane, courts developed the doctrine of impracticability, which has been adopted by the U.C.C. and the Restatement impracticability has changed the objective, albeit often harsh, rule of impossibility into a subjective analysis with few guiding principles. Under the impracticability standard, some courts choose to focus on how closely the facts come to the common law categories of excusable cases. Other courts, however, undertake an equitable weighing of the hardships to determine which party should bear the loss. This court adopts yet a third common approach, which focuses on the language of the contract to determine if the risk of impracticability was allocated in some fashion. Although most courts do not excuse performance on the basis of a loss of a supplier, the court here found that because. Superior was expressly mentioned in the contract, the risk of loss was allocated to Selland (P).

## ■ CASE VOCABULARY

IMPRACTICABILITY: A doctrine courts use to excuse a party's performance under a contract when an unexpected event makes such performance impossible or extremely difficult.

# Canadian Industrial Alcohol Co. v. Dunbar Molasses Co.

(Buyer of Molasses) v. (Seller of Molasses)

258 N.Y. 194, 179 N.E. 383 (1932)

## A COURT WON'T EXCUSE CONTRACT PERFORMANCE IF THE SELLER FAILS TO TAKE REASONABLE MEASURES TO ASSURE PERFORMANCE

■ **INSTANT FACTS** Canadian (P) entered a contract with Dunbar (D) to purchase a supply of Dunbar's (D's) molasses, but Dunbar (D) failed to deliver the agreed amount because the sugar company didn't produce enough sugar to supply Dunbar (D).

■ **BLACK LETTER RULE** If a seller fails to take all due precautions to ensure a steady supply of raw materials to complete his goods, then the court will not excuse his performance when such raw materials run out.

■ **PROCEDURAL BASIS**

Appeal from judgment for Canadian (P) on an action for breach of contract.

■ **FACTS**

Canadian (P) entered into a contract with Dunbar (D) to purchase a supply of Dunbar's (D's) molasses, but Dunbar (D) failed to deliver the agreed amount because the sugar company didn't produce enough sugar to supply Dunbar (D). Dunbar (D) never made nor attempted to make a contract with the sugar company.

■ **ISSUE**

If a seller fails to take all due precautions to ensure a steady supply of raw materials, will the court excuse his performance when such raw materials run out?

■ **DECISION AND RATIONALE**

(Cardozo) No. If a seller fails to take all due precautions to ensure a steady supply of raw materials to complete his goods, then the court will not excuse his performance when such raw materials run out. Here, Dunbar (D) never made a contract with the sugar company to ensure a steady stream of raw materials that were necessary to make the molasses. Furthermore, Dunbar (D) never even tried to make such a contract. Such a contract would've helped to avoid the damages suffered by Canadian (P). Judgment affirmed.

**Analysis:**

The UCC states that a seller's performance is excused if (1) the buyer and seller considered the supplier of raw materials as being the exclusive supplier of such materials; and (2) the seller has taken all due precautions to make sure that the supply of raw materials will be sufficient. Do you think the court would've changed its mind had it known that Dunbar (D) had a long-lasting relationship with the sugar company, such that Dunbar (D) had always received a sufficient and steady supply of sugar? Perhaps

Dunbar (D) naturally and perhaps even reasonably assumed that it (D) would again receive the same, dependable service without having to bother with a contract. Consider how to balance ideas of fairness with the law's general emphasis on predictability.

### ■ CASE VOCABULARY

ALEATORY ELEMENT: This means the existence of uncertainty or fortuitous events.

CONTRIBUTORY FAULT: This means that plaintiff was partly at fault for his own injuries or damages.

IMPLIED TERM: This is a term of a contract but it is not made explicit in the contract; nonetheless, it still exists.

# Eastern Air Lines, Inc. v. Gulf Oil Corporation

(Airline) v. (Fuel Supplier)

415 F.Supp. 429 (S.D. Fla. 1975)

THOSE WHO ASSERT THE DEFENSE OF COMMERCIAL IMPRACTICALITY BEAR THE BURDEN OF SHOWING THAT THE CIRCUMSTANCES ARE UNJUST AND UNFORESEEABLE

■ **INSTANT FACTS** In the midst of an oil embargo, Gulf Oil attempts to get out of its requirements contract with Eastern Air claiming the increased cost of oil made performance impracticable.

■ **BLACK LETTER RULE** The party seeking to establish commercial impracticality bears the burden to show that the events causing impracticality were not foreseeable and that the cost increase complained of was unjust.

■ **PROCEDURAL BASIS**

Judgment of district court in breach of contract action, following entry of a preliminary injunction against defendant.

■ **FACTS**

Please see facts as summarized on page 19 of this book.

■ **ISSUE**

May a seller be excused from supplying goods under a requirements contract when the cost of raw materials to the seller dramatically increases to the point where the seller claims the contract is no longer profitable?

■ **DECISION AND RATIONALE**

(King) No. To excuse a seller from performing a contract because costs have unforeseeably increased, the unforeseen costs "must be more than merely onerous or expensive. It must be positively unjust to hold the parties bound." A mere showing of unprofitability, without more, will not excuse the performance of a contract. Gulf (D) contends that the escalator indicator did not work as intended by the parties because of the advent of the two-tier pricing of government controls. It also argues that crude oil prices increased substantially without a similar rise in the pricing indicator. But, the language of the contract is clear and unambiguous. It is clear that the parties intended to be bound by the specified entries in *Platt's* which has been published at all times material here, and which is still published. With regard to Gulf's contention that the contract has become "commercially impracticable" within the meaning of U.C.C. § 2–615 because of the increase of the market price of foreign crude oil, the court finds that the tendered defense has not been proved. On this record the court cannot determine how much it costs Gulf (D) to produce a gallon of jet fuel for sale to Eastern, whether Gulf (D) loses money or makes a profit on its sale of jet fuel to Eastern, either now or at the inception of the contract, or at any time in between. The party undertaking the burden of establishing "commercial impracticability" by reason of allegedly increased raw material costs undertakes the obligation of showing the extent to which he has suffered, or will suffer, losses in performing his contract. The record here does not substantiate Gulf's contention on this fundamental issue. Gulf (D) transfers oil from one subsidiary to another. Each of the various subsidiaries charges the buyer subsidiary different prices. As a result, Gulf (D) is able to shift the tax consequences of the profits it earns from one subsidiary to another. But because of the use of such accounting practices, it is impossible to determine Gulf's actual costs for fuel sold to Eastern. This is especially true in light of the fact that Gulf (D) earned substantial profits during the periods in question. Under no theory of law can it be held that Gulf (D) is guaranteed preservation of its intra-company profits. The burden is upon Gulf (D) to show what its real costs are, not its "costs" inflated by its internal profits at various levels of the manufacturing process. But, even if Gulf (D) had established great hardship under U.C.C. § 2–615, which it has not, Gulf (D) would not prevail because the events associated with the so-called energy crisis were reasonably foreseeable at the time the contract was executed. If a contingency is foreseeable, it and its consequences are taken outside the scope of U.C.C. § 2–615 because the party disadvantaged by fruition of the contingency might have protected himself in his contract. The record is replete with evidence of the volatile situation in the Middle East, and Gulf (D) assumed the risk that the OPEC nations would do exactly what they have done. With respect to Gulf's argument that "two-tier" was not "foreseeable," the record shows that domestic crude oil prices were controlled at all material times, that Gulf (D) foresaw that they might be de-controlled, and that Gulf (D) was constantly urging the Government that they should be de-controlled.

### Analysis:

A mere increase in the expense of performing does not give rise to a defense of impossibility. Consider an official comment to the UCC, which states that "increased cost alone does not excuse performance unless the rise in cost is due to some unforseen contingency which *alters the essential nature of performance.*" It goes on to say that "a severe shortage of raw materials or of supplies due to a contingency such as war, embargo, local crop failure, unforseen shutdown of major sources of supply or the like, which causes a marked increase in cost is within the contemplation of this section." On the surface, it seems that Gulf's (D) position fell squarely within the contemplation of the UCC and it was entitled to the defense. Ultimately, however, Gulf (D) lost because of a failure of proof; it could not prove its increased cost to supply Eastern (P). Moreover, due to its own efforts to alter price controls, the court decided that the risk of a change in such controls was foreseeable by Gulf (D) and, accordingly, should have been addressed in the contract. The law was on Gulf's (D) side; the facts were not.

### ■ CASE VOCABULARY

U.C.C. § 2–615 (in pertinent part): "Except so far as a seller may have assumed a greater obligation .... (a) Delay in delivery or non-delivery in whole or in part by a seller ... is not a breach of his duty under a contract for sale if performance as agreed has become impracticable by the occurrence of a contingency the non-occurrence of which was a basic assumption on which the contract was made ...."

# Krell v. Henry

(Hotel Owner) v. (Hotel Renter)

2 K.B. 740 (1903)

## A COURT CAN EXCUSE PERFORMANCE EVEN THOUGH IT'S NOT IMPRACTICAL BUT MERELY DUE TO FRUSTRATION OF PURPOSE

■ **INSTANT FACTS** Krell (P) rented a room in his hotel to Henry (D) and both believed that the room would be used to watch the King's coronation.

■ **BLACK LETTER RULE** Even though performance isn't Impractical, a court can still excuse performance on the basis of frustration of purpose as long as there is a non-existence of events which both parties considered as the foundation of the contract.

■ **PROCEDURAL BASIS**

Appeal from judgment for a breach of contract.

■ **FACTS**

Krell (P) announced on his window that his hotel would rent rooms to see the King's coronation. Henry (D) saw this written announcement and paid Krell (P) a deposit in advance for those days when the King would have his coronation ceremony. But the King got really sick, and the ceremonies were canceled. Krell (P) demanded the balance of the hotel rent- Henry (D) refused. Krell (P) claimed breach of contract.

■ **ISSUE**

Even though performance isn't impractical, can a court still excuse performance on the basis of frustration of purpose as long as there is a non-existence of events which both parties considered as the foundation of the contract?

■ **DECISION AND RATIONALE**

(Vaughn Williams) Yes. Even though performance isn't impractical, a court can still excuse performance on the basis of frustration of purpose as long as there is a non-existence of events which both parties considered as the foundation of the contract. Here, performance wasn't impractical. Nothing in the written contract stated that the room was rented to view the coronation. Thus, Henry (D) could still use the room even though the coronation didn't occur. But the purpose of renting the room was frustrated because the coronation was canceled. moreover, both Krell (P) and Henry (D) had assumed that the coronation was the foundation of the contract. Without the coronation, there was no purpose for Henry (D) to have rented the room, and as evidenced by his (P) announcement of the event, Krell (P) knew it. Appeal dismissed.

**Analysis:**

The Uniform Commercial Code hasn't explicitly recognized the doctrine of frustration. However, most American courts, like the English court in *Krell* have adopted the doctrine of frustration. The first and second Restatements have also adopted it. The Restatement lists four requirements to show frustration of purpose: (1) the event must have substantially frustrated the party's main purpose; (2) the nonoccurrence of the event must have been a basic assumption of the contract; (3) the frustration must not have occurred by the party seeking to be excused; and (4) the party seeking excuse must not have assumed a greater obligation than the law imposed. Notice that the four requirements in the Restatement are very similar to its requirements for impracticability of performance.

■ **CASE VOCABULARY**

AFFIDAVIT: This is statement made under oath.

DISCHARGE: To "discharge" performance means basically the same thing as to "excuse" performance.

# Swift Canadian Co. v. Banet

(Lamb Pelt Seller) v. (Lamb Pelt Buyer)

224 F.2d 36 (3rd Cir. 1955)

## FREE ON BOARD DESIGNATION CAN DEFEAT A CLAIM OF FRUSTRATION OF PURPOSE

■ **INSTANT FACTS** Banet (D) contracted with Swift (P) to buy lamb pelts from Swift (P) but a government regulation prevented their importation into America.

■ **BLACK LETTER RULE** A buyer cannot claim frustration of purpose—and thus be excused from performance—even if a supervening event prevents him from receiving his goods, as long as a free on board term (F.O.B.) allows the seller to complete his duties simply by delivering the goods to a carrier, and the seller then actually delivers the goods to that carrier.

■ **PROCEDURAL BASIS**

Appeal from granting of summary judgment for Banet (D) on an action for breach of contract.

■ **FACTS**

Banet (D) contracted with Swift (P) to buy lamb pelts from Swift (P). Their contract contained the following words: "F.O.B. Toronto." Toronto was Swift's (P) working plant. There was also the provision that "when pelts are sold F.O.B. seller's plant, title and risk of loss shall pass to buyer when product is loaded on cars at seller's plant." Swift (P) loaded the lamb pelts on a train in Toronto and shipped them to Banet (D) in America. But the U.S. government passed regulations which in effect prevented Banet (D) from importing the pelts. Because he couldn't import the pelts, Banet (D) claims frustration of purpose and wants to be excused from performance of having to pay Swift (P).

■ **ISSUE**

Can a buyer claim frustration of purpose—and thus be excused from performance—even if a supervening event prevents him from receiving his goods, as long as an F.O.B. clause in the contract allows the seller to complete his duties simply by delivering the goods to a carrier, and the seller then actually delivers the goods to that carrier?

■ **DECISION AND RATIONALE**

(Goodrich) No. A buyer cannot claim frustration of purpose—and thus be excused from performance—even if a supervening event prevents him from receiving his goods, as long as an F.O.B. clause in the contract allows the seller to complete his duties simply by delivering the goods to a carrier, and the seller then actually delivers the goods to that carrier. Here, the government regulation was definitely a supervening event which neither party contemplated while entering the contract. But there was an F.O.B. designation in the contract. This F.O.B. designation allowed Swift (P) to complete his duties simply by delivering the goods to the train. Once they were on the train, Banet (D), according to the F.O.B. clause, assumed all responsibility, including the consequences of a supervening event. Judgment reversed with instructions to enter judgment for Swift (P).

**Analysis:**

What would happen if the contract provided "F.O.B. Philadelphia," which is Banet's (D) home? For the obligations of the seller, see Uniform Commercial Code § 2319(1)(b). Here, the judge discussed the F.O.B. clause basically to determine the intent of the parties. The bigger picture illustrated by this case is that parties are free to allocate the risk of frustration of purpose. When such risk is allocated between the parties, the doctrine of frustration will not be used to defeat their intent.

■ **CASE VOCABULARY**

FREE ON BOARD (F.O.B.): This clause means that the seller will pay for all shipping and handling costs to the destination indicated.

# Chase Precast Corp. v. John J. Paonessa Co.

(Producer of Dividers) v. (General Contractor)

409 Mass. 371, 566 N.E.2d 603 (1991)

## FRUSTRATION OF PURPOSE CAN EXCUSE PERFORMANCE AS LONG AS THE CONTRACT DIDN'T ALLOCATE RISK TO A PARTY

■ **INSTANT FACTS** Chase (P) contracted with Paonessa (D) to supply concrete dividers but a supervening event obviated the need for Paonessa (D) to buy more dividers from Chase (P).

■ **BLACK LETTER RULE** A court can excuse performance on the basis of frustration of purpose only if the contract didn't allocate to one of the parties the risk of a supervening event.

■ **PROCEDURAL BASIS**

Appeal from judgment on an action for breach of contract.

■ **FACTS**

Massachusetts contracted with Paonessa (D) for some street construction, including putting in concrete dividers. The contract was a standard one offered by Massachusetts. In the contract, Massachusetts reserved the right to delete any portions of work found unnecessary. Paonessa (D) then contracted with Chase (P) to provide Paonessa (D) with concrete dividers. In Paonessa's (D) contract with Chase (P), there was no provision which allowed Paonessa (D) to delete any portions of work found unnecessary. In the subsequent months, angry residents protested the use of the concrete dividers instead of grass dividers. Massachusetts told Paonessa (D) to stop installation of the concrete dividers. Remember: according to its contract with Paonessa (D), Massachusetts could delete unnecessary work. But by this time, Chase (P) had already produced about one-half of its production order for such dividers. Paonessa (D) paid Chase (P) for everything that it produced. But Chase (P) wanted Paonessa (D) to pay for even the future production of dividers. Paonessa (D) claims frustration of purpose and wants to be excused from its duties.

■ **ISSUE**

Can a court excuse performance on the basis of frustration of purpose if the contract didn't allocate to one of the parties the risk of a supervening event?

■ **DECISION AND RATIONALE**

(Lynch) Yes. A court can excuse performance on the basis of frustration of purpose even if the contract didn't allocate to one of the parties the risk of a supervening event. Chase (P) argues that Paonessa (D) had assumed the risk of the supervening event, and therefore, it (D) has no excuse for nonperformance. Chase (P) points to Paonessa's (D) contract with Massachusetts as the main evidence. In that contract, Massachusetts reserved the right to delete any work which was unnecessary. Chase (P) argues that Paonessa (D) was fully aware of this provision and nonetheless still assumed the risk of a reduction in work orders. But Chase (P) was also aware of such risks. Chase (P) had contracted with Massachusetts in the past and signed contracts which contained the same standard provision as in Paonessa's (D) contract.

**Analysis:**

The court states here that frustration of purpose and impossibility both involve a supervening event, and they differ only in the effect of the supervening event. Assuming neither party caused the supervening event and neither party assumed the risks, under impossibility, both parties are excused from performance if a supervening event occurs that undermines a basic foundation of the contract. In other words, performance is basically impractical. But for frustration of purpose, the effect of the supervening event is less significant. Performance is still possible, but the value of the performance has been destroyed by the supervening event. The court in *Chase Precast* also compared the definition of frustration of purpose in Restatement (Second) of Contracts § 265 with the definition of "commercial impracticability" in Uniform Commercial Code § 2615, noting that they both were nearly identical.

■ **CASE VOCABULARY**

DOCTRINE OF IMPOSSIBILITY: This is a defense to a charge of breach of contract. If one succeeds with the argument of impossibility of performance, the party is excused from performance without being liable for damages.

# Northern Indiana Public Service Co. v. Carbon County Coal Co.

(Electric Company) v. (Owner of Coal Mine)

799 F.2d 265 (7th Cir. 1986)

---

BY AGREEING TO A FIXED-PRICED CONTRACT, THE PARTIES ASSUME THE RISKS OF MARKET PRICE CHANGES

---

■ **INSTANT FACTS** Northern Indiana Public Service Company (P) (NIPSCO) entered a contract with Carbon (D) which was a long-term contract that didn't allow NIPSCO (P) to renegotiate its terms.

■ **BLACK LETTER RULE** Even though there is a force majeure clause (a clause which lists certain events that are beyond the control of the parties and thus excuses performance), a party has assumed the risks for market fluctuations if that party has agreed to a fixed-priced contract.

---

■ **PROCEDURAL BASIS**

Appeal from judgment on an action for court declaration excusing performance.

■ **FACTS**

NIPSCO (P) is an electric company. It (P) contracted with Carbon (D) to buy Carbon's (D) coal which would be used to run NIPSCO's (P) electric plant. The contract stated that NIPSCO (P) would buy 1.5 million tons every 20 years. The contract wasn't a requirements contract (a type of contract where seller agrees to furnish everything that buyer needs and where buyer agrees to buy exclusively all of his goods from the particular seller), and so NIPSCO (P) was bound to buy all 1.5 million tons no matter how much it actually needed. Moreover, the contract didn't allow NIPSCO (P) to renegotiate the terms. The contract also contained an "elevation clause" (this allows a party to raise the contract price from time to time according to provisions of the contract) such that Carbon (D) could raise the price. Finally, the contract contained a force majeure clause which excused NIPSCO from accepting and paying for Carbon's (D) coal for "any cause beyond [its] reasonable control....which wholly or partly prevented...the utilizing...of the coal." About five years after NIPSCO (P) and Carbon (D) entered the contract, a state commission regulating NIPSCO (P) issued an order preventing NIPSCO (P) from shifting its (P) costs to its (P) customers. So when NIPSCO (P) entered a long-term, nonnegotiable, restrictive contract with Carbon (D), it (P) bore the risk of being unable to purchase at lower prices elsewhere and not being able to shift the costs to its (P) customers. NIPSCO (P) discovered that Carbon's (D) competitors were offering lower prices. NIPSCO (P) wanted to exercise its force majeure clause and sought excuse of performance from the court.

■ **ISSUE**

Even though there is a force majeure clause, has a party assumed the risks for market fluctuations if that party has agreed to a fixed-priced contract?

■ **DECISION AND RATIONALE**

(Posner) Yes. Even though there is a force majeure clause, a party has assumed the risks of market fluctuations if that party has agreed to a fixed-priced contract. Here, there was a force majeure clause

---

excusing performance if there are certain supervening events. But the clause was never triggered. NIPSCO (P) claims that it was triggered because the state commission's orders prevented NIPSCO (P) from shifting the costs to its (P) consumers. But obviously, this doesn't prevent NIPSCO (P) from actually performing its duties—accepting the coal and paying for it. Moreover, NIPSCO (P) had explicitly assumed the risks for market fluctuations by signing a fixed-priced contract. NIPSCO (P) gambled that the fuel costs would rise over the life of the contract. If the gamble paid off, NIPSCO (P) would save money through this fixed-priced contract. If the gamble didn't pay off, NIPSCO (P) agreed to live with the consequences. Thus, NIPSCO (P) is bound to perform its duties because NIPSCO (P) explicitly agreed to assume the risks of market fluctuations and because the force majeure clause was never triggered. Judgment affirmed.

---

**Analysis:**

The force majeure clauses. Specifically, the force majeure clause is a response by contract drafters to overcome the inadequacies in the substantive law. For quite a while, the law didn't recognize the ideas of legal impossibility, impracticability, or frustration of purpose. Thus, contract drafters included these force majeure clauses in order to protect the parties from supervening events that rendered performance onerous. Now, this effort by the contract drafters has of course found its way into the substantive law. Judges are likely to infer the presence of force majeure clauses in those contracts that lack them. The Uniform Commercial Code and the Restatement (Second) of Contracts have adopted the purpose behind force majeure clauses. See UCC § 2–615 and Restatement § 265, comment a.

---

### ■ CASE VOCABULARY

ELEVATION CLAUSE: This allows a party to raise the contract price from time to time according to provisions of the contract.

FORCE MAJEURE CLAUSE: A clause which lists certain events that are beyond the control of the parties and thus excuse performance.

REQUIREMENT CONTRACT: A type of contract where seller agrees to furnish everything that buyer needs and where buyer agrees to buy exclusively all of his goods from the particular seller. Elevation clause: This allows a party to raise the contract price from time to time according to provisions of the contract.

# Young v. City of Chicopee

(Bridge Repairer) v. (Bridge Owner)

186 Mass. 518, 72 N.E. 63 (1904)

A PERSON WHO AGREES TO DO A REPAIR JOB BEARS THE RISK OF THE LOSS OF THE ITEM BEING REPAIRED

■ **INSTANT FACTS** Young (P) contracted with Chicopee (D) to repair Chicopee's bridge, but a fire burned and destroyed the bridge.

■ **BLACK LETTER RULE** If a supervening event renders performance impractical for a repair contract, the owner must compensate the repairer only to the extent of actual repair done on the owner's property.

■ **PROCEDURAL BASIS**

Appeal from judgment on an action to recover for work and materials furnished under a repair contract, not for repairer's supplies.

■ **FACTS**

Young (P) contracted with Chicopee (D) to repair Chicopee's (D) bridge. The contract stated that Young (P) couldn't begin his work until material for one-half of the repair is on the job site. After Young (P) had done some repair, but prior to his completion, a fire burned and completely destroyed the bridge. The fire also burned and destroyed the wood that Young (P) had brought onto the job site near the bridge. Young (P) now wants compensation for the wood that was merely resting on the job site.

■ **ISSUE**

If a supervening event renders performance impractical for a repair contract, must the owner compensate the repairer only to the extent of actual repair done on the owner's property?

■ **DECISION AND RATIONALE**

(Hammond) Yes. If a supervening event renders performance impractical for a repair contract, the buyer must compensate the repairer only to the extent of actual repair done on the buyer's property. Here, Young (P) had actually done some repair on Chicopee's (D) bridge. For the actual work done, Chicopee (D) properly compensated him even though a supervening event completely destroyed it. However, Chicopee (D) doesn't need to compensate for Young's (P) supplies—the wood that merely rested on the job site near the bridge. This is because such wood was never used as part of the repair. Nor did Young (P) ever give Chicopee (D) the right to use the wood. The wood was entirely Young's (P) and never constituted a part of the repair work. Thus, Chicopee (D) doesn't need to compensate Young (P) for this wood on the job site.

**Analysis:**

Young (P), as the repairman, seems to have really "burned his bridges" in this case. Would he have been better off if he had the job of erecting the bridge, instead of merely repairing it? Probably not. If a contractor agrees to build something (like a bridge), and a supervening event destroys it prior to completion, then the contractor is bound to rebuild it! The court will not let him use the defense of impracticability because the contractor is still able to rebuild it. Yes, rebuilding will cost money, and yes, the obligation seems unfair. But that's what insurance is for. The policy reason for such law is that predictability is essential.

## ■ CASE VOCABULARY

IMPLIED ASSUMPSIT: This is Latin for implied agreement. It is also a common law form of action available for a party to recover for damages for breach of contract.

IMPLIED CONTRACT: This is not an explicit verbal or written contract. It is an agreement that is implied from the circumstances surrounding the contract.

MATERIALS WROUGHT: This is a phrase we don't see often these days. It basically means the materials that were actually built into the bridge, not just sitting on the ground next to it.

# CHAPTER TEN

## Third Parties: Rights & Responsibilities

### Lawrence v. Fox

**Instant Facts:** Fox (D) fails to fulfill his promise to Holly to pay off a loan which Holly owes to Lawrence.

**Black Letter Rule:** Privity is not needed to recover damages by a third party creditor beneficiary.

### Seaver v. Ransom

**Instant Facts:** Judge Beman fails to fulfill his wife's deathbed wish, as he promised, giving the house or an equivalent amount to their niece, Marion Seaver.

**Black Letter Rule:** Any third party beneficiary donee has the right to bring an action on a contract made specifically for his/her benefit.

### Rathke v. Corrections Corporation of America, Inc.

**Instant Facts:** Rathke (P) sued the Corrections Corporation of America (D) over a failed drug test, alleging that he was a third-party beneficiary of a contract between Corrections Corporation (D) and the State of Alaska.

**Black Letter Rule:** When determining whether a person is a third-party beneficiary of a contract, the required intent to benefit that third-party may be manifested by a promise to render performance directly to the third-party.

### Verni v. Cleveland Chiropractic College

**Instant Facts:** Verni (P) sued Makarov (D), claiming he was a third-party beneficiary of Makarov's (D) employment contract with Cleveland Chiropractic College (D).

**Black Letter Rule:** There is a strong presumption that a contract was executed for the sole benefit of the parties, and a third-party is not a beneficiary of the contract unless the terms of the contract directly and clearly express the intent to benefit the third-party or any class of which the third-party is a member.

### Grigerik v. Sharpe

**Instant Facts:** Claiming status as a third-party beneficiary, a buyer of a tract of land filed suit against the sewage engineer hired by the seller to develop a drainage plan which would be approved by the town sanitarian.

**Black Letter Rule:** The intent of both, not just one, of the parties to a contract determines whether a third party is to be afforded third party beneficiary status under a contract.

### Sally Beauty Co. v. Nexxus Products Co.

**Instant Facts:** The exclusive distributor of beauty products delegates his best effort obligations to the subsidiary of direct competitor.

**Black Letter Rule:** The duty of performance under a "best efforts" exclusive distributorship may not be delegated to a competitor without the obligee's consent.

### Herzog v. Irace

**Instant Facts:** As consideration for a doctor's promise to perform surgery for no up-front payment, Gary Jones assigned his payment rights under a pending personal Injury action to the doctor, but Jones later attempted to revoke the assignment.

**Black Letter Rule:** An assignor must dearly demonstrate his intent to relinquish any rights to the assignee, and thus an assignor may not retain a power of revocation.

### Bel-Ray Company v. Chemrite (Pty) Ltd.

**Instant Facts:** A company which had assigned to it a contract for the rights to distribute certain chemical products sought to avoid arbitration as required by the contract on the ground that the assignment made to it was void because consent was not obtained from the obligor.

**Black Letter Rule:** Contractual provisions limiting or prohibiting assignments operate only to limit a parties right to assign the contract, but not their power to do so, unless the parties' clearly manifest an intent to the contrary.

### Delacy Investments, Inc. v. Thurman & Re/Max Real Estate Guide, Inc.

**Instant Facts:** Thurman (D) assigned his unpaid real estate commissions to Delacy (P), but Re/Max (D) refused to pay Delacy (P).

**Black Letter Rule:** An assignee's rights are subject to the terms of any contract that creates the rights of the assignor.

### Chemical Bank v. Rinden Professional Association

**Instant Facts:** Rinden Professional Association (D), the buyer in a lease-purchase agreement, waived all warranties when the right to receive payments was assigned to Chemical Bank.

**Black Letter Rule:** When the right to receive payments on a sales contract is assigned, the original buyer may waive all warranties on the products.

# Lawrence v. Fox

(Promisor) v. (Third Party Beneficiary)
20 N.Y. 268 (1859)

## PRIVITY FOUND UNNECESSARY FOR THIRD PARTY CREDITOR BENEFICIARIES

■ **INSTANT FACTS** Fox (D) fails to fulfill his promise to Holly to pay off a loan which Holly owes to Lawrence.

■ **BLACK LETTER RULE** Privity is not needed to recover damages by a third party creditor beneficiary.

■ **PROCEDURAL BASIS**

Appeal from the Superior Court affirming trial court judgment for the plaintiff for legal damages.

■ **FACTS**

Holly lent $300 to Fox (D); Holly already owed $300 to Lawrence. So in order to pay back Holly, Fox promised Holly to repay the $300 debt that Holly owed Lawrence (P), directly to Lawrence (P). Fox (D) failed to pay Lawrence (P) the $300, as Fox (D) had promised Holly. Lawrence (P) brought this action against Fox (D). Fox (D) claimed that his agreement with Holly lacked consideration. Fox (D) further claimed that since there was no privity between Fox (D) and Lawrence (P), there was no basis for a suit. The trial court overruled the motion and the jury found in favor of Lawrence (P).

■ **ISSUE**

Whether a lack of privity prevents a third party beneficiary from recovering damages?

■ **DECISION AND RATIONALE**

(Gray) No. First of all, Fox (D) received sufficient consideration from Holly in exchange for his promise to pay Lawrence (P) the agreed to sum. This was the sole reason that Holly lent Fox (D) the money. Fox (D) then had a duty to remit the money to Lawrence (P) following the principle, "that a promise made to one for the benefit of another..." is actionable if the promise is breached. Fox (D) was in the same position as if he were the holder of a trust fund, rather than the holder of a short term loan. The $300 which Holly lent to Fox (D) was intended to, eventually, benefit Holly's creditor, Lawrence (P), and relieve Holly of the task of repaying the loan to Lawrence (P) himself. Fox (D) promised Holly to relieve him of that task in exchange for the $300 loan. Since the intent of the contract between Holly and Fox (D) was to benefit Lawrence (P), the lack of privity between Lawrence (P) and Fox (D) has no relevance. Lawrence (P) is entitled to damages for the breach of contract.

■ **DISSENT**

(Comstock) Since Lawrence (P) was neither the promisee, nor the provider of consideration, and was therefore not in privity, he is unable to maintain an action against Fox (D). Only a promisee or someone with a legal interest in the agreement has privilege to bring a suit.

**Analysis:**

Few contract cases are as significant as *Lawrence v. Fox.* Here, the court establishes the principle of a creditor beneficiary. A promise made to a promisee does not necessarily have to benefit the promisee directly. Any promise made in exchange for an act, a forbearance, or a return promise will provide sufficient consideration, if that is the intent of the promisee. When there is an underlying promise and the promisee receives the indirect benefit of the promise, the primary intent to benefit the third party would appear to make the argument of privity seem virtually irrelevant. The fact that someone other than a promisee benefits from the execution of a contract cannot mitigate the promisor's obligations.

### ■ CASE VOCABULARY

ANNUL: To make empty or void of meaning.

BENEFICIARY: One who receives some benefit as the result of another's acts or promises.

CESTUI QUE TRUST: Benefitor of a trust which has vested in another.

COUNTERMAND: To change orders that were already given.

DISCHARGE: Performance by one of the principal parties in a contract, of an act which relieves that party of further contractual obligations.

INURE: Conclude or result

PRIVITY: The relationship of two parties as a result of an agreement between them.

PRIVY: The intimate knowledge that one has of thoughts or actions of any person or thing.

TRUST: The holding of property for the benefit of another.

TRUSTEE: The person who holds property for the benefit of another.

# Seaver v. Ransom

(The Niece) v. (Judge Beman's Executor)
224 N.Y. 233, 120 N.E. 639, 2 A.L.R. 1187 (1918)

ANY THIRD PARTY BENEFICIARY DONEE MAY MAINTAIN AN ACTION AGAINST THE BREACHING PARTY

■ **INSTANT FACTS** Judge Beman fails to fulfill his wife's deathbed wish, as he promised, giving the house or an equivalent amount to their niece, Marion Seaver.

■ **BLACK LETTER RULE** Any third party beneficiary donee has the right to bring an action on a contract made specifically for his/her benefit.

■ **PROCEDURAL BASIS**

Appeal from the affirming judgment of the appellate court for plaintiff for recovery of damages.

■ **FACTS**

Shortly before her death, Mrs. Beman requested that her husband, Judge Beman, make out her will. In the will she left $1000 to Seaver (P), the use of the house to her husband for life and small amounts to various relatives and the ASPCA. Mrs. Beman then decided to change the will and give the house to her niece, Seaver (P), and leave the rest of the will unchanged. Mrs. Beman didn't believe she would live long enough for her husband to draw and execute a new document. But her husband, Judge Beman, swore an oath to leave Seaver (P) a sufficient amount in his own will to make up the difference. However, when Judge Beman died, his will made no provision for Seaver (P) as promised, and Seaver (P) brought suit. Ransom (D) is one of the executors of Judge Beman's estate.

■ **ISSUE**

Whether a third party beneficiary, who is neither a creditor nor a member of the immediate family, may maintain an action for damages without privity?

■ **DECISION AND RATIONALE**

(Pound) Yes. The trial court found for Seaver (P), based on the theory that Mrs. Beman was fraudulently induced to execute the will by her husband. But Seaver's (P) action is maintainable on grounds defined in Lawrence v. Fox [supra] "... the right of the beneficiary to sue on a contract made expressly for his benefit...." Such a right is "just and practical" since it allows the party who is benefiting from the contract to enforce it against the party who is in breach. The right of a third party to enforce a contract, to which he/she is the intended beneficiary, has been upheld in various situations. This case presents a category of beneficiary that is yet to present itself. The Bemans were childless and Seaver (P) was, virtually, the daughter they never had. The contract between Judge and Mrs. Beman was for the sole benefit of Seaver (P) and she is the only person "substantially damaged by its breach." The fact that Seaver was not a member of the immediate family in no way should prevent her from seeking recovery. The personal relationship between the Bemans and Seaver (P) is certainly worthy of consideration. It defines the moral obligation that the law seeks in establishing the intentions of the parties in a contract. An arbitrary line of demarcation between members of a family, based merely on marital status and lineage, fails to account for relationships that develop over a period of time, without a traditional legal status. The fact that Judge Beman, intentionally or unintentionally, failed to redraw the will as promised, does not change the promise or the intent Mrs. Beman had to give the house to Seaver (P), as a third party beneficiary. Seaver (P) was the intended beneficiary donee of the contract between the Bemans and is, therefore, entitled to recover damages. The judgment, with costs, is affirmed.

**Analysis:**

Writing for the lower court, Kellogg, P.J., wrote, "The doctrine of *Lawrence v. Fox* is progressive not retrograde. The course of the late decisions is to enlarge, not limit, the effect of that case." The New York court truly takes this language to heart in reaching its decision in *Seaver*. Although the case involved a family member, it is clear that a familial tie is no longer necessary. The court recognizes the legal rights of a third-party beneficiary donee in order to enforce the intent behind a contract. The court abandons any prior legal pretense that prevents the intent of a contracting party to give a benefit to whomever he/she pleases, as an intended recipient donee. Furthermore, the court forcefully concludes that the intended donee has the legal right to enforce such contracts without the need to demonstrate justifiable reliance on the promise. An intended beneficiary, according to *Seaver,* has greater legal authority than the common law legal authority once granted children and spouses. Such is the power of a valid contract.

■ **CASE VOCABULARY**

AVOUCH: To guarantee

BEQUEATH: Usually the giving of personal property by will rather than real property

COLLATERALS: Relatives not directly related for purposes of inheritance, such as cousins.

EQUITY: Fairness

EXECUTOR: Someone who is appointed to act in the place of the deceased in order to carry out their wishes as expressed in their will.

INTESTATE: Dying without leaving a will

LEGACY: Refers to a general legacy, providing a gift of personal property or money by means of a will.

PECUNIARY: Concerning money or its equivalent.

RESIDUARY LEGATEE: a person who gets whatever is left over after the specific gifts have been given.

TESTAMENTARY: Refers to any sort of document which fails to take effect until after the death of the individual who is making it.

TESTATOR: Anyone who leaves a will and is now dead.

TESTATRIX: Specifically, a dead woman who has left a will.

# Rathke v. Corrections Corporation of America, Inc.

(Inmate) v. (Prison Administrator)

153 P.3d 303 (Alaska 2007)

INMATES MAY SUE NONGOVERNMENTAL PRISON SERVICE PROVIDERS

■ **INSTANT FACTS** Rathke (P) sued the Corrections Corporation of America (D) over a failed drug test, alleging that he was a third-party beneficiary of a contract between Corrections Corporation (D) and the State of Alaska.

■ **BLACK LETTER RULE** When determining whether a person is a third-party beneficiary of a contract, the required intent to benefit that third-party may be manifested by a promise to render performance directly to the third-party.

■ **PROCEDURAL BASIS**

Appeal from an order dismissing the plaintiff's complaint and granting summary judgment.

■ **FACTS**

Rathke (P) was an inmate at a prison located in Arizona and operated by the Corrections Corporation of America (CCA) (D) under contract with the State of Alaska. He was disciplined after a drug test administered by PharChem, Inc. (D) showed that he had marijuana in his system. The level of marijuana in Rathke's (P) system was within the limit allowed by Alaska law, but exceeded the limit allowed by Arizona law.

Rathke (P) brought an action against CCA (D) and PharmChem (D), claiming he was a third-party beneficiary of their contracts with the State of Alaska. The specific contract was a final settlement agreement entered into by the state in a prisoner class action suit known as *Cleary v. Smith* (referred to as the *Cleary* FSA). The *Cleary* FSA gave certain rights to prisoners who were in held by the State of Alaska. The trial court dismissed Rathke's (P) claim, holding that he was not a third-party beneficiary of the contract between the state and CCA (D). The court held that the duties in the *Cleary* FSA ran only from the state to the inmates, and the duties in the contract between the state and CCA (D) ran only between the state and CCA (D).

■ **ISSUE**

Was Rathke (P) a third-party beneficiary of the contract between the state and CCA (D)?

■ **DECISION AND RATIONALE**

(Carpeneti, J.) Yes. When determining whether a person is a third-party beneficiary of a contract, the required intent to benefit that third-party may be manifested by a promise to render performance directly to the third-party. The parties' objective motive—rather than their subjective intent—is determinative.

The state owes certain legal duties to all Alaska inmates, including those housed in Arizona. Those duties are set out in the *Cleary* FSA. The *Cleary* FSA is incorporated by reference into the contract between Alaska and CCA (D). In addition, many of the provisions of the *Cleary* FSA are repeated virtually word for word in the CCA (D) contract. For example, parts of the discipline section of the CCA (D) contract that were allegedly breached in Rathke's (P) case are virtually identical to the *Cleary* FSA. In addition, the *Cleary* FSA sets out a presumption of innocence and a requirement that guilt be based only on a preponderance of the evidence presented at a disciplinary hearing. This provision is restated in the CCA (D) contract with Alaska. Given the identity of provisions between the two agreements, the inmates are the third-party beneficiaries of the portions of the CCA (D) contract with Alaska that are taken directly from the *Cleary* FSA. The result of the trial court's order would be that Rathke (P) could sue the state for violations of the *Cleary* FSA, but he could not sue the state or CCA (D) under identical provisions in the CCA (D) contract. Such a result would deny the Alaska inmates in Arizona direct redress against the very institution charged with their day-to-day care and discipline.

Rathke (P) is not, however, a third-party beneficiary of the state's contract with PharmChem (D). Prisoners are not mentioned in that contract, except in some attachments. The PharmChem (D) contract refers to "specimens" to be submitted for testing. Although prisoners may be said to benefit from competent drug testing, the fact that they are not even mentioned in the contract makes it impossible to say that the circumstances show that inmates were the intended beneficiaries of the promised performance. Affirmed as to PharmChem (D), reversed as to CCA (D).

## Analysis:

In recent years, many state and local governments have found it cost effective to contract with private companies to provide governmental services. These companies, especially those that operate correctional facilities, are often accused of violations of constitutional or statutory rights. Many plaintiffs have adopted Rathke's (P) theory that they are third-party beneficiaries of governmental service contracts, and this theory has generally met with success. Increasingly, however, service providers are insisting on contractual clauses that state specifically that members of the public impacted by the provision of services (such as prison inmates) are not intended to be beneficiaries of the contract.

## ■ CASE VOCABULARY

THIRD–PARTY BENEFICIARY: A person who, though not a party to a contract, stands to benefit from the contract's performance. For example, if Ann and Bob agree to a contract under which Bob will render some performance to Chris, then Chris is a third-party beneficiary.

# Verni v. Cleveland Chiropractic College

(Former Student) v. (School)

212 S.W.3d 150 (Mo. 2007)

---

THIRD–PARTY BENEFICIARIES ARE NOT PRESUMED

---

■ **INSTANT FACTS** Verni (P) sued Makarov (D), claiming he was a third-party beneficiary of Makarov's (D) employment contract with Cleveland Chiropractic College (D).

■ **BLACK LETTER RULE** There is a strong presumption that a contract was executed for the sole benefit of the parties, and a third-party is not a beneficiary of the contract unless the terms of the contract directly and clearly express the intent to benefit the third-party or any class of which the third-party is a member.

■ **PROCEDURAL BASIS**

Appeal from an order of the Western District Court of Appeals reversing an order granting Cleveland Chiropractic College's (D) motion for judgment notwithstanding the verdict, and denying Verni's (P) motion for additur or a new trial.

■ **FACTS**

Verni (P) was a student at the Cleveland Chiropractic College (D). He was dismissed for selling advance copies of an exam given by Makarov (D), a member of the faculty at the College (D). After his dismissal, Verni (P) sued Makarov (D), claiming that Makarov's (D) dealings with him violated the provisions in the faculty handbook that required faculty members to observe standards of decency in dealing with students. Verni (P) claimed that the faculty handbook was a part of the employment contract, and that Verni (P) was a third-party beneficiary of that contract. The jury found in favor of Verni (P).

■ **ISSUE**

Was Verni (P) a third-party beneficiary of the contract between Makarov (D) and Cleveland Chiropractic (D)?

■ **DECISION AND RATIONALE**

(Wolff, C.J.) No. There is a strong presumption that a contract was executed for the sole benefit of the parties, and a third-party is not a beneficiary of the contract unless the terms of the contract directly and clearly express the intent to benefit the third-party or any class of which the third-party is a member. A mere incidental benefit to the third-party is not sufficient to make him or her a beneficiary.

The question is resolved by looking at the language of the contract. Makarov's (D) employment contract was a one-page document that required him to be on campus for a certain amount of time every week and that outlined his teaching duties. The contract also set out Makarov's (D) salary and benefits. There was no clear expression of intent that Makarov (D) was undertaking any duty to benefit Verni (P) or a class of students. The contract also required Makarov (D) to comply with the policies and procedures in the College's (D) faculty handbook. The handbook required faculty members to treat students with courtesy, respect, fairness, and professionalism. The handbook also stated that students were entitled

---

to expect such treatment. Assuming that the faculty handbook is a part of Makarov's (D) employment contract, there is still nothing that overcomes the strong presumption that the contract was executed solely for the benefit of Makarov (D) and the College (D). Because Verni (P) was not a third-party beneficiary, he had no standing to raise the breach of contract issue. Standing issues are reviewed by the court *de novo*. Reversed.

## Analysis:

In his suit, Verni (P) denied that he sold advance copies of Makarov's (D) exam. His claim against Makarov (D) was based on Verni's (P) contention that Makarov (D) had asked students to draft the exam questions, and the exam was ultimately based mostly on questions drafted by Makarov (P). An anonymous informant allegedly saw discarded copies of the questions, and falsely reported Verni (P) as selling the questions.

## ■ CASE VOCABULARY

ADDITUR: (Latin, "it is added to.") A trial court's order, issued usually with the defendant's consent, that increases the damages awarded by the jury to avoid a new trial on grounds of inadequate damages. The term may also refer to the increase itself, the procedure, or the court's power to make the order.

# Grigerik v. Sharpe

(Buyer of Land) v. (Drainage Engineer)
247 Conn. 293, 721 A.2d 526 (1998)

THE INTENT OF BOTH CONTRACTING PARTIES DETERMINES WHETHER A THIRD PARTY MAY BE DESIGNATED AS A BENEFICIARY TO A CONTRACT

■ **INSTANT FACTS** Claiming status as a third-party beneficiary, a buyer of a tract of land filed suit against the sewage engineer hired by the seller to develop a drainage plan which would be approved by the town sanitarian.

■ **BLACK LETTER RULE** The intent of both, not just one, of the parties to a contract determines whether a third party is to be afforded third party beneficiary status under a contract.

■ **PROCEDURAL BASIS**

Appeal to the Connecticut Supreme Court to review the decision of the Appellate Court, which, partly on the ground that jury was incorrectly charged as to third party beneficiaries, reversed the trial court's judgment entered after the jury returned a verdict for the plaintiff.

■ **FACTS**

Joseph Grigerik (P) contracted to buy a tract of land from Edward Lang for $16,000. As part of the sale Lang agreed to get the approval for the tract as a building lot. To that end, Lang hired Gary Sharpe (D) to prepare a site plan for drainage that would be approved by the town sanitarian. Although evidence showed that Sharpe (D) was told the plan was necessary to obtain town approval and effect the sale to Grigerik (P), Sharpe (D) denied having been so informed. Nevertheless, Sharpe (D) prepared the plan, which was approved by the town sanitarian, and the sale went through. When Grigerik (P) applied for a building permit, a new town sanitarian and state authorities claimed the tract was unsuitable for a septic system. Grigerik (P) filed suit against Sharpe (D), claiming, in addition to negligence, his entitlement as a third party beneficiary of the services contract.

■ **ISSUE**

Is only the intent of the promisee to be considered when determining whether a person not a party to the contract is entitled to status as a third party beneficiary?

■ **DECISION AND RATIONALE**

(Borden, J.) No. The intent of both, not just one, of the parties to a contract determines whether a third party is to be afforded third party beneficiary status under a contract. We disagree with those commentators which argue that the concept of intent is too "obscure and elusive" to determine the rights of third parties. If the intent of the parties can serve to determine the inception and meaning of a contract, it certainly may determine whether a third party should be granted rights under a contract. Furthermore, § 302 of the Restatement (Second) states, in essence, that a beneficiary is an intended beneficiary if recognizing him as such effectuates the "intention of the *parties*." Applying this standard to these facts lead us to conclude that Grigerik (P) cannot prevail on his breach of contract claim. Although the jury found that Grigerik (P) was a foreseeable beneficiary, that fact is insufficient to grant him rights as a third party beneficiary. Application of the foreseeability concept to the law of contracts would severely limit the power of the parties to control the scope of their contractual duties. Reversed and remanded.

---

**Analysis:**

The existence of an intent to confer a benefit is often the critical inquiry in the area of third-party beneficiaries. The test of intent differs significantly among jurisdictions. Some courts hold that only the intent of the promisee (the seller Lang in this case) is dispositive. However, other courts recognize that the intent of the promisee should carry more weight, but make the promisor's intent a factor in the total inquiry. The court here adopts a test that requires consideration of the intent of both contracting parties to determine whether a third person is entitled to third-party beneficiary rights. The court here also rejects the concept of the foreseeable third party beneficiary, reasoning that giving merely foreseeable parties enforceable rights may take the contract out of the contracting parties' hands. In a jurisdiction that recognizes foreseeable beneficiaries, the parties are forced to include a provision in their contract denying such party any enforceable rights. In Connecticut, however, the foreseeable (but not intended) beneficiary is automatically denied third-party beneficiary rights, unless the parties include a provision providing otherwise.

---

### ■ CASE VOCABULARY

FORESEEABLE BENEFICIARY: A person who is not a party to the contract, but which the contracting parties could have foreseen would directly benefit from the contract.

INTENDED BENEFICIARY: A person to whom the parties to a contract intend to confer a benefit arising from the contract.

# Sally Beauty Co. v. Nexxus Products Co.

(Assignee-Competitor) v. (Obligee)
801 F.2d 1001 (7th Cir. 1986)

## PERFORMANCE MAY NOT BE DELEGATED TO A DIRECT COMPETITOR WITHOUT OBLIGEE'S CONSENT

■ **INSTANT FACTS** The exclusive distributor of beauty products delegates his best effort obligations to the subsidiary of direct competitor.

■ **BLACK LETTER RULE** The duty of performance under a "best efforts" exclusive distributorship may not be delegated to a competitor without the obligee's consent.

■ **PROCEDURAL BASIS**

Appeal of summary judgment by the District Court for a breach of contract.

■ **FACTS**

The Best Barber Beauty & Supply Company was acquired by the Sally Beauty Company (P). Sally (P) succeeded to Best's rights and interests, in all of Best's contracts, including an agreement to exclusively distribute Nexxus Products (D) in Texas. Nexxus (D) renounced all of its obligations, upon the occurrence of the merger, because Sally Beauty (P) was a wholly-owned subsidiary of Alberto-Culver, a direct competitor of Nexxus (D). Nexxus (D) held "great reservations about a competitor acting as a distributor of Nexxus (D) products. Nexxus (D) claimed its agreement with Best was based upon "personal trust and confidence which precluded an assignment to Sally (P) absent Nexxus' consent. Sally Beauty (P) argued that the contract was between corporations and the expected performance would not be altered by Sally Beauty (P). The trial court affirmed a motion for summary judgment, brought by Nexxus (D), "based upon a relationship of personal trust and confidence.

■ **ISSUE**

Whether an exclusive distributorship contract may be assigned to a direct competitor of the assignee without the obligee's consent?

■ **DECISION AND RATIONALE**

(Cudahy) No. The exclusive distribution agreement called for Best's "best efforts to distribute Nexxus (D) products. Nexxus (D) refused to accept that Sally (P), the subsidiary of a direct competitor, Alberto-Culver, could carry out its "best efforts" In good faith. The "... duty of performance under an exclusive distributorship may not be delegated to a competitor... without the obligee's consent." It is reasonable that Nexxus (D) believed that the "best efforts" it had bargained for would be different under the control of a competitor, Alberto-Culver. Sally's (P) contention, that it should be allowed to proceed to trial to prove that it could perform with "best efforts to Nexxus' (D) satisfaction, is not consistent with a "best efforts contract, which is nondelegable, without Nexxus' (D) consent. An obligee cannot be forced to accept a delegation of a performance in which the obligee cannot have full confidence in the best efforts of the assignee. Sally (P) has an obvious conflict of interest as a wholly-owned Alberto-Culver subsidiary. Therefore, the contract between Nexxus (D) and Best was not assignable to Sally (P), absent Nexxus' consent. Summary judgment affirmed.

## ■ DISSENT

(Posner) Since General Motors sells cars manufactured by Isuzu, why couldn't Sally (P) be expected to perform with "best efforts" to distribute Nexxus' (D) products? In the long run it would appear to be an incredibly poor business decision to sabotage Nexxus' (D) products, in a futile effort to monopolize the market. Not only would that violate federal antitrust acts but also create unwanted negative publicity. Furthermore, there is no reason to think that the one-year obligation to promote their competitor's products would so seriously injure Sally (P) that they would violate their assigned contract for a risky competitive advantage. If Nexxus (D) had any concern over Sally's (P) best efforts, they should have "demanded assurance of due performance."

## Analysis:

"Best efforts" contracts are generally non-delegable since they are generally based on a personal relationship or personal knowledge that one party has with another. "Best efforts implies a subjective standard for judging the adequacy of another party's abilities to perform to the satisfaction of the obligee. The technical skills that might be required for the particular performance are secondary to the good faith efforts that are expected by the obligee. Good faith or best efforts are not measurable quantities, but qualities that can only be assessed in the most subjective fashion. An obligee who "feels" uncomfortable with the best efforts of an assignee cannot be expected simply to accept the delegation of a performance to that assignee. And despite the logic of the dissent, it would truly be odd to expect one corporation to accept categorically that a direct competitor would give its best efforts to promote and distribute a product that would damage the competitor's own profit margin.

## ■ CASE VOCABULARY

ANTITRUST ACTS: Statutes that prevent unlawful price fixing and monopolies.

DELEGATE: To transfer a duty to perform from one party to another.

MERGE: The absorption of one company by another causing the loss of the absorbed company's identity.

MONOPOLY: Total control by one company over a particular supply of goods or services.

OBLIGEE: A party to whom a promise to perform is made *per se*, by itself, in and of itself

RENOUNCE: Absolute and unequivocal rejection or abandonment

SUBSIDIARY: A company that is under the control of another company.

# Herzog v. Irace

(Surgeon) v. (Attorney)
594 A.2d 1106 (Me. 1991)

AN ASSIGNOR RETAINS NO POWER OF REVOCATION AFTER MAKING AN ASSIGNMENT

■ **INSTANT FACTS** As consideration for a doctor's promise to perform surgery for no up-front payment, Gary Jones assigned his payment rights under a pending personal Injury action to the doctor, but Jones later attempted to revoke the assignment.

■ **BLACK LETTER RULE** An assignor must dearly demonstrate his intent to relinquish any rights to the assignee, and thus an assignor may not retain a power of revocation.

■ **PROCEDURAL BASIS**

Appeal of order affirming judgment for breach of assignment of personal injury settlement proceeds.

■ **FACTS**

Gary Jones needed surgery to fix a shoulder injury, but he could not afford to pay. However, Jones was expecting to receive a substantial amount of money in settlement of a personal injury action he had instituted earlier. Thus, in lieu of payment, Jones attempted to assign his right to the settlement monies to the surgeon, Dr. Herzog (P). Dr. Herzog (P) notified Jones's attorneys, Anthony Irace (D) and Donald Lowry (D), regarding the assignment. Nevertheless, after Jones received a $20,000 settlement award, Jones instructed Irace (D) and Lowry (D) not to pay Dr. Herzog (P). Thereafter, Dr. Herzog (P) filed a complaint in an attempt to enforce the assignment. The trial court rendered a judgment in favor of Dr. Herzog (P), the Superior Court affirmed, and Irace (D) and Lowry (D) appealed again.

■ **ISSUE**

Does an assignor retain a power of revocation of an assignment?

■ **DECISION AND RATIONALE**

(Brody, J.) No. An assignor retains no power of revocation over an assignment. In an assignment, the assignor transfers some right to the assignee. For an assignment to be valid and enforceable, the assignor must make clear his intent to relinquish the right to the assignee and must not retain any control over the right assigned or any power of revocation. In the case at hand, Jones validly assigned his right to a portion of the pending settlement to Dr. Herzog (P), demonstrating an intent to permanently relinquish all control over the assigned funds. He therefore had no right to revoke the assignment by instructing Irace (D) and Lowry (D) not to pay Dr. Herzog (P). Furthermore, Irace (D) and Lowry (D) were under no ethical obligation to honor Jones's instruction in disbursing the funds. Maine's Bar Rules say nothing about a client's power to assign his rights to proceeds from a pending lawsuit to third parties. Affirmed.

**Analysis:**

An assignments essentially a transfer of some right from one party (the assignor) to some third party (the assignee). All that is required is a clear intent for the assignor to relinquish his right. And while the party who must perform to the assignee (the obligor) need not consent to the assignment to render it valid, the assignment must not significantly alter the burden imposed on the obligor. While each of these rules is important, the only one essential to this case is the notion that an assignor may not revoke the assignment after it has been made. Perhaps this rule is overly general. Suppose Jones executed a written assignment to Dr. Herzog (P), but that Dr. Herzog (P) had a change of heart and agreed to perform the operation for free. Wouldn't it make sense to allow Jones, the assignor, to revoke the assignment since Dr. Herzog (P) had not detrimentally relied on it? Perhaps the better rule is based on an estoppel theory, namely that an assignor may not revoke an assignment after the assignee has materially changed position in justifiable, detrimental reliance on the assignment.

### ■ CASE VOCABULARY

ASSIGNEE: A third party to whom some contractual right is transferred.

ASSIGNMENT: An action demonstrating an intent to transfer a contractual right to a third party.

ASSIGNOR: A party who transfers his rights under a contract to a third party.

OBLIGOR: A party who, following an assignment, must render performance to the assignee rather than the assignor.

# Bel-Ray Company v. Chemrite (Pty) Ltd.

(Patent Licensor) v. (Assignee)

181 F.3d 435 (3d Cir. 1999)

**CONTRACTS ARE FREELY ASSIGNABLE AND COURTS WILL INTERPRET PROVISIONS RESTRICTING ASSIGNMENT NARROWLY SO AS TO FURTHER THE POLICY FAVORING FREE ASSIGNABILITY**

■ **INSTANT FACTS** A company which had assigned to it a contract for the rights to distribute certain chemical products sought to avoid arbitration as required by the contract on the ground that the assignment made to it was void because consent was not obtained from the obligor.

■ **BLACK LETTER RULE** Contractual provisions limiting or prohibiting assignments operate only to limit a parties right to assign the contract, but not their power to do so, unless the parties' clearly manifest an intent to the contrary.

■ **PROCEDURAL BASIS**

Appeal to the Third Circuit Court of Appeals to review an order of the district court, which compelled a foreign party to submit to arbitration.

■ **FACTS**

The Bel-Ray Company (P) entered into a series of agreements ("Agreements") with Chemrite Ltd. (D), a South African corporation, giving Chemrite (D) the right to blend and distribute certain lubricants. When Lubritene Ltd. (D) acquired Chemrite (D), Lubritene (D) had assigned to it all of the rights under the Agreements. Bel-Ray (P) was informed of the transfer and it continued to do business with Lubritene (D). Bel-Ray (P) then filed an action against Lubritene (D) in federal District Court in New Jersey, alleging fraud and violations of the Agreements. Bel-Ray (P) sought and was granted an order compelling Lubritene (D) to submit to arbitration on the ground that the Agreements contained valid and enforceable arbitration clauses. Lubritene (D) appealed the order. Lubritene (D) argued that it was not required to submit to arbitration because the rights under Agreements were assigned to Lubritene (D) without Bel-Ray's (P) consent, which was expressly required by the language of the Agreements. Hence, Lubritene (D) argued, there was no written agreement to arbitrate between it and Bel-Ray (P).

■ **ISSUE**

Is an assignment of contractual rights automatically voided when it is in breach of a provision restricting the assignment of such rights?

■ **DECISION AND RATIONALE**

(Stapleton, Cir. J.) No. Contractual provisions limiting or prohibiting assignments operate only to limit a parties right to assign the contract, but not their power to do so, unless the parties clearly manifest an intent to the contrary. This rule mirrors § 322 of the Restatement (Second) of Contracts, which provides that, unless a contrary intent is manifested, a contract term prohibiting the assignment of rights under the contract gives the obligor a right to damages for breach of the terms forbidding assignment but does not render the assignment ineffective. An assignment made contrary to the terms of the contract will be voided only where the parties expressly provide that such is to be the consequence of such assignment.  The Agreements at issue here contain no language which would suggest an intent to void assignments made without the consent of Bel-Ray (P).  Accordingly, the assignment made by Chemrite (D) to Lubritene (D) is enforceable and Lubritene(D) is required to submit to arbitration.  Affirmed.

**Analysis:**

This case illustrates the majority rule regarding the contractual provisions that purport to restrict the assignment of rights accruing under the contract.  Although early cases suggested that such terms effected an unlawful restraint on allenation, the rule that prevails today is that restrictions on the assignment of rights are to be construed only as promises.  Unless the contracting parties clearly state otherwise, an assignment of rights made contrary to the terms of the contract will give rise only to a claim for damages, and will not act to negate the assignment.  Since the damages that would usually flow from an extra-contractual assignment are likely to be minimal, anti-assignment clauses are practically ineffective if they are phrased improperly.  Article 9 of the Uniform Commercial Code makes ineffective all clauses that purport to prohibit the assigment of an "account", as that term is defined by the UCC Article 2 has a similar provision regarding the assignment of a right to damages, a right to payment for goods delivered, and a right to the receipt of goods already paid for.

■ **CASE VOCABULARY**

ANTI-ASSIGNMENT PROVISION:  A contractual term which is aimed at restricting the parties from assigning their rights accruing under the contract.

# Delacy Investments, Inc. v. Thurman & Re/Max Real Estate Guide, Inc.

(Lender) v. (Real–Estate Agent) & (Real Estate Brokerage)

693 N.W.2d 479 (Minn. Ct. App. 2005)

---

## AN ASSIGNEE HAS NO GREATER RIGHTS THAN THE ASSIGNOR

---

■ **INSTANT FACTS** Thurman (D) assigned his unpaid real estate commissions to Delacy (P), but Re/Max (D) refused to pay Delacy (P).

■ **BLACK LETTER RULE** An assignee's rights are subject to the terms of any contract that creates the rights of the assignor.

---

■ **PROCEDURAL BASIS**

Appeal from an order granting summary judgment for Re/Max (D).

■ **FACTS**

On November 11, 2001, Thurman (D), a real-estate agent, entered into an agreement with Delacy Investments (P), d.b.a. Commission Express (P), called a "master repurchase and security agreement." The agreement provided that Thurman (D) granted to Commission Express (P) a security interest in all of his current and future accounts receivable. In exchange for the assignment, Thurman (D) would receive immediate funds from Commission Express (P). Commission Express (P) duly perfected its security interest by filing a financing statement.

On February 25, 2003, Thurman (D) entered into an independent contractor agreement with Re/Max (D). The agreement provided that Thurman (D) would pay certain overhead expenses to Re/Max (D). The agreement also provided that Thurman (D) would be entitled to receive only that part of his commissions that exceeded his past-due obligations for overhead expenses. The portion of Thurman's (D) commissions that did not exceed his past-due obligations was deemed to belong to Re/Max (D), to be used to offset arrearages. The legal relationships of the parties made Commission Express (P) the "assignee," Thurman (D) the "assignor," and Re/Max (D) the "account debtor."

In April 2003, Re/Max (D) executed an acknowledgment of Commission Express's (P) security interest in Thurman's (D) commission from the sale of a home on Javelin Avenue. Re/Max (D) directed that Thurman's (D) commission be paid directly to Commission Express (P). Later that month, Commission Express (P) and Thurman (D) entered into an agreement whereby Commission Express (P) agreed to purchase a $10,000 receivable related to Thurman's sale of a property on Keller Lake Drive. On June 7, Re/Max (D) terminated Thurman (D) for poor performance, failure to deposit earnest-money payments on time, and customer complaints. Re/Max (D) claimed that Thurman (D) owed Re/Max (D) $11,126.38 in overhead debts. Re/Max (D) refused to pay Commission Express (P), saying that Thurman (D) was not entitled to be paid because his past-due overhead obligations exceeded his commission.

Commission Express (P) brought suit against Thurman (D) and Re/Max (D). Thurman (D) did not plead, so judgment by default was entered against him. The trial court granted Re/Max's (D) motion for summary judgment, holding that Thurman (D) was not entitled to receive a commission from the sale of the Keller Lake Drive property, and that it was impossible for Commission Express (P) to obtain a greater right in the commission than Thurman (D) had.

---

## ■ ISSUE

Was Commission Express (P) entitled to receive the commission?

## ■ DECISION AND RATIONALE

(Halbrooks, J.) No. An assignee's rights are subject to the terms of any contract that creates the rights of the assignor. Section 9–404(a)(1) provides that the rights of an assignee are subject to the terms of the agreement between the assignor and the account debtor. A valid assignment grants the assignee the same rights that the assignor had in whatever was assigned. Thurman (D) was not entitled to collect a commission while he owed Re/Max (D) for overhead expenses. There is no question that Thurman (D) was in arrears on his payments to Re/Max (D), and he was therefore not entitled to collect a commission on the Keller Lake Drive sale. Because the rights of Commission Express (P) were subject to the agreement between Thurman (D) and Re/Max (D), Commission Express (P) was not entitled to collect the commission from Re/Max (D). It was impossible for Commission Express (P) to obtain a greater right in the commission than Thurman (D) had in the commission. Commission Express (P) could have contracted so that it was not bound by the agreement between Thurman (D) and Re/Max (D), but it did not do so.

Commission Express (P) argues that U.C.C. § 9–404(a)(2) bars Re/Max (D) from refusing to pay, because it had notice of a previously executed assignment. Commission Express (P) further argues that there are limits to the setoffs an account debtor, such as Re/Max (D), may assert against payment to an assignee after notice of the assignment. Commission Express (P) says that Re/Max (D) had notice of the assignment from the filing of the financing statement, and that it had actual notice from the delivery of the notice regarding the Javelin Avenue property, as well as the notice of the assignment of the Keller Lake Drive receivable. But U.C.C. § 9–404(a)(1) provides an exception to the general rule. Although Re/Max (D) had notice of the assignment between Thurman (D) and Commission Express (P) before the independent contractor agreement was entered into, the independent contractor agreement limited payment to Thurman (D) to the commissions that exceeded his past-due financial obligations to Re/Max (D). Commission Express (P) could take no greater rights than Thurman (D) had. Affirmed.

---

### Analysis:

The court notes that Commission Express (P) could have, if it had chosen to do so, negotiated its contract so that its right to receive payment would not be subject to Re/Max's (D) right to withhold commissions for unpaid overhead. An easier course of action may have been to make inquiries before advancing any money. It appears that there was no blanket agreement that automatically obligated Commission Express (P) to advance commissions, as the court refers to separate agreements made for each transaction. Commission Express (P) could have avoided the whole issue by verifying with Re/Max (D) whether Thurman (D) owed Re/Max (D) any money before agreeing to advance commissions.

---

## ■ CASE VOCABULARY

INDEPENDENT CONTRACTOR: One who is hired to undertake a specific project but who is left free to do the assigned work and to choose the method for accomplishing it. Unlike an employee, and independent contractor who commits a wrong while carrying out the work does not create liability for the one who did the hiring.

PERFECTED SECURITY INTEREST: A security interest that has completed the statutory requirements for achieving priority over other security interests that are subject to the same requirements.

# Chemical Bank v. Rinden Professional Association

(Institutional Lender) v. (Law Firm)

126 N.H. 688, 498 A.2d 706 (1985)

A BUYER MAY WAIVE ANY CLAIM FOR BREACH OF WARRANTY ON A PRODUCT WHEN THE OBLIGATION TO PAY FOR THE PRODUCT IS ASSIGNED

■ **INSTANT FACTS** Rinden Professional Association (D), the buyer in a lease-purchase agreement, waived all warranties when the right to receive payments was assigned to Chemical Bank.

■ **BLACK LETTER RULE** When the right to receive payments on a sales contract is assigned, the original buyer may waive all warranties on the products.

■ **PROCEDURAL BASIS**

Appeal of master's favorable report in action seeking to enforce waiver-of-warranties provision.

■ **FACTS**

Rinden Professional Association (D), a law firm, entered into a lease-purchase agreement with Intertel for the installation of a telephone system, Intertel assigned its rights to the lease payments to Chemical Bank (P). Rinden's (D) office manager assented to the terms of the assignment, which required Rinden (D) to continue making payments to Chemical Bank (P) regardless of any claims they might have against Intertel. However, after the phone system began to malfunction, Rinden refused to make further payments to the bank. Intertel had gone bankrupt at the time, and Chemical Bank (P) brought suit to enforce the waiver clause. A master issued a report favoring the bank, and Rinden appealed on grounds that the waiver clause was unenforceable.

■ **ISSUE**

When the right to receive payment for an installment-sale transaction is assigned, may the purchaser validly waive the sales warranties?

■ **DECISION AND RATIONALE**

(Douglas, J.) Yes. When the right to receive payment for an installment-sale transaction is assigned, the purchaser may validly waive the sales warranties. In order for the waiver to be valid, pursuant to the UCC and Massachusetts law, there must be an agreement by the buyer, who is not a consumer, to waive defenses against an assignee. Furthermore, the assignment must have been made for value, in good faith, and without notice of a claim or defense. In the case at hand, Rinden (D) agreed to the waiver-of-defenses clause, and Rinden (D) did not claim to be a consumer. In addition, the assignment to Chemical Bank (P) was made for value, as the bank paid Intertel over $8,800. There is no basis for concluding that Chemical Bank (P) was not acting in good faith, or that it took the assignment with notice of Rinden's (D) claim or defense. Moreover, there is no validity to Rinden's (D) argument that consideration was required to make Rinden's (D) waiver valid, as modifications under the UCC need no consideration. Finally, this decision is in accord with the general policy of encouraging the supply of credit and insulating the lender from lawsuits over the quality of goods. Affirmed.

**Analysis:**

While the court's analysis, upholding the validity of the waiver, appears to be consistent with the relevant statutes, it certainly leaves Rinden (D) in an unenviable position. Rinden (D) was unfortunate enough to foolishly assent to a waiver of defenses (gaining nothing in return), and now the law firm is paying the price. Thus, even though the leased phone system was a complete dud, Rinden (D) had to continue making payments to Chemical Bank (P) because it effectively agreed not to complain about any defects. This clause certainly seems harsh and oppressive, but apparently neither the master nor the state supreme court believed that it was unconscionable. Nevertheless, the powerful Chemical Bank (P) seems to completely take advantage of Rinden (D) in this case. Although Rinden (D) was a professional law firm, it could make a valid claim that it was an inexperienced "consumer" of telephone services. It this were so, then the statute at hand would not apply. Unfortunately for Rinden (D), it failed to prove this point.

### ■ CASE VOCABULARY

MASTER: A judicial officer appointed to assist courts with specific duties, including making preliminary findings of fact and conclusions of law.